T5-DGC-177

Hometown Horizons

Robert Rutherdale

Hometown Horizons: Local Responses to Canada's Great War

UBCPress · Vancouver · Toronto

15 14 13 12 11 10 09 08 07 06 05 04 5 4 3 2 1

Printed in Canada on acid-free paper

Library and Archives Canada Cataloguing in Publication

Rutherdale, Robert Allen, date
Hometown horizons : local responses to Canada's Great War / Robert Rutherdale.

Includes bibliographical references and index.
ISBN 0-7748-1013-0

1. World War, 1914-1918 – Social aspects – Canada. 2. Lethbridge (Alta.) – History – 20th century. 3. Guelph (Ont.) – History – 20th century. 4. Trois-Rivières (Québec) – History – 20th century. 5. World War, 1914-1918 – Canada. 6. Canada – History – 1914-1918. I. Title.

FC557.R87 2004 940.3'71 C2004-903586-X

Canadä

UBC Press gratefully acknowledges the financial support for our publishing program of the Government of Canada through the Book Publishing Industry Development Program (BPIDP), and of the Canada Council for the Arts, and the British Columbia Arts Council.

This book has been published with the help of a grant from the Canadian Federation for the Humanities and Social Sciences, using funds provided by the Social Sciences and Humanities Research Council of Canada, and with the help of the K.D. Srivastava Fund.

UBC Press
The University of British Columbia
2029 West Mall
Vancouver, BC V6T 1Z2
604-822-5959 / Fax: 604-822-6083
E-mail: info@ubcpress.ca
www.ubcpress.ca

For Myra and Andrew
and in memory of my father, John A. Rutherdale,
and
my grandfather, Angus MacGregor,
veterans of two world wars

Contents

Illustrations

Acknowledgments

On completing this book, my thoughts turn to the collective, often collaborative effort it represents. The manuscript benefited from exchanges I greatly valued with Jack Granatstein, whose knowledge of Canada's Great War and military and political history throughout the twentieth century guided a generation of younger scholars who began graduate work at York University. I feel fortunate to have been part of that community, and remain indebted to all whom I know as friends, peers, and now colleagues across the country. I must also extend a special thanks to the several history departments that encouraged me to combine research with teaching, and to experiment in developing new courses that fed directly back to this book. Memorial University of Newfoundland, the University of Northern British Columbia, University College of the Fraser Valley, and the University of British Columbia provided that support and my appreciation extends to Andy den Otter, Joe Cherwinski, Bill Morrison, Ken Coates, Eric Davis, Jean Barman, Veronica Strong-Boag, Neil Sutherland, Mona Gleason, Leslie Paris, Allan Smith, Chris Friedrichs, Robert McDonald, Dianne Newell, David Breen, and Charles Humphries. I owe thanks as well to Alvin Finkel of Athabasca University. I am happy to thank the many students with whom I had the privilege to work, who shared their own research in progress on war and society topics across fall, winter, spring, and summer courses that took me from St. John's to Prince George. As a follow-up to a recent University of British Columbia 'War and Society' student seminar, modified portions of chapter two on recruitment will appear in a forthcoming issue of *Histoire Sociale/Social History* as 'Send-offs During Canada's Great War: Interpreting Hometown Rituals in Dispatching Home Front Volunteers.'

My research in local and regional repositories provided the adventure of living and working in distinct environments for extended periods, and I owe a debt of appreciation to archivists, local historians, and regional experts, on whose knowledge of the varied meanings of locale my work depended. I extend a special thanks to the work of the late Dr. Alex Johnston and Greg Ellis in Lethbridge. I also thank François Roy of Trois-Rivières for his friendship, and I am indebted to the patient staff of the Archives du Séminaire de Trois-Rivières. Guelph's Museum and Archives and Wellington County's Museum and Archives also provided excellent research support.

In my sojourns across and beyond Canada I have been sustained by strong friendships including those of Deanna Reder, Holly Kavanaugh, Alan Kavanaugh, Alison Peel, Doug Peel, and Katie Pickles, Ross Bragg, Larry Woods, and Elizabeth Buchanan. Jean Wilson at UBC Press must be thanked for wise counsel when the manuscript approached its final form, as must Emily Andrews for manuscript acquisition editing, and the anonymous readers for valuable critique. For editorial production, my thanks to Holly Keller and Darcy Cullen, and for her skilled copy-editing I owe Audrey McClellan considerable gratitude. I also appreciate Eric Leinberger's work in producing the maps.

My time spent researching and writing involved blurring the boundaries between the domestic and professional lives of two historians, my partner Myra and myself. Both Myra and our son, Andrew, gave generously, and my debts to them are beyond estimation. So too is what I owe my parents, Jack and Jean, and brother John, who never lost faith in my efforts to write history and to, perhaps, finally settle down to a home community in Sault Ste. Marie with a good high school for our son and a welcoming home for family visits. My thanks also go to Algoma University College, which furnished an especially friendly academic home for this book's final stages, and to Bill Newbigging, who has provided the best of collegial support.

Introduction

The First World War is considered by many historians to have been a critical conflict, a turning point. The notion that the twentieth century began in 1914 has shaped the social memories, as well as the historiographies, of the countries that fought in the war. The period was marked by very real shifts in global power, by the demise of the European empires, and by the development of industrial weapons and tactics. Britain's pre-eminence as an imperial force waned, America's grew, and the Hapsburg, Hohenzollern, and Romanov dynasties collapsed, along with what remained of the Turkish Ottoman Empire. Eric Hobsbawm's recent study of that century, which emphasizes the acceleration of causal events in overlapping eras of catastrophe and transformation, recounts yet again the ruptures that began in early August 1914. He begins by considering the war's immediate cause, the diplomatic crisis after the assassination of Archduke Franz Ferdinand in Sarajevo. He addresses the war's underlying origins, from imperialism, nationalism, and militarism to the system of European alliances, before moving on to highlight the significance of the destruction and dislocation that followed.[1]

To a degree, his approach is conventional. He works toward coherent explanations for past events, however destructive and irrational the outcomes. His work presents, in other words, reasons rooted in mistaken ideologies for the many disastrous, often misguided, decisions that have framed global histories to the near-present. He studies nation-states and empires. He considers what maintained them and what their populations produced and consumed. He addresses why various peoples invaded, killed, resisted, or revolted within and beyond their borders. He presents the century as short, brutal, and of ominous consequence.

In so doing, Hobsbawm also considers news of violence broadcast by a new breed of war correspondents reporting from scattered locations in Africa and Asia. Sparing us any detour into semiotics, he suggests that proliferating print media romanticized clashes between the major powers in colonized regions, deliberately cast as exotic, foreign and Other. During the long epoch of infrequent hostilities along the borders of major powers that paralleled endemic conflicts in disputed territories on the edges of empire, military spending was often justified as a necessity in contests of imperial hegemony. In broader terms, therefore, the oft-noted hiatus, from 1815 to 1914, of major warfare in Europe itself referred to little more than a fictional 'peace' between the powers. Apart from brief wars in the Crimea (1854-56), during German and Italian unification, in the Balkans, or between France and Germany (1870-71) and Russia and Japan (1905), armed encounters, mobilizations, and wartime planning occurred either in colonized zones or through the output and projects of factories, shipyards, military academies, and military strategists. Buildups in land forces and naval inventories, most notably the dreadnought race between Germany and Britain, took place against a backdrop of popular images of distant wars, feeding distorted perceptions of colonization and hostile encounters far from Europe.

Such images of conflict and compelling Otherness in colonized regions not only intersected with new technologies and productive capacities to amass land and sea arsenals, they also often validated use of these new weapons in the modern world. Meanwhile, through a growing popular press and book-publishing industry, audiences consumed multiple images of sexualities, racial differences, and violence in cross-cultural encounters. 'Such exotic conflicts,' Hobsbawm notes, 'were the stuff of adventure literature or the reports of that mid-nineteenth-century innovation the war correspondent, rather than matters of direct relevance to most inhabitants of the states that waged and won them.' Against the gilded, heroic, imperial warriors of popular imagination, the arms race and march toward the catastrophic carnage that began in Belgium becomes, in Hobsbawm's story as in countless others, a threshold, a one-way door. Its long-term trajectories, from dynastic overthrow and economic collapse to the rise of fascism, have been repeatedly classified and reclassified in many grand narratives, few of which share Hobsbawm's sophistication. On the impact of the First World War on mass societies and cultures in the West, he writes simply: 'All this changed in 1914.'[2]

By examining Canada's part, especially how home front populations perceived and experienced the war's many demands and consequences, historians can begin to understand more fully how relationships of empire, nationality, gender, class, and public power began to shift in significant ways during this four-year crucible. These ruptures were not just directed by empires and large-scale business interests. However self-serving imperialism and capitalism were, neither the great powers nor the financial backers of empire and industry could sustain their activities in a vacuum. Rather, they operated within fluid cultural spheres of information, images, and ritualizations. Hometown sites were frequently used to represent a 'great' war of European powers, overseas dominions, and far-flung colonies, a struggle often shaped in hometown communities through popular and public experiences. This book examines relationships between public perceptions on a local level and the making of a national home front in Canada, which was part of an imperial system undergoing shifts and transformations, as the fighting overseas intensified.

The use of routinely generated materials, from hometown newspapers to the private records of local residents, does not dispute projects like Hobsbawm's, but adopts alternative positions to examine how the war was perceived on a popular level and how it evoked public responses. This is a study of locally situated evidence – of the settings and circumstances in which ordinary Canadians at home came to experience a distant war overseas. It is thus, in many respects, a study of a war imagined. It considers how people in three very different Canadian cities witnessed and actively interpreted this intense period of conflict by examining what they used to see it through or with. What circulated as newspaper texts, illustrations, or photographs, what was staged as parades or march pasts on city streets, or what was expressed as orations or songs were usually commonplace, replicated in one form or another in urban spaces across the country. They were also very powerful. Many of the public displays and demands of the war meshed with everyday life to produce significant cumulative effects, but it is difficult for historians to reach unqualified generalizations about these effects.

The multiple sites of war-related discourses considered here also point to the importance of isolating public events in the cultural spaces people ordinarily inhabit, of selecting localized, culturally constituted domains in which particular information and images circulated. Through them we can learn much more about how recruitment, enemy alien treatment, conscription, or veteran re-establishment were experienced and understood by ordinary people than we might by considering accounts from politicians and commanders alone. Public events and information flows in specific cities produced novel emotions and ideas as people imagined, felt, and invented interpretations of how the war was affecting them and how it might shape their future.

As a study of hometown horizons, this book places the flow of social interaction and cultural representations on the countless intersections between local, national, and international histories, between the immediacy of parochial settings and a war fought on two fronts. Such an approach offers particular advantages for historians as it keeps us focused on what many people saw first-hand and experienced most directly. It also prompts us to consider how specific discourses worked, how communication was linked to social differentiation, how movements from signs to boundaries enforced crucial divisions in society: recruits from civilians, enemy aliens from the host society, men from women, conscription supporters from their various opponents, or returned soldiers from civilians. That social differences of gender, ethnicity, class, and age helped to configure other social barriers created by the war cannot be understood without examining how everyday communications inscribed these differences. In this way, the themes pursued here seek to show how ordinary, home front Canadians made visible, and circulated, perceptions of a distant war that had fundamental effects on them as they lived through an extraordinary period of history.

Recent histories of culture and communication show a greater sensitivity to relationships between everyday life in a particular social domain and the authorized powers of distant decision-making centres. Instead of viewing government as a command centre and different, scattered populations as the lower, suppliant part of a top-down hierarchy; instead of assuming an impermeable split between the power of national authorities and the power of local knowledges; instead of overlooking the often reciprocal and fluid exchanges between ruler and ruled, these recent histories not only acknowledge the importance of ordinary modes of experience, but also consider those positions as crucial domains in repositioning studies of socio-historical movements or inertias. There have been significant shifts in methods and conceptual approaches across the disciplines, as well as in their inquiries and objects of study. For historians this has meant reorienting their investigations, moving from studies of overarching structures to multiple networks, from quantifiable social categories to lived experience, or from societal norms to individual tactics and strategies.

In Canada during the war, evidence of local, public expressions of action and sentiment remains scattered. Although responses to the fighting varied, few Canadians were isolated entirely from the war's carnage. Yet what they used to interpret events was often situated close to home, though its referents, from Ottawa's command decisions to the carnage overseas, usually were not. From the first reports of the outbreak of fighting in Belgium, to the letters of condolence that came later, to fantastic accounts of enemy alien sabotage or stories about the injured bodies of returned men, news of the war reached home front populations through a series of ordinary, local channels that circumscribed how people imagined or understood events outside their immediate surroundings. Studies of selected sites used to broadcast images and specific understandings of the war – a school classroom, a civic meeting, a patriotic rally, an editorial, a commemoration ritual – can help to uncover how people came to view the war and to interpret its wider implications. The texts, practices, and varied sites of encounter that transported signs of the war – whether they were as typical as battle coverage in a city newspaper or as unique as the Lethbridge enemy alien internment camp located on that city's exhibition grounds – often provided not simply windows to wider worlds, but distorting mirrors, misleading settings, and illusionary situations. They could be very powerful. Sites like these, where local knowledges confronted war-related discourses, can help us understand how home front populations perceived their circumstances and acted in the context of a world war.

As well, we need to recognize that public events, and publicly invented interpretations of events, could have significant consequences beyond the cities and regions in which they took place. War-related communication across the country may be seen as complex oscillations from margins to centres and back again – from Ottawa or from the front or from mass-circulating depictions of the hated Kaiser or the martyred Edith Cavell to the pinpoints of particular responses, shaped by local means and perceptions. This book probes the home front as an evolving sequence of exchanges between hinterland populations and centres of command, objects of fascination, and apocalyptic fighting fronts that produced massive killing and loss. It addresses how Canada's home front was shaped by local horizons and responses during more than fifty months of destruction that we now call the First World War.

Between Canada at War and City Life

My research stems largely from routinely generated evidence, the kind produced in comparable ways in all the belligerent countries from August 1914 to the initial phase of veteran re-establishment. Local newspapers, dailies and weeklies, provided diverse depictions of everyday life considered here, from public ritualizations to more incidental evidence of people living through the war. Their photographs, descriptions of local events, editorials, and reports on the war overseas opened avenues to revisit home front experiences from the perspectives of local participants and observers. They presented complex and wide arrays of representations, from local to national politics, from gendered images to those of ethnic and class relations, all in hometown settings depicted in local texts that circulated widely and, like any successful press, strove to attract both readers and advertising. I worked to piece together the histories and unravel the languages of voluntary clubs and associations, military documents, municipal minutes, school and church records, and personal and family papers.

I also chose a comparative approach and gathered evidence pertaining to home front responses in three very different Canadian cities: Trois-Rivières, resettled by Europeans of the *ancien régime* at the confluence of the Mauricie and St. Lawrence rivers; Guelph, a city in mid-southern Ontario that grew from a townsite laid down in the early nineteenth century; and Lethbridge, a more recently urbanized, southern Alberta locale in a rapidly populated province created, with Saskatchewan, less than a decade before the outbreak of war. Studies of public sites in these cities can uncover how peoples in different regions defined themselves in relation to national demands and constraints. There are often revealing gaps between the context of a country at war and the local texts that result. Local responses that interested me most were those shaped by hometown horizons of understanding, perception, and imagination. The distances between wartime circumstances and hometown-produced responses necessarily mediate flows in either direction between national imperatives and urban spaces and discourses. This book addresses their many ambiguities as encounters between command centre directives and local peculiarities. Military historians of Canada and the war, for instance, have referred often to Sam Hughes' snap decision at the outbreak to scrap a recruit mobilization plan already in place. Instead, the Department of Militia and Defence sent 226 night telegrams asking for enlistments to militia commanders across the country. Brief chaos resulted. Trois-Rivières' previous militia commander, Lt.-Col. Louis-Phillipe Mercier, got one of these calls for troops and had to remind Ottawa that his unit had just been disbanded. The breakup in June 1914 of the 86th Three Rivers Regiment had already prompted bitter reaction from one city newspaper, and it underscores the complete absence, at a crucial time, of a local recruiting desk for a significantly large regional centre in Quebec.

Meanwhile, Guelph and Lethbridge papers joined the popular press across Canada in generating vivid descriptions of crowded armouries, 'official' pronouncements, and the first send-off rallies staged by local communities: the announcement of war, the sight of young civilians crowding around the armoury, the recruiter's desk, documents, medical examinations, marching drills, all were followed by frenetic send-off displays. Each part of this process was liminal, ephemeral, immediate, and situated. Such sites activated parochial experiences, measured by the perpetual distances between a country at war and the complexities of varied urban populations. By critically examining hometown horizons as local responses mediated on local sites, we can particularize a wide variety of questions concerning homefront perceptions. What did recruits represent? Why were enemy aliens a threat? On what grounds should conscription be supported or opposed? How should veterans be treated?

Answers to these questions, of course, were far from singular. During the conscription crisis, for instance, when Lester Pearson's father, the Rev. Edwin A. Pearson, pastor of Guelph's Norfolk Street Methodist Church, declared that 'the principle reason why I support Sir Robert Borden and the Hon. Hugh Guthrie and Union Government is my entire family of three sons are at the front,' he offered a position for others to see a contentious issue.[3] His brief oration, reprinted in the local press, can be compared to an address by the Rev. W.J. Hindley, a war veteran, delivered before a crowd attending a first-ever Chautauqua show at Lethbridge's Eckstorm auditorium. Hindley was said to have animated his audience when he spoke about conscription as an unneeded measure in western Canada. He described the West as a patriotic heartland, fiercely loyal to Canada and to Britain, a region which had already paid far more than its fair share. 'The east,' Hindley claimed, 'has said that the west is materialistic, but when the war broke out, the four western provinces proved themselves by the enlistments of men and by the generosity of their gifts.' Muscular patriotism, as he put it, was a virtue of Canada's West. 'Wild ruggedness and loyal hearts,' he declared, 'go to make up the westerner.'[4]

Examining how such evidence was formed or 'situated' – how it was said, where it was said, and by whom – helps us to interpret both its content and effects. What, for example, was the relationship between send-off rallies and the making of recruits as hometown products at the beginning of the war? How in Guelph did a military inquiry, staged to investigate veteran care in one of its hospitals, both express and influence how its patients saw themselves shortly after it ended?

As Joan Scott has argued, subjects in situations analogous to these encounter signifying acts that become symbolic not simply as 'an experience,' but because they are experienced in active ways. The proposition that 'experience' becomes significant when subjects replace prior interpretations with new ones is particularly applicable here. As the intensity of many challenges mounted, Canadians at home during the war were repeatedly required to develop new interpretations of what lay ahead in their appropriation of public discourses. As local participants, audiences, or principal actors, city inhabitants also helped to 'make' their hometown horizons both visible and potent. Conceptions and reconceptions were continually derived from complex flows of sensory information, typically found in local situations. Conceptually, as Roger Chartier has put it, the 'history of the construction of social identities thus becomes a history of relations of symbolic force.'[5] On the home front, these histories can often be located in accessible, familiar, and local texts and the sites on which they circulated.

I selected these particular cities because of their obvious differences as medium-sized urban spaces in francophone, anglophone, industrial (both Trois-Rivières and Guelph), and agricultural regions (especially Lethbridge); because of the richness of local, archival evidence; and because each supported particularly detailed and revealing local newspapers that were preserved, reasonably legible, and topically comprehensive. Although the same might be said for comparable materials drawn from other locales, in terms of scale (between eight and sixteen thousand inhabitants), regional variation (land-use histories and corresponding ethnic geographies), and record survival, these choices avoided the empirical hazard of amassing too much material from too many regions while affording core samples sufficiently rooted in local peculiarities and perspectives.

I would not say, however, that this book emphasizes local or even regional identities; only that these became part of a much more complex perceptual mix when it came to representing the war publicly and to fashioning the many boundaries that divided home front populations. A large and very useful historiography has accumulated that considers Canadian responses, and the responses of some of Canada's regions, to the war. Descriptive overviews include, most notably, Desmond Morton and J.L. Granatstein's *Marching to Armageddon* (1989), though both authors have published, individually and with others, detailed studies of conscription, Canada's overseas war ministry, and veteran re-establishment.[6] On regional histories of the home front, John Herd Thompson's study of the Prairie provinces is joined by a much earlier work on the conscription crisis in Quebec by Elizabeth Armstrong. Donald Avery, Howard Palmer, and Bill Waiser have each examined the plight of enemy aliens in the western provinces, perceived by the host society of mainly white, Anglo-Saxon Canadians as 'dangerous,' close to the bottom of an ethnic 'pecking order,' and ultimately subject to internment and forced labour that included major projects building roads and facilities at Jasper, Banff, and Yoho national parks in Alberta and British Columbia. Other works have concentrated on specific topics related to military affairs or military-civilian relations based on regional or provincial histories. Jean-Pierre Gagnon, for instance, presented a detailed social-historical analysis of the 22nd Battalion, recruited largely in Quebec, while more recently Paul Maroney examined cultural aspects of recruitment in Ontario.[7]

Generally, historians in the past have paid close attention to developing the war's political and diplomatic chronologies and have highlighted its significance as an armed encounter that fundamentally altered Canada's relationship to Britain and the Empire. From A.F. Duguid's officially authorized version of events, presented in 1938, to G.W.L. Nicholson's subsequent account of the Canadian Expeditionary Force, published in 1962, their emphasis on military history remained faithful to a compelling politic in Canadian history writing: to bring to light a more independent role for Canada. The war became a sign, a watershed, for the colony-to-nation school. This theme has since been reinforced in broad surveys of Canada's military history by C.P. Stacey, Stephen Harris, and Desmond Morton, among others, that embrace the war years.[8] These more traditional approaches, which ostensibly seek to explain decision-making processes, battlefield outcomes, and reconstruction efforts, also demonstrate a remarkably consistent enterprise of connecting selected aspects of Canada's national identity to its participation in the Great War. 'Even though Canadians fought as allies of the British,' as Morton and Granatstein put it, 'for Canada the Great War was a war of independence. By 1918, the self-governing colony that had trusted its fate to British statecraft was not only committed to speaking with its own voice in the world, it had won on the battlefield the right to be heard.'[9]

Nation-building was fostered in a variety of ways. Veterans, for instance, as Morton and Glenn Wright have shown, waged a 'second battle' in their struggle for better re-establishment programs that the authors present as a precursor to the subsequent development of the modern welfare state in Canada. On the other hand, social memories of the war, as Jonathan F. Vance's recent turn toward cultural history points out, coalesced around themes of sacrifice, duty, and honour that also produced a new and popular sense of nationhood built on mythical conceptions of the ultimate meaning of the death and destruction it caused. Vance unearthed a vast range of middlebrow literature and commemorative practices, and he focused his interpretive efforts on their role in shaping a new and more distinct national identity. He emphasized that throughout the interwar period, popular exercises of myth-making 'added the nation-building thesis' to a remarkably persistent effort across the country to derive positive meaning from what had been such a costly and disastrous event. Many wished to believe that great sacrifices had been made by a new and now greater nation, a country made whole, not torn apart, during the strenuous tests of 1914-18.[10]

Though this was hardly a reality during the conscription crisis or when dealing with enemy aliens or during efforts to reintegrate returned soldiers, to note major exceptions, Vance was looking at something quite different. His work considered the subsequent 'uses' of a cultural sense of the past. It examined how the memory of the war became a national heritage project, based on sanitizing myths fashioned to ennoble those who had made the supreme sacrifice. Such illusions could be powerful. 'By encouraging people to focus their thoughts on a time when the nation appeared to be united in a common cause, the memory of the war could prove that the twentieth century did indeed belong to Canada.'[11] Striving for political and military independence, in other words, rested in part on the invention of idealized versions of the war, imagined and remembered through popular discourses, from commemorative rites to middlebrow fiction and consumer advertising.

While these studies show a marked consistency linking wartime experience to nation-building, it is equally important to note that significant shifts in topics and methods have taken place as well, from military, diplomatic, and political history and biography to social and, most recently, cultural histories of the war. These changing historical practices should be placed in a broader context, revealing a new emphasis on home front histories and away from the fighting itself. While in the 1970s Eric J. Leed's and Paul Fussell's work considered the war experience as a crucial break for the soldiers themselves – a liminal transition for the troops who survived the horror of no man's land, according to Leed, and a significant shift in subsequent languages and literary genres, according to Fussell, and later Samuel Hynes – Modris Eksteins subsequently went beyond these domains in his examination of many parallel aspects of the war as a cultural break from tradition. Eksteins considered its impact across Western societies, and his book joined a growing body of work that relocated the many consequences of war well back from the actual fighting, deeply embedded in the societal and cultural contexts ultimately affected by the carnage. The work of social historians in particular, from the collaborative projects of Jay Winter to new studies and edited collections of women and the war, has examined war's consequences behind the lines through studies of the complex systems of social structure and cultural exchange on different national home fronts.[12]

In two important collaborations, *The Upheaval of War* (1988) and *Capital Cities at War* (1997), Jay Winter and others presented new work that emphasized the quantitative social history of home front conditions, primarily through comparative studies of living standards, family life, workers, women, and youth.[13] While the latter book, based on studies of Paris, London, and Berlin, emphasized social and demographic assessments, it left consideration of popular culture, particularly interpretations of local representations, open to further study and alternative approaches. Although the volume remains a useful examination of urban spaces and wartime experience, and purports to 'turn to the social history of material life in Paris, London, and Berlin' to 'trace the history of social relations of work, wages, and consumption, attending both to quantitative evidence and to the perceptions of contemporaries,' it falls short in tracing histories of perception. Only one of the sixteen essays – on the image of the war profiteer – tackles representations per se as a central object of study.

Nonetheless, as a study primarily of social relations and structural change, this project achieved other aims admirably, following an introduction that addresses the relationship between localized and national experiences of Europeans at war. Winter observes that the history of the Great War has been told within various 'national frameworks.' Nations, however, do not wage wars, he reminds us. 'Groups of people organized in states do.' Only in an 'abstract, legal' sense did France and Britain wage war on Germany, he suggests. On the one hand, 'a declaration of war was ratified by the appropriately empowered bodies; funds were earmarked, and enabling acts opened the way to armed conflict'; on the other, local differences made armed mobilization and home front support a more complex process. The 'concrete, visible steps taken by Frenchmen, Germans, or Englishmen,' Winter argued, 'to go to war, to provision the men who joined up, and to adjust to the consequences – the human dimension of war – were almost always taken within and expressed through collective life at the local level: communities of volunteers or conscripts; communities of munitions workers; communities of the faithful and bereaved.'[14]

While the nation, to invoke Benedict Anderson's thesis, is an imagined experience, local life is often less so. Living locally entails direct encounters and interactions. A sense of national belonging, however, is framed much more by the symbols of an imagined community, those patent, traditional, often patriotic signs that are shared across a population experiencing life within the nation-state on different levels simultaneously. Images of a warring nation, as a clear example, are powerful to the extent that they bring local life and national community into close communion. Studying their points of intersection, Winter indicated, helps us understand how this war was waged, lived, and experienced. Problematically, however, he relied on a static notion of 'community' to emphasize this fundamental point: 'We take "community" to mean social and geographical entities around which ordinary people construct their daily lives. In this sense a neighbourhood is an "experienced community"; a "nation," as Benedict Anderson tells us, is an "imagined community"; a city is at the meeting point of the two, with both an imaginative and a visible existence, one much closer to the neighbourhood than the nation.'[15]

Distinctions between experienced and imagined communities are not easily drawn. Parades, for instance, were often organized to frame perceptions of what lay beyond the environs of town and city. In these local situations, where did the nation begin and the street, neighbourhood, or city recede into the background? If local sites are used to see much larger pictures, then clear distinctions between microhistorical events and macrohistorical circumstances remain elusive. 'The distinction,' Winter conceded, 'between "experienced" and "imagined" communities is best understood as a heuristic device.' As he saw it (and this is where my work departs from his most) the effects of cultural signs – what people use to communicate with or through – can be distinguished from those of material settings – what people face as material circumstances. He implies a dichotomy between 'lived perceptions' and 'lived conditions.' He also assumes that wartime demands increased the force of the latter. Reading the signs of home front experiences becomes secondary to analytical assessments of the 'physical realities' of wartime demands and conditions, from enforced laws to shortages to morbidity rates. 'One of the challenges of such research has been to escape the trap of idealism in social history, to avoid the fashionable current in which only representations exist,' Winter writes. 'Wartime cities were full of such images, but the realities of daily life in wartime all too frequently deflated them by bringing to the fore the physical realities of conscription, shortages, and spiraling food prices.'[16]

I do not think they were necessarily deflated or that some representations paled in comparison to the actual conditions. Without assuming, reductively, that locally experienced lives were constituted by discursive strategies alone, historians are increasingly challenged to examine relationships between actual conditions and actual responses. The signs and the practices of local life mediated an awareness of various physical 'realities' – of death, danger, hardship, or loss. 'Urban populations,' as Winter put it himself, 'faced these tangible, visceral difficulties in one way or another every day of the war.'

But encounters with these 'realities' did not displace other signs of the war, somehow relegated to the background as murmurs or noise. Indeed, the most tangible and visceral of wartime referents were made real through interpretations of their ordinary, popular, and local signs. 'All we can claim,' as he concluded before turning to the studies themselves, 'is that these levels of perception and adaptation can be explored more effectively on the local level than on the national level.'[17] About this we are in preliminary agreement. Since most work to date has paid little attention to what people in local settings typically used as signs or as symbols to see the war with, or through, I would emphasize that the local level becomes a crucial plane of experience on which national-level 'realities' were lived, while retaining Winter's other point – that assessing the evidence of local life often becomes crucial in determining wartime perceptions.

I had much to choose from. From Trois-Rivières, for instance, there was the *Bien Public* itself, the city's most widely circulated newspaper and vanguard for French Catholicism. There was the *hôtel de ville* (city hall), where speeches endorsing the Canadian Patriotic Fund were delivered; the St. Lawrence River waterfront, where troopships bound for England steamed downstream, while those carrying the wounded or returned moved upriver; the Canadian Pacific station platform, with a military guard posted, watchful of unruly soldiers stepping off for a smoke while local citizens scuttled by in fear of contracting the *peste blanc*, tuberculosis. Guelph had its Grand Trunk Railroad platform, which most troops left from or returned to; its exhibition grounds; and its armoury, which, with many of its churches, created settings for send-off ceremonies at the beginning of the war and welcome-home and memorial services afterwards. In Lethbridge, the Department of Militia and Defence had converted a portion of the city's exhibition grounds into a prison camp for enemy aliens. Half a dozen escapes, several drawn-out military inquiries, and a series of newspaper reports later helped to conjure fantastic images of enemy aliens, a fear built on demonization efforts situated close to home.

This is not a study of three cities during the war. In Habermasian terms, the public spheres or lifeworlds one finds in them were far from holistic: there was no single 'Lethbridge,' Alberta, or 'Guelph,' Ontario, or 'Trois-Rivières,' Quebec, from which the evidence of the war could be seen or read or constructed in only locally identifiable terms. As Geertz remarked famously, it is not villages that anthropologists study, but rather what takes place within them.[18] I would like to say the same of my approach. Ordinary perceptions of civilian-military relations, even as the war dragged on and its effects became vastly general, were constrained by place, by localized referential modes, and by pre-existing patterns of expression and understanding (despite the fact that telegraph, telephone, and rail had significantly reduced the time taken to traverse or to communicate).

The framing was communicated in public spheres that varied, but remained site-specific. It could introduce novelty or notions of the meaning of the battles overseas. Trois-Rivières's location on the shores of Canada's main waterway access to the interior, for instance, provided moments of experiential connection to the war that could not have been duplicated in inland communities like Lethbridge or Guelph. As people paused to gaze out from the municipal waterfront, they often saw large vessels moving up or down the St. Lawrence, comprising an important share of Canada's North Atlantic sea traffic. In several press reports, these ships and the river soon came to symbolize a sense of local connection to the fighting overseas. One afternoon in June 1915, for example, news of a troopship passing the city upstream carrying wounded from the Canadian Expeditionary Force's first battles attracted onlookers, described quite differently from those who applauded Pearson's remarks or cheered Hindley vociferously. Instead, this gathering was said to have watched in near silence as the vessel moved out of sight, in a moment conducive to imagining a very different war. 'Quite a number were on the wharf Sunday to see the S.S. *Missanabie* go up,' the *Newcomer* described the scene, 'as there were quite a number of wounded officers and soldiers on board.'[19]

The deceptive and crucial distances between what people immediately construe and what actually happens elsewhere increased in many home front situations. This gives historians fair scope to juxtapose interior, localized, vertical perspectives, perhaps those of the crowd of onlookers gathered at Trois-Rivières's city wharf, with imagined horizons of the fighting overseas and home front conditions generally. War-related discourse and practices were formulated, amplified, and exchanged on 'known' or 'knowable' sites, seldom distant from everyday life but far removed from their referents or motivating aims. The spate of myth-making, propagandizing, demonizing, hero-worshipping, or fear-mongering that is ordinarily found in the vehicles of public culture, from newspaper sensationalism to street theatre, is approached here as a series of messages that could open considerable gaps. Popular interpretations, perhaps created by a grotesque report of enemy alien sabotage, often repressed a corresponding reality of, for instance, young Hungarians from Lethbridge on the march to forced labour in Banff National Park. This book considers how reports like these in Lethbridge, Guelph, and Trois-Rivières operated as transports of Otherness, fashioning on the parochial sites of urban spaces a potent dissonance between popular discourses and the wartime realities that others experienced, from enemy aliens to front-line soldiers.

Throughout, I consider how verbal and pictorial texts or military and civilian rituals were placed in power struggles on these sites, where prior knowledge was deployed, as narratives and social memories, to adjust, inscribe, or reconstitute aspects of wartime identity. How did narrative clusters – patriotic, gendered, religious, or nationalistic – demonize enemy aliens, proclaim loyalty, or delineate boundaries between veterans and other Canadians? How were they used to circumscribe or to police gendered margins, or to delineate positions for or against compulsory military service? Evidence in these forms, multiple as codes and meanings, can tell us much about how home front perceptions were fashioned within the fluid environs of a city. It also suggests how the differences we view as the most fundamental divisions created by the war across Canada came into being through the immediacy and contingency of everyday life.

Hometown Horizons

1
Places and Sites

A farmhand, Albert, has been living for some twelve years with a French Canadian family, the Moisans, on one of the thousands of narrow Laurentian strip farms on the St. Lawrence River. Their small but just sufficient thirty-acre parcel is close to Trois-Rivières. During the threshing of 1914, Albert begins spending his evenings doing something he had never regularly done before – reading the local paper. These days, of course, its pages are filled with sensational accounts of fighting overseas. They appear in story after story, from those under bold headlines to serial reports that run alongside minute local notices in the back pages. Albert tries to brush aside early news of the German advance through France, the country of his birth, but seems absorbed in an exercise of intense reading over several evenings that will soon lead to a crucial decision in his life.

His employer, Euchariste Moisan, is also disturbed by recent news of war. Moisan is a farmer, a descendant of the agricultural society of rural Quebec that continues its lurching transitions toward modernity. Moisan sees his whole life as one linked to the land, its kinship networks, and its local pasts. He tries to imagine why such killing has begun so far away. What prompted such hatreds, such passions, such massive military responses? On the one hand, he thinks of how France, the land of his ancestors, is spoken of by the people he knows best, his friends and neighbours, in tones of deep respect, a distant motherland that even the simplest and rudest would not dare shame with their vulgarisms. On the other, this strange news of war seems not only to have upset deeply seated tranquilities, more imagined than real; it reminds him also of a parish curé who had warned that, some day, France would be punished for getting rid of its priests.

A few nights later, Moisan's trusted hired hand, Albert, turns pale and tosses his newspaper aside. As reliable as the seasons ordinarily, he suddenly disappears that night. He returns the next morning to tell Moisan of his difficult decision: He is going to return to France to rejoin the army he had deserted for a new life in Quebec more than a decade ago.

Moisan suddenly realizes that even his scant thirty acres, a place so seemingly distant from the war, and this harmless man who helped him work it can not remain isolated from what this upsetting, new confrontation will come to mean for many: departure, separation, and loss. Surely, he tries to reassure himself, his own sons will stay. The war has nothing to do with them. To put this moment in its original terms, we hear Albert say:

> 'Monsieur Moisan, il faut que je parte,' il se rendit compte que ce qui se passait là-bas, si loin d'eux, était venu toucher au fond d'une calme paroisse du Québec un homme paisible qui jamais pourtant n'avait apparemment souhaité de mal à âme qui vive, qui jamais n'avait désiré la terre ni la maison du voisin. Il comprit surtout que la guerre, c'était le départ. Ses fils à lui ne partiraient pas, puisque cela ne les touchait point. Mais il pouvait bien en être autrement de l'homme qu'il avait en face de lui, de cet homme qui jamais n'avait été complètement des leurs, malgré onze ans passés sur les mêmes trente arpents de terre, cette terre-ci.[1]

Moisan listens as this quiet man speaks of the 'damned Boches' in France, images that ultimately drove him, Albert Chabrol, a deserter, back to his native land and into uniform. At the same time, Albert pauses to consider why just a few words in a newspaper came to mean so much to him and so little to his employer, a man of the soil not far from Trois-Rivières.

This scene is drawn from Philippe Panneton's (Ringuet's) masterwork, *Trente Arpents,* which first appeared, in French, in 1938. The story of two generations of family life on a small farm near Trois-Rivières, this novel has since become a classic depiction of how modernization came, step by step, to change the lives of ordinary people on the rural countryside in Quebec. Throughout, Panneton, who grew up in Trois-Rivières, constructs vivid portraits of rural life in Quebec well into the interwar period, based on a series of intersections between broad historical shifts and local socio-cultural landscapes.

The war became yet one more event that even a parochial farmer could not turn his back on entirely. The pathos of *Trente Arpents* is underscored by this basic point, that no people can really become an island unto themselves, no matter how much they may wish or even try to do so. In an immediate and significant sense this is how the war affected all Canadians, whether young men choosing to abandon the seasonal cycles on the Laurentian lowlands in search of work in Trois-Rivières; or longstanding residents of British origin in Guelph, Ontario, an industrialized service centre in the mid-southern region of the province; or recent arrivals in the new city of Lethbridge, incorporated less than a decade before the war as the largest service centre in southern Alberta.

How local populations in Canada came to respond to the war stemmed from how they used local sites to activate a coherent sense of what seemed to be happening overseas or elsewhere, often well beyond immediate referents of locale – the sights, sounds, feelings, and meanings that local, war-related experiences generated in the midst of a significant period of historical change. The war, in other words, often unfolded as a story that had to be told and retold, through sermons, parades, speeches, editorials, gossip, and a host of local events that broadcast in very ordinary terms what many understood, quite correctly, was an extraordinary period in history. The printed news, posters, rituals, or snatches of conversation used to fashion specific reactions were both produced and embedded in the local spaces that people used to broadcast them. We begin, then, as Albert Chabrol did, at the margins of local setting and international news.

Toward the Outbreak of War: Local Populations, Heterogeneous Domains

Trois-Rivières, Guelph, and Lethbridge, as unique locales, represent Canada's vastly different regional social pasts. Trois-Rivières, Quebec, the oldest by far as a post-contact population centre, was colonized by Europeans during the early sixteenth century as part of the *ancien régime* in New France. The French began by developing trade relations with the Montagnais, Huron, and Algonkians who lived and travelled along the watersheds of the north shore of the St. Lawrence. War with the Iroquois, who intercepted St. Lawrence fur trade traffic on its way to Tadoussac, lent strategic importance to the confluence of the Rivière St-Maurice and the St. Lawrence River, where Trois-Rivières came to be located.

In 1632, annual trading became regularized when a small fort was established there under the command of Laviolette, a fur trader commissioned by Champlain. The Jesuits set up a permanent mission within the stockade that same year. Situated on a three-pronged delta, Trois-Rivières's physical features offered water-travelling traders and its first settlers a convenient name. The site was consistently occupied by settlers, their descendants, and newcomers, and grew to be the third largest city in Quebec by the eve of the First World War.

Some two centuries after Trois-Rivières's founding, in an era of rapid commercial expansion, Guelph grew from a townsite laid down in the 1820s by the Canada Company, a land-based enterprise set up to profit from control of agricultural settlement in mid-southern Ontario, then part of Upper Canada. From its original settlers to its social geography in August 1914, Guelph remained a predominantly British locale, rooted in the transition from a fledgling commercial and milling settlement in the 1830s to a regional manufacturing and transportation service centre in the early twentieth century. Compared to the settlements along the St. Lawrence, Guelph was one of many medium-sized cities in southern Ontario that had followed a more dispersed pattern of urban growth, fuelled by commercial and industrial expansion since settlement in the era of the two Canadas, Upper and Lower.[2]

Finally, located in the centre of the southern prairie grasslands, a vast region resettled rapidly between 1885 and 1914, Lethbridge stands in further contrast. As the nineteenth century drew to a close, the city's sudden appearance and growth was due partly to government-sponsored concessions, but mainly to the rapid development of a grain-growing region. Irrigation projects and new railway spur lines, combined with a significant influx of newcomers of diverse ethnic origins lured by the promise of a better life in the Canadian West, gave Lethbridge by 1914 a relatively diverse social mix and a pattern of resettlement experiences.

Given such enormous dissimilarities of location and of patterns of Euro-Canadian colonization, we might consider population compositions in each city as a starting point for historicizing their enormous ethnic differences, from a striking homogeneity of francophone Catholics in Trois-Rivières (over 95 percent) to the significant diversity among newcomers in Lethbridge. Comparing different origins and local factors affecting population growth since the late nineteenth century gives us useful entry points for contrasting local social differences that came to shape very different perceptions and responses to the war.

According to the census of 1911, respective populations stood at 13,691 inhabitants in Trois-Rivières; 15,175 in Guelph; and 8,050 in Lethbridge. In each case, growth patterns began to accelerate markedly after the turn of the century. Economic development had certainly stimulated very different in-migrations in each case. During the five decades of in-migration to each city from 1871 to 1921, as Trois-Rivières received inflows from the surrounding countryside, while migrants from outside Canada poured into the Lethbridge area, growth in each locale corresponded to rising labour demands, from primary commodity production to professional services, given the particular metropolitan-periphery niches each local economy served. Of course, quite dissimilar pull factors – the coal and wheat production of southern Alberta, the mixed economies of southern Ontario, and the lumber and textile industries of the Mauricie – attracted and sustained populations of diverse origins, though ethnicity in Trois-Rivières remained predominantly French Canadian. That all three cities underwent growth spurts indicates the extent to which a sense of novelty and change, dampened by the recession of 1913, had become part of everyday life, particularly for recent arrivals who had often left very different lives behind, whether in European homelands or on the rural countryside in Canada.

Though these changes were experienced differently by individuals, families, and communities criss-crossed by class-based, gendered, and ethnic diversity, few citizens could overlook changed circumstances in their lives. Many millworkers, displaced by depressed agricultural conditions in the surrounding area, worked for low wages in Trois-Rivières's textile industry, while immigrants from Eastern Europe faced exploitative and dangerous conditions in the coal mines of Lethbridge. Whether coping with the rising cost of living as wage earners or with income shortfalls as business or farming families, or in struggles to move up the social ladder or simply to maintain their status, most Canadians were adapting to new work conditions and practices connected to volatile rates of social mobility and accelerating patterns of geographic transiency. Rapid change from the latter nineteenth century onward created crowded and often poor housing conditions in urban locales, often worse from those only a generation before. For most city dwellers, who lived in the more densely concentrated working-class neighbourhoods, the future seemed uncertain, particularly during the general economic downturn of 1912-13. Economic cycles connected to population growth throughout most parts of Canada remained part of an ongoing struggle to impose, maintain, or resist local hierarchies, contests that often came into sharp relief during the war. A brief tour of each city's distinctive districts and local peculiarities will help to set the stages on which these contests were played out after the outbreak of war.

Trois-Rivières

Conversion and expansion from pre-industrial commercial capitalism to an industrial locale with ideal water shipping access for the pulp, paper, and timber products of the Mauricie prompted a burst of in-migration and growth in Trois-Rivières in the early twentieth century. This had long been a favoured location for commerce and manufacturing, for forest products processing in the latter nineteenth century, and for textiles production in the twentieth. The city also retained its importance as a regional service centre and central location for educational, religious, and other cultural institutions during this period of industrial transformation. Accelerated growth came with the expansion of logging on the Laurentian shield in the latter nineteenth century and with the construction of pulp and paper and textile mills in the early twentieth century. Significant changes in the material contexts of everyday life brought with it changes in community formation, in cultural life, and in the mental outlooks of rural populations linked by kinship networks, by regional histories, and by that complex cultural web that historians inspired by the *Annales* school have called the *mentalité* of given populations. As René Hardy and Normand Séguin concluded in their study of forestry and social formation in the Mauricie region, it was the peasantry and, later, the new colonization parishes that provided the manpower for the forestry sector: 'La masse paysanne des anciennes paroisses du bord du fleuve, et plus tard des nouvelles paroisses de colonisation, a fourni la substance humaine à cette mainmise sur le domaine forestier et à l'occupation du nouvel œcumène.'[3]

Population growth in Trois-Rivières, the third largest urban centre on the St. Lawrence next to Montreal and Quebec City, reflected in-migrations from adjacent agricultural areas on both sides of the St. Lawrence, including Francheville, Le Centre-de-la-Mauricie, and Maskinongé to the north, and Bécancour and Nicolet-Yamaska to the south. Many men and women sought work in the labour-intensive textile industry established by the Wabasso Cotton works, or in more capital-intensive timber processing, industries that expanded in uneven spurts up to the 1930s to meet the demands of external markets. As a general pattern, these in-migrations of people, who were overwhelmingly francophone, Catholic, and indigenous to the region for several generations, were not new.

In terms of European colonization, over four centuries of occupation by French-born newcomers and their descendants had created a social geography distinct from that of Guelph or Lethbridge. After Aboriginal contact, which began with Cartier's voyages in the sixteenth century, the St. Lawrence lowlands became the heartland of New France in fairly discrete stages. Samuel de Champlain's influence was significant, particularly in terms of constructing fortified settlements in the early seventeenth century. He ordered one for Trois-Rivières in 1634. Its location was strategic, connecting the Rivière St-Maurice valley to the St. Lawrence and affording convenient midpoint contact between Montreal and Quebec. Trois-Rivières's importance as an administrative centre began when it acquired a *gouverneur* in 1663. Between then and the Conquest a century later, the population increased marginally to six hundred inhabitants.

Figure 1 illustrates population increases between 1871 and 1921. The rate of increase for Trois-Rivières exceeded both Quebec's and Canada's from the turn of the century. Between the census of 1911 and that of 1921, the recorded population for the city rose from 13,691 to 22,367 inhabitants as newcomers secured work in an increasingly diversified economy. In manufacturing alone, employment increased almost three-fold between 1871 (871 employees) and 1911 (2,323 employees).[4] With the forest industry's expanding influence in the region, firms like the Wabasso Cotton Company, established in 1907, and Wayagamack Pulp and Paper Ltd., founded in 1910, exploited the advantages of an abundant labour supply, proximity to suppliers and customers, and relatively cheap power furnished by the Shawinigan Water and Power Company. Some twenty-five other manufacturers included in the 1911 census employed growing numbers of workers, supplied in large part from surrounding areas. The resulting pattern of intra-regional migration into the city led to a high degree of ethnic homogeneity immediately preceding the war years.

Even by 1914, Trois-Rivières's ethnic homogeneity was striking in comparison to most cities and towns in Canada. Guelph had an Ontario-born proportion of 74.1 percent. In Lethbridge, a recent spate of development

Figure 1

Percentage changes in population in Trois-Rivières, Quebec, and Canada by decennial intervals, 1871-1921

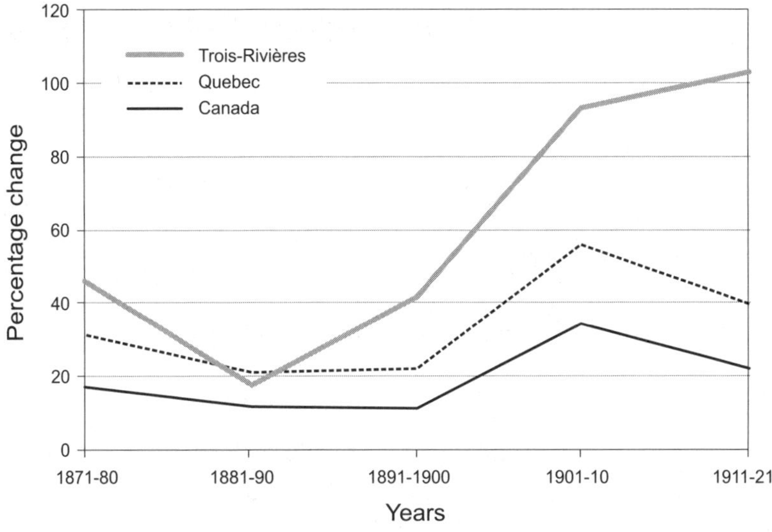

Source: Sixth Census of Canada 1921 (Ottawa: King's Printer, 1924), vol. 1, Table 12, p. 235.

and rise in labour demand, based on servicing grain-growing and coal production, had brought large numbers into the city, most from the rest of Canada or from Europe. This regional process, which took off after the Canadian Pacific Railway (CPR) opened in the mid-1880s, left Lethbridge's Alberta-born population at just 14.6 percent by 1911. As of 1911, however, the formal census recorded 13,259 of Trois-Rivières's 13,691 inhabitants (96.8 percent) as Quebec-born (see Figure 2).

Figure 3 underscores as well the predominance of French Canadian ethnicity in Trois-Rivières. A very high 95.6 percent claimed 'French' as their national origin. Overall, the entire province of Quebec stood at 80.1 percent. The proportion of Roman Catholics was even greater. In 1911, 97 percent of Trifluviens (13,328 of 13,691) were enumerated as Catholics, while Quebec as a whole reported 86.1 percent. Minority Protestants in the city, as a tiny fraction, were led in absolute numbers by Anglicans (152), Presbyterians (92), and Methodists (22).[5]

Since the turn of the century, Trois-Rivières had been in the midst of a sustained period of industrial development that fluctuated but did not show long-term decline until the 1930s. Many of its neighbourhoods, particularly those in the east end, had expanded in class-based patterns, with an increase in single-family residential blocks closer to the downtown core,

Figure 2

Proportion of population by birthplace in Trois-Rivières, Quebec, and Canada, 1911

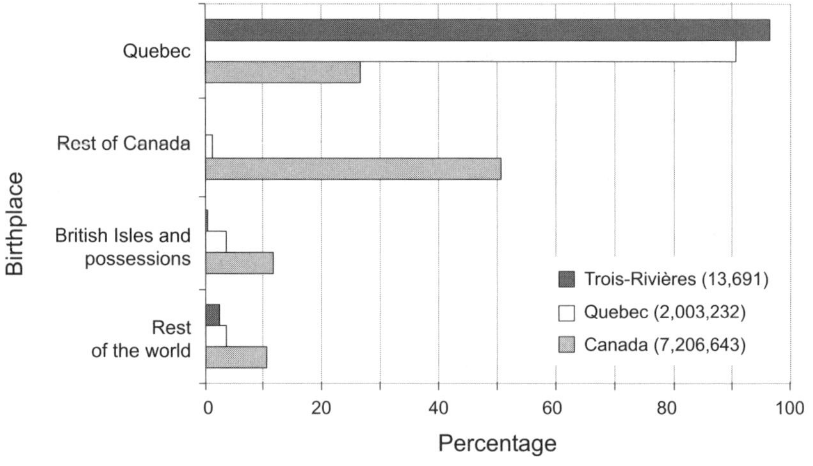

Source: Fifth Census of Canada 1911 (Ottawa: King's Printer, 1913), vol. 2, Tables 16 and 17, pp. 433, 441, and 443.

Figure 3

Proportion of population by national origin in Trois-Rivières, Quebec, and Canada, 1911

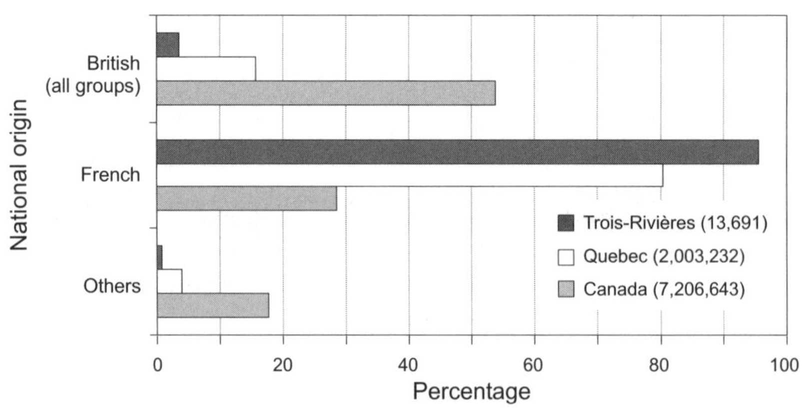

Source: Fifth Census of Canada 1911 (Ottawa: King's Printer, 1913), vol. 2, Tables 7 and 8, pp. 256, 312, and 340.

and new rows of low-cost dwellings in working-class neighbourhoods built in each of the surrounding city blocks.

Bounded by the St. Lawrence to the south, the St-Maurice to the east, the CPR lines to the north, and its spur connector to the west, four fairly distinct city quarters had developed by 1914: St-Phillipe, St-Louis, Notre-Dame, and Ste-Ursule. Each radiated outwards from the downtown core. Expansion had taken place on their peripheries, particularly in the far east end, but each had remained largely intact up to our period, and the municipal government was routinely using them as administrative zones. Much of St-Louis and Notre-Dame had been rebuilt in higher density housing to accommodate influxes since about 1900. The Roman Catholic Church had

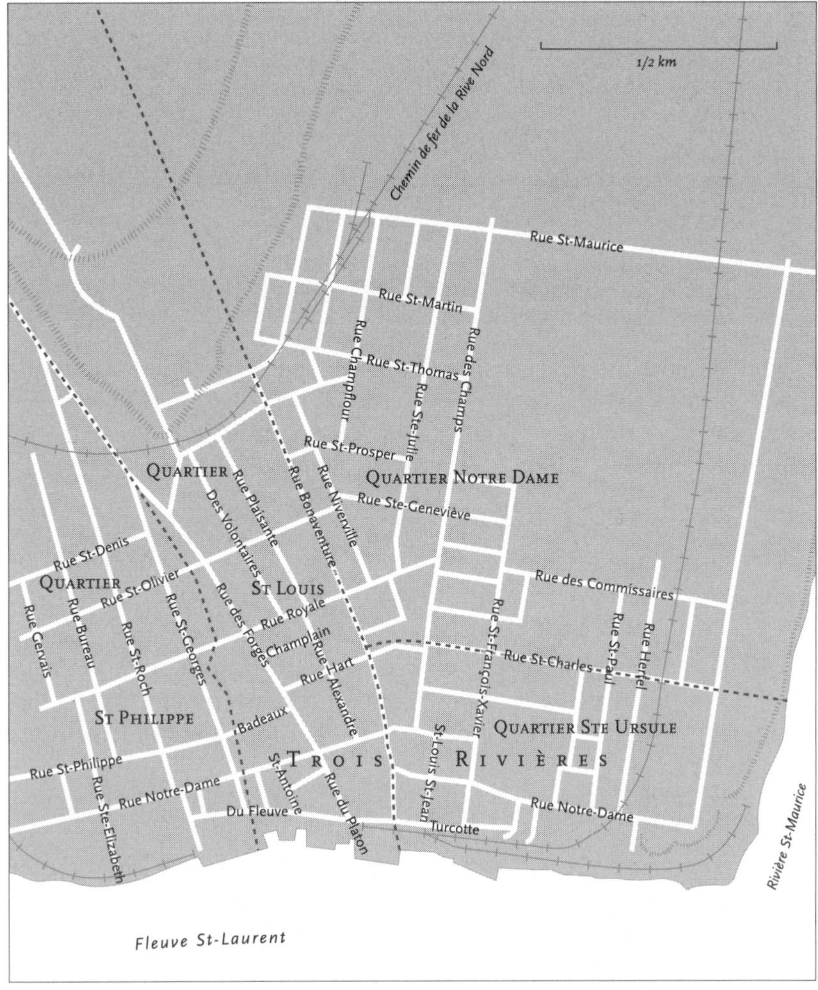

Major streets and municipal quarters of Trois-Rivières, Quebec, before 1914

designated four parishes for the city, beginning with the oldest, established in 1678. The others were new, all designated after 1909.[6]

In 1905, as part of a Canada-wide armoury construction program, the city's *manège militaire* was erected on rue St-François-Xavier. The genteel ambiance of the Quartier Notre-Dame streets changed, however, as one moved east toward rue Ste-Cécile and the Rivière St-Maurice and encountered newly constructed row housing. This more recently developed half of Notre-Dame was dominated by the new manufacturers driving Trois-Rivières' local economy: Canada Iron Foundry Limited, the Wabasso Cotton Company, and Wayagamack Paper Company overshadowed an industrial zone served by a local installation of the Shawinigan Water and Power Company and by a railway spur connecting this riverfront area to the CPR main line.

Below this area, to the east and toward the St. Lawrence, lay the architecturally historic quartier Ste-Ursule. Older buildings included the city's original post office (relocated on rue des Casernes in 1918), Monastère des Ursulines, École Ste-Ursule, and De La Salle Academy, the provincial jail, and the Wesleyan (Methodist) and St. James (Anglican) churches. Housing in the east and north sectors of this quarter was primarily low-income rentals for the city's expanding working class. Most of the older area, west of rue Hertel, remained comparatively unchanged, with fairly low residential densities of mixed socio-economic status.[7]

Four newspapers circulated in Trois-Rivières during the war: the *Bien Public*, a Roman Catholic paper; the *Nouveau Trois-Rivières*, a Liberal paper; the *Courrier*, a Conservative paper; and the *Newcomer*, the city's sole anglophone paper, edited by a Presbyterian minister, the Rev. J.A. Clark. In their compendium of Quebec newspapers founded in this era, André Beaulieu and Jean Hamelin provide circulation figures for the *Nouveau Trois-Rivières* as well as brief notes on proprietorships, editorial positions, and lifespans of each. The *Nouveau Trois-Rivières* (1908-17) began with a circulation of 750 in 1909 and rose to a peak of 5,000 in 1911 before plummeting to 850 in 1913. It dissolved in April 1917. The *Courrier* (1902-17) discontinued shortly afterwards, in August, leaving the *Bien Public* the only francophone paper. Beaulieu and Hamelin provide no circulation figures for the *Courrier* or for the *Newcomer* (1914-18). The latter's Anglo-Protestant readership was a tiny minority in Trois-Rivières, and the paper struggled to collect subscriptions throughout its brief life.[8]

The *Bien Public*, the city's leading paper, was representative of a particular genre of Quebec journalism known as the Catholic press, or *la bonne presse*. These newspapers were influential in this period, something historians of Quebec journalism frequently note.[9] Roman Catholics, from bishops to parishioners, often used *la bonne presse* to circulate commentaries on a wide variety of topics concerned with industrialism, urbanism, social questions, and the problem of French Canada's minority status within an English-speaking milieu across the continent. If, as many clerical elites held, Quebec Catholics were to pursue a civilizing mission in what was seen as a veritable sea of Anglo-Protestantism, then such papers played no small part in spreading their message. Theological perspectives shaped much of their content, and a provincial editorial committee under the bishop's direction closely governed what was printed and what was not. As Jean Hamelin and Nicole Gagnon noted, 'La presse catholique s'affirme une force sociale non négligeable. Le Comité central permanent de l'Action sociale de Québec entreprend d'unir tous les journaux catholiques dans une action commune, "dont l'object principal est la défense des intérêts religieux" et le souci premier, "une entière soumission à l'autorité ecclésiastique."'[10] Reorganized in 1914, this centralized, ecclesiastical body, whose task was to defend religious interests, exercised its influence on a variety of Catholic periodicals and newspapers, including the *Bien Public*.

The *Bien Public* began publishing its weekly editions in 1909 and affiliated with *la bonne presse* in 1911, when the bishop of Trois-Rivières, Mgr François-Xavier Cloutier, entered into a proprietorship with Joseph Barnard, its editor. Support of Catholic interests, whether of local or general concern, became its raison d'être from then on. Within a year, circulation reached 3,500 copies. Its popularity grew to 5,425 copies by the middle of the war and may have increased by 1917.[11] 'Quite obviously,' William F. Ryan stated in his study of the Catholic Church's role in Quebec's economic development, 'the paper was meant to educate as well as provide local news. If we can accept the circulation figures claimed by the *Bien Public* – 5,000 copies in a diocese of less than 90,000 at the end of 1910, with the energetic promotion work just at its beginning – and take into consideration the large size of the average family, this newspaper must have been available to the majority of the Catholics in the diocese, especially in the later years.'[12] The city's population was expanding at this time, and the paper's distribution included the surrounding rural areas as well. The population of the diocese of Trois-Rivières, at which the *Bien Public* was targeted, stood at 102,622 in 1917, over seven times the size of Trois-Rivières.[13]

By the autumn of 1914, Trois-Rivières's four urban zones combined to situate the hometown life experiences of over fourteen thousand people, almost entirely French Canadian citizens. Describing its spatial divisions and diverse social environs helps to introduce the public spaces and sites where the common constraints and conditions of Canada's home front were made immediate, challenged, or valorized. And although the construction of a newspaper text or accessible outdoor display or institutional setting might seem generic, how local settings framed understandings and responses to external demands remains crucial, yet little explored.

Shortly before war began, for instance, a conflict over symbolic display took place during an incident on the edge of the city that captured press attention. It concerned a ban on religious symbols traditionally used in the ceremonies of French Canada's volunteer militia. The military ordinance enforcing it, Regulation No. 156, became effective in June 1914. Customary processions involving Canada's militia could no longer follow established practice. Armed, uniformed troops, either permanent forces or voluntary militia corps, were now prohibited from marching alongside religious orders, the Papal Zouaves, crucifixes, or virtually any overt display of religious allegiance.[14] This new measure, which immediately provoked condemnations from the Catholic Church that were echoed in francophone editorials throughout Quebec, did little but alienate the province's French and Catholic militia volunteers. It was roundly condemned in all three of Trois-Rivières's francophone newspapers. It became, as well, a confrontation of more than words for French Canadian Catholics, who saw their interests at stake just when militia volunteers from a number of Quebec regiments assembled at the training camp grounds, located to the northeast of Trois-Rivières proper.

As the end of June approached, troops from Quebec's 12th Infantry Brigade, 1st Grenadiers, 3rd Victoria Rifles, and 65th Mount Royal Rifles arrived at a camp that soon swelled to some 2,500 men.[15] In the first few days of what became three weeks of training and manful camaraderie – a masculine rite of summer in many parts of Canada at that time – Roman Catholic troops had put up a temporary altar to celebrate the Mass. This itself was acceptable, provided that no troops under command and bearing arms assembled next to the altar itself. At the same time, several units announced their arrival by parading through Trois-Rivières's downtown core, forming a march past of citizen-soldiers that was said to have produced a powerful spectacle as they moved through the city's principal streets. They drew attention as well, perhaps, because something was missing, and it seems that local citizens knew and felt this absence as a slight from an English Canada personified by an Orangeman, Sam Hughes, minister of militia and defence. The soldiers marched in Trois-Rivières, but they tramped to and from the downtown streets for the first time without any sign of religious heritage, in full compliance with Regulation No. 156. What the *Bien Public* called 'la stupide ordonnance de M. Hughes' circulated as an outrage just when troops were putting up tents and preparing for militia exercises.[16] With the exception of the anglophone *Newcomer*, the city newspapers ran several stories highlighting the insulting absence of any sign of Catholicism on parade.

As part of the first week of events, Trois-Rivières's mayor, Joseph-Adolph Tessier, who also served as minister of roads in Quebec's Liberal government, was joined by his spouse in hosting a colourful reception for the camp commandant and his officers.[17] But this only seemed to gloss over the problem. Nothing had been resolved concerning Regulation No. 156. Then an incident took place that, in the end, buried everything but the anger. During preparations for the Mass held at the camp several days later, on the

1 Taken at Trois-Rivières's exhibition grounds, this scene displays the neatly-erected tents and well-groomed horses of a militia summer camp, a popular annual rite for young men and officers across Canada before the war. This depiction of order and routine, maintained by cavalry troops who are not shown, was framed a decade before the fiasco of July 1914, when Regulation No. 156 seemed to break any semblance of order and decorum at this camp's first Sunday morning mass, held just over a month before the outbreak of war. *Courtesy of Archives du Séminaire de Trois-Rivières, FN-0064-49-04*

first Sunday of July 1914, a young and defiant captain from one of the assembled units, Eugene Bourassa, formed an armed guard of honour in front of the makeshift altar, determined to act in deliberate violation of Hughes's new regulation. The camp commandant, however torn he might have been, would not permit this. He immediately ordered the guard turned out, shutting down the whole symbolic act. The Liberal *Nouveau Trois-Rivières* noted that this command, which upheld the new and hated regulation, caused great uproar among the camp soldiers and Catholic officers.[18] Even the Conservative *Courrier* described the outcome as based on an 'injuste et injustifiable' directive by militia minister Sam Hughes.[19]

Less than two months before war broke out, another news report challenged the propriety of a symbolic gesture by Mayor Tessier. At the same time Hughes was being widely castigated as the villain who ran roughshod over traditional rites, Tessier was chastised as a partisan of confused loyalties, a Liberal French Canadian who chose to fly a Union Jack at city hall and another at his home. As the *Courrier* reported: 'Plusieurs citoyens nous ont fait remarquer que "l'Union Jack" flottait sur l'Hôtel de ville et la résidence de son honneur le maire.'[20] In Trois-Rivières, it was not easy for a politician to walk the line between the city's French Catholic heritage and a Dominion that remained part of the British Empire.

Mayor Tessier knew this well, as did the local member of Parliament, Jacques Bureau, also a Liberal. The city's St-Jean Baptiste Day observances of 24 June were said to have been celebrated with unusual enthusiasm that same year. One report noted that 'Nous avons peut-être eu tort de vouloir que cette démonstation de la St-Jean Baptiste soit toujours ici de plus en plus belle, et surpasse en grandeur les célébrations des années précédentes.' In the early hours of the morning, numerous fleurs-de-lis appeared in front of shops, offices, and homes in the downtown area and along rue Royale and rue Laviolette, greeting those who filed into Trois-Rivières's towering Cathédrale. After a special Mass and a day of celebrations held in sweltering heat, the evening was capped off with an enthusiastic reception rally, said to have drawn over eight thousand spectators to the parc Champlain in the heart of the city. The large crowd was entertained by music performed by Trois-Rivières' popular orchestral ensemble, Union Musicale. They joined the band to sing patriotic songs, punctuated by several speeches, including one from Tessier and another from Bureau, who was to carry the riding virtually uncontested during the conscription crisis.[21]

With the coming of war, symbolic exhibitions in the city sought accommodation with changed circumstances: French Canadian nationalism and the imperial-nationalism of the rest of Canada seemed to achieve a temporary, if uneasy, coexistence. At times the boundaries blurred considerably. After the dramatic news from Europe and from Ottawa, no paper spoke out against the municipal authorities when they hoisted, directly in front of city hall, French and Russian as well as British flags, signifying support for an Allied victory.[22] Hughes, the federal government, and military officials throughout the country would soon be busy adopting measures affecting local communities across Canada. But our pre-war tour of Trois-Rivières points to mixed settings and cultural positions of some fluidity, even in a city where residents' native tongue and religious affiliation were predominantly French and Catholic. Three years later, however, the divisive implementation of compulsory military service would greatly harden local feeling against Prime Minister Borden and his Union government – far more, of course, than Regulation No. 156 could have done in the summer of 1914.

Guelph

In Guelph, places of birth, ethnic origins, and religious affiliations were much more diverse than they were in Trois-Rivières, mediated by the fundamental fact that anglophones predominated and, more particularly, that two-thirds of them had descended from British immigrants or were themselves from Britain. At the outbreak of the war, many of Guelph's citizens rode the huge wave of sentiment in support of the imperial tie for obvious reasons – they were, or saw themselves as, British.

As part of English Canada, Guelph's beginnings in the 1820s and Lethbridge's in the 1880s reflected regional resettlement patterns dominated numerically by British newcomers and their descendants, and configured spatially by colonization and resource exploitation schemes controlled by a handful of British and Anglo-Canadian capitalists. There is also a coincidental connection through the Scottish-born poet, novelist, and commercial speculator John Galt. Galt was key to the founding of Guelph as a private enterprise initiative in Upper Canada. His son, Alexander Tilloch Galt, and grandson, Elliott Torrance Galt, later became key figures in the financial backing and management of Lethbridge. Both cities can be considered Galt-backed businesses that ultimately succeeded – Guelph in an era of commercial capitalism, wagon roads, and agricultural resettlement; Lethbridge in an era of industrial capitalism and transcontinental steam rail that both consumed Lethbridge coal and shipped grain from the surrounding region.

Guelph's origins can be traced back to the early 1820s when wealthy Upper Canadians lobbied for the transfer to private speculators of large land tracts held by either the Anglican church, known as the Clergy Reserves, or the Crown. The Canada Company, a commercial settlement firm set up by John Galt, bridged the gap between Upper Canadians, who wanted their colony resettled by Europeans and exploited by their economies, and British politicians and capitalists willing to support such ventures. What became Guelph lay on Crown land in Wellington County, a primarily agricultural district. It was sold to the Canada Company, and Galt named the town in honour of Britain's Hanoverian monarchy, descendants of a group of German ruling families known as the Guelph party.

Guelph's first settlers included a group of fifty-seven men, women, and children known as the La Guayrans. In 1825 these would-be farmers were lured by the Colombian Company and tried their luck in Caracas, Venezuela. When lavish promises came to nothing, they left Latin America and ended up in Philadelphia, on the doorstep of the British Consul. There they were told of Galt's scheme, which seemed their only viable option. Those who survived the journey and the adjustment to life in Guelph faced high credit charged by the Canada Company store. But after the La Guayran families had worked off the cost of their passage, Galt gave them each small, fifty-acre plots of land and they joined others with a stake in Guelph's future. Seventy-one town lots had already been sold in 1827, before the La Guayrans took up their land, on a township site located on the Speed River and connected by wagon roads to York and Eramosa.

The settlement then developed as an Upper Canadian mill town and later as an Ontario service centre in a rural hinterland. By the 1890s, Guelph's

Figure 4

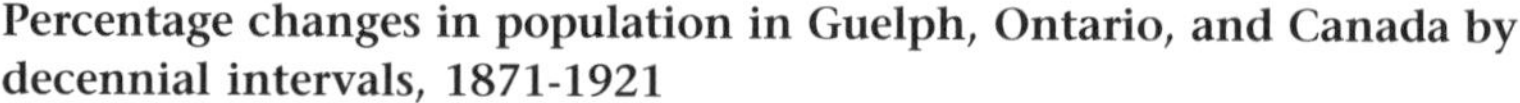

Percentage changes in population in Guelph, Ontario, and Canada by decennial intervals, 1871-1921

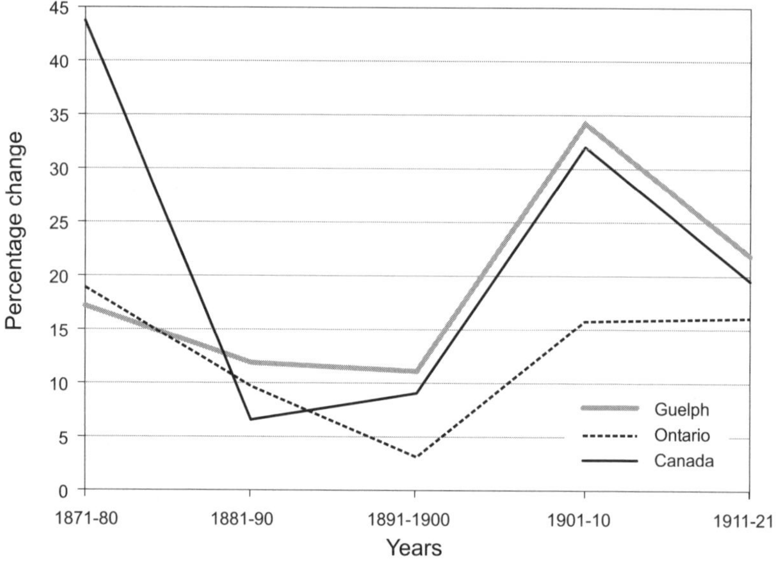

Source: Sixth Census of Canada 1921 (Ottawa: King's Printer, 1924), vol. 1, Table 12, p. 235.

location also placed it within a larger matrix of industrial integration and expansion across southern Ontario's mid-sized urban locales. A study of its population growth provides a measure of this transformation. Looking at the long-term pattern illustrated in Figure 4, we see this shift take place at the turn of the century, as an industrial-based economy supplanted a commercial one. Guelph's population increased rapidly, from 2,290 inhabitants in 1840 to 15,175 in 1911.[23] During the two decades preceding the war, the town's growth rate paralleled manufacturing and service-sector expansion throughout southern Ontario.

A high proportion of these new arrivals came from outside the province. Measures of ethnic and religious differences, as enumerated in 1911, provide useful comparisons between Guelph and the other cities under consideration. It is also worth comparing Guelph's figures to Ontario's and to Canada's as a whole. Figure 5 highlights that a higher percentage of Guelph's inhabitants had been born in the Empire (19.5 percent), most from Britain, compared to Ontario (15.0 percent) or to Canada as whole (11.6 percent).

Moreover, as Figure 6 shows, comparatively more claimed an English heritage in Guelph: 42.1 percent against 35.1 and 25.3 percent for Ontario and Canada respectively. Scottish ancestry was also higher at 19.8 percent, compared to 16.8 percent for Ontario and 13.8 percent for Canada overall. Of

Figure 5

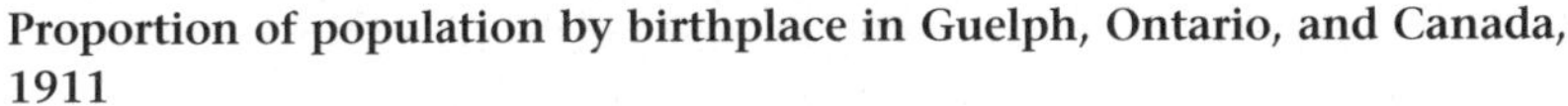

Proportion of population by birthplace in Guelph, Ontario, and Canada, 1911

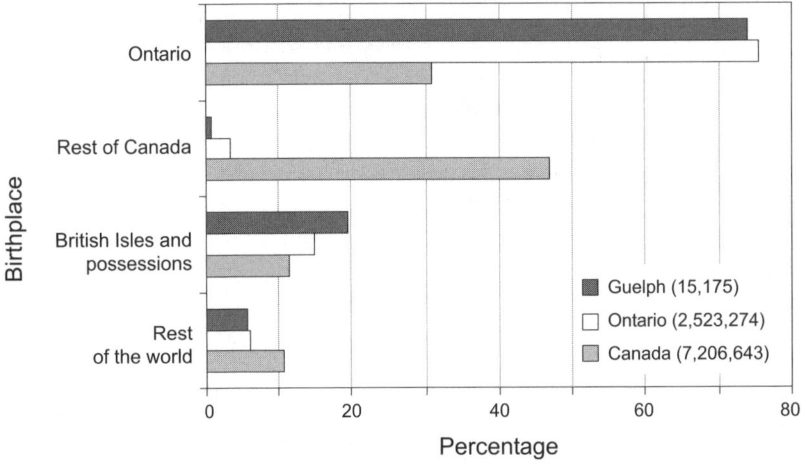

Source: Fifth Census of Canada 1911 (Ottawa: King's Printer, 1913), vol. 2, Table 2, pp. 82-83.

note concerning wartime fears of enemy aliens, a slightly higher proportion in the city, 8.3 percent, identified Germany as their original nationality, compared to 7.6 percent across Ontario and 5.5 percent across Canada. Fewer claimed Austro-Hungarian backgrounds (just 0.1 percent), but that figure should be placed against 0.5 percent for the province and just 1.8 percent for all of Canada. Clearly, the most salient feature, which might account for the many speeches that made mention of Guelph's British heritage, is the fact that over two-thirds of the city laid claim to such origins in 1911.

Turning to the distribution across religions in what had come to be called the 'Royal City' of Guelph (so named since John Galt's day, as he put it, 'in complement to the Royal family'), this predominantly British population showed a mixture of denominational affiliations.[24] Roughly equal proportions, as presented in Figure 7, of Anglicans, Methodists, Presbyterians, and Catholics were divided into active, well-established church congregations throughout the city. Fairly even percentages stated they belonged to Canada's four largest churches, which stood locally as Presbyterians (24.1 percent), Methodists (23.3 percent), Roman Catholics (20.4 percent), and Anglicans (20.1 percent). These proportions were close to those for Ontario as a whole.[25] Baptists came next at 4.2 percent, largest amongst Guelph's smaller (less than 5 percent for any) religious groups. These figures indicate that as a mid-sized, mid-southern-Ontario city, Guelph contained diversities in population that were hardly atypical and, indeed, parallelled those of many towns and cities in the province and across English Canada generally.

Figure 6

Proportion of population by national origin in Guelph, Ontario, and Canada, 1911

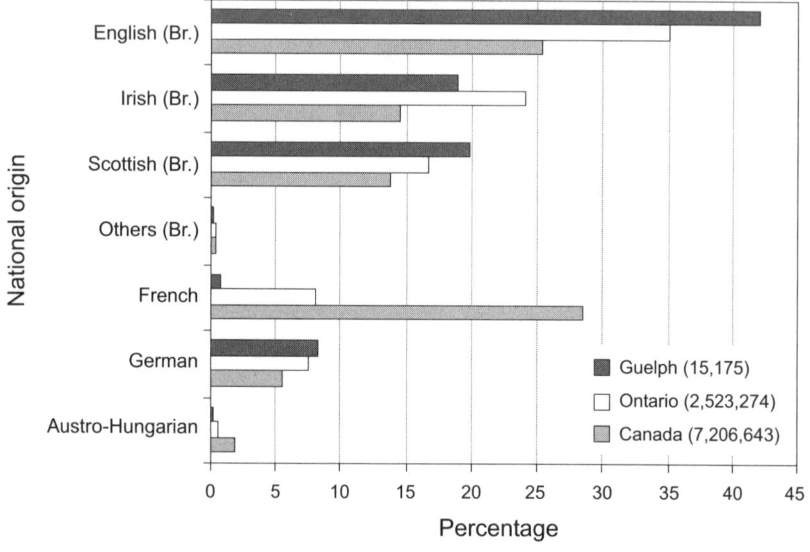

Source: Fifth Census of Canada, 1911 (Ottawa: King's Printer, 1913), vol. 2, Tables 7 and 9, pp. 162, 204, and 252.

From its colonial beginnings, Guelph's favourable location on the Speed River had fuelled its first grist and saw mills, monitored by commissioners of the Canada Company from a log house known as the Priory in the centre of town. This company mill town later supported manufacturers that served either nearby or distant markets – from Sleeman's Silver Creek Brewery to the White (formerly Raymond) Sewing Machine Company and the Bell Piano and Organ Company – while continuing to provide agricultural service needs in Wellington County and hinterlands beyond. Throughout the city there were economic ebbs and flows – Raymond Sewing Machine and Bell Piano and Organ, for instance, were taken over shortly before the war by American and British firms respectively – and social problems – St. Patrick's ward faced a huge sewage problem in 1914 – that moved in tandem with southern Ontario's rapid industrialization and urban growth up to that point.

Guelph's regional importance comes into focus when we consider its spatial patterns, its places of institutional and cultural life, and its transportation corridors, which placed the city in an inter-urban network between Toronto and Windsor, east and west, or between Hamilton and Owen Sound, north and south. Less then two generations after the first town lots went up

Figure 7

Religious affiliations in Guelph by proportion of the population, 1911

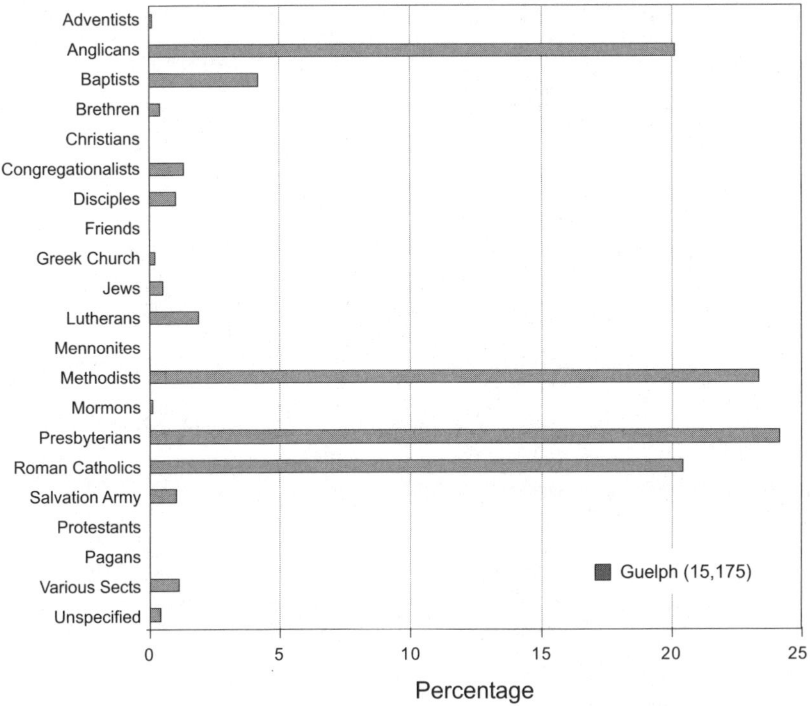

Source: Fifth Census of Canada 1911 (Ottawa: King's Printer, 1913), vol. 2, Table 2, pp. 82-83.

for sale, the Grand Trunk and Canadian Pacific rail lines crossed near the site on which the Priory still stood. Rail traffic linked Guelph closely to the provincial and national economies, now ruled more anonymously by regional, national, and international buyers and markets. From the beginning these had included labour pools that brought people from Britain and from the rest of the world to settle temporarily, or more permanently, in a city that before the war was administered as six municipal wards.

From a bird's-eye view, the city's neatly concentrated downtown hub sat at the focal point of residential streets and later industrial sites fanning outwards along its key thoroughfares. First coach and carriage, and later electric rail, truck, and automobile traffic converged at the city centre. From the south, Brock Road followed the route of the Guelph and Dundas wagon road, first used by the Canada Company in the 1820s. Running east and west, Waterloo Avenue, another old Canada Company route connecting Guelph to Waterloo, bisected the city. It began carrying streetcar traffic to

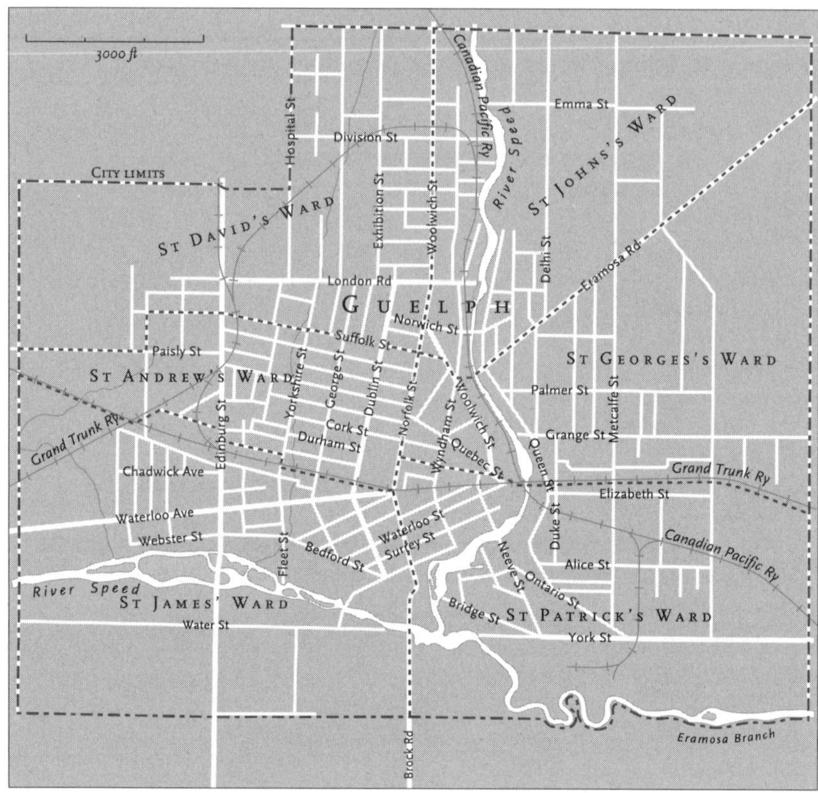

Wards and principal streets of Guelph, Ontario, c. 1908

and from the central core in 1895. Woolwich Street entered the city from the north and also carried electric rail passengers. From the northeast, the Eramosa Road ran to the downtown, connecting a farming township of the same name to the expanding services, diversities, and problems of Guelph city life. Until the war's outbreak, the recent growth had been concentrated in the largely working-class St. Patrick's ward. Within the expanding industrial development of this era, Guelph's steady growth positioned it as a medium-sized city among many across southern Ontario's sprawling hinterlands. It was linked in innumerable ways to the outside world, but remained contained in appearance by those last streets and roads that stood at its municipal boundaries that divided city from countryside. Guelph's urban and new suburban spaces were bordered by rural and largely agricultural townships that made this contrast, and its city limits, visibly obvious.

The city's central core contained what we might expect – from a city hall, court house, and main post office to financial houses, newspaper offices, and a few prominent hotels. Its other institutions – a prison, an asylum, an agricultural college, two large hospitals, and a Jesuit novitiate – were located near, or just outside, Guelph's perimeters.

The prison, actually a prison farm built just inside the city's southwest boundary, was a provincial reformatory, intended to rehabilitate its inmates in a medium-security setting through agricultural labour. When incarceration rates eased during the war, planning began to convert facilities like these into military hospitals. This carceral in a semi-rural setting enters our story as the newly converted Speedwell Military Hospital, a chronic-care facility that specialized in tubercular rehabilitation for veterans. It became, as well, a site for dissent. Its new inmates, returned soldiers, came to see themselves as almost equally incarcerated there, with little political voice in the early phases of post-war reconstruction.

Just north of Guelph stood the St. Stanislaus Novitiate, a Jesuit seminary, which was where Marcus Doherty – son of Canada's solicitor general, who had helped to draft Canada's conscription law – was arrested in June 1918 for dodging the draft. He and his fellow novices raised the suspicions of some Protestant clergy in Guelph, who believed they were residing there simply to avoid conscription, possibly even in violation of the Military Service Act.

As elsewhere, public events often brought the local situation to bear on national imperatives. At the beginning of the war, when troops marched north along Dublin Street, turning west on London Road toward the exhibition grounds in the centre of St. David's ward, onlookers lined the streets en route to see them off. A rally with songs, speeches, and prayers for the troops, hastily organized and staged at the city's exhibition grounds, was described as the largest single demonstration ever witnessed in Guelph. Such innocent enthusiasm soon evaporated across Canada and opened gaps in enlistments, culminating in the conscription crisis three years later. This shift was also revealed through ordinary, localized discourses. When Lester Pearson's father, Edwin, spoke in support of compulsory military service from his pulpit as pastor of Norfolk Street Methodist church in St. Andrew's ward, he described himself as a father of three sons overseas who saw the need for others to support their efforts.

John McCrae, who wrote the most frequently used verses in the English language to memorialize fallen soldiers, grew up near the banks of the Speed River. But whether they were from McCrae's neighbourhood, one of the longest settled in the city, or from the working-class districts in St. Patrick's ward, or from St. George's to the north, or from St. John's north of that, Guelph's inhabitants came to understand war-related events and issues through local place and circumstance. Obscure and even seemingly bizarre practices helped to shape perceptions, however ephemeral they might appear as local events.

The *Mercury*'s report in early November 1914 of the actions of a group of 'braw Scotsmen' might be a case in point. The gang, it seems, threw mud at the statue of the Laird of Skibo to protest Andrew Carnegie's supposed pro-German sympathy (the statue stood near the public library on Nelson Crescent, built with a Carnegie endowment). Their action suggests a localized response to the 'enemy' and to what was perceived as pro-German sympathies. Even as a burst of masculine bravado, such truculence was hardly accidental, nor insignificant in relation to similar incidents. The public sphere of Canada's home front cannot be approached as an anonymous space where communication took place spontaneously. Local sites, local organizations, and local associations supported historical subjects acting, in countless ways, as the most immediate and most potent vehicles of communication. Institutional affiliations, especially enrolment in schools of higher learning, served as prime sites for recruitment. Like other colleges and universities in Canada, many of Guelph's early enlistments were drawn from the city's Ontario Agricultural College. From that time forward, residents across the city scanned the pages of its largest paper, the Guelph *Mercury*, a Liberal organ. This paper and the Conservative *Herald* became the key channels for wartime news from within and beyond the city. A huge crowd in Guelph celebrated the outbreak of war as first news of it was posted in front of the *Mercury* newspaper office on McDonnell Street, in the heart of the downtown core. A few weeks later, middle-class women met at the Macdonald Institute, across from the Ontario Agricultural College, to raise funds and procure medical supplies for families at home and men overseas. At the Collegiate Institute in the city's west end, working-class men met to drill for the short-lived home guard. These examples underscore the point that wartime practices developed in localized settings, commonplace, everyday sites normally activated to communicate something substantial about the war.

Parochial communication ordinarily took place in this way. Information, perspectives, or impressions from outside one's immediate social circle, hometown, or everyday experience were conveyed on communicative sites that combined the familiar with the new. In innumerable ways, public spaces could be appropriated to connect the local scene to outside worlds, with hometown backdrops serving as intimate theatres for imagined phenomena, spectacles, or exotica. A very ordinary recollection by a pharmacist, John D. Higinbotham, who grew up in Guelph before taking his trade to Lethbridge, suggests parochial contact points between local settings and the famous travelling circuses of the late nineteenth century, which often featured public displays of technical innovation. What child, he wrote six decades afterwards, cannot recall vividly the marvellous wonders of Forepaugh's circus or the spectacular displays staged more famously by P.T. Barnum? Higinbotham describes a Barnum circus that came to Guelph 'with his wonderful hippodrome, which by the way was nearly wrecked by a terrific thunderstorm, creating pandemonium among the spectators. It was on this occasion that the first incandescent lights were exhibited in Canada.' Whether true or not, Higinbotham also described in some detail how another instrument of this particular era of invention fascination was displayed in public: 'A demonstration of the first phonograph – or talking machine, as it was then called – to the citizens of Guelph was given in 1878 by Professor Gillespie before an excited audience in the Town Hall. It was a large cylinder covered by tinfoil and turned by means of a handle. Bandmaster Wood was invited to the platform, and upon his cornet he played "Wait for the Wagon" into the diaphragm, which Professor Gillespie, after reversing the record, repeated with distinctness.'[26] Accounts like this remind us how the world outside one's immediate, local environ is often seen through familiar settings that serve as mediating modes of perception.

Like Galt family businesses, Higinbotham headed west, taking his pharmaceutical skills from Guelph to Fort Macleod and then Lethbridge in 1884. He became that city's first druggist, serving also as its postmaster until 1910. Too old to enlist when war broke out, he continued to build up his drugstore, relocated at the corner of 2nd Avenue and 5th Street South. Throughout the war he fashioned himself into a particularly active and patriotic citizen, volunteering for many organizations and carrying out a host of war-related tasks. He kept his hand in local affairs and had connections to a staunchly anglophilic network of local elites. As the war moved from the celebrations of August to a prolonged stalemate, Higinbotham joined the millions of Canadians who continued to perceive events from parochial vantage points, from their own hometown horizons.

Lethbridge

Lethbridge's early growth and development epitomized the goods, services, and population flows anticipated by Canada's National Policy, a scheme that concentrated industrial production in the East and agricultural production in the West.[27] Up until the first of many disastrous harvests in the 1920s, the city transformed itself from a coal-supply to an agricultural service centre, and population growth throughout the period remained consistent up to the end of the Galt era.[28] Overall, Lethbridge's rapid population growth, depicted in Figure 8, indicated on a local scale the massive in-migration to the western provinces that began with the completion of the CPR. In this case, a small coal-mining venture expanded quickly to exploit rich deposits and, after 1905, to supply and service a grain-growing hinterland. Lethbridge was incorporated as a city that year. By then, its collieries had become just part of its economic function as a major irrigation and agricultural service centre. Spurred by new settlement, rapid urban growth, and

Figure 8

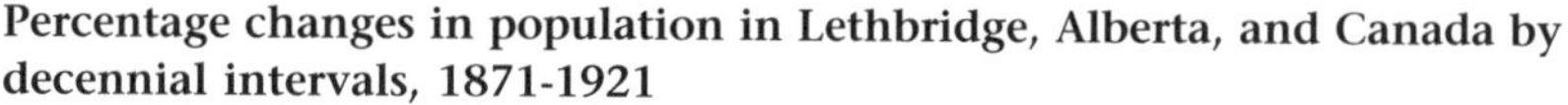

Percentage changes in population in Lethbridge, Alberta, and Canada by decennial intervals, 1871-1921

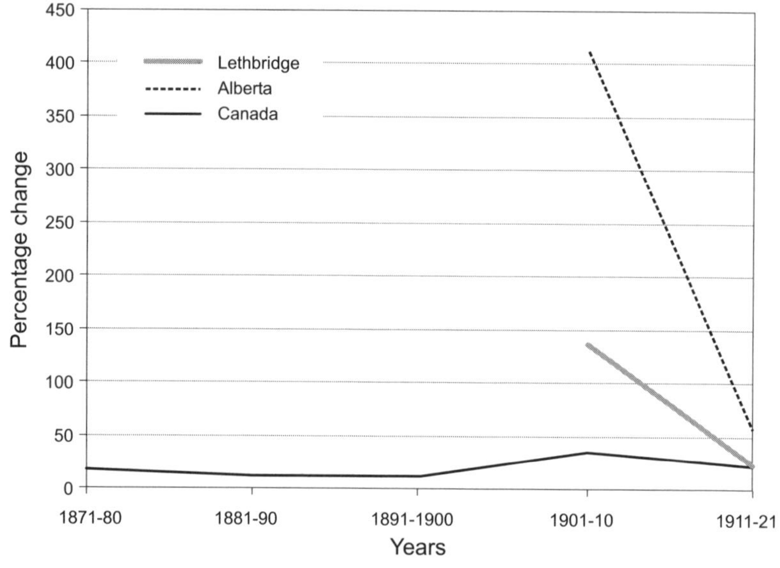

Source: Sixth Census of Canada 1921 (Ottawa: King's Printer, 1924), vol. 1, Table 12, p. 235.

the completion of a boom-and-bust cycle that collapsed with the recession of 1913, Lethbridge can be approached as a city transplanted, not transformed.

When Higinbotham arrived, the settlement was little more than a fledgling work site, based almost entirely on coal extraction. Resettlement had started as a company town, Coalbanks, which served several collieries owned by the North-West Coal and Navigation Company (NWC&NCo). The mines were located on the banks of the Oldman River, just east of Fort Whoop-Up, which had ended its days as a whiskey trading post when the North-West Mounted Police arrived only a decade earlier. The townsite proper, just east of the riverbank mine shafts, was renamed Lethbridge, after the NWC&NCo's president William Lethbridge, in October 1885. The displacement of Aboriginal people, who had long been part of a fur trade economy, was a recent event and, apart from a few small reserves, unmitigated.

Three years after the Mounted Police's arrival, in 1877, the Mik-kwee-yene-wak (Blood) people, who had winter-camped on the nearby Belly (Oldman after 1915) and St. Mary rivers, became part of Treaty 7, a Department of Indian Affairs administrative zone that was occupied by the Sarcee, Blackfoot, Blood, Stoney, and Peigan peoples and covered most of what was to become southern Alberta.[29] Aboriginal cultures had adapted to more than a century of trade with the North West and Hudson's Bay companies, but nothing could match disruptions caused by the encroachment of white resettlement. Already a series of infectious epidemics had taken heavy tolls: smallpox in 1781 and 1837; scarlet fever in 1865; smallpox again in 1869. The natives came to call the flood plain where the St. Mary and Belly met Sow-kee Akainuski, or the 'prairie where many people died.'[30] Then came the deliberate and sustained slaughter by whites of the bison along with large numbers of deer, pronghorn, and elk. All this was but a prelude to the survey teams, railway gangs, and thousands of homesteaders who followed.

Coal extraction, the first industry after the fur and whiskey trade to gain any lasting importance, actually began on a small scale more than a decade before the completion of the CPR. In the autumn of 1874, a whiskey trader turned prospector, Frank Sherman, began hand digging a rich, black seam on the upper banks of the Belly River. He sold the coal as a heating fuel to the Mounted Police stationed to the west at Fort Macleod and to merchants at Fort Benton across the border on the Missouri. Sherman's find and small venture soon drew the attention of a Canadian government official, Elliott Torrance Galt, grandson of John Galt who had played such a key role in the founding of Guelph.

Elliott was then stationed in the region as an assistant to the Indian Commissioner, Edgar Dewdney, who administered Treaty 7. The younger Galt's post, however, took him into the field to survey what lay ahead for the region's economy and settlement potential, rather than for its Aboriginal peoples. While inspecting the area along the Belly, near Fort Whoop-Up, in 1879, he took samples from the blackened seams around Sherman's mine. His father, Sir Alexander Tilloch Galt, then serving as Canada's first High Commissioner to Britain, had been urged by Ottawa to use his position to secure capital for land development projects in western Canada. The coal find came at just the right time. Subsequent surveys by Nova Scotia mining engineer Nicholas Bryant and William Stafford of the Acadia Coal Company confirmed the younger Galt's expectation that the site offered a lucrative and steady fuel supply for the stream of rail traffic about to commence across the West. The Galts were able to secure from Ottawa a land concession to construct a narrow-gauge rail line connecting their operation to the main CPR line. Almost ideally located, the Coalbanks mines proved profitable, a cheap and ready coal source. Thus, by combining London-based capital and federal land grants to create the NWC&NCo. in 1882, the younger Galts struck, in this prairie dry belt district, the same successful mix of capital and land concessions that John Galt had achieved in the agricultural heartland of Upper Canada fifty years earlier.

As the CPR main line neared completion, Coalbanks grew to some four hundred miners, carpenters, engineers, and saloon keepers, some with families not listed in the original census. According to an early description, service demands supported 'six stores, five saloons, four billiard rooms, two barbershops, one hotel and a livery stable.'[31] Higinbotham recalled the Lethbridge Hotel, where he spent his first few days in town, as a rather crude, cramped, and boisterous stopover place. But until his dispensary was ready for business, he and his brother, Ed, had nowhere else to put up. 'The noise and general roughness of the place were too much for me.' Even when his store first opened, it too was seconded as a temporary roof overhead for passersby. According to Higinbotham, 'It was no uncommon thing to have a dozen or more men occupy the floor space between and behind our counters, where they spread their blankets ... Most of our over-night guests were stage-passengers from Macleod, Pincher Creek and outlying ranches.'[32] Many, too, would stay on in Lethbridge in search of work.

The decade that followed the arrival of the railroad proved a hectic period of in-migration, business formation, and installation of the social and cultural institutions, from churches and schools to voluntary associations, associated with urban life in a frontier setting – indicative, in short, of an 'emergent society,' one that may be seen as an experiment of grafting structures and practices established in the East onto an entirely new landscape. In the process, Lethbridge and the surrounding area were transformed by irrigation projects, dryland homesteads, a high-level bridge and further rail branch lines, and rapid urban development. As local services and amenities took root, the city grew, not just as a coal-mining operation, but also as a local service centre for agriculture with a complex mix of occupations, social classes, ethnic diversity, and social hierarchies.

After a repeal of the CPR monopoly in the spring of 1889 and a lucrative 6,400-acre-per-mile land subsidy from Ottawa, the NWC&NCo. was recapitalized in London as the Alberta Railway and Coal Company (AR&CCo.). This reorganized, expanded company completed a line to Montana in 1890. By then the coal business and growing service requirements had attracted a small group of local stakeholders who were active in municipal politics and social affairs. Ontario-born Charles A. Magrath came first as the NWC&NCo.'s land commissioner and resident manager. A key organizer of Lethbridge's proliferating voluntary associations, he became in 1891 the town's first mayor as well as the local member for the North-West Territorial Council. Harry Bentley moved from Medicine Hat, where he had operated a retail store for an Ontario firm, to become a wealthy retail and wholesale merchant as well as Lethbridge's second mayor. Frank Hamilton Mewburn, first company doctor with the NWC&NCo., married Louise Nelson, a governess from Prince Edward Island. Mewburn served two mayoralty terms before 1905. A lawyer, Charles F.P. Conybeare, joined this group, as did Higinbotham, who served as the town's postmaster while establishing his drugstore business.

As Lethbridge grew, so did its separate operations, which amalgamated once again in 1903 into the Alberta Railway and Irrigation Company

(AR&ICo.), with Elliott Galt as president. Urban growth became pronounced after 1906, when grain production surpassed coal as Lethbridge's prime export commodity. Although the most concentrated selling of town lots and dryland homesteads in the immediate vicinity lay a few years off, Galt industries continued to promote the sale of irrigated lands. Their firms also enjoyed the support of the Liberal government in Ottawa, which forgave surveying dues owing on its existing land grant.

This gave Galt and Magrath leverage to develop irrigated lands. For their first venture, Mormon settlers provided the labour, with wages paid half in cash, half in land. Beginning in August 1898, some three hundred teams dug over 150 kilometres of canals south to the town of Stirling within two years. Water entered the main canal from the St. Mary River, close to the Montana border. Water diversion schemes were vigorously promoted, with fair success in this case. The farmer, as one promotional brochure put it, 'would become his own rainmaker.' Irrigation projects, however, incurred higher start-up costs and maintained fewer families per acre than the 160-acre homestead allotments allocated under the federal Homestead Act. In the long run, though, after the war, dryland farming failed to live up to its promotional billing in campaigns that were far more extensive than those staged by Galt and Magrath.

In the early years, before the war, the development of Marquis wheat and further experimentation in dryland farming techniques contributed to frequent land-buying frenzies, a rapid granting of homestead concessions, and population in-migration. Securement applications for homesteads in the surrounding districts peaked in 1910, with 4,952 approved. This came at the midpoint of speculative land turnovers, and from 1907 to 1912 there was a flurry of city lot subdividing in Lethbridge itself. Similar patterns occurred elsewhere in the province, which prompted passage in Edmonton of the Alberta Town Planning Act of 1912, legislation that curbed excessive property subdivision and helped to stem the tide of prairie boosterism in a climate of almost unbridled optimism.[33]

Lethbridge's boosterism was marked by the formation in 1907 of the 25,000 Club. Composed of optimistic citizen-stakeholders, these boosters backed a drive to accelerate city growth to 25,000 inhabitants by 1912. While they got less than halfway there, ready access to cheap coal did attract several manufacturers, while at the same time grain production secured its place as the mainstay of the local economy. The Lethbridge Foundry (Lethbridge Iron Works after 1900) began operating in 1898; the Lethbridge Brewing and Malting Company in 1901; two milling and elevator companies, Ellison and Taylor, in 1906; and the Lethbridge Woolen Company was wooed from Medicine Hat that same year. Other firms followed in the boom years, embraced by boosters who saw future prosperity in industrial diversification in their newly incorporated prairie city.

While both Trois-Rivières and Guelph grew at faster rates than their respective provinces, Lethbridge's rapid development as a settlement-frontier city within a fast-populating Alberta, far surpassed municipal growth rates for most locales east of Manitoba up to 1914. Until the war began, newcomers from different social classes and diverse national communities formed patchwork communities in this Prairie city, within settlement patterns marked more by social boundaries than by rapid integration. Nonetheless, local government, educational structures, and cultural institutions adapted readily to demands and opportunities produced by town-making processes where, up to the war at least, very real economic opportunities and labour demands had been created. Employment demands continued to affect the structure of the labour force, to a large degree newcomers from eastern Canada, from Europe, and from the United States. Class and ethnic differences continued to segregate peoples struggling to transplant themselves culturally and institutionally. As a job-frontier settlement, Lethbridge had a male-to-female ratio of 1:24 in 1911, compared to the unsurprising balances in this figure for more established cities like Guelph or Trois-Rivières.[34]

Figure 9

Proportion of population by national origin in Lethbridge, Alberta, and Canada, 1911

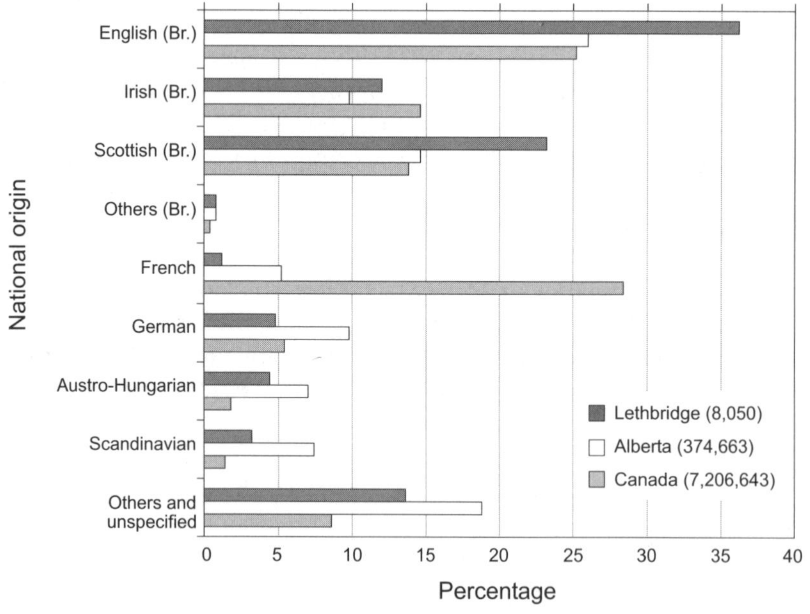

Source: Fifth Census of Canada 1911 (Ottawa: King's Printer), vol. 2, Tables 7 and 9, pp. 162 and 164.

But male predominance, created largely by a bachelor workforce in the coal mines, was only part of a much larger picture of urban and rural re-resettlement. More significant was a growing sector of newly-arrived nuclear families that made up most of this city's comparatively young, growing, and diverse population.

Compared to the province as a whole, Lethbridge at this time had a higher proportion of inhabitants claiming British national origins, of English or Scots ancestry in particular. German and Austro-Hungarian proportions were also lower than provincial averages, but remained much higher than the country as a whole (see Figure 9). In 1911, within a total population of 8,050, 385 claimed German ancestry, with nearly an equal number, 362, claiming Austro-Hungarian origins. With respect to religious affiliations, Presbyterians made up the largest proportion at 27.5 percent, closely followed by Anglicans at 24.1 percent. Methodists and Catholics stood at 18.0 and 11.7 percent respectively (see Figure 10). The overwhelming majority of the population had arrived within the previous fifteen years, comprising

Figure 10

Religious affiliations in Lethbridge by proportion of the population, 1911

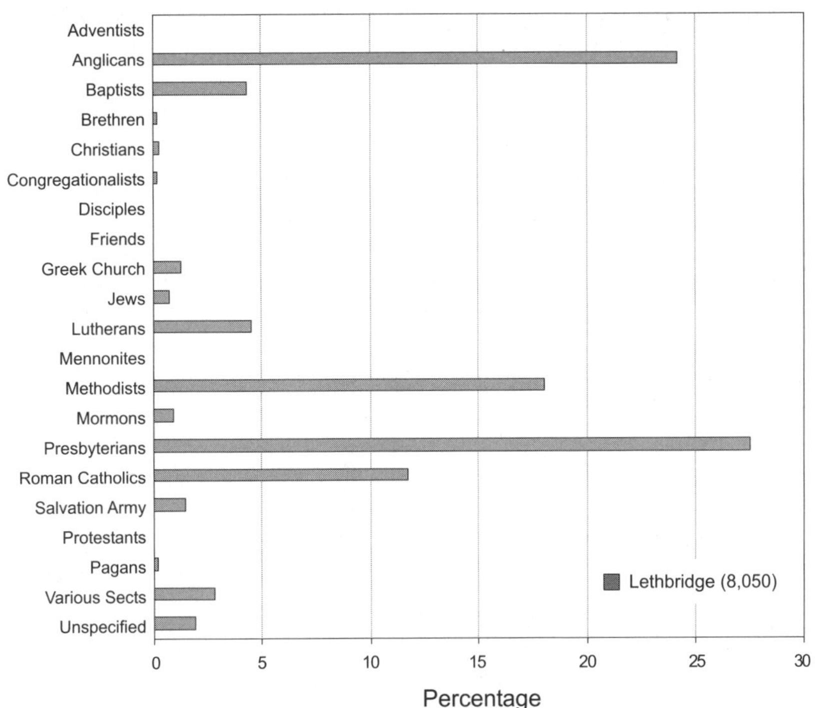

Source: Fifth Census of Canada 1911 (Ottawa: King's Printer, 1913), vol. 2, Table 2, pp. 82-83.

a polyglot conglomerate of communities that often remained separated by differences of language and religion. Local politics and businesses, however, remained under the control of an Anglo-Protestant majority, conforming to the broad pattern of Anglo conformity and nativism in Alberta at this time.[35]

From the completion of the CPR in 1885 onward, the concentrated arrivals of ethnically diverse peoples, the sudden rise of the coal industry, and the expansion of wheat farming had transformed both the Galts' investments and the area's human geography into a prosperous yet subordinate regional economy within the national framework. Since the development of the Coalbanks site and the founding of Lethbridge, eight separate companies had built 355 miles of railway and 150 miles of irrigation canals, and controlled coal mines that could turn out two thousand tons per day. However, coal and grain profits remained subject to external markets and decisions made in the East. Like many large-scale enterprises in the West, they were tightly controlled by outside capital and by investors who wielded enormous power over local workforces and populations. The Galt era ended two years before the start of the Great War, when this still viable operation was sold to the CPR. By then Lethbridge was a bustling frontier centre, touting itself in typical booster style as an ideal spot in the 'last best West,' with a population approaching nine thousand by 1914.

Despite such dramatic changes on such a large scale, newcomers who came to settle often romanticized their early years in the West. They saw their surroundings, new only to them, as almost unaltered, even untouched. The prairies, W.L. Morton wrote years later, echoing this theme, 'remained, for modern civilization, a virgin *tabula rasa*, a blank sheet with no writing, an unmarked parchment, unscraped, unoiled, unprepared.'[36] Popular memories of settlement, right up to the war, depicted arduous struggles against a harsh climate and the unforgiving challenges of making homesteads into farms. As myths, mixing fact with fiction, these tales of 'pioneer' days circulating in local newspapers, in popular histories, and in autobiographies often spoke of the 'opening' of a rich territory, the 'taming' of a wild frontier – a West wilder, freer, and more perilous than it could have been in reality. The much-heralded and hailed advances of progress, from land speculation to irrigation projects, indeed converted land usage to new economies, but the prairie's growing number of workers and working families struggled within metropolitan-hinterland imbalances that constrained, often severely, individual, family, or group initiative.

In mythologizing this process through a retrospective gaze, Higinbotham saw himself and many of his neighbours weaving, through stubborn effort year by year, a social fabric covering the rough and rude remnants of the past. A formidable landscape also emerges in his account, with freezing winters warmed occasionally by chinooks or blistering summers sometimes cooled by thunderstorms; a setting more brutal at its worst than the average easterner faced. Its Otherness and, at times, horrific strangeness, cast by Higinbotham under the title *When the West Was Young*, remained romantic and imaginary, if not illusionary. Higinbotham's tales of prairie fires and winter blizzards exoticized ordinary encounters by placing them on an extraordinary frontier. The West, as he saw it, was tamed just enough for settlement to begin. As a train passenger, he recalled his first impressions, 'there being nothing on which the eye could rest but the vast uninhabited wilderness, now all fenced and cultivated with thriving towns and villages.'[37] Here Higinbotham alluded to the emergent boosterism on an 'unvarnished' frontier, a series of civic promotions in which the young pharmacist joined many in Lethbridge in lending his active support.

Throughout, his stories converged on a territory he saw as only recently occupied by Natives, who were cast as unruly nomads on the brink of extinction, however bold and masculine their popular image as buffalo hunters had been.[38] The North-West Mounted Police, or what Higinbotham called in one chapter the new 'Riders of the Plains,' became a heroic instrument of territorial salvation, 'quenching prairie fires and sounding out the fords of swift-flowing rivers, carrying mail to outlying settlers, showing the newcomer the way to his homestead, teaching the red men the virtues of honesty, work, temperance, and peace.' The old-time Mountie was many things: the rancher's second pair of eyes, the whiskey trader's scourge, the gambler and drug peddler's nemesis. In all, they remained but 'single men in barracks,' as Higinbotham rehumanizes them, 'just like you.'[39]

Lethbridge's new economies, of coal first and wheat second, were directly linked to national ones. Yet everyday life for many local settlers took shape as a 'frontier' encounter, where community-building often developed as an inaugural process that melded booster idealism with the stark realities of a fledgling, Prairie city setting. Settlement remained, for many in this period, a struggle of transplantation imagined through ethnocentric lenses typified in both the daily discourse of city papers, the Lethbridge *Herald* and the *Telegram*, as well as in accounts like Higinbotham's. The prairies were seen and described as a natural landscape in the process of being reshaped through 'development,' 'expansion,' and the implantation of 'civilized' modes of life, from numbered streets to the frequently lauded hubbub of a busy downtown core, with new retail and commercial outlets opening each season. On the margins of this vision, partly embedded in what was indeed happening in Lethbridge, rested romanticized figures of a recent past: buffalo-hunting tribes, whiskey traders, and the first detachments of the North-West Mounted Police.

Actual development was fostered by many of the short-sighted plans on which boosterist city councils tended to pin Lethbridge's future hopes. Concessions to new businesses of free building sites, water, and power, and tax-free horizons of a decade or more, came on a platter. Growth in local

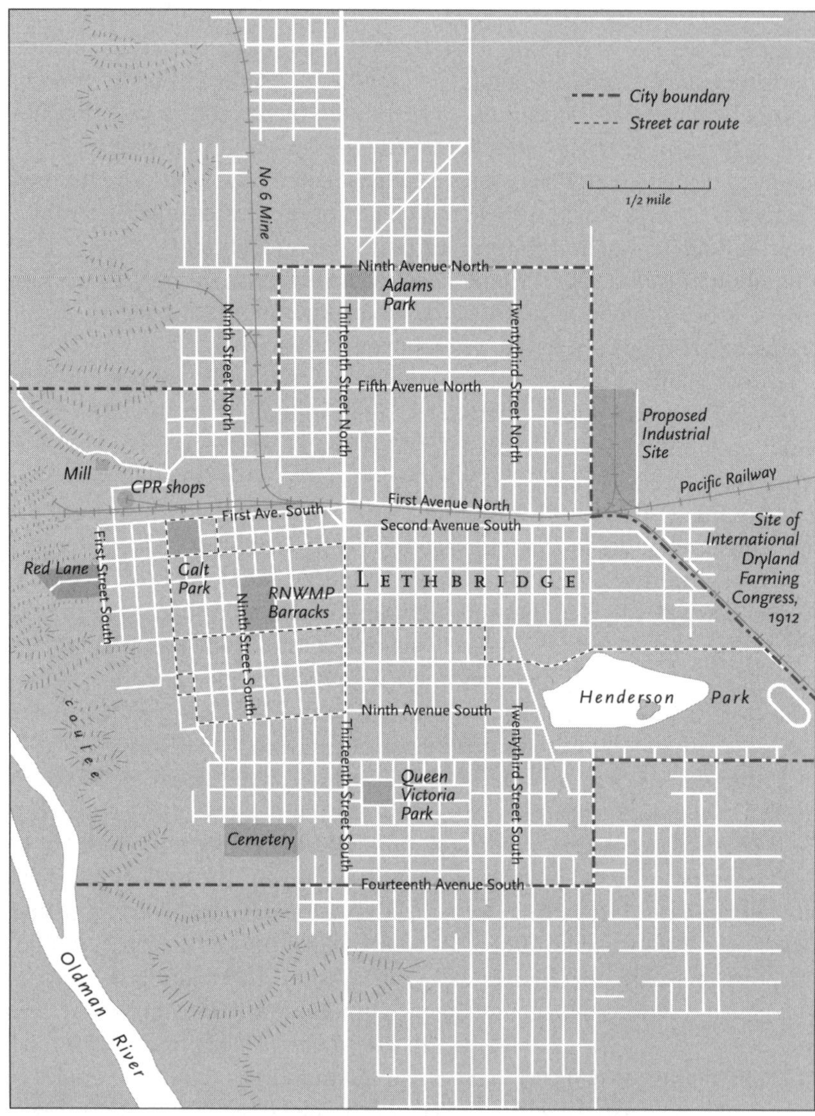

City of Lethbridge streets and selected points of interest, c. 1914

industries ultimately compromised Lethbridge's municipal revenue base, a problem that worsened in the years leading up to the war. The municipal debt deepened as the city prepared for its largest pre-war event, the Seventh International Dry Farming Conference, which was held in October 1912 to the delight of local boosters. Over five thousand delegates from some fifteen countries, including representatives from China and Persia, poured into a city of about eight thousand.[40] With visitors crammed into hotels, billeted in residents' homes, even accommodated in special tents, this event, successful in itself, promoted what proved disastrous for many farm families in the dust bowl decades following the war – grain growing in southern Alberta's dryland agricultural belt.

Nonetheless, the conference prompted improvements in local amenities totalling $1.5 million. The city built the 9th Street overpass, crossing the Oldman River. A streetcar system, water filtration, public property landscaping, and the erection of a grandstand and spectator seating at Henderson Lake Park in the southeast end all reflected the enormous hopes placed on an improved public image such upgrades might generate.

An intense period of speculative optimism and signs of real growth preceded a sudden collapse of the real estate boom in 1913. City council gave free rein to developers who were then in the process of subdividing properties located on the municipality's peripheries. The village of Stafford, the southern portion of the North Ward, and North Lethbridge each were subdivided. In the downtown area, lots on 5th Street priced at $1,000 per foot in August 1912 sold for $1,200 by September. By the time the bubble burst, the city itself was facing a severe financial crunch linked to overdevelopment without corresponding extensions of its tax base. A municipal debt that stood at $175,000 in 1906 skyrocketed to $2,515,676 by 1912.[41] There was also some $600,000 in uncollectable invoices, all eventually discarded. The city desperately needed a sounder fiscal management and planning strategy. On 1 January 1914, commission government took charge, created through an amendment to the city's charter. William Duncan Livingstone Hardie, a past mine manager for the Galts, became mayor and also served as commissioner of finance. Land surveyor and former mine operator A.M. Grace was named commissioner of utilities. Daily municipal administration was henceforth directed by Arthur Reid. All three presided over a period of economic collapse and recovery during the war years.

Signs of the city's diverse social makeup and the contested presence of some groups remained on the fringes of Lethbridge. Most prominent was the Point, a red-light district overlooking the steep coulees to the south of the mine shafts, which housed several brothels in use since the 1890s. Presbyterian and Methodist preachers, led by the Rev. Charles McKillop of Knox Presbyterian, a moral reformer who had fought liquor law violations in the past, and by the Rev. W.T. Perry of Wesley Methodist, had railed against the city's illicit yet most popular 'tourist' industry. In 1909 they joined forces with Higinbotham to form a Moral Reform League, which petitioned city council. Some eighty-one supporters signed a resolution demanding that city hall take immediate action 'toward closing up such houses and suppressing the social evil to the full extent of your legal power.'[42] At that point, this Segregated Area, as it was also known, which had operated for over a decade with the knowledge and tacit consent of municipal authorities, appeared to be expanding. Perry estimated that some twenty-two prostitutes and six or seven Chinese cooks and servants were employed there. 'I have it from the people living off the street leading to the district,' he claimed, 'that the drunken rowdyism, obscene language, and fighting there is more than they can bear. It is depreciating the value of their property to say nothing of the abomination of the thing.'[43]

Nothing substantial was done at that time to eradicate the brothel-based sex trade on the Point, however, and it remained a distinct area in this Prairie city, still in the midst of a boom period of expansion but deeply divided along class and ethnic lines. A year after the Moral Reform League's unsuccessful petition, city hall passed a discriminatory bylaw that ordered the removal of all laundries operating in a designated quarter of the downtown core occupied by several Chinese laundries. This move followed on the heels of several ugly public incidents that hinged on anti-Asian sentiment, including a riot that wrecked a local Chinese restaurant. 'The Celestials,' the Lethbridge *News* reported, 'are much wrought up over the matter and have banded together to see if something cannot be done to amend the present by-law.'[44]

In many respects, Lethbridge on the eve of war remained a city comprised, more than either Guelph or Trois-Rivières, of newcomers not yet accommodated to divisions of history and identity that cut across urban populations established in central and eastern Canada at this time. The war would do little to overcome these barriers anywhere in Canada. Yet, as elsewhere, the great struggle was often portrayed in the Lethbridge papers and in many speeches and sermons in the city as a great forging force, one that drew civilians and soldiers together in a common cause. Such depictions described merely the surface of events, cast through the culturally specific lens of Anglo-conformist newspapers that routinely reported public occurrences from the skewed perspectives of mostly white, Protestant residents, who generally stood in support of the early war effort. Their story began not just with the news of war, but also with a series of impromptu, if not spontaneous, ritualizations that expressed support for Canada's backing of Britain's entrance, following the fateful expired ultimatum to Germany. While the most imperial-nationalistic segments of the city's inhabitants quickly endorsed the war, a diverse and often divided set of communities in Lethbridge could never be truly united in an enterprise that excluded on the basis of race as well as on the newly-constituted basis of 'enemy alien' ethnicity.[45]

The Outbreak and the Festival of August: A Masculine Ritualization

In Canada news of the coming war prompted many public demonstrations of support for the Allies as Europe drifted inexorably from expired ultimatums and declared war to armed mobilizations. Within two weeks of the end of July, armed divisions from Britain and the continent, poorly prepared for the kind of fighting that soon developed, were engaged in the crucial first battles and the race to the sea from Belgium to the coastline of France. All of this took place within imperial systems connected, of course, by that disastrous bipolarity of diplomatic alliances that included Britain and, by an extension of tradition though not by constitutional requirement, Canada. Most Canadians felt simply that support for Britain was justified, even imperative.

When news of an actual war footing was first broadcast, hastily assembled crowds across the country expressed an enormous sense of anticipation, often enthusiasm, to be part of it. In urban centres from Halifax to Vancouver, local groups, communities, and the public at large witnessed a dense series of parades, orations, concerts, and sermons, often with intense interest and enthusiasm rather than passive curiosity. Downtown streets, theatres, church pews, and exhibition grounds in every region, including Quebec, filled with news-seekers and with those who came to cheer, even to celebrate the moment. While their appearance was sudden, the actual performances themselves were planned and orchestrated. They conformed to prior forms of public ritual, from parades and singing crowds to specific orations and band concert recitals. But invariably, in every city, public displays did not appear as generic replications that simply echoed across the country.

In Lethbridge, the *Herald* spoke of large, news-hungry crowds appearing in front of its office for several days, 'all agog' with piqued anticipation just before the outbreak. Late in the afternoon of 3 August, 'the largest crowd ever' gathered in front of Lethbridge's Galt Gardens bandstand to hear the latest bulletins. The reporter underscored the imperial tie between Lethbridge's Anglo-Canadian majority, the rest of Canada, and the Empire as a whole. Heritage appeared not as actual history, but as imagined bonds. Yet people responded and seemed to enjoy being part of an event they had made themselves to celebrate an invented sense of lineage and a racialized concept of nation. The most compelling moment came, as the eyewitness reporter put it, when Canada's official offer of assistance to Britain was met by 'the mightiest cheer that ever rent the atmosphere that hovers over the tranquil city of Lethbridge.' The 'multitude,' it was said, displayed unequivocal loyalty: they 'testified beyond the shadow of a doubt that if the sentiment was as strong all over the Dominion as it is in Lethbridge, Canada is ready to meet any emergency into which the Motherland may be precipitated.'[46]

Despite the variety of ways in which such messages were understood – their polysemic nature – the crowds were indeed large, noisy, ubiquitous, and unprecedented in scale, particularly those gathered in front of newspaper offices. Among 'the people in general,' the editor of the *Canadian Annual Review* put it, 'there were many demonstrations of loyalty and patriotism' among large numbers that assembled in the several days leading up to the climactic expiration of Britain's ultimatum on 4 August.[47] In Guelph, 'huge crowds gathered to hear the very latest war news,' publicized as soon as telegraphed bulletins were posted by the city's daily paper.[48] Along with predominantly English Canadian crowds in most parts of Canada outside Quebec, numerous reports from that province described anglophones and francophones united in celebration. In Montreal, mixed throngs of French and English marched along 'the streets carrying French and British Flags, singing songs such as the Marseillaise and Rule Britannia.' In Quebec City, 'English and French and Irish paraded together in an outburst of combined patriotism.'[49] Midway between, in Trois-Rivières, a smaller crowd gathered in front of the city armoury. One anglophone reporter boasted, nonetheless, that his city 'was not behind other cities in her devotion to the King and Mother country.'[50] The *Bien Public* spoke of the unity symbolized by English and French Trifluviens marching together. Led by the Union Jack and fleur-de-lis, and singing patriotic songs, they headed for city hall, where they were addressed by, among others, Jacques Bureau and the Rev. J. Aitken Clark, a Presbyterian clergyman. The demonstration was said to celebrate the city's part in 'la victoire des Anglais sur les Allemands.'[51]

The war began for most Canadians simply as news, celebrated and displayed. Popular expressions of what was taking place quickly materialized and circulated through local means that can tell us much about what people believed, felt, and understood. The sudden appearance of cheering and singing throngs, fascinated by their imagined sense and vicarious understandings of what lay ahead, created spectacles that allow us many points of entry.

Their apparent spontaneity was often little more than an illusion. Public spaces, in most cases, were carefully used to stage displays in fairly conventional forms for the purpose of both broadcasting information and mounting public displays of local reactions. Speeches cast in tropes of sentimental patriotism, or civic band concerts featuring patriotic music, or militia march pasts and send-offs described by the press as public spectacles staged to educate attending audiences or readers did just that: Beginning with what local populations, ordinary participants in an urban crowd, already knew, believed, or understood about their past and present in general terms, such spectacles offered visual, aural, and often symbolic moments through which the purposes of at least a formalized version of the war as a new situation could be communicated and experienced. Though the detailed press descriptions that remain are themselves constructed texts, they do provide a useful means for delineating social differences as well as the salient claims they often made for citizen support for a British and Canadian victory. The passage presented below allows us our first close examination of the setting, form, and textual representation of several patriotic displays in Lethbridge.

The detailed coverage it received in the *Herald* was typical. Though it parallels an international pattern of public celebration, what Gordon A. Craig once described as 'an almost carnival gaiety' with which the war in Europe began, we begin confined.[52] We begin one late-summer afternoon in Lethbridge, at the war's outbreak.

Lethbridge Proclaims Her Loyalty to the Great British Empire

'Breathes there a man with soul so dead,
Who never to himself hath said,
This is my own, my native land.'

How deeply this sentiment stirred the hearts of the vast crowd assembled outside the Herald Office last night, was vividly portrayed by the wild scenes of enthusiasm which greeted the announcement that war had been declared between Great Britain and Germany.

Amidst excitement which baffles description, the despatch stating that Germany had declared war on Great Britain was megaphoned to the eagerly awaiting crowd. The people listened in tense silence until the despatch was finished and then one yell – you could not describe it as a cheer – rent the air, hats were thrown, sky high and for a moment the people went mad. Many a deeply muttered 'Thank God' was heard as everyone realised that Great Britain, true to her past traditions, meant to carry out her obligations in the spirit in which they were made, as well as to the letter, no matter at what cost to herself.

It was a Goliath's task to corral the members of the Citizen's Band, but once they learned of the happenings it did not take them long to fall in line. Commissioner Grace invaded the band rooms, where a rehearsal was in progress and enlisted the support of Bandmaster Cline and those present. The fire chief's 'red devil' was next appropriated and transformed into a van. Within an hour the instruments were collected and the procession lined up. During the pilgrimage No. 2 fire hall was visited, and there was found a half score of lusty Britons eager to join in an expression of patriotism. Though compelled to stand guard over the city they were none the less patriotic.

The vast assemblage in front of the Herald Office were enthused to the breaking point, when the parade led by the fire chief's squadron and followed by the band and a throng of citizens with flags, marched out onto 6th avenue. Cheer after cheer arose amid the greatest of excitement. The band was vociferously cheered after each contribution to the general uproar. Then they played 'Rule Britannia,' 'The Red, White and Blue,' 'Bonnie Dundae,' 'Men of Harlech,' 'Cock o' the North,' 'The 81st Regimental March,'

'The Maple Leaf,' 'O Canada,' and 'God Save the King.' Much credit is due the band boys for the masterful manner in which they located their members. The demonstration would have fallen flat had it not been for the stirring tunes supplied by the Citizen's Band.

Bulletins were announced at intervals by Mr. McCarty from the Herald window, each being separately cheered. Fireworks exploded and rockets spluttered and went heavenward. The fire department turned out and shot a stream of water into the air, the effect along with the rockets reminding one of an engagement on the North Sea.

First Intimation

If excitement reigned on the streets, the state of mind in the Herald Offices was one of fever beat. The declaration came in shortly after seven o'clock and a special was on the press within 30 minutes. The very first intimation given to Lethbridge that the Motherland had declared war, came to the few who gathered at the office when the first special off the press was allowed to flutter to the street from an upper window. The Union Jack soon floated from the masthead, and the news was out.

The newsies could get no farther than a few feet into the crowd, that sprung up like magic, and the entire edition was soon sold out.

At the Starland the lights blazed forth, the orchestra played 'God Save the King,' a likeness of His Majesty was flashed on the screens, and extras scattered through the crowd. A cheer arose and from that moment the news spread like wild fire.

As the crowd increased, the bulletins were megaphoned out the window.

In the procession was seen a French flag and during the course of the demonstration the 'Fleur de Lis' nation was given three lusty cheers.

The crowd called on our popular mayor for a speech and he immediately responded.

'Ladies and gentlemen and fellow subjects of the British Empire,' said our Mayor, 'you are assembled now at the most momentous moment in the history of the British Empire, to which it is our proud privilege to belong. The war has been thrust on us, we have not sought it. But now it has come we are ready and I know that every citizen of the City of Lethbridge is ready to do his duty at any sacrifice to himself. The German Kaiser has been going around for some time with a chip on his shoulder and the time has come for us to knock that chip off. The Kaiser has been seeking trouble and has now started something, and I tell you, citizens of Lethbridge, that by the time the trouble is over, there will be no Kaiser and we will have put the 'Dutchman' where he belongs.' (Cheers.)

Mr. David Elton, our worthy magistrate, made an impressive speech. 'This war has been thrust on us,' he said, 'The Kaiser has been skating round a hole in the ice for some time and now we are going to put him in the water.

> (Voice from the crowd, 'Under the water.') We have wanted peace with honor, but never peace with dishonor. What is the good of crying, 'Peace, peace, when there is no peace?' We are ready, and when this war is over it will have had the effect of welding together the whole of the Anglo-Saxon race as one entity, covering a space from the centre of the earth to its circumference. I know in this crisis that every man in Lethbridge will do his duty to the Empire. The scene in front of him reminded him of the time when as a toddling mite, his uncle returned to Worcester from the Afghan war, where he had been fighting under Earl Roberts.' (Cheers and cries of 'Good old Bob.')[53]

This report has many limits. It can lure, mislead, beguile if the potential modes of its construction are overlooked. Within it, many things seem suspect. Its viewpoint is certainly skewed. We learn of the fever beat of the *Herald* office, the extras, the first intimation of war as an offering (the single copy that floated down from the office window) or the ignition of a rumour (through the circulation of a few hot extras at the Starland theatre). McCarty's shouts from an open window become a pivot for events driven by the latest 'intimations' from Europe. It is news through a newsmaker's eyes. Its purpose, from that perspective, is to arouse further the excitement it described and to sell newspapers. What are we to make of the admission that the demonstration might have fallen flat if it hadn't been for the Citizen's Band? Was the crowd really smaller than suggested? Or was its reported size really just a pat on the back for the band? The report's biases, the distortions caused by its intentions and situated horizons, may be numerous. But they too can offer something to the historian. Interpreting such sources, constructing a secondary reading from a constructed primary reading of an event itself constructed, may suggest layers of communication that are far from direct, but worth pursuing.

Roger Chartier has noted his reservations about approaching human activities, especially public events, as texts to be read – as the schemata of power relations, social structure, and experience. When we try to read one through the other, we encounter an unavoidable problem. The logic of written expression and that of 'practical sense' are not identical.[54] To this, Robert Darnton, whose textual readings in the *Great Cat Massacre and Other Episodes in French Cultural History* (1984) prompted much debate on the utility of 'thick descriptions,' responds that the real task is to move successfully back and forth between text and context.[55] We might thus consider how such shifting consciousness, awareness, or 'local knowledges' became significant within their local realms because of their links to other worlds – connections to other places, other histories.

For our purposes, we can approach the text above as a complex ensemble, grounded in both local experience and much wider pasts. We might also look for signs of how collective experiences, outside of any particular urban space, are shaped by local immediacy and everyday life in a specific locale. Readings might be offered concerning constructions of patriotism, assertions of masculinity, the appeal of social memories – the use generally of symbols that might at times promote a sense of connection between 'official' culture, expressions by governing spokespersons standing behind Canada and Britain at war, and the contrasting perspectives of groups divided by class, occupation, age, gender, and ethnicity.

The 'wild scenes of enthusiasm' among crowds that seemed to spring 'up like magic' were described in similar terms in other city newspapers. Their portraits could be of different ethnic groups, men and women,[56] and young and old,[57] joined in song, cheering, and witnessing spectacles like those described in front of the *Herald* office. Such crowds did not form spontaneously. Their members were aware of news concerning the likelihood of war and certainly knew where the latest reports could first be seen – as headlines posted on bulletin boards in front of newspaper offices in the downtown core. The use of bulletin boards, megaphones, stereopticons, speaking platforms, musical bands, flags, posters, and bunting provided hastily fashioned but suitable settings for symbolic communication. Commissioner Grace, in the Lethbridge case, appeared almost frantic in his efforts to create a spectacle. Another report placed him atop a building, draping a huge sheet over its wall to be used as a screen for slide projections of several public figures, including Lord Kitchener.[58] Crowds often formed in front of newspaper offices when crucial news was anticipated. Accounts across Canada compared the demonstrations that greeted the war's outbreak to those prompted by news of the Boer War, though public responses reflecting division between French and English Canada were absent in August 1914, and this frequently drew comment.

In part, this prompts us to consider ephemeral moments in public gatherings when barriers might have broken down and even permitted certain thresholds to be crossed. We might address, in other words, liminal moments during public ritualizations that greeted the war. From speech making and patriotic singing to posting bulletin board news or hastily assembling parades, sites of shifting sentiments and attitudes seem evident in many reports. For these we might consider Turnerian approaches to local rituals, readings that consider how established social boundaries are abandoned, temporarily, during intense moments of public display. The music, marching, chanting, listening, and applauding that took place may have often blurred distinctions between crowds and performers. Lines between spectators and participants might have suddenly shifted or dissolved. For those most affected, August 1914 may have induced a temporary transcendence of prior relationships and boundaries, or what Turner called anti-structure.[59] Although it must be stressed that such moments are short-lived, their liminal potential, their capacity to produce experiences in which fundamental interpretations of the world as it is are substituted, one for another, is worth keeping in mind as we go on to look at how recruitment took place and how civilians organized themselves to support it.

The Lethbridge text might also lead us to interpret constructions of patriotism, nationalism, and imperial-nationalism. This leads into a complex web of meanings. Each, for example, needs to be considered in a plural sense to do justice to the varieties of Englishness, Frenchness, Canadianness, and so on we might encounter. Unravelling cultural communication on the home front often impinges on relationships of imagined community, of race, people, country, or empire. The same could be said about gender. The good work of the 'band boys' thrown together in a 'Goliath' effort, or the 'lusty cheers' heard that afternoon, are described with phrases borrowed from conventional forms of gendered language often used to translate events. So too were the speeches and rejoinders made to knock a chip off the Kaiser's shoulder or to sink him altogether. Moreover, the configurations of many scenes, with a marching band, a fire truck hosing the sky, or male civic leaders addressing audiences in masculine terms, leave us something else to consider. Masculine forms were ordered in relation to other practices. As signs of men's social power, embedded in many sources of cultural representation, they provide us a means to probe relationships between lived experience and fantasy worlds, the places of imagined manhood.

Both invented traditions and social memory also come into play. The *Herald* text includes reference to Great Britain as 'true to her past traditions.' The fireworks and water cannon show also conjured images of naval warfare. Mayor Hardie exploited a usable past to connect his audience to the history of the British Empire. And for David Elton, an imperial militarism set in the past, his family history, and his manful boasting to put Kaiser in his place all combined to shape his speech. Social memories, particularly at the national level as Fentress and Wickham have suggested, can be reworked to produce idealized representations of the past, especially in wartime.[60] Invented traditions also can be mobilized as symbolic reminders of such pasts. How parades, flags, speeches, and songs were used as symbols implies a relationship of representation between traditional practices and public display. As inherited emblems of identity – of 'imperial-nation' of 'a people,' of 'a glorious history' – national symbols in particular can both evoke emotions and be used for cognitive purposes. When, as the *Herald* claimed, the Union Jack was hoisted over the newspaper's headquarters on 4 August, a powerful symbol framed the coming of war once again. The 'old flag' stood atop a 'young Dominion' at this moment. A new war against Germany and its allies was proudly marked wherever local sites could be found to stir the imagination. The crowd's reaction in front of this newspaper office would have constituted an ideal event for individuals predisposed to supporting Canada's part in the war to channel

2 In a pre-electronic era of mass broadcasting, about a decade before radio, city streets during the First World War served as important sites for public theatre, often readied by local citizens of all social ranks to deliver dramatic war-related messages. Here we see eager spectators beneath Union Jacks, strung between the buildings overhead, waiting during wartime to see the floats, the military regiments, or the civilian groups and dignitaries file by, along Wyndham Street in Guelph's downtown core. This particular scene appeared on a set of local postcards. *Courtesy of Guelph Museums, 986.18.224*

their feelings toward a collective, and fundamentally imagined, sense of the war as it unfolded. There was often no better arena for 'educating' sentiments of patriotism, imperial-nationalism, militarism, or demonizations of the enemy than a wartime crowd, gathered downtown. If social memory served as an underlying fabric, binding imperial-national communities across Canada to a sense of tradition and identity, then public spaces provided convenient sites to display what many English Canadians recognized as their most cherished signs. The street theatre of August 1914, in particular, depended heavily on patriotic songs, symbols of the Empire in many forms, and a constant discourse of imperial-national rhetoric and commemoration.

The procession, music, and speeches of observance and commemoration described also suggest possible meeting grounds between official and vernacular cultural expressions. As John Bodnar has argued with respect to public memory, 'official culture' is rooted in the interests of leaders from all levels of society, be they small towns, ethnic communities, or the bureaucracies of government, education, or the military. Such elites, powerful within existing institutions and social relations, tend to favour the status quo. Civic, educational, religious, economic, and governmental spokespersons most typically prefer order and harmony over any significant rival, especially radical, movement. They concern themselves with social cohesion and stability, with protecting existing institutions. In the ordinary discourses of oration, sermon, and editorial commentary they tend to convey public messages through a 'dogmatic formalism,' one that relies on idealistic concepts of a timeless, sacred past. And they present interpretations of the past and present that alleviate the concerns of competing interests. They seek a 'higher' goal through the use of imagined nationalisms that encompass the whole of society and mediate the interests of its diverse vernacular cultures.[61]

What Bodnar identifies as 'vernacular' cultures make up sub-elements within the society. They are numerous. Workers, women, ethnic affiliations, or the poor are examples of these. Such collectivities, whenever and wherever they arise, tend to restate perceptions gained through direct experience within their respective social segment rather than through any powerful, imaginary connection with the nation as a whole. They often convey how they feel about their particular social situation rather than what society in general should become for all its constituent elements. They are often patriotic, but unlike promoters of official culture they seek to defend their own interests against the threat of others. Though we might consider them 'ordinary people,' they are not necessarily representative of a working class. They may reflect the politics of gender, class, or ethnicity, but vernacular experiences can be formed by countless other relationships and shared histories. While official culture tends to draw its promoters from a broad group of middle-class professionals, all social stations can contribute to vernacular cultures, be they immigrants, students, workers, professionals, militarists, or pacifists. Effective communication between official and vernacular cultures takes place through rituals, metaphors, and symbols that convey a unitary conceptual framework capable of connecting discordant interests to shared images of some ideal. That is its purpose.

Attempting to evaluate rituals strictly in terms of their functional characteristics, however, leaves us with static explanations. This is found, for instance, in Robert Bocock's argument that rituals can either bind 'people's feelings into the existing organization of society' or help 'them to become critical and independent of it.'[62] True, but the spectrum of mixed purposes between these extremes is daunting enough for us to consider alternatives. Bocock's approach, like that of Edmund Leach, seems constrained, given the fluidity our cases suggest.[63] Once war was declared, newspapers became crowded with stories of recruitment procedures, march pasts, patriotic rallies, farewell dinners, dances, or railway station send-offs. 'Social control' or 'functionalist' interpretations of these events tend to see them as holistic, hegemonic efforts to impose interpretations from above to serve the interests of the ascendant orders.

However, home front populations did not simply choose at times to reflect or to reject demands communicated by various social elites. Instead

Canada's vernacular components – people divided by class, gender, ethnicity, and age – engaged in a perpetual battle for power on the home front. Fundamental social boundaries did not dissolve, but became the wedges through which consensus or conflicts took shape, especially as the war dragged on. The study of specific calls that public, or 'official' voices made through customary rituals – speeches, sermons, parades, or rallies – to serve the nation at home or overseas should not be seen simplistically as a top-down system of signification that either succeeded or failed to win over given, and rather static, target audiences. Instead, we need to develop approaches that highlight what were often ambivalent, multivocal, and polysemic forms of communication and experience.

Catherine Bell's conceptual work on strategies of ritualization offers a more flexible encounter with the variety of home front rituals considered here. Bell sees ritual as a dynamic process, 'a strategy used for the construction of certain types of power.'[64] During the voluntary recruitment period, there were reports of home guard units forming and the ubiquitous drives for fresh enlistments were undertaken. Both were accompanied by strategic home front rituals – parades in special uniforms, speeches that appealed to manhood and to public duty. As public performances enacted to communicate constructions of patriotism, nationalism, gender, or social memory, they often adopted strategies based on the ritualization of existing power relations. At times they sought to reaffirm old boundaries; at others, to establish new ones.

Imagining a distant war through local places and sites takes us often to horizons of expectation, communication, and perception. Such activities, of course, were cultural. The experiential worlds through which local populations imagined distant events and the worlds they lived in, as sites of popular communication and ritualizations, turned out to be the same place. I address the proposition that active subjects, someone, for example, like Albert Chabrol 'poaching' from a newspaper text to imagine the war overseas, cannot return entirely to what he once was. To consider this, we need to ask how everyday experiences served to connect the immediate experiences of the familiar and the known to the otherness of an imagined war overseas. We need to approach textual evidence, in very different forms, as material compilations of conventionally recognizable signs – verbal, aural, and visual – that provoked symbolic interpretations, particularly those that seemed, for a given individual or group in these cities, most fathomable, most comprehensible, most identifiable, most effective.

Their potency, in these respects, derived from their local, often parochial referents. The familiar and recognizable discursive acts they incited and exchanged, within a church congregation, amongst a reading audience, or during the structured encounter of a government board of inquiry, lent them, in various ways, their communicative power. What follows, then, considers how a specific set of civilian-military relations, from recruiting to veteran re-establishment, were imagined in codes and formed inscribing social differences. We move on to examine how local experiences of everyday life on the home front – the fluid exchanges between perceptions and consciousness made possible by newspapers, public displays, and traditional ritualizations appropriated for wartime purposes – constituted systems of belief and practice dividing recruits from others, enemy aliens from others, veterans from others, men from women, and supporters from opponents of compulsory military service.

2
Dancing before Death

The fictional representation of Albert Chabrol's decision to enlist, encountered in the previous chapter, isolates a moment of decision spurred by newspaper reading and his response to a demonized enemy. Chabrol left Canada to join the French army, becoming part of a generation of soldiers who paid a heavy price for their part in history. But men like him could hardly foresee their future nor do much about it even if they did. Most volunteers and conscripts from the belligerent countries entered the war, as Chabrol did, with little idea of what lay ahead. Evidence of what contemporaries felt and saw survives in many memoirs from the period. We might consider one that circulated years later under the title *The Great War As I Saw It*. Written in the early 1930s, the Rev. Frederick George Scott's popular account placed him, in early August 1914, on the margins of the crowd around the bulletin boards in Quebec City as the huge gathering reacted with shouts, songs, and cheering to first news of the war.[1] Scott writes of being an onlooker pulled into the vortex of the day's excitement, a perilous current that would soon tear him away from many things he had valued. His claim, constructed in hindsight, was no doubt conditioned by the catastrophe he spent the next four years witnessing. 'I had a queer feeling that some mysterious power was dragging me into a whirlpool, and the ordinary life around me and the things that were so dear to me had already begun to fade away.' Celebrations of war brought the festive and the pensive face to face. When peace between Britain and Germany ended with an expired ultimatum two days later, 'all civilization seemed to be tottering,' as he saw it. The 'world seemed suddenly to have gone mad.' He entered the whirlpool and enlisted a few days later.[2]

At the outbreak, Canada had, in round numbers, some 77,000 peacetime militia in volunteer units throughout the country, and a permanent force of 3,000. Most of the militia with family or jobs stayed home at first. A short war was all they expected. For those who did join up, two-thirds of whom were British-born, peer pressure and economic necessity may, as often as not, have been greater inducements than the patriotic reasons they gave such great voice to.[3] Moreover, a naïve hope, often concealed under the cloak of far greater ideals, that a great adventure awaited overseas seemed to underscore their urges. Newspapers often played this up and certainly did not hide a kind of vicarious excitement as they reported events at or near the recruiter's desk. The rush to get into action, above all else, reflected the general ignorance at that time of the destructive stalemate that loomed.

The rise and fall of voluntary enlistment across Canada was a marriage of localized intentions and national strategies pursued by the federal government. It ended in estrangement for some in English Canada and in a riot in Quebec City after conscription came. Most accounts describe how in Ottawa, and soon after at Valcartier – the huge training base set up in Quebec to receive recruits – Robert Borden's Conservative government and his minister of militia and defence, Sam Hughes, authorized the raising of men and materiel. It was a sloppy affair, poorly organized and directed by an energetic but single-minded politician-turned-military commander. Nonetheless, it produced Canada's first contingent of some 22,000 men. At the same time, across the country, official directives from the militia department were met with enthusiasm, espoused patriotism, and collective action. Hometown settings became significant because they blended the power of local experience with a constantly shifting sense of a distant war and its imperatives. Across the country, recruitment depended on local networks of civilians eager to support the war effort and willing to translate what Ottawa intended, and what Hughes managed to accomplish, into demonstrations of civic endorsement for Canada's commitment to enlisting, provisioning, training, and dispatching so many males, mostly youths, overseas.

Opinion makers of all kinds, from mayors and editorialists to preachers and teachers, readily took up opportunities to pontificate on the war's various meanings, its origins, causes, purposes, and inevitable outcomes, as culturally specific impressions and visions. Pro-war orators and journalists exploited a repertoire of cultural discourses, from social memories and moral justifications for the war to predictions of how and why the Allies would win, to mark the moments of departure for local troops. Their roles in the public sphere as propagandists proved crucial, as they became conduits of information and interpretation concerning the war. The interests and attitudes of their audiences and readers were far from ready-made, pre-existing, or singular. Yet as contested as the images and ideals of the conflict in Europe were across a mosaic of pacifists, enemy aliens, and others who opposed the war, a majority throughout the country, even in many parts of Quebec, shared much of the innocent enthusiasm of early August. For local crowds and observers, the march pasts, send-offs, and patriotic rallies organized in every town or city in Canada that dispatched troops, which distanced raw recruits from family and friends, did so by making mundane realities seem purposeful, by making of hometown settings the first place where the significance of leaving for the front, as a threshold experience, could be imagined.

Ordinary citizens frequently took part in the public events recruiting required, to reaffirm social and political hierarchies and to reiterate the moral values of a society preparing for war. Apart from the few people in each city who actually organized these events, large crowds and mass readerships heard or read the orations and sermons that accompanied them, typically framed to mask social divisions in shaping popular interpretations of their audience's or readership's imagined relationship with the world beyond their city. When Hugh Guthrie, a Liberal MP representing Guelph and Wellington County, addressed an inaugural rally for the Canadian Patriotic Fund by stating that 'there is no statesman in England at the present time who doubts the value of the colonies, and no colonial who doubts the connection with Great Britain,' he tapped into a powerfully mythical reciprocal relationship, frequently used at this time to justify Canada's support for an imperial war.[4] Or when the Rev. G.H. Cobbledick of Lethbridge's Wesley Methodist Church quoted a passage from the book of Exodus before a send-off for Lethbridge troops held in his church, imploring the fresh recruits to 'Fear not, stand in marching order, and see the salvation of God,' before adding on behalf of friends and families looking on, 'Our hearts and minds are with our boys who will go to the front,' he drew from religious pastoral, a regular tactic in public speech in August 1914, yet important to our understanding of how orators deployed social narratives to justify recruiting.[5]

The popular press in Quebec, as elsewhere, joined in endorsing Canada's support for the Allies and the Empire, prompting historians since to comment on the apparent unity with which Canada went to war. At a city hall meeting in Trois-Rivières, called to inaugurate the local chapter of the Canadian Patriotic Fund, Mayor J.-A. Tessier led several other speakers in soliciting donations. 'Chacun de ces orateurs persuadait pendant quelques minutes le public de l'idée patriotique,' the *Nouveau Trios-Rivières* reported, 'qui avait présidée à cette démonstration en notre cité, et généralement dans toutes les villes du Canada.'[6] Such rhetoric helped to instill an imagined sense of why support was necessary and of what others were doing across the country to maintain it. A short war was generally expected; the slaughter in the trenches was not. In all cases, however, recruitment began in hometown settings, and its success or failure ultimately reflected the uncertain connections between Ottawa's requirements and local conditions.

Phases of Voluntary Enlistment: National Strategies and Local Patterns

Recruitment strategies, which depended on centralized tactics and favourable local conditions, certainly began with little foresight on the part of Ottawa.

The reality of this simple fact ultimately shaped changing approaches and policies on both levels. In general, as manpower demands increased from August 1914 until conscription was implemented in the summer of 1917, recruitment responsibilities shifted from the national to the local level. In the end, decidedly local or 'community-based' efforts became little more than a last-ditch attempt to revive enlistment through localized affiliations of men by place, by ethnicity, even by community-based associations. In broad terms, instead of the militia department assuming an increased role as manpower needs grew, which proved ineffective from the Valcartier fiasco on, existing and subsequent military units were given increased control over a task that depended on local networks, local appeals, local control, and local resources. Ottawa only brought in conscription as a last resort after an assortment of local efforts, from county to 'pals' battalions, failed to maintain adequate enlistment levels.

By the autumn of 1917, two-and-a-half years later, voluntary recruitment and send-off ritualizations had passed through three discernible stages, which we might designate as the 'Valcartier,' 'militia regiment,' and 'community regiment' phases. Their sequence in raising volunteers reflected the general Ottawa-to-local shift in emphasis and resources. Guelph and Lethbridge became part of this primarily English Canadian tactic. Given French Canada's more limited commitment to military service within the British Empire, and given the sudden demise of the city's only militia regiment shortly before the war, recruitment patterns in Trois-Rivières took quite a different course from the very beginning in August 1914.

Raising the CEF began that month with an experiment in central control, now well documented, that was directed in a single-handed manner by the minister of militia and defence, Sam Hughes. Hughes began by scrapping a quite viable mobilization plan, drawn up by his senior staff, which would have decentralized recruiting. Instead, he favoured establishing one large-scale training depot located in Valcartier, Quebec.[7] Instead of equipping, housing, and training recruits wherever their particular regiment was located, over 36,000 volunteers travelled by rail to Valcartier, an extensive training facility Hughes had personally selected on a site located sixteen miles northwest of Quebec City on the east bank of the Jacques Cartier River.[8] The minister took charge of daily operations. It only lasted two months, from the outbreak of the war to 6 October, but it produced Canada's First Overseas Contingent and in the process contributed to how the public across Canada perceived these first soldiers as volunteers. Throughout this phase, marked by administrative confusion and Hughes's unorthodox leadership style, command, if not control, remained tightly concentrated in Ottawa. Militia units across the country, nonetheless, remained the initial contact points of communication, enrolment, and mustering procedures.

This process began on 6 August, when militia unit commanders across

3 This photograph of Trois-Rivières's *manège militaire* (armoury) was taken about five years after its completion in 1905, when it served as the headquarters of the 86th Three Rivers Regiment. The breakup of this unit, just weeks before the onset of the war, dislodged a local militia organization at a time when it was most needed for recruitment from the city and surrounding rural districts. *Courtesy of Archives du Séminaire de Trois-Rivières, FN-0064-49-06*

the country, with the exception of cavalry officers, received one of some 226 night lettergrams calling on them to provide lists of eligible volunteers, by name and qualifications.[9] The lettergram specified requirements for physical stature, age, and marital status, as well as a 'high standard' in marksmanship. Senior officers from each regiment were asked to designate these first enlistees and, if possible, have the men examined by an Army Medical Corps officer. 'When all the names have been received officers commanding units will submit direct to Militia Headquarters descriptive rolls of those who have passed the required medical examination,' the instructions read.[10] Then – and this step caused a delay of about a week for most units waiting to hear back – Militia Headquarters in Ottawa set a quota for each regiment. Two days later, Hughes's department notified all militia commanders that 'not more than 125 men and officers will be accepted' from either rural or small city regiments; the preliminary lists for Lethbridge and Guelph stood at this number.[11] The 30th Wellington Rifles recruited and dispatched Guelph's first CEF troops, its limit of 125, during the hectic Valcartier phase, as did the 20th Battery, Canadian Field Artillery, from Lethbridge. Because the Department of Militia and Defence had recently disbanded the 86th Three Rivers Regiment, volunteers from that area could not enlist locally. As far as can be determined from scattered press reports, only a handful of Trifluviens came forward during the first call for recruits.

Apart from the comparatively weak response among francophones in Quebec, the real difficulty faced in Lethbridge, Guelph, and units across English Canada was not finding the men, but having to turn them away. Added to this was the broader problem of how best to equip, train, and dispatch the chosen men overseas. The dusty, chaotic camp life at Valcartier was perhaps indicative of a country unprepared for the demands of organizing for a war of unprecedented scale, though we might speculate on how different the original plan may have made things. Given a fledgling military bureaucracy and numerous problems of direction, supply, even morale, it soon became quite clear, even to Hughes, that something beyond a centralized strategy was needed. The militia regiment recruiting and training approach that replaced it was adopted on 6 October, when the Canadian government offered Britain a second contingent of twenty thousand men.[12] In Ottawa, responsibility for raising this force was initially delegated to Maj.-Gen. W.G. Gwatkin, chief of the general staff, assisted by the deputy minister of militia, Maj.-Gen. Eugène Fiset.[13] But primary control lay in the hands of existing and newly commissioned military units across the country.

Given the anticipated number of recruits needed once the stalemate set in early 1915, sheer necessity gave rise to this larger and more locally sensitive system.[14] In practice, control over recruiting was handed back to Canada's six military divisions and three districts, administrative zones between the Maritimes and British Columbia that served as intermediate command posts between local militia units and Ottawa. Though state authority in Ottawa continued to direct everything from official censorship procedures to material support, control over their specific application, from displaying posters to delivering speeches, shifted effectively to local officers in concert with civilian women and men associated with Canada's recruiting establishment. Military and civilian coordinators in each locale thus used their particular regiment or battalion as a recruiting node that ultimately fed into the national system, as recruits continued to stream into the CEF. In practice, this greatly enhanced the importance and influence of local situations, which were rapidly adapting to the changed conditions of a country at war. Lethbridge was in Military District 13, with headquarters in Edmonton. Guelph reported to the 1st Division in London, while Trois-Rivières was commanded by the 4th Division in Quebec City.

As these divisions and their respective militia units assumed control, fresh recruits were inducted and trained at designated locations, usually at or near the hometowns or cities their particular regiment drew recruits from, until movement orders were received. From then on, the sustained presence and impact of local recruiting, training, and troop dispatches became part of the routine of home front life generally, up to the adoption of conscription measures in the summer of 1917. The Department of Militia and Defence, with Hughes's support, also dealt with the need to establish

4 The 16th Battery, Canadian Field Artillery, is pictured here in front of Guelph's armoury on Wyndham Street, which was constructed just six years before this photograph was taken in 1915. This unit was recruited during the 'militia regiment' phase, when local facilities and training grounds were used to equip and train volunteer regiments within an expanded, decentralized regimental system. Most units to the Canadian Expeditionary Force's Second overseas contingent had strong regional links – of kinship, schooling, or recent employment history – to a home region. Posed regimental portraits like this one were staged to reflect a sense of pride and *esprit de corps* among local volunteers during the early war. *Courtesy of Guelph Museums, 981.289.4*

institutional bridges to French Canada through the creation of new francophone units. These newly created regiments and battalions, most notably the 22nd Bataillon along with the 41st and 57th, eventually drew far higher numbers from Trois-Rivières than could have been expected without them. Militia regiment approaches produced the 20th and 39th Batteries from Lethbridge, and the 34th Battalion, the 16th and 29th Batteries, and part of the 71st Battalion from Guelph.

Within a year, however, enlistment levels began to drop precipitously, before plummeting in the fall of 1915. This led the Department of Militia and Defence to supplement the existing system with the community regiment strategy by September 1915. This used cultural means to obtain military ends. Individual towns, cities, counties, or even local ethnic or social networks, such as the Highlanders or certain groups of 'pals,' raised their own units, with far greater control in naming and inventing their regimental identities. Often these appeals amounted to little more than convenient tactics to promote yet one more genre of regimental identity, and, of course, recruits joined up who were neither local, Scottish, or at all connected to their unit's label or ethos.[15] Community regiments used their invented distinctions as a marketing ploy that met with mixed results in most locales. The drive for greater numbers, nonetheless, consumed the attention of each regiment's staunchest backers, the civilian volunteers who made up part of each town or city's recruiting clique. In this final phase of voluntary recruitment, fully stepped-up local recruiting campaigns became an important means to get these units filled and trained in a preliminary way before the journey overseas. Lethbridge produced the 113th Lethbridge Highlanders' Battalion; Guelph contributed to the Wellington County's 153rd Battalion.

This final effort may have attracted as many enlistees as possible under any voluntary system, but failed to supply the numbers required. As national totals continued to decline overall, arguments in favour of compulsory service gained support during 1916, coming to a head with the conscription crisis the following year. By then, the voluntary system as a whole in Canada, from Valcartier-based central planning to community-based local regiments, reached a systemic limit. Its implementation at local levels, at sites that disseminated compelling images of wartime masculinity and signalled the liminality of enlistment and departure, had brought together networks of family, institutional, and community relations. Send-off ritualizations served to demarcate the new boundaries between recruits and civilians that sanctioned the dispatch of thousands of mostly young men to idealized causes and imagined purposes. Interrogating these signs helps us understand how, in separate ways as either enlistees or civilians, recruits and their home front supporters crossed these thresholds.

Ritualizations of Departure: The Valcartier Rehearsals

While the military bureaucracy was being hastily assembled in early August 1914, grafting new and sometimes contradictory directives onto old procedures, volunteers lined up at militia armouries or other recruiting stations throughout the country. Most had never served in the militia; two-thirds were British-born. Many felt disillusioned about Canada's future in the economic depression, which seemed like it might only get worse. A paid-fare trip back home in a short, decisive war seemed promising.

The militia commanders were familiar with recruiting routines, a task undertaken many times before.[16] Specifications were checked, medical inspections completed, and lists drawn up, often within a day. The difference now, of course, was the deluge of volunteers they faced.

After the huge demonstrations that greeted the coming war, the press scrambled to cover scenes of jammed armouries, with 'scores of able-bodied' men, as the Guelph *Mercury* put it, signing up. Official procedures tended to structure application processes, in part, by blocking them from the public. Civilians in Lethbridge and Guelph faced events at the local armouries as a closed affair, part of military business. Onlookers were on hand, but most would read about it in the next day's papers. In the generic discourse of masculinity and patriotism, so much a part of ordinary press reports at this time, news stories advertised the fiction that every 'man jack of those who crowded into the armories was full of fight and anxious to get a chance to give battle to the enemy'; yet only a select few would be picked, 'men of brawn and muscle, capable of standing hardship and long marches.'[17] These images, of gallant, eager, muscled men facing harsh battles of movement, give us some measure of the style and metaphorical frames through which local perceptions took shape, apart from readers' individual sensibilities.

Such stereotypes helped to prop up what Ilana R. Bet-El called the myth of the Great War volunteer, the soldier as 'a man who enlisted in a spirit of intense patriotism: a brave knight who took himself off on a crusade of chivalry and sacrifice.'[18] As a mythopoeic masculinity, an appeal of immediate utility, this image certainly shaped much of the associated discourse generated by city presses across English Canada. In Lethbridge, the call to the colours was said to kindle the patriotic fires 'in many a breast' in early reports that tended to downplay the mundane realities of the recruiting station – the queues, questionnaires, and automatic commands, so much a part of army life.[19] Despite attention given to glorifying events, occasional passages point to more monotonous routines. While masculine-imperial images of 'Old Countrymen,' filled with love for the motherland and fight for the Kaiser, became an instant genre embedded in codes both hackneyed and current, one Guelph man, a husband and father, admitted simply that he could not keep his family on three days' work a week. They would, he was to have said, 'be much better off if he were at the front,' a murmur that the desperation of 'hungerscription' began with the war itself.[20]

At the beginning of the war, crowds of curious onlookers appeared from across the social spectrum. Most public stagings were re-presented, in itemized detail, on the front pages of city dailies, offering some onlookers and readers doubled layers of signification: first they saw an event, then they read about it. They also introduced cleavages embedded in the insurmountable gaps between the experience of soldiers and the experience of the communities that produced them. Recruiting and dispatching fresh troops from cities like Guelph and Lethbridge, as inscribed through their public spaces, offered vicarious and refracted sensations of war, both for the crowds assembled and for the men who at first had little idea of what actually lay ahead. Local circumstance intersected crucially with the horizons of masculinity, imperial-nationalism, and social memory active in the social body and meta-narratives of the country as a whole.

In Guelph, a parade and concert were held before a final send-off rally dispatched the county's first contribution to the CEF's first contingent. On the evening of 14 August, Wyndham and Woolwich streets, between the city's armoury and its exhibition park, became lined with spectators. The procession began at the official recruiting site, the armoury itself, led by two standard-bearers representing both army and navy constituents of the local veterans association. The Guelph Musical Society band came next. Like other city bands, the GMS band had helped bring a local presence to many public events as part of the civic boosterism so important in urban life at this time. Veterans of the Boer War followed, then the enlistees. At the rear were decorated automobiles carrying militia officers, city council members, and the mayor. At the exhibition park an audience, which had paid a small admission in aid of soldiers' families, was entertained by musical selections from 'Rule Britannia' to 'O Canada.' Mayor Carter's speech, true to form, referred to the war as 'a straight fight for civilization, and Germany was in the wrong.' In closing, trumpeter W. Aspen stepped forward and played, among several standards, 'The Roll Call' and 'The Cavalrymen's Last Post.'[21]

Though from the names mentioned in press reports it appears many middle-class women actually took the lead in organizing send-off rallies in Guelph and in Lethbridge, the marching, band concerts, speeches, and prayers that both solemnized and celebrated what was taking place showed militarism and masculinity conjoined in displays of military power: a manful assertion of garb, gesture, and gait. Musical selections were drawn from a repertoire recited in varied forms in towns and cities throughout English Canada. Such events, as this Guelph example shows, tended to communicate through sentiments structured by tradition; its meanings were no doubt appropriated in diverse ways, but its staging was far from accidental.

As performances, send-off rallies also seemed to alternate between two directions: from staged spectacle to audiences and back again. Reciprocal elements were suggested as crowds, in many instances, were described as 'spirited' or displaying an enthusiasm 'aroused' by their experiences, as the one was in Guelph's exhibition park. There, entertained by a patriotic concert, by renditions of songs from 'Old England' and Canada's national anthem, their experience of the whole performance seemed far from passive.[22] These participatory elements, as oscillations between performance and applause or between speeches and responsive singing while the band played on, also suggest how these events displayed popular social memories, the past as heritage rather than as actual history. A unified line of descent from British stock to Canadian people was a favoured theme across both lyrical verse and formal orations, and the most common purpose seems to have been to promote wartime unity by signifying a sense of imperial-nationalism as a unified genealogy, a tradition of imperial achievement, however nostalgic and invented it was in fact. The march past itself followed the customary rites then established for urban parades, with a salient military presence.[23] The order of procession, with a square of Boer War veterans succeeded by two larger companies of mostly green recruits, conveyed a sense of continuity with the past, a rejuvenated rather than fading line of succession.

In a sense, send-off crowds served as a ready market, appropriating what was supplied yet helping to shape the images as well. Symbolic references to this appeared ubiquitously in the metonyms and keywords used to transform popular, imagined views of war into a forceful cultural commodity. They certainly served, in parades, rallies, or send-offs, as the coded currencies by which recruits might be purchased and presented. The impending catastrophe increased the value of a discourse that valorized the noble volunteer, but in so doing it distanced home front perceptions from overseas realities. That family and friendship ties tended to personalize the departure of an entire military unit while the recruits filed by in the panoply of a march past, or waved good-bye at the frenetic scenes of railway platforms, indicates the inescapable layers of localized, immediate, and parochial circumstances through which perceptions were also derived. Their intersections with popular myth in countless moments of final departure served to activate the commonplace, infused with mixed emotions.

Guelph's first railway platform pull-out began with a departing march past from the armoury on the morning of 19 August. Wyndham Street in the downtown core was said to have been lined with thousands of spectators, eager to catch sight of the city's first volunteers. Led by the GMS band, recruits selected through the 30th Wellington Rifles joined members of the Army Service Corps to form a line of eighty men. To the beat of martial music, they marched through the rain to the Canadian Pacific station and onto its crowded platform, depicted as a 'sea of umbrellas.' They broke ranks to strains of 'Auld Lang Syne' and 'The Girl I Left Behind Me' and began boarding. A series of farewell scenes with family and friends in tears were described, set amid the intense activity and ambiance of the CPR platform.[24]

Corresponding scenes appeared in the *Mercury* the following week as recruits selected through Guelph's 11th Artillery Battery left the city in an organized send-off, with Mayor Carter and members of city council also on hand. 'There must have been several thousand citizens packed and jammed in every available corner,' according to one report. The 'boys' were 'cheered repeatedly' as they swung from Wyndham to Carden Street, this time toward the Grand Trunk station. It seemed difficult to dissuade the crowd from disrupting the 10:00 a.m. boarding. A halt had been ordered en route to give families and friends a last chance to say good-bye, a common scene at any march past to the station. Ritualized as an embrace, a handshake, and a few conventional phrases of encouragement, these gestures served to encapsulate what was most feared – a final parting. Perhaps for this reason, the interruption failed to satisfy everyone's need to stay as close as possible to the troops before, or even as, they pulled out, to maintain a final contact. 'There was no holding back the crowd,' as the reporter put it, 'which swarmed up on to the tracks and crowded right up to the coaches on which the boys entrained.'[25]

Many at the station would have attended a huge public ceremony for the volunteers held the week before. There, recruits from Guelph and surrounding areas, including Harriston, Elora, Fergus, Drayton, and Mount Forest, displayed new uniforms in their first parade as an artillery unit. During their march from the armoury to the exhibition grounds they adopted the standard order of procession: the GMS band, remustered from the send-off for the 30th Wellington recruits that morning, led a formation of Boer War veterans followed by the new recruits. A 'round of cheers' greeted the marchers as they filed by on Wyndham Street. One reporter, sensing that the 'citizens who lined the streets seemed to realize for the first time that the boys were really going to war,' recorded his impressions after witnessing a ceremony that included an important and, for Guelph, novel element – organized prayer.

When the procession arrived at the exhibition ground, the troops broke off to form a square in front of the bandstand. To one side sat the surpliced choirs of St. James and St. George's churches, both Anglican. 'Thousands' present were said to have 'joined in the singing' of hymns. The Rev. C.H. Buckland of St. George's and Archdeacon Davidson of St. James conducted a joint service. In reference to perils of the battlefield, soon to become a constant horror for those left behind, Buckland's sermon called for the 'safe return' of the troops, who then stood between him and an audience which was modelled, through its attendance and participation, as a congregation of Christians rather than a 'patriotic' crowd of imperial-nationalists. The danger faced, however dimly its scale was foreseen, was communicated through a religious ritualization, from hymn singing to the sermon itself. Moreover, Buckland's oration moved from the secular formalism we might associate with a public official to the sacred tropes of a cleric. 'All of you,' he said, 'will fight under one great banner – the banner of victory – the flag that represents liberty to all mankind.' That standard, as he put it, 'was the banner of Jesus Christ.' Mayor Carter then took the stage and called for three cheers for the recruits, which were 'heartily given.'[26]

Despite its salient religiosity, placed in the context of the send-off for the 30th Wellington recruits that morning or the prepared rally staged on August 14, this event bore some functional resemblance to the others. There was nothing new in the fact that the street audience cheered, as others had done, at the sight of the troops, *their* troops as it were, marching by. The exhibition ground audience may have felt a closer connection to the real danger of war when many sang, listened, or saw the young men in standing formation, but this is only suggested in the prayers and Buckland's sermon. Carter's call for three cheers seemed an attempt to revive the tone of celebration witnessed on the streets, to clear the air of certain tensions, apparently fostered in the ceremony. The obvious signs of ritualized militarism as a kind of martial masculinity, characteristic of the militia parade genre, also seemed to turn during the service, instead cultivating a mood hinging on the promise of death. Hints of this had surfaced the week before when trumpeter Aspen played the sombre notes of 'The Cavalrymen's Last Post.' Even Mayor Carter noted then that not every volunteer would return: 'they'll need our sympathy and prayers.'[27] But here, the tension between sympathy for the soldiers and dread for their worst fate was rendered more tangible through the church-led ceremony, which for a very large stadium audience that could hardly have been entirely Anglican was conducive to moments of Turnerian *communitas*, when public gatherings experience a strong sense of transcendence from the social barriers that divide them in other contexts.[28]

As a usual climax, those closest to the troops gathered to catch a final glimpse of the men, in street clothes or in uniform as complete units, making their way to the last place that many set foot upon at home, the train platform. The *Mercury* in Guelph delivered, for instance, a scene of 'gray haired mothers, sad-faced wives, proud sisters, and heart-broken sweethearts' left standing on the railway station platform, a gendered and maudlin depiction to be sure. But what we can draw from such an account, which also reads, 'there were tears in many an eye, and many a prayer was whispered for the brave sons of Canada,' is a sense of the emotional intensity of that time and place.[29] Whereas perceptions of the war overseas remained, on hometown horizons, a heavily edited set of images and nothing more, local send-offs took shape as experiences both lived and imagined. Sentiments at hometown send-offs, from fear to pride, took shape through the directness of human senses. They were also shaped by the local and very unique spaces on which they were produced, from the confusion of crowded wooden planks and steam engines hissing on the Grand Trunk platform, to the meditative silence of a clergyman's call for prayer.

Unit officers marched new recruits along city streets throughout the first year of the war. During pre-announced march pasts, crowds of curious onlookers ordinarily appeared to cheer or even sing in unison, many focusing on the familiar faces of loved ones or friends just signed on. Once the regiments had pulled out of their respective local depots for further training, soldiers started to write letters home that served as key links between fighting front and home front, sometimes maintaining (despite censorship measures) descriptive links between the two, at least before the soldiers themselves witnessed firsthand whatever awaited them overseas.

A mixture of earnest hope, fateful preparation, and boyish innocence ran through many. 'Dear Mother,' Pte. Cliff Allan, part of the Second Contingent's volunteers from Guelph, wrote from the Royal School of Artillery in Kingston in the summer of 1915. 'We are leaving on Monday next – and sail I think on Thursday. I'll not get home again before sailing.' He then, as all new recruits were required to do, shifted attention to his few assets: 'I've written the [militia] department – asking them to send $35 per month to father, and deposit the remainder to my account in the Quebec Bank at Ottawa.' He added that his 'insurance policies are all with Ainslie Greene 5-8 Primrose Ave. of Ottawa also my will which [a notary] made out for me. I left a trunk at 261 Laurier West – containing some photos jewelry etc. There were also a number of books. I think that's about all.' The rest shifts back to details of an unfolding adventure, picked up in later letters, of his journey overseas – to England, exciting London, training in Kent, a glimpse at the French coast. He could hardly wait. At this point, though, the parades and rallies in Guelph had brought him little farther than a stay with family friends near his unit's current base. From there, near the shores of eastern Lake Ontario, he imagined finally getting to the 'big show' in France:

> I am writing from the Smythes in Kingston. Two of the 38th officers are here. They are leaving tomorrow. We expect to go on the same boat but we were switched to a week later. I think the rest of the troops on our ship are from London so that probably some of the Guelph Battalion will be on loan. We will be in England some weeks before we get over to the big show. We are doing great work in camp just now. Tomorrow a route march to Gananoque is on the boards ... The other two officers in our draft are awfully fine chaps and we are taking a good bunch of men. Remember me to all the Guelphites.[30]

Early send-offs served, in part, to feed such optimism. The first public ceremonies to honour new recruits in Guelph and Lethbridge were organized by citizens closely connected to imperial-national organizations: members of the Alexander Galt IODE and the Sons of England in Lethbridge, or the Ladies Garrison Club and the Army and Navy Veterans Association in Guelph took active parts. They staged several send-offs and remained active in groups like the Canadian Patriotic Fund to aid families with breadwinners overseas. A group calling itself the 'Overseas Club,' launched just days before in Lethbridge, took charge of the city's first send-off rally. Its acting-secretary, Charles Westley, was past-president of Alberta's Sons of England, while another organizer, A.J. Blackburne, would soon be helping to revitalize Lethbridge's Red Cross chapter.[31] In both cities, the local recruiting and war relief organizers solicited the participation of civic bands, mayors and city councils, and local clerics, along with assorted recitalists, clergy, civic officials, and other speakers. Blackburne, for instance, had organized a decoration committee in preparation for the 'big send-off' set for 18 August, while others were asked to prepare clothing parcels, later distributed just before volunteers departed. Their efforts, carefully staged, celebrated the power and purpose of Canada's armed response at this time, but always with a local signature. The salient and interconnected themes of imperial-nationalism, militarism, and masculinity, symbolized by decorated automobiles, uniformed men on parade, podiums adorned with Union Jacks and bunting, musical selections featuring 'patriotic airs,' and speech after speech that justified the war, were expressed in hastily but deliberated planned and orchestrated affairs.

As such, these displays served to define recent events. Imperial-nationalist sentiment had been promoted by many voluntary associations and ethnic groups during the nineteenth and early twentieth centuries in local communities across English Canada. Lethbridge, a young city in 1914, was still in the process of laying down its institutional roots. The Alexander Galt chapter of the IODE, established in February that year, would grow to 250 members during the war and be joined in 1917 by the Jack Ross chapter, named to commemorate a local officer killed in action.[32] While members of benefit societies like the Sons of England pledged to uphold the 'character and traditions of England,' or ethnic affiliations like the Lethbridge Kentish Association, which helped find jobs for English newcomers, expressed particular loyalties for groups of men, women's voluntary associations like the Mathesis Club joined the IODE and local Red Cross chapters to espouse broader 'patriotic' aims by providing support for winning the war.

But what many imagined that great victory to be seemed as varied as the vernacular elements that combined to speak or perform for it. As their various constitutions and activities indicate, these groups embraced a variety of purposes and sentiments, from the militia units themselves to the many local associations that endorsed their recruiting efforts. The 25th Battery, Canadian Field Artillery, had been active in Lethbridge since 1908, and its yearly training camps, drills, and parades instilled or reinforced a military ethos.[33] The same was true for the 30th Wellington Rifles, stationed in Guelph, with a militia history dating back to European settlement in Upper Canada. Added to this, the proliferation of voluntary associations of gendered, class, or ethnic compositions, found in everything from the fraternal orders to religious groups, also served as pre-existing networks that channelled countless efforts toward the fighting overseas.

Voluntary associations could be divided according to their aims and interests. From the beginning, however, it was important to construct rituals, from parades to speeches and sermons, to signify the ideal of national unity. Notwithstanding the problem posed by enemy alien minorities or pacifists or others either neutral or even opposed to the war, support for Canada's participation was far from uniform across the country, and recruitment patterns in Quebec were proving it. Typically, however, when mayors, public officials, or other local elites addressed large audiences, they emphasized common goals, usually in terms of fighting for a moral ideal, rather than, for instance, saying how the war should be fought, or by whom. While the IODE, the militia, veterans, or smaller groups from church choirs to school assemblies represented specific claims on the meaning of war, speeches by civic officials like mayors Samuel Carter in Guelph or William Hardie in Lethbridge served to channel interpretations of a British or, as some more narrowly saw it, an English war into something transcendent and abstract: a 'just cause,' a 'fight for civilization,' or some variant of 'liberty over autocracy.' What were often called 'patriotic' speeches usually contained little more than secondary references to England or Canada. Their appeals helped to mediate vernacular interests, many devoutly patriotic. A Kentish immigrant in Lethbridge, for instance, might know what it felt like to be at war, but the more 'official' discourses from city hall typically emphasized what the war should mean for the broader audiences they targeted. In general, civic performances tended to express something that John Bodnar has described as a conceptual meeting ground for the most effective forms of public expression – those that tend to meld vernacular feelings (that were rooted in the aspirations of specific groups) with official messages (that reflected the policies of the nation as a whole).[34] The results, of course, tend to appear as a kind of dogmatic formalism, statements that usually divide audiences the least by highlighting little that might distinguish one potentially dissenting group from another.

Francophone audiences in Quebec, however, could not subscribe to the same formal references to Canada within the Empire that might draw cheers in places like Guelph and Lethbridge. In Trois-Rivières at this point, former commander Lt.-Col. Louis-Phillipe Mercier was saddled with the vexing task of reminding Ottawa that he simply had no troops to send after he, too, through some oversight, was delivered one of the 226 night lettergrams requesting enlistment rolls.[35] Few, if anyone, had volunteered from there in August. The city's sole anglophone newspaper had heard of no one who had joined as yet, a conspicuous absence given that nearly two hundred potential recruits had recently undergone training at the now disbanded 86th.[36]

At the same time, the English Canadian press closely monitored news of preparations at Valcartier, as senior militia officers coped with the systemic problem of delays in communication from the militia department. Not only was recruitment a dominant preoccupation in places like Guelph and Lethbridge, but local organizers were eager to represent the process symbolically through an ensemble of cultural forms, from parades and patriotic concerts to send-off rallies.

It was, in part, a sense of mission that underlay many such displays, but a mission that brought together many elements of imperial-national identity. These displays rehearsed over and over again what the war should mean as young men marched toward it. Send-offs, in all their forms, were far larger and enthusiastic during the Valcartier phase, when so little of the actualities of war could be known, than during the militia regiment and community regiment phases that followed. As soon as Lt.-Col. J.J. Craig in Guelph and Maj. J.S. Stewart in Lethbridge received word to move their men to Valcartier, plans got underway to arrange the first and most spectacular public send-off in both cities described above.[37] City newspapers covered them in great detail, emphasizing the attachment between hometowns and their troops.

These events had multiple functions, from their potential to sanitize state authority in expressions of glorified tradition to simply reminding other men considering enlistment of what might lie ahead of them. But fundamental to most was their capacity to signify the great threshold that was being crossed. A very obvious structure was both imposed and solemnized publicly: it took men, mostly youths, out of their past lives and bureaucratically conveyed new and distinct identities upon them as enlistees. Finally, and most importantly for our purposes, came the public events themselves, which displayed these first handfuls of recruits from each armoury or other sign-up facility as the men selected first. The August crowds that turned out were not only larger than they would ever be again, but were also described in qualitative terms difficult to sustain in the latter phases as their naïve enthusiasm and hopefulness gave way to a very different climate of perception brought on by subsequent casualties and the stalemate in the trenches.

The first big send-off in Lethbridge, at first glance, seems a curious contrast to Guelph's. A religious aspect is not absent, but appeals to imperial-nationalism, combined with a display of masculine esprit de corps, seemed more amplified. Its function as a liminal ritualization – a three-step process of formal recruitment procedures, public display, and final departure – seems equally apt. Though the speeches and a presentation of recruits were actually held in two churches – Wesley Methodist, built the year before, and St. Augustine's Anglican – they were not overtly religious observances. Wesley's preacher, the Rev. G.H. Cobbledick, did deliver one of several addresses, but he spoke just briefly, defining the war as one of basic principles: 'Liberty and Democracy pitted against despotism and autocracy.' His words, though not his presence, suggested nothing beyond a secular message. Cobbledick also spoke last, after Mayor Hardie, long-time Lethbridge resident and lawyer Charles Conybeare, and, most noticeably, regimental commander Maj. J.S. Stewart had each addressed the gathering.

The entire program, organized by the Overseas Club, began at 8:00 p.m. and lasted until the troops finally boarded the train at 1:00 a.m. Two bands,

Lethbridge's thirty-piece Citizen's Band and the Kilty Band, led the troops to Wesley's auditorium, where the first reception took place. From there they marched to St. Augustine's hall, where the Alexander Galt IODE had prepared a special dinner and where its rector, Canon Murrel-Wright, spoke of the Cross and the flag as conjoined in true patriotism. While the Overseas Club presented what became a long evening of events in a 'program that went off without a hitch,' it was the recruits and their commander who stole the show. The scene in the Wesley church, which held a smaller, more select audience than the huge crowd in Guelph, offered a departure toward the androcentric culture of the military unit, rather than to anything explicitly religious.

Major Stewart presented his 'battery boys' in an overt display of masculine camaraderie. His attention, deliberately focused on the regiment, gave family and friends on hand a chance to view the men in terms of an ideal manhood. As Stewart rose to speak on behalf of the regiment, he was said to have been applauded 'vociferously' by the audience and given 'three lusty cheers' by the men seated on the platform beside him. He depicted their devotion to duty as part of their manfulness. Stewart spoke 'mostly of the boys, their loyalty, their willingness to sacrifice, and the zeal for the Motherland.'[38]

His own experience, and what can be documented concerning the field battery he led, serves as a useful backdrop, not only for his choice of words but also for the frequent blurring of genres, of manful association and military rites, evident that evening. A comparatively long-serving militia commander, Stewart, a Lethbridge dentist by profession, had led the 25th Battery since its inception in 1908 and had served in the Boer War as a trooper in Strathcona's Horse. Like other units across Canada, the 25th had undergone training at summer camps authorized by the Department of Militia and Defence. These were often events of gregarious display and bravado that would have little tactical significance overseas, but may best explain how these men experienced their final send-off.

During their last camp, held the month before at the Sarcee training grounds, they got their first taste of live shell practice and, according to one member, nearly blew themselves up with a missing round.[39] Despite such mishaps, these camps were part of a voluntary militia movement that had undergone significant reforms under Sam Hughes's direction. Funding had been increased in recent years, and a series of baronial, red-brick armouries were built in cities across Canada. To redirect masculine behaviour, in fact to patrol it through the discipline of a militia directive, Hughes also introduced strict prohibition for the camps, which had hosted their fair share of drinkers in the past. Moreover, equipment, training exercises, and inspections were taken more seriously each year. By 1914, some 55,000 volunteers had taken part in militia summer training, up from less than half that number a decade before.[40] In recent years, the 25th Battery had welded itself into a close group. As one member recalled, the 1914 camp had 'boosted the esprit de corps of the unit to a marked degree.' But the exercises were still more a sport than a serious business. They had just competed and won the Czowski Cup, awarded for a second-place showing against groups across Canada in battery manoeuvres. These kinds of experiences, of 'playing' together in imaginary wartime exercises, which more 'modern' approaches to military training had scarcely begun to stifle at this point, also underscore the appeal to manhood with which the war began.

The evening of their departure at summer's end that year became, partly because of the 25th's recent past, a celebration of manful loyalty and pride, coupled with a sense of mission that leaving for the front together helped to dramatize. In the Wesley auditorium, Stewart introduced each recruit individually, pausing to salute him with a few words on his conduct and character. For him, as he put it, it was their manhood that counted, which in this case was cast in terms of unity, strength, and a just cause. He drew cheers when he stated that they would be fighting 'shoulder to shoulder with a combination the world could not beat.' After the dinner the recruits marched to the CPR platform where the

> band played several musical selections and escorted the party to the station, where the largest crowd ever assembled out-of-doors in Lethbridge waited to say the good-byes and God-speeds. Members of the battery were carried aloft of the shoulders of their comrades, and cheer after cheer followed them down the platform. The reservists were also the property of their friends and relatives during the last few moments. When the train pulled in the special coach was ready, and the crowd prepared for the final wrench that would take their heroes away. Three cheers and the singing of 'God Save the King,' led by the city band, accompanied the music of the moving wheels, and the Lethbridge contingent of the Overseas forces had a last look at their home town that will remain with them throughout their campaign, no matter where it may take them.[41]

The affair was hailed in the next day's *Herald* as the most 'momentous occasion' in Lethbridge's history.

Though reports like these were mediated through the lens of popular journalism, which produced texts that sanitized and glorified local events, fairly detailed and comparable descriptions of send-offs accumulated in city newspapers across Canada. They depict two parallel currents of popular culture. An imagined 'community of August,' to combine approaches to nationalism and war found first in Eric Leed and now more famously in Benedict Anderson, was being rapidly manufactured. August 1914 celebrated promised escape from the countless burdens of the present, whether these were

5 This railway station pull-out of members of the 20th Battery, Canadian Field Artillery, at the Lethbridge CPR station signified the distance established between enlisted men and families, friends, and other well-wishers crowded at the wooden platform. This particular unit was awaiting transport to Camp Shilo in Manitoba, June 1915. Such scenes, of more disciplined armed formations during the railway station 'good-byes and God-speeds' moments were typical of the 'militia regiment' phase and marked a contrast with the August 1914 farewell for the 25th Battery, with its exuberant hoisting of station-bound soldiers on comrades' shoulders and the looser intermingling of civilians and recruits. *Courtesy of Sir Alexander Galt Museum and Archives, P19981035042*

unemployment or the entrapments of bourgeois respectability.[42] The send-offs to war, in this period of innocent enthusiasm, combined a fear of death with a celebration of life away from the mundane and stifling travails of home. It was a set of localized experiences felt and expressed across Western societies entering the war. In addition, the displays of masculinity, imperial-nationalism, and social memory in early recruiting did not mean that the unofficial propaganda of the press, public events connected to send-offs, or even institutional support for the war were collectively imposed on populations. Rather, they arose from local circumstances and were organized by pre-existing groups and interests. Usable settings and localized experiences, from those of voluntary civilian associations to militia units, became vehicles mobilized on a wide array of sites, isolated here in the send-off ritual, to communicate how people saw and understood what was taking place. Their own interpretation of events took shape at the intersections between the immediacy of staged scenes, like Major Stewart and 'his boys,' and the imagined horizons of Canada and the Empire at war.

The description of Lethbridge's first send-off rally and the journalists' customary penchant for inflation, so pronounced at this time, provide an opaque window through which people came to understand what was taking place, one in which patriotic language, imperial-national symbols, and gendered forms of militarism shaped meanings. Its participants sought to use these sites for their own ends, to derive a subjective sense of the war beyond the hometown horizon that suited their purposes. By looking at their operations as communicative vehicles, we can move beyond the obvious similarities of form found in other locales, in the order of parade processions, or the mix of public officials, clerics, and proponents of imperial-nationalism, to consider intersections between specific, localized acts of ritualization, of cheering, orations, and gestures, and more general conditions. It is also possible to consider how this was used in much smaller recruitment patterns and send-off rituals, like those in Trois-Rivières.

Farewells in Trois-Rivières

From the beginning of enlistment processes in Trois-Rivières, a noticeable divide between language, history, social memory, and popular culture of English and French Canada was coopted locally for particular purposes by religious and political interests. Recruitment patterns and send-off rituals also signified masculinities there, but local contexts distinguished French from English. Unlike English Canadian towns and cities, there were no rousing rallies or send-offs staged in Trois-Rivières at the very beginning of the war. Sustained enthusiasm for what was really a war of empires remained muted across French Canada, and of course inverted into outright hostility during the conscription crisis. When Mayor Tessier spoke of unity between French and English Canadians at the outbreak of the war, his words seemed to echo street demonstrations in Quebec City, Montreal, and Trois-Rivières itself, but failed to translate into significant enlistment numbers locally. From the beginning, recruitment patterns in Trois-Rivières suggested quite different sentiments in the small anglophone minority and in the city as a whole.

Varied interpretations connected to religious sensibilities sprang from this overwhelmingly francophone Catholic milieu. While recruitment was slow, attention to events remained high for some, who saw the war as either regenerative or apocalyptic and certainly a significant event in history. The view of one veteran of Europe's battles between religion and politics can be discerned in the correspondence of Gédéon Désilets, who had left Trois-Rivières in 1868 as a young man to join a regiment of Papal Zouaves in defending Catholic Rome against Garibaldi.[43] Just days after Germany's march through Belgium, Désilets disclosed his sense of unfolding events in a letter to his son, then a teaching brother at Montreal's Écoles chrétiennes au Mont-Lasalle. According to Désilets, Europe had been swept into a merciless sea of self-destruction because its citizens and their governments had lost contact with God. This dreadful war, which he claimed to have long anticipated, was a scourge promoted by the atheism of governments and the corruption of man's moral spirit. As he put it, 'c'est le fléau animé par l'athéisme des gouvernements et la dépravation des moeurs chers.' Désilets also conveyed a lingering loyalty to France, but particularly to Catholic France in his concluding thoughts on the war. 'Pour moi,' he wrote, 'Lourdes et Montmartre garantissent le succès final de la France ... et je fais des voeux pour le triomphe de la France catholique.'[44]

The editor of the *Bien Public*, Joseph Barnard, cast the beginning of war as an irruption, signifying the impoverishment of religiosity and sacred concern. So did the Bishop of Trois-Rivières, Mgr François-Xavier Cloutier, who interpreted its coming as a sign that modern society had gone astray in pursuit of secular goals, from commercial and industrial exploitation to technological advance.[45] Perhaps the best literary sample of local sentiment is found in the work of Nérée Beauchemin, the gifted and celebrated poet of Nicolet, located directly across from Trois-Rivières on the St. Lawrence. Beauchemin was best known for *Patrie intime*, a collection that explores his response to Quebec's European heritage. Shortly after the invasion of Belgium he wrote: 'Amende honorable à la France, / A la mère des bons Français, / Qui triomphe plus que jamais, / Des mille morts de la souffrance. / Le sang chrétien n'est point tari.'[46] Like imperial-nationalists in English Canada who, in comparable terms, used images of the English motherland to connect people to a cause, Beauchemin's sense of connection to a war involving France seemed a curious voice from a former colony. But such appeals meant far less to most French Catholics in Quebec. Others in Quebec spoke of the outbreak in terms of the necessary partnership between English and French in a just war, not an imperialist one. Of course, this appeal, too, would soon hold little sway and collapsed with conscription. Evidence specifically from Trois-Rivières expressed palpable tensions between French and English Canada leading up to the fragile entente of August 1914.

These signs had surfaced most recently in the editorial columns of Trois-Rivières's newspapers that commented on Regulation 17 in Ontario, a measure restricting French-language instruction in that province; on the flying of the Union Jack at city hall, for which Mayor Tessier was criticized; on Ottawa's decision to disband the 86th Three Rivers Regiment; and, most recently, on Militia Regulation No. 156, the reviled new restriction that forbade the display of religious icons alongside armed militia assemblies. The city's English minority seemed aware of the tensions these events contributed to. Recently, for instance, the *Newcomer* had commented on the embarrassing fact that during the last Victoria Day holiday, several 'people in this town' had the temerity to fly 'the Canadian Flag upside down.'[47]

As a prominent Liberal, Mayor Tessier had commanded the 86th before handing its command over to Mercier, another staunch *rouge* supporter. Disbanding the 86th because of its alleged connection to the Liberal Party no doubt hurt recruitment, particularly at the beginning of the war, but when this was followed by the notorious decision to impose Regulation No. 156, francophone Catholics throughout Quebec were incensed. Led by Archbishop Bruchesi in Montreal, French Canadian clerics issued strong protests. They were joined by papers like the *Bien Public*, outraged by a move seen plainly as undue interference. Clerics and press expressed anger at Hughes's motives and cast the minister as an ultra-Protestant anglophone – a fanatic in this respect. The *Bien Public* ran a series of commentaries in June and July, just before the war's outbreak, that added fuel to a province-wide editorial outcry. Hughes's well-known association with Canada's Orange Order was attacked, as was his department's aberrant deviation from what the paper saw as the more 'prudent' policy of avoiding laws or regulations offensive to Catholics and to francophones in Quebec.[48] Regulation No. 156, and Hughes's unswerving support for it, was an affront. News of Captain Bourassa's defiant transgression, forming an armed guard before a summer training camp altar (described in Chapter 1) appeared in the *Nouveau Trois-Rivières* under the caption, 'L'insulte se continue – Encore le fanatisme de Sam Hughes.'[49]

While official suppression of Catholic symbols in the militia was no doubt an irksome factor, the absence of distinctly French Canadian militia units did far more to delay recruiting across francophone Quebec generally. The initially dismal levels from Trois-Rivières could certainly be attributed to this, and it was a problem Hughes himself raised on behalf of francophones seeking French Canadian regiments. Just before he left for England as the Valcartier phase ended, Hughes informed Prime Minister Borden that, in addition to returning to the militia regiment scheme for all further recruiting, provisions would be made to raise a French Canadian brigade. 'Our French Canadian country fellowmen would, under this plan,' Hughes wrote, 'have the opportunity of furnishing a brigade of four regiments.'[50] But until these newly designated francophone-led and -supported units could begin their enlistment campaigns, the appeal of English Canadian battalions and regiments in Trois-Rivières and throughout Quebec remained limited.

As part of Quebec's militia regiment phase, the creation of the 22nd Battalion, authorized in December 1914, began to draw Quebec francophones from mainly urban parts of the province.[51] Its first commander, Col. Frédéric-

Mondelet Gaudet, a Trifluvien officer serving in the permanent force, quickly established a recruiting program coordinated from the former barracks of Montreal's 65th Regiment located on the avenue des Pins.[52] Recruitment still remained comparatively weak in Trois-Rivières. Although the city's anglophone newspaper, the *Newcomer*, claimed optimistically that Trois-Rivières was 'beginning to awake to a sense of the importance of the Great War,' only ten men were reported to have 'volunteered for the French Canadian Contingent forming in Montreal' shortly after recruiting for the 22nd began.[53] According to an extensive socio-statistical study of the 22nd Battalion's history, by the end of the war these numbers increased to a total of fifty-six from Trois-Rivières in its ranks, though conscripts from the city are not identified.[54] While these numbers are small relative to English Canada, the formation of this unit marked an important step toward creating francophone units in the CEF. The 'Vandoos,' as they came to be known famously, would do more than any other battalion in Quebec to instill a tradition of French Canadian participation in both world wars.

But the 22nd recruited from across the province, and its traditions grew as a French Canadian battalion for the province and country as a whole. No military unit was established to recruit locally in Trois-Rivières at any point during the war. In October 1915, some anglophones sought a revival of the 86th, but the Department of Militia and Defence, perhaps preoccupied with so much else, did not act. In contrast to both Guelph and Lethbridge, no militia nor community regiment process applied in Trois-Rivières, a conspicuous absence for a city this size, even in Quebec. Sporadically, anglophone youths left for English Canadian regiments or, in the wake of several recruitment drives, francophones enlisted singly or in small groups in some other unit.

Networks connected to the places young men interacted socially, from universities to work sites, were important to recruitment patterns across Canada, and this seems true for the small numbers of men who did sign on in Trois-Rivières. With respect to the anglophone minority in Trois-Rivières, large employers in the city, such as the Wayagamack Pulp and Paper Company, the Wabasso Cotton Company, and the Canadian Iron Corporation, supplied from their clerical and managerial ranks many of the city's English Canadian volunteers. Lance-Cpl. John B. Adams, manager of Wayagamack's Rat River logging district, was one of the handful of recruits who joined the first contingent.[55] Killed in action the following spring, 'Jack' was commemorated in the *Newcomer* as one of several 'well known and highly respected young men' who 'gave up a lucrative position' at Wayagamack to join Montreal's 5th Royal Highlanders.[56] Another employee, R.A. Gillis, later enlisted in the McGill University Officer Training Corps, as did Peter Clark, son of the Rev. J. Aitken Clark of St. Andrew's Presbyterian.

Gillis was given two farewells: first in late June 1915 by the Three Rivers Rifle Association, which presented him, as the first of its number to join the active forces, with a silver wristwatch; then, on a Saturday evening the following month, three months after Adams was killed, the Wayagamack office staff held a 'quiet little ceremony' at the Canadian Hotel to honour the step Gillis was taking. One co-worker 'wished Mr. Gillis a safe and speedy return. He also hoped that Mr. Gillis "might get the Germans and that they would not get him."' As an office worker-turned-recruit, Private Gillis was then presented with a purse containing $65, on which was inscribed: 'From your friends and the staff at Wayagamack.'[57]

Wayagamack employees later that autumn also bade farewell to co-worker Richard J. Hamilton who, on the night before he left, was presented with an inscribed silver watch and a sum of money.[58] Earlier that summer, those who knew James Fotheringham through their mutual employment at the Canadian Iron Corporation had given him a farewell supper the evening before he left to join Montreal's 73rd Royal Highlanders. He too received a wristwatch and send-off speech, as the 'evening was spent in songs and social intercourse.' One report added that Fotheringham's employers 'have done well as regards [sic] volunteers.'[59] Hamilton was later joined at the 73rd by V. Elsden of the Wabasso Cotton Company.[60] Both men had roomed at the same boarding house, known as 'The Hutch,' and several reports place them on leave, returning to visit old friends there.[61] Occupational status, place of residence, and other individual circumstances combined with ethnicity to produce the scant patterns of recruitment that can be found for Trois-Rivières.

In place of the large and vocal public send-offs of Lethbridge and Guelph, some employers and work peers in Trois-Rivières held these more intimate, closed affairs to honour the decisions employees or friends had made to serve their country. The basic purposes served by these small group send-offs, however, were the same. The 'quiet little ceremony' for Gillis, for example, became a special dinner gathering of supportive supervisors and co-workers and a hopeful recruit. It served as a practical way to deal with local circumstance. The farewell suppers, send-off speeches, presentations of inscribed watches and money, songs, and 'social intercourse' not only served to model valued relationships; they also signified recognition of enlistment as an honourable act of service made by young men in response to the war. While their form was different, these send-off rituals may have held functions comparable to the public displays in English Canada. But they produced quite different experiences for all gathered, who appeared as English-speaking workers and enlistees separated, if not isolated, from the city's overwhelmingly French inhabitants.

Two months later, when several of Gillis's former office mates learned that he was sailing for England aboard the SS *Missanabie*, slated to moor briefly near Trois-Rivières, arrangements were quickly made for a large number of the Wayagamack staff to greet the vessel aboard the *Eric R*, a company tugboat. When the tug drew alongside and hailed the troopship, the *Missanabie*'s railings were soon lined 'with solders who heartily responded to the cheers from those on board the tug.' Gillis's departure as a soldier aboard ship was observed partly through his connection to his co-workers. 'The tug saluted the liner in the orthodox manner, and the liner responded, as she swung from her moorings and headed downstream with the 'ERIC R' in close attendance.'[62] But as they did when they presented him with a watch and a sum of money, what his apparently boisterous pals configured symbolically in that moment on the St. Lawrence, signified through their cheers, was an effort to bring themselves as close as possible to Gillis the pal and Gillis the soldier in a way that saluted the civilian/soldier distance between tugboat and troopship as an obvious but not complete break from his past. The *Eric R* in 'close attendance,' chasing the troopship off to sea, suggests the scamper alongside for a step or two that children make with soldiers marching to war.

At the same time in Trois-Rivières, French Canadian recruits joined their own regiments, led by the 22nd and, later, the troubled 41st Battalion. The 41st first signed on over seventy men, though this would more than double to take in the bulk of francophone troops from the immediate area. On two occasions the departure of volunteers prompted send-off rallies. These were much smaller than those of English Canada, but their purposes seemed the same. Surviving descriptions of Trois-Rivières's parades, for instance, suggest this: the men assembled publicly, marched, and were in turn accompanied by a band and onlookers that got to see their troops in full parade display before they left. The departure of the 41st Battalion was ritualized with a procession 'throughout the principal streets' of Trois-Rivières, led by the city's Union Musicale band.[63] This particular unit, however, was soon plagued with serious morale problems.[64] Desertions soared after the unit moved from the Citadel at Quebec, where the Trifluvien troops were first stationed, to Valcartier in June 1915.[65] A few, possibly from Trois-Rivières, deserted even sooner. Within a month, according to the *Newcomer*, several had been apprehended in the city.[66] Another was arrested in early July, just before the main wave of desertions that followed the regiment's move to Valcartier.[67]

Nonetheless, French Canadian regiments kept the pressure on recruiting in Quebec in a series of enlistment campaigns. As elsewhere, they appeared as anticipated public displays, strategically staged, very likely with recruiting posters and other advertising forms. Given its location and size, Trois-Rivières certainly got its fair share of these itinerant shows, which typically featured an officer appealing from some stage or podium for more men and for a crucial victory overseas. Near the end of June 1915, for instance, the *Newcomer* reported in a brief note that a 'couple of officers from Québec were in town last week trying to pick up a few recruits.'[68] By summer's end, public rallies for particular regiments and for more French Canadian volunteers became commonplace throughout Quebec, especially in its urban centres. In late August, Mayor Tessier, along with Maj. Firmin Bissonette and several officers from the fledgling 69th Regiment, 'addressed a meeting in the City Hall. The meeting was held with the object of raising funds for the Regimental Funds of the 69th Regiment of Montreal, also to try secure [sic] some recruits.'[69] Trois-Rivières's city hall was a frequent site for recruitment drives and for the Canadian Patriotic Fund campaigns, considered in our next chapter.

These efforts, along with local enlistment drives by other French Canadian units, met with some success. Ten men from Trois-Rivières joined the 69th Regiment in the wake of Bissonette's campaign for funds. But this was overshadowed entirely the following week when a further 182 signed on with the 41st Battalion and another 18 joined the 57th Regiment – a veritable peak in voluntary francophone enlistment on any Trifluvien site. An officer from the 57th, one report noted, also expected 'to leave, as soon as harvesting is finished for the northern part of the province, where he believes a large number of good men may be found.'[70] Tapping rural areas in Quebec often proved difficult, however, sometimes due to seasonal variations in the pool of willing men.

But for the volunteers leaving for Valcartier with the 41st and 57th, 'a good send-off,' as the *Newcomer* put it, was expected. Arrangements for 'bands to play them to the station and a big crowd to cheer as they leave' were underway as soon as the news was made public.[71] Once again the Union Musicale led a parade and station platform send-off. The affair likely attracted a larger and mostly francophone crowd, as compared to the tugboat crew of office workers who hailed Gillis's troopship past the city that same week. This underscores that recruitment and send-offs took place within separate spheres in this city.

Hometown horizons marked by cultural differences reflected deeply divided local responses. The apparent unity between French and English Canadians of August 1914, so often cited by the press and contemporary observers as expressed in public demonstrations elsewhere in Quebec, simply could not be sustained in a city so dominated by francophone culture. Relatively closed and rare English-dominated send-off rituals can be found, but they occur within a sustained pattern of sporadic and less successful recruitment drives in this city throughout the war, certainly when compared to drives in Guelph, Lethbridge, or English Canadian cities generally. From August 1914 on, most francophone volunteers from the city joined francophone-speaking units, and probably all, French or English, signed on with units based in Montreal or Quebec City. In total, recruitment throughout Trois-Rivières probably did not exceed three hundred by the end the war.

Both military authorities and supportive civilians recruited and dispatched troops in ways that reflected and reinforced the separation of French from English. For anglophones in the city, organizers of a home guard unit known as the Three Rivers Rifle Association formed a gun club that provided an early setting for recruitment for a few men. Men like Peter Clark came from families affiliated with one of Trois-Rivières's two Protestant churches, St. Andrews Presbyterian and Wesley Methodist. Middle managers of local manufacturers, in turn, held send-off gatherings that further privatized the city's anglophone minority. Meanwhile, from early 1915 to the end of 1916, recruitment drives for the 22nd Battalion specifically sought French Canadian recruits. Numerous factors, from peer-group processes to established social networks, obviously influenced individual decisions to join. And yet the comparatively low number of Trifluvien French Canadian enlistments, from a population almost uniformly French and Catholic, seems indicative of deeply rooted differences. This indicates that recruitment as a cultural process divided people by their regional and ethnic histories. Horizons of culture and of motivations in this hometown's voluntary recruitment period reflected such barriers.

The Militia Regiment Phase: Guelph and Lethbridge

During the militia regiment period, two artillery batteries, the 20th Field Battery and the 39th, were authorized for recruitment and training in Lethbridge by the Department of Militia and Defence. But until September 1915, when community regiments began to appear alongside units like these, the department still held the upper hand in initiating and naming new units. The 20th began recruiting on 6 October 1914, starting with a nucleus of officers and men left behind by the 25th Battery when that unit left for Valcartier. The 25th's commander, Major Stewart, remained behind, in charge of what was then a redesignated unit. There was 'no doubt,' the *Herald* noted, 'that the majority of the men' would come from the remnants of the 25th Battery, though they would have to 'leave their name behind.'[72] By the end of November 1914, recruiting was completed and training commenced, with barracks construction underway at the Lethbridge exhibition grounds.[73] A month later, Maj. Alvin Ripley, formerly the city's postmaster, took command of the new 140-man unit, and its quarters were built and occupied in early January 1915.[74] Even the *Herald*, which like most papers usually acted as a cheering reporter for all men in training and their units, referred briefly to the new regime of reveille, stable chores, and guard duty as a monotonous routine. No doubt it was. As the paper put it, 'kit inspection' had become 'one of the most exciting events of the day.'[75]

Highlights of the 20th Battery's hometown training included a farewell dance, a mock battle, and a public send-off. The farewell dance, by then a formalized event for many troops-in-training, was held at the city's Masonic

Hall on 23 March 1915. Its twenty-dance program, ending with the 'Home, Sweet Home Waltz,' offered a socially choreographed presentation of the battery. Its ornately printed Program and Invitation listed the hierarchical designation of the unit itself, its officers and non-commissioned officers, sergeants, corporals, and bombardiers. They were distributed, and the men were invited to bring 'a lady.'[76] The regimental dance, a very common event at this time, combined with many other community-based events. The dinners, gift giving, care packages, and later, during the community regiment phase, a special presentation of drums to the Kilty Regiment by the IODE, lent a local signature to passages from home to front. Unlike the brief Valcartier phase with which mobilization began, and which drew the largest crowds, subsequent units often spent months at or near home. At their departure, smaller crowds, usually made up of immediate family and friends, turned out for a final farewell at the rail station. Certainly the frames through which the war was viewed had shifted considerably as often-alarming news from Europe circulated.

Prolonged exchanges through the press, public events, or direct everyday contact typified the histories of these regiments and batteries, which dined and danced as units about to ship out after months of drill close to home. From their inception, esteem for both militia regiments was a journalistic staple. Signs of local pride depended often on exploiting a variety of spaces and settings, from front-page coverage to formalized farewell dances and suppers. The men themselves may have been sequestered for days at a time at restricted barracks and grounds located in their towns and cities, but they remained embedded in the life of their families and of the communities they came from. The fact that most trained nearby and passed through a series of ordinary experiences, undoubtedly reflected in local gossip, gradually eroded the mystique of the whole process. Many signs of this survive in local newspapers at this time. When the men got new barracks and equipment, paraded in drilled unison, or appeared at concerts and finally at farewell suppers and dances, it still made the news, but did so as local notices, not real war news. There were exceptions. Special training exercises that involved mock battles could give rise to more exotic kinds of reports. In some cases the *Herald* still courted public fascination with reports of mounted troops getting out on the prairies for a simulated game of war as great adventure. Using terms like 'military authorities,' 'word from the commander,' 'orders given,' these reports certainly seem designed to attract the attention of the armchair soldier.

Against the lustreless life of the ordinary man in uniform, these reports inserted references to men dedicated to perfecting their war games – stories that seem strangely detached from other news about the boys from home, the sons, brothers, husbands, lovers, and friends everybody knew. On a mundane level the *Herald* spoke often of local 'battery boys,' who had during their recent training in the city become 'part and parcel of Lethbridge life for the past six months.'[77]

In similar terms, the *Mercury* in Guelph began a series of columns called 'With the Troops,' constructed as a running commentary on workaday life at the barracks, which ran for several months beginning in the spring of 1915. A front-page feature, its indulgent highlighting of the local as local featured personal portraits and detailed descriptions of armouries, camps, and quarters, enlivened by the reporter's endless store of gossip. Training in Guelph appeared in serialized parodies: tales of plucky troops in training, their unpretentious chivalry masked by boyish pranks in military guise. A sanitizing instrument of inquiry, its reference to the simple virtues of home, 'our boys,' 'our city,' 'our bit,' combined a local sense of pride with a running tidbit column on camp life. This lighthearted column stood opposite sensationalized coverage of Canada's first major battle, at Ypres, and subsequent front-line reports in the summer and fall of 1915 that did little to hide the adversity and horror overseas that readers craved as well.

The reports of war games staged at facilities and fields nearby, which placed local units on familiar spaces from exhibition ground barracks to the open prairie, authorized an imagined link between civilians and the soldiers they read about. 'Local Battery Engage in Mimic Battle' ran a front-page report in the Lethbridge *Telegram* on 22 April 1915. This particular item depicted a battery exercise as a sporting contest, but with a noticeable emphasis on procedure and efficiency. The entire drill was put in terms of a formal display of machine-like precision in which the making of new and expert sets of soldiers was reflected in the attention they paid to the rightness of detail and quick response. Readers learned of a mock battle between the 'Red' and 'Blue' forces of the 25th. The Reds, led by Lieut. W.H. McLelland, 'had been driven from Lethbridge toward the boundary and were making for Raymond' sometime in the middle of the night, to begin a game of hide-and-seek. First a mounted Blue patrol of nine men, led by Sgt. S.V. Perry, left the barracks at 5:28 a.m. At 6:05 a.m. the Blue's main body, led by Captain Ripley, also on horseback, set out due south, turning east at Kirkham's farm, then southeast on the Stirling trail toward Raymond, some twenty miles away. Messages, timed to the minute, went back and forth between the patrol and Ripley's force. 'Several rifle shots were heard by the party at Wilson at 9:15 a.m.' Thirty-five minutes later, action speeds:

> At 9:50 a.m. the following was received: Hostile battery S.E. corner Felger's Farm. Horses in readiness guns facing east of it. Observation party some distance in front.
>
> After moving about 1000 yards the guns were located north of the observation station.
>
> According to the rules of war the Red force was put out of action.[78]

6 John Newstead Jr. of Guelph Ontario, c. 1915. It appears that this young lad on a tricycle, with his uncommitted gaze, was fitted for his own uniform, patterned identically to those of the Canadian Expeditionary Force. *Courtesy of Guelph Museums, 995.11.8*

Like the carefully dug trenches with right-angled corners and immaculately stacked sandbags that were used for public display in some cities, this report seemed intent on transforming the ordinary lives of local soldiers into a kind of mythical construct, of men learning specialized procedures needed for the fields of real battle. The militia regiment period in both Lethbridge and Guelph introduced an illusionary sense of recruits in training in their home regions. Most prominent were references to manful camaraderie, transcending but never transgressing the constraints of uniformed life, of cheerful goodwill among men facing a rarely faulted bureaucratic machine that dictated their day-to-day manoeuvres and fate. An obvious sentimental attachment to the men was conveyed as they passed from recruits to trainees to departing soldiers, passages retold through items designed for their families, loved ones, friends, and any local reader proud of her or his community. As a common theme of war coverage, tales of troops-in-training became a recurrent, undoubtedly profitable, vehicle for local presses. It was often quirky but always good news on the home front for these boys, these noble men. News of the departure of Guelph's 34th Battalion for further training in London, Ontario, appeared in the *Mercury* under the subcaption 'SORRY TO LOSE 'EM.'[79]

The militia regiment phase brought one more unit to Lethbridge. Ottawa designated the 39th Battery, Canadian Field Artillery, seven months after the departure of the 20th. Its enlistment filled fairly quickly, reaching its 140-man complement in just two days, all signed on by 11 October 1915. It was 'a matter of congratulation, not only for this fact, but for the fact that the entire battery was recruited within the city of Lethbridge' the *Herald* boasted.[80] Although, according to its unit register, compiled by Sgt.-Maj. F.G. Holyoak in 1919, 'no barracks were available, training commenced immediately, the men falling in daily outside the Herald office on 6th Street South, and a fatigue party being put to work to make ready a building at the Exhibition Grounds to serve the purpose of a barracks, into which the Battery moved on the 1st of December following.' Holyoak's record of the 39th is indicative of a genre in regimental histories: accounts prepared by former members that painstakingly itemize a unit's origins and progress while emphasizing its achievements.[81]

While these memoirs are useful in countless ways, their authors, collectively, wished to leave a commemorative record of the men in the Great War. They stressed esprit de corps, local pride, and worthy service. Holyoak's chronicle certainly corroborates the *Herald*'s claim that the battalion was very much a local product, with numerous references to the men's backgrounds and contributions as hometown heroes. Offered in plain language, it remained focused on the ordinary. 'This book,' he put it, was 'written by a man in the ranks, for the men in the ranks, of the life of the men in the ranks, claims nothing more than to have set out that life.' As a gendered text, it describes paths to an authentic manhood that, Holyoak suggested in numerous passages, belonging to this regiment instilled. Even when training almost next door to one's family and friends, army routine at the barracks, or training exercises in the fields nearby, served to mould a new kind of military masculinity defined by discipline to routine, though the realities of the front would be much worse. Holyoak stressed how life in uniform helped young men to mature, to break habits formed in a coddled civilian past. 'The barracks appeared to some at first a little tough,' this former sergeant-major, recalled:

> although, had they had the chance to sleep in the same place a year later they would have considered it palatial.
>
> Undoubtedly the Army breaks one in gently. Home to barracks, barracks to barn, barn to grass covered field, field to the rain-sodden and muddy shell hole, though the latter was often not despised.
>
> Some of the 'City Gentlemen' not at first fully realizing that they were now in the army, changed nightly into garments of many and varied hues, and thus won for themselves the name of 'The Pajama Brigade' but reveille being at an early hour, and noticing that those who slept half dressed thereby obtained an extra five minutes in bed on a cold winter morning, they forsook their former genteel habits and thus somewhat subconsciously assumed a phase in army life.
>
> The food was good and plentiful, though this was not always appreciated, practically all the Battery not on duty leaving barracks nightly for their homes, or a meal down town.[82]

Local training, despite its drawbacks as a close-to-home experience, its dreariness, and its fabricated hardships, did introduce many young men to a soldier's life before they faced battle, and gave many civilians a more immediate sense of barracks life.

In the end, though, it failed to meet its recruiting targets. Militia units assembled volunteers and sustained a national training system, but they could not meet constantly increasing demands for men. Although the Department of Militia and Defence routinely approved new recruitment drives through either existing or newly authorized local units (seventy-one new infantry battalions were created in this period), it soon became apparent across Canada that the pool of eager recruits, which had seemed inexhaustible in the fall of 1914, showed signs of abating by the beginning of 1915.[83]

Guelph's part in the militia regiment phase certainly reflected this. Recruiting for its 34th Battalion started as an uphill battle only six months after the war began. Less than a week after its first volunteers signed on, in mid-January 1915, enrolments collapsed to about one per day. The tendency for British-born men to dominate many rolls also continued. As the *Mercury* noted, the 'majority of those who have already signed up, and who have been passed by the medical examiner' were 'old countrymen, English, Irish and Scotch.'[84] One recruiting officer asserted that Canadians were 'just as brave' as the British-born, but they were 'apparently of the opinion that they are not needed in the field of battle.' His second point was more telling: 'Many of them are drawing good wages here, and are adverse to accepting the wages offered by the Militia Department.'[85]

When the 29th Battery began recruiting in June 1915, only thirty-four men signed on during the first week. With little prospect of improvement, it was decided to transfer this group as a 'first batch' for training at the Carling Heights camp in London, Ontario. Its send-off bore no resemblance to the excitement and crowds of the early war. 'There was very little enthusiasm as the train pulled out' with the men aboard, one reporter stated.[86] The situation only got worse when yet another battalion, the 71st Infantry, opened its recruiting doors in late August. An unrealistically high quota of 280 men was set for Guelph, compounded by the *Mercury*'s hopes that it could be met within two weeks.[87] Only eight volunteers signed on during the first day. Despite the paper's overstated claim that recruiting for the 71st was off to a 'good start,' it was obvious that local recruiting campaign efforts could not meet their initial quotas.[88]

As the fighting bogged down overseas, enlistment drives and public displays intensified in every town and city. From posters and orations to the rituals of the recruitment drive, the period from the summer of 1915 to the following year became a frenetic, often frustrating, time for recruiters trying to get as many men as could be persuaded into uniform. Illustrated recruiting posters appeared in local newspapers and became a near ubiquitous sight. Many were produced by the regiments themselves or by civilian volunteers within individual military districts, something Paul Maroney has noted for Ontario. In District 2, which included Guelph, for instance, 'a series of at least seventeen different recruiting posters, one of which was a copy of a British design,' were used during the war. Civilian recruiting agencies joined battalions in this effort and, as Maroney observes, 'thousands, perhaps tens of thousands, of such posters were issued and posted. Once in place, an effective poster, with a strong pictorial element and deftly related verbal message, could act as a silent recruiting sergeant, appealing to countless passers by.'[89] Their themes, from hypermasculine militarism and guilt-directed condemnations of unmanliness to demonizations of the enemy, touched on every conceivable aspect of wartime service. They, and the recruiting exercise as a whole, soon became more a record of what recruiters imagined might work best than anything else. Efforts applied at the local level, however, clearly could not sustain the CEF's thirst for further enlistments by the late summer of 1915.

On 3 September 1915, Labour Day, the bulk of Guelph's contribution to the 29th Battery and 34th Battalion, numbering some one hundred men, along with a medical inspection team, returned briefly to their hometown to help turn things around in the city.[90] Their presence on parade and at rallies did draw crowds, but not high numbers. To support their drives for recruits on a more permanent basis, the 29th and 34th Battalion joined with the newly-created 71st Battalion to open a recruiting office on Upper Wyndham Street. This gave one veteran wounded at St. Julien, Cpl. Joe Fitzgerald, a public relations role as a local fixture for local recruiting. Fitzgerald had briefly resided in Guelph before enlisting with a Montreal regiment, which took him to France where 'he did his "bit" and was one of the first to fall from a German bullet.' As a note on his background put it, the 'Dominion government ... saw fit to send him to Guelph to aid in the recruiting for the 71st Battalion.' Fitzgerald, as the *Mercury* cast him, had 'a knack' for 'inducing the boys to sign on,' and one upbeat report stated that the new uptown office was 'doing fine.' But it was not. Far short of the 280 men first called for, Fitzgerald managed only 20 enlistments for the 71st in his first week, before he took up his first speaking engagements.[91] His tactics were more personal than public. As the *Mercury* put it, Fitzgerald's efforts depended on the 'personal appeal method' of recruiting in the city. 'Light of limb, broad of shoulder, strong of heart and with an Irish smile on his Celtic face, Corporal Joe Fitzgerald, veteran of St. Julien, beckons the men of Guelph, and with his soft Irish brogue induces them to sign on with the 71st Battalion, at the recruiting station recently established on Upper Wyndham street.' But it was hardly an easy task for the 'hustling Irish recruiter.' As he explained:

> Many of those who walk Wyndham street, if they are going up, turn their eyes to the left when they pass the recruiting station, and to the right if they are going down. Many of them are afraid to look at the streamers, which flaunt in their faces, begging them to enlist. They are not the kind we want. What we want is whole-hearted men who are not afraid to make a sacrifice, and more than that, whole-souled women – sisters, mothers, sweethearts and wives – who will place no obstacle in the way of their sons, lovers or sweethearts and try to stop them enlisting.[92]

Women faced blame from time to time in the Lethbridge *Herald* as well. This reflected the patriarchal attitudes enforced in this war and a journalistic stance common in much of what was said about the problems of recruitment. In editorials and numerous separate reports in the *Herald* and other papers at this time, the notion that family ties and female lovers could be obstacles to one's duty as a real man in uniform was reiterated over and over again. True bravery could be found only in the hearts of real men. Hearth and home, on the other hand, were portrayed as feminine domains that no man could abide in time of war.

However, women could not be blamed for the fact that Fitzgerald's appeals fell far short of his quota: only seven more men enlisted with the 71st three days after the last recruiting drive ended, and the men helping out from the 29th Battery and the 34th Battalion returned to barracks in London. Smaller companies of soldiers, backed by military bands, staged several more enlistment rallies, organized by officers and volunteers at the Wyndham Street office. They still featured Fitzgerald's entertaining, but ineffective, orations.

Such scenes had become commonplace. Activating an imaginary vision of masculine adventure in uniform remained an ongoing campaign across the country. It made use of congested public spaces and well-advertised recruiting rallies. Recruiting drives began to fill both weekend and weeknight programs, and the sounds of bands and speeches filled the air in Guelph as elsewhere. As their appeals faded, local recruiters across Canada tried new schemes, and concerns grew that one regiment's drive for recruits would eat into the dwindling pool of another. That often happened, especially in the more densely populated areas of southern Ontario. In terms of raising the number of new volunteers, no more than a trickle by this time, just several a day, could be drawn from a city the size of Guelph.[93]

While the enlistment rate was still holding firm in Lethbridge, with its proportionately higher British-born population and relatively depressed local economy, circumstances elsewhere in English Canada generally contributed to downward trends as the CEF entered its second year of wartime recruiting.[94] Enlistments were down 8 percent in September 1915 and plunged a further 23 percent by the end of October.[95] By the spring of 1916 the pool of willing and able recruits had all but dried up.[96] Moreover, the existing system simply could not keep up with the relentless demands of the slaughter overseas. Lower inflows and higher casualties prompted a change from militia regiment recruiting in favour of a new community regiment approach, the last of the procedures that depended on viable partnerships between local settings, military organization, and recruiting strategies for the CEF before compulsory military service was imposed.

Last Calls Before Conscription: Guelph, Lethbridge, and Community Regiments

To some recruiters the community regiment phase must have seemed like a last-ditch effort to raise and fill as many new regiments as possible before the implementation of conscription in October 1917. Sam Hughes, who endorsed the move toward community-based regiments, thought, with his usual optimism, that he might locate some groundswell of untapped sympathy for the war effort at the local level.[97] With the determined network of speakers and patriotic leagues still fervently campaigning for more volunteers across the country, he hoped, or perhaps conceded, that simply giving them more control over the creation and filling of new units might stimulate a new influx. As one study of this move noted: 'In the fall of 1915 the Department announced that henceforth the local regiments of Militia would be bypassed in the recruiting effort and the individual citizens and communities would be authorized to raise battalions on their own if they would assume the costs of recruiting.'[98] It proved to be Ottawa's last nationwide strategy to increase volunteers and maintain a system fast reaching its absolute limit. It also depended even more heavily than the existing militia regiments did on local support.

Giving local groups and associations, or interested citizens, more latitude to form their own regiments, provided that they met costs, was one thing, but creating some new affiliation, real or imagined, that might appeal to those not yet signed on was another. Community regiments tried to incorporate some element of ethnicity, 'moral character,' or even physical stature in their particular symbolic identities. Except for Canada's two 'Bantam' battalions, for men less than the required five feet, two inches, community regiment appeals were usually based on selling a particular regimental image or identity, whether it be Scottishness, Irishness, sobriety (battalions from Winnipeg and Toronto promised strict temperance), or 'sportsmanship' (two others came to be known as 'Sportsmen' battalions).[99] Apart from the very real niche filled by the Bantams, these battalions were designated, quite deliberately, as a bottom-up method, and more than any other phase of recruitment they reflected the importance of local initiative.

Lethbridge's 113 Highlanders, the Kilty Battalion, began as part of this phase in the winter of 1915-16 and appealed for volunteers as a local Highland regiment until the following spring, when it was sent on to a militia department training camp at Sarcee, Alberta. The basis for the battalion's local backing was also rooted in ensuring that Lethbridge got its fair share of the monetary benefit of outfitting, feeding, and housing what early organizers hoped would be a thousand men. Mayor Hardie and the Board of Trade felt that Lethbridge had already paid its fair share of 'brawn and muscle,' over one thousand men, the *Herald* pointed out, and yet was only housing and provisioning a mere 140 trainees then in town with the militia department's 39th Battery.[100] If the city gave, then it should get; the campaign for one more regimental unit with a distinctive stamp could not be disentangled from hopes for far more tenders, contracts, and money from Ottawa.

After some discussion, W.S. Ball, a lawyer and local Conservative Party organizer, and E.C. MacKenzie, also a lawyer, travelled to Ottawa to lobby Sam Hughes directly. It was late October 1915, and enlistments had just taken the sharpest month-to-month drop to date. Ball and MacKenzie asked that an existing battalion be moved to Lethbridge or, in lieu of that, that the 39th be brought up to full battalion (1,100 men) strength. Hughes would do neither. He did promise to set up a permanent recruiting station and to give some thought to approving another unit for the city. Official authorization for a new unit came through just before the delegates headed home.[101] They could do what they wanted, but they would have to do it themselves, with Ottawa only agreeing to meet costs once the unit was in place.

In granting approval, Ottawa designated a Highlanders battalion for Lethbridge, probably on the suggestion of Ball and MacKenzie. The task now was for its backers in the city to get a battalion up and running in, they hoped, short order. Under the banner of the '113th Lethbridge Highlanders,' the *Herald* noted, its members were to wear the 'Balmoral' or 'Glengarry' cap, with a special khaki doublet. Uniforms reflecting invented tradition, however, had to be tailored to needs. A complete Highland uniform, with kilts, might provide men with colourful parade uniforms, but it would not serve as the most practical gear for battle. Kilts were out, first because of expense (estimated by the Quartermaster General's office at $30,000, twice the cost of khaki), and also because of problems the men might encounter with barbed wire, or so it was explained in a letter from the Quartermaster's office to Mayor Hardie.[102] The *Herald* also reported that the city's Kilty Band joined as a complete unit, which no doubt delighted organizers and suggests that there might indeed have been something Scottish in the new battalion's makeup.[103]

That competing efforts to recruit for other corps anywhere in southern Alberta were shut down entirely, and that it took seven months to get the 113th even close to full strength, illustrates some measure of the difficulty of attracting enlistments by this time. Meanwhile, the *Herald* played its part with headlines like 'Recruiting for 113th Away at Good Swing,' 'Kilties Get Recruits at Good Rate,' or 'Steady Stream of Recruits for new Kilty Battalion' with less than 10 percent of its volunteers signed in the fall of 1915.[104] In comparative terms, however, the Kilties were by no means a failure as a community regiment. A reported 200 men were in the ranks by early December, half of their target of 400 for that date, with 900 of the 1,100 quota signed on by the spring of 1916.[105]

The unit's commander, Lt.-Col. A.W. Pryce-Jones, a Welsh-born militia officer who had settled in Calgary in 1910, was appointed in December 1915.[106] His junior officers received their appointments in early January 1916. The sense of identity and esprit de corps men felt within their regiments served many purposes, and this was true with the 113th Kilties, but with community regiments in particular, civilians often came to expect a little extra display of colour and presence. The *Telegram* complained that the battalion had seldom been on parade, and when it was, some men were still in 'civies' while others trudged in assorted uniforms.[107] Both the *Herald* and the *Telegram* expressed concerns over this, while the Kilties struggled to attract enough men to train as a unit. The *Telegram* also reprinted in full a letter from the Quartermaster's office concerning the style of uniform to be worn by the men, indicating the appeal of creating a battalion with its own symbols and tradition. Both papers also maintained that big plans were underway for a special public event: a demonstration of traditional Highland sports as part of a full afternoon of manful Scottish display by the men before they were dispatched to Sarcee, Alberta, as a completed force for further training. 'The program is of considerable variety,' the *Telegram* reported

7 Here enlistments of the 78th Battalion, a depot regiment that supplied other units, perform a marching drill in front of the Royal North-West Mounted Police Barracks in Lethbridge, summer 1917. As was common in local communities, these exercises drew the attention of onlookers – in this case, a group of older men (huddled on the left edge of the photograph). *Courtesy of Sir Alexander Galt Museum and Archives, P19760217063*

on 4 May, 'and included tugs-of-war, putting the shot, and many other feats of strength and endurance, in addition to the usual sprints and long distance races. One of the features of the day will be the old Highland sport of "Tossing the Caber."'[108] For whatever reason, the event did not come off at all.

While traditional Scottish exertions may have been difficult to reinvent on this prairie setting among men from across southern Alberta, the key to maximizing enlistment with units like this often lay in fostering a sense of local identity, if possible by appointing some well-known figure to head up the unit, at least until the end of its initial training. Recruiting for Wellington County's 153rd Battalion seems typical in this respect. As its former commander and chronicler, R.T. Pritchard, noted, the formation of 'D' company 'as a wholly Guelph Company commanded by Guelph officers provided a stimulus to recruiting.'[109] The fact that 340 men enlisted with this all-Guelph unit, a figure that would have delighted recruiters for the militia department's 71st Battalion, indicated how the community-based approach to recruiting could, in some cases, work better than the more top-down militia regiment approach it supplemented.

The 153rd was one of a large number of Ontario's 'county' battalions, which sprang up throughout the province in 1916. They could not meet Borden's ambitious pledge of November 1915, to increase the total CEF compliment to 500,000 men. But nothing could, many soon argued, short of compulsory service. Once authorized, the 153rd called upon recruiting organizers from Guelph to get together with others in nearby towns and villages. 'A' Company was composed of initial volunteers, most of whom were from Guelph; 'B' and 'C' Companies later recruited separately in areas surrounding Fergus and Mount Forest respectively; while 'D' company drew the last wave of recruits, again from Guelph. 'To assist in recruiting the battalion up to full strength,' Pritchard recalled, 'a recruiting league was organized in Guelph with Judge Hayes, of Guelph, as Honorary President, James Beattie, of Fergus, as President, and Alderman H. Westoby, of Guelph, as secretary-treasurer.'[110]

Later, in the spring of 1916, when the 153rd established its four companies, its commander recalled, 'A succession of meetings were held and recruiting posters and literature distributed. Grants were obtained by the recruiting league from County and City councils. With the aid of the Branch Committees throughout the County, and the officers in charge at the different centres, a list of the men in the County eligible for military service was compiled, and letters sent to each man, putting the question of his duty before him. At the same time meetings were held throughout the county by the officers in charge and men already enlisted organized a vigorous visiting campaign.'[111]

Voluntary recruitment in its final phase featured drives, supported by local elites and organized by citizen committees, that included compiling lists of names and addresses and making direct contact with as many eligible men as possible. The community regiment period could not hope to raise half a million men as volunteers across Canada. But in terms of what was accomplished, the recruiting drives of Lethbridge's Kilty Battalion and Guelph's 'D' Company of the 153rd relied heavily on local participation. The creation of these units depended on exploiting a sense that hometowns, not Ottawa, were in charge of attracting as many volunteers as possible from men who still walked the streets out of uniform and unenlisted.[112]

Soldiers Mustered, Trained, and Dispatched in Local Settings

Popular perceptions of the men who signed on, trained, and left for overseas service were never communicated for a single purpose. Yet even when the initial enthusiasm for recruitment, rallies, and military display all but collapsed, the call for public ceremony never really stopped. 'The war is on,' the *Telegram* reported more than a year before the Kilties departed.

> As the conflict deepens we become day by day more impressed with its realities. Behind it creeps a long line of domestic tragedy. It is coming nearer to us in the list of local casualties. We are not depressed. Far from it. But confident in the ultimate end it is equally essential that a cheerful spirit be retained. We cannot forget the war. It is bound while it continues to be ever with us as the one supreme interest of the day.

> But while remembering this it is at the same time good for us not to unduly dwell on it. More now than ever an occasional tonic will be good for us. We need to be drawn more together, to mix with the crowd under cheering and inspiring opportunities. A community spirit needs encouraging. We are all one in one great common desire, the triumphant success of our armies. Let us emphasize this. Public music to bring the crowd together is necessary. We have four bands in the city. How much do we hear from them? Why not have an afternoon, or an evening, every week with a band in Galt Gardens, varied by volunteer singers, in the shape of an open air concert?'[113]

That this event seems never to have got off the ground indicates the emotional distances that had set in between the festive performances that marked the outbreak of war and the arrival of news of the disasters overseas. Enthusiasm and local opportunities for ongoing recruitment and volunteer dispatches shifted with the chronology of the war, as the editorial above makes clear. The crowds at send-offs to Valcartier waned precipitously as many faced death as a more palpable reality for their friends or loved ones. The orations of the speakers leagues, recruiting posters, and an increasing number of editorials calling for conscription implied an intensified commitment of support for the forces overseas, an often frenetic imperative to stay the course for those first killed in action or wounded. But their appeal could not be sustained.

Public speakers, reporters, newspaper editors, and many others who made up local recruiting establishments nonetheless persisted. Long after the extent of the catastrophe overseas had become obvious, they reiterated the same messages and themes that erupted at the beginning of the war. When publicly displayed in hometown settings, voluntary recruitment's public face expressed intimate connections between home and overseas. Throughout each phase of a process, from Valcartier to community regiments, that in the end could not keep up with demand, hometowns and their shifting horizons of expectation remained primary settings for the social history of recruitment in Canada. As we have seen, toward the end of voluntary recruitment, local networks often proved practical in organizing community regiments like the Lethbridge Highlanders or the Wellington County regiment. And from the very beginning, local parks, streets, armouries, and other sites, including city newspapers, served as the most powerful contexts for communicating to Canadians as a whole what the war meant as a great and terrible reality.

First, they helped to validate offering men's bodies to certain ideals. In so doing they politicized the sacrifice by connecting ideals to action. Second, both public and, in Trois-Rivères, private affairs held to recognize the significance of civilian-to-soldier transitions marked a very real and localized process of social differentiation. The boundaries drawn between the raw recruit and his family, friends, and other civilian ties could be made to seem both ominous and necessary. 'They'll not all come back again,' Guelph mayor Samuel Carter stated with unusual realism at the beginning of the war, 'and they'll need our sympathy and our prayers.'[114] Assertions like this helped to make what was taking place as a military exercise coherent as a cultural event for local audiences, if not for the troops themselves. The everyday sights and sounds of wartime mobilization on the streets, in newspapers, and at armouries, exhibition grounds, and railway stations across the country inscribed meanings – militaristic, imperialistic, nationalistic, gendered, and religious – to the innocent enthusiasm with which the country went to war. The troops left, but the same war-supporting messages were reiterated at home, bolstered by the additional reference to justifying a great sacrifice once the casualities mounted up. To the extent that battle-hardened soldiers gave up on such rhetoric, we find (in Chapter 7) that it may have helped to distance veterans from their home communities.

It is misleading, though, to consider send-offs as a break between those leaving and those 'left behind.' Their impact remained in memories of civilian audiences that experienced warfare vicariously, but actively. As public performances, each depended as much on crowd presence and participation. Spectators interpreted the signs as symbols of recruitment from hometown horizons that fractured any sense of English Canada's home front as a coherent whole – a single society, a single imperial-nationalism, or a single vision of war. As gendered scripts they ritualized the exclusivity of military manhood, a boundary that both barred women and sought to effeminize the 'slacker' who failed to enlist. The social cleavages between the recruit and his most immediate communities emerged as outcomes, culturally inscribed through local means first, while enforced by official bureaucracies and procedures. Send-offs took place on local sites, confined by the perspectives of hometown horizons. It is also useful to look at how they changed, less than one year into the fighting, from the flurry of fast recruiting at the beginning of the war to the slide in enlistment once the stalemate in the trenches solidified. From that basis, we can move on to consider how established relationships of social hierarchy mobilized a new discourse endorsing voluntary civilian contributions to patriotic causes. Like recruitment, war relief was also orchestrated through local responses, deployed at the nexus of home and nation.

3
Hierarchies

'So ends 1914 with its stormy, troublous times,' Julia McWilliams of Puslinch, near Guelph, wrote in her diary on 31 December of that year. 'Fiercest war ever waged going on between Germany and Austria against Russia, Britain, France and Belgium. Very uncertain as to how peace may come to us again. Very many lives lost and trouble all over the world.' Her son, Albert, would later join Guelph's 64th Battery, only to embark for Europe just as the war ended.[1]

Between the stalemate, firmly established by the end of 1914, and the cease-fire almost four years later, casualty lists, reprinted in local newspapers, offered one more marker of the war's plummeting course. Released through the press, the dreaded tabulations by name, regiment, and often place of death or battle became a public way to disseminate notices of men killed in action, something most deeply felt by families receiving letters of condolence. As the war dragged on, simply reading newspapers, or overhearing word of the names, gave many on the home front a deepened sense of the losses suffered in local communities and by the country as a whole. Depending on how close one's personal ties were to the men overseas, home front life became an unending vigil. As it was for McWilliams, the troubled world 'outside' was something most could only imagine as a distant struggle, while the faces and memories of those overseas provoked much deeper emotions. The disillusionment with the present was very real. So was fear for the future. The 'uncertainty,' the 'many lives lost,' the 'trouble all over the world' that this mother noted at the end of 1914 placed the war in an atmosphere of growing chaos and confusion. McWilliams's pessimistic outlook was justified. Neither peace, nor Canadians at war, would return any time soon.

The apocalyptic depictions of the Great War that civilians generated often bring us closer to how the war was understood and codified by contemporaries than to how it actually proceeded as a sequence of events. As opaque glimpses, they inscribe subjective versions of events, derived simultaneously from immediate surroundings and from dark visions of the carnage overseas. As we have seen in the previous chapter, an aging Gédéon Désilets, who had left Trois-Rivières as a youth in 1868 to join the Papal Zouaves in Italy, described the present war as a struggle for redemption before God. As conflicted souls in tumultuous times, as he put it, man must place himself at the foot of his sovereign master, and nowhere else. Désilets saw 'la France du Sacré-Coeur et de la Ste-Vierge' rising above the ashes of destruction 'pour remettre l'ordre dans le monde: Dieu à la première place, et l'homme son indocile serviteur à la sienne, c'est-à-dire aux pied du souverain Maître.'[2]

The *Bien Public*'s editor, Joseph Barnard, saw the war in similar terms, a portent heralding the return of France's Catholic traditions. 'Hier,' Barnard wrote in one of his bylined, front-page commentaries, 'c'était la renaissance du culte de la patrie; fasse le ciel que demain ce soit, sous l'épreuve, la renaissance du culte de Dieu.'[3] As bishop of the surrounding diocese, Mgr François-Xavier Cloutier depicted what was taking place as a diabolic manifestation in his 'Circulaire au Clergé' of 1915. Cloutier referred to a year eclipsed by 'le terrible fléau de la guerre, qui ravage actuellement l'Europe et le monde' – the terrible scourge of war that raged across Europe and the world. In its materialism and its use of new technologies, the modern world had lost faith in God in its headlong pursuit of earthly rewards. Cloutier's conservative and theological image of peace on earth paralleled that of Désilets and Barnard: 'Supplions le Dieu des miséricordes d'accorder au monde la paix dans le rétablissement de son règne et dans la soumission pleine et entière à son Eglise.'[4]

In different themes and narratives, as we have also seen, popular scripts for a war of heroic volunteers, of boys becoming men, of overseas adventure and certain victory, circulated as unofficial propaganda, the kind of sustained journalistic discourses one might sample from the *Mercury* or the *Herald*. From the raised pulpit to the private diary, subjective interpretations accumulated. People peered at the fighting overseas just beyond such hometown horizons. Deeply rooted anxieties at home not only grew commonplace, but also intersected with the practices of civilians who organized home front relief. Unlike troops huddled under the shelling, local people in voluntary associations, social reform groups, and other networks could at least try to do something while the war's casualties mounted. At first glance that might seem why some did get involved. We find, however, another motive at play, and it was as conservative as that of our Catholic commentators above. Many not only wished through nostalgia to turn back the clock and see their loved ones returned home or divine power resurrected; many also did not want the social order greatly altered as the war dragged on. They did not want to see the world they had known before the war disappear. This was particularly true for the middle-class women and men who were settled residents and stakeholders in Lethbridge, Guelph, and Trois-Rivières before August 1914.

How contemporaries represented themselves in organizing home relief expressed their corresponding preferences for existing and stable social hierarchies and relations – marked by class, gender, and ethnic differences. That they expressed concern for the future security of Canada and of its populations and acted on that concern is not at issue, but that they communicated such messages through signs of social difference that conformed to their sense of an ideal or model world can present another reading, one that allows us to probe local perceptions and actual power relations. In varied genres, from advertisements to editorials, pro-war prescriptions of the citizen's duty accompanied coverage of the fighting in virtually every city daily throughout the war. Battle news itself appeared in fantastic accounts that passed the censor's gaze because it posed no real threat to the government's aim of winning the war. Together, the citizen's duty and the horrible cost of war echoed as themes through much of the public discourse considered here. Strangely, war relief workers reflected this constantly – that the war was costly and that citizens had responsibilities – but here we consider how that became translated into exercises of self-preservation, self-interest.

When civilians tried to do their bit, to contribute in some way to projects they saw and presented as worthy, ameliorative, and practical, they quickly began to narrate: to themselves, to others they hoped might contribute or join them, and to those who might criticize or attack their efforts. How they positioned themselves through their causes, rather than the causes themselves, we might consider as entry points, as strategies adopted to justify the purposes of their projects based on the societal models they used to comprehend their world. As fighting in Europe and other fronts dragged on, possibilities diminished for sustaining war relief through voluntary approaches alone, particularly in terms of raising monies for soldiers' families. Examining how relief organizers represented their own views of society as a set of unequal relations, nonequivalent identities, and uneven powers can help us understand why many attempted to sustain war relief's cheapest first method: voluntary donation and redistribution.

Many causes placed special emphasis on their ability to attract donations from a broad social spectrum. Their claims, though overstated, had some foundation in what took place. Even religious pacifists, as we shall see, could be drawn to contribute to the support of soldiers' families in need during the war. That so many forms of war relief appeared soon after the outbreak, and increased in scale and scope as freshly trained units left for the front, demonstrated the appeal of voluntarism, particularly among middle-class Canadians, both women and men, who were economically established in their respective locales, especially those who had been active before in voluntary associational life. Those connected to small and large businesses often saw themselves, rather than government, as the initiators of civilian support for the effort, particularly in war relief work.

In fact, their interests as wealthier citizens were at stake. Ottawa introduced taxation in 1917, partly in support of soldiers' dependents. This began an eclipse of voluntary charitable support for aid to soldiers' families and veteran re-establishment, which had proved inadequate on its own. Addressing why charitable relief took on its tasks, especially in the early war, and how organizers, many operating businesses large and small, coordinated local and national efforts sheds light on how they perceived social relations and boundaries and how they hoped economic redistribution might be sustained without increased taxation.

Relief, Not Charity

War relief embraced a myriad of charitable funds and other projects in support of the Canadian and Allied effort, from IODE projects to the Canadian Patriotic Fund, established at the beginning of the war to supplement the family loss of a male breadwinner at home. Appeals for war relief were constructed as a special circumstance and response. Organizers used them often enough, and in forms consistent enough, to present self-elevating portraits of themselves as mission-bound with a common sense of purpose. Through these notions, they saw themselves leading a society very different in its makeup but supposedly united by the war's great imperatives. All reasonable citizens, however humble or eminent, it was said, must do their duty. The organizers' conceptions of unity, of the common causes taken on to aid, for instance, families with men at the front, the men themselves, or the innocent in Belgium that Britain pledged to protect, can, however, be read as signs of difference. War relief organizers often generated texts and practices embedded in a society construed as differentiated. Charitable approaches, in particular, conformed to a failed project, a hierarchical model of society that ultimately failed to become a practical model for directing a society at war.

By any definition sanctioned by the many voluntary causes taken on, war relief was recast as something quite different from charity. For example, popular images of Belgians facing atrocities and brutalities at the hands of a German army suggest tactical measures to sensationalize 'little Belgium's' losses and devastation by depicting the invaders in monstrous terms designed to shock, horrify, and solicit donations. Patriotism as a sentimental and duty-bound tie to country became itself an appropriated ideal, applied to name the most important cause in this category of activities, the Canadian Patriotic Fund (CPF). Perhaps its title served as the first convenient extension of past practice, since a fund of the same name had been organized for the families of South African volunteers from Canada. The 'patriotic' aims of the Fund, formed in 1914, were to spring not from devotion to winning an imperial war, a sentiment that French and English Canada would never share, but from duty to protect the country's soldiers' families. The shared duty seemed rooted in the rhetoric of support for the working-class breadwinner's dependants enduring rising cost-of-living hardships. As we shall see, francophone support in Trois-Rivières relied on appeals of this sort, thus avoiding entanglements with imperial-national connotations that could be turned around to feed nicely into fundraising efforts in Guelph and Lethbridge. Some social reform movements, like prohibition, found increased relevance during the war, when abstinence was linked to new codes of societal discipline, though war-induced campaigns against alcohol consumption were not prominent in the cities considered here. Measures seen as practical, voluntary, and supportive of the Canadian soldiers' families while their primary providers risked their lives against an evil aggressor did, in fact, quite easily cross the divide over the contested meaning of patriotism, so obvious when comparing French to English Canada. Practical sense made more sense than patriotic zeal.

On a national scale, Canada's many voluntary war relief organizations can be divided into two broad categories, though both engaged in similar, often overlapping, activities. First there were the established organizations that took on war relief projects, like the IODE, the Canadian Red Cross, Women's Institutes, local women's councils, the YWCA and YMCA. Quickly springing up alongside these groups were many new organizations, most directed at specific fundraising campaigns created by the war: the CPF, the Belgium Relief Fund, and at the very beginning of the war, local Overseas Clubs. Later, pro-veteran groups like the Next-of-Kin Associations or the Khaki Leagues appeared as the advocacy needs of veterans and their families increased.

Whether it took the form of a prisoner of war fund, a tobacco fund, or funds to purchase machine guns or ambulances overseas, civilian war relief was distanced discursively from the stigma of financial need, and certainly from poverty. They were championed as 'patriotic' causes, wartime measures that expressed and privileged voluntary, civilian activities. They were cast, too, by newspapers and by the organizers themselves in 'civic' terms as the contributions of specific towns or cities, often boasting of their success in comparison to rival municipalities or regions.

Civic rivalries helped promote the CPF as the largest and most significant of all Canada's war relief funds. As we shall see at the local level, middle-class citizens across the country, operating on the basis of class, gender, and ethnicity, became involved on a significant scale almost immediately after war broke out. They struck committees, secured necessary start-up donations of office space and supplies from local businesses, and began door-to-door and other local campaigns to raise money for the CPF. As we shall also see, those same local networks raised funds for those left displaced in Belgium, for military hospitals or Red Cross stations near the front, for prisoner of war funds, or for the host of other causes that depended on local action and voluntarism. Collectively, they became war relief workers.

Thus, as a keyword, 'relief' displaced 'charity' to designate even campaigns not aimed directly at Canada's fighting men, like the Belgium Relief Fund. The word, however, applied broadly. The CPF's national executive, for instance, saw itself as doing two basic things: financing the Fund, that is raising money for it; and 'relief,' or giving it to deserving families. They assigned themselves what they saw as the final basic task, or 'third responsibility': policing relief disbursements, a set of activities that stood between 'finance' and 'relief' and underscored the fact that prior relationships between philanthropic patronage and charitable donation had not in fact disappeared – 'relief' was a process screened by the conventions, prejudices, and perceptions of those who distributed it. Relief was seen as something different from charity, especially by those who organized its projects and sought to distance their recipients from any sense of stigma – and themselves from any further burden. In Guelph, for instance, a group of women formerly known as the Fireside Circle renamed themselves the College Heights Relief Association in 1915 and raised money to provide medical supplies for wounded Canadians hospitalized in England. As we shall see in Chapter 6, the renaming reflected their sense that charity in peacetime and relief in wartime were not the same. Extreme social inequalities made charity necessary in past times; preserving social order marked by class differences in wartime now required relief to soldiers' families most in need.

But in fact, charity and relief were the same. As hierarchical configurations assembled from the very beginning of hostilities, what mostly middle-class volunteers executed as duty-bound imperatives, from securing material supplies to aiding soldiers' families, served as concealments for power systems that sought to maintain boundaries of social difference and inequalities in wealth on the home front.[5]

In fact, a gap had opened between discourse and intent. The stated objective of the CPF, to isolate the most salient example, was to provide legitimate relief to soldiers' dependents. But as the secretary of the national body himself recorded in his chronology of the Fund's activities, redistributing relief from wealthier to poorer regions and policing the allocation of benefits revealed a politic and agenda determined by the Fund, not by its beneficiaries. Philip H. Morris, executive secretary of the CPF, who compiled and edited a report of the Fund's aims and activities, claimed that political partisanship and religious differences did not determine the Fund's priorities, either in financing (garnering donations) or in relief (distributing monies). Much of his revealing text offers information that we can approach, however, as a strategy of representation. It outlines how the Fund was financed, provided relief, and administered the distribution of its resources, both financial and in the form of social services. While the issue of political partisanship did indeed prove unimportant, his detailed and descriptive history and reports of chapter-by-chapter activities, including those of the three cities examined here, map out the salience of other boundaries.

The national executive of the CPF was gendered from the start, as men monopolized honorary, executive, and senior administrative positions. Women assumed administrative tasks at the local level. Thus, though both sexes mapped out gendered fields, as more active agents, women gained powers through the expansion of the Fund's home visits and moral regulation initiatives. Ethnicity, too, operated to exclude non-whites from holding any office, but not from donating: strident efforts by the Fund's national executive and by local branches to applaud subscriptions received from Chinese, First Nations, and enemy alien donors revealed the presence rather than the absence of such barriers. As noted below, the manner in which such contributions were represented, both in Morris's report and in local newspaper accounts, demonstrated how boundaries of gender, class, and ethnicity could be invoked by the Fund and by the journalistic discourse that accompanied its activities in Lethbridge, Guelph, and Trois-Rivières.

The CPF ultimately failed to meet many of the needs so stridently addressed at the war's onset, particularly the maintenance needs of poorer families. The inadequacies of voluntary, charitable approaches to fill the needs of soldiers and their families were as obvious as casualty rates. By 1917, demands for state initiatives were raised, often by the veterans themselves. What we are left with in the evidence of local initiatives and national strategies shaping war relief are the anxieties of more financially secure citizens, prompting action under the guise of redress for those most in need in time of war. Through their words and actions we see efforts to redistribute wealth in order to preserve the social order as a measure for increased security on the home front after the first enlistments had left for Valcartier.

Fundraising and the Priorities of Voluntary Relief

A Canadian precedent for a patriotic fund dates to 1812, when a sum of £13,841 was raised, mainly from outside Upper Canada. Contributions assisted disabled militiamen and their families, with the balance spent on designing a commemorative medal for the War of 1812. The Crimean War prompted a fund of £46,575 in 1855-56, collected by the Receiver General of Canada and redistributed to British and French families in Europe. Canada's participation in the Boer War led to the charter of another fund in

1900, this one marking the first case in which fundraising and disbursement primarily, though not exclusively, took place within the Dominion itself. This original Canadian Patriotic Fund nonetheless replicated the pattern of prestigious patrons garnering donations in support of volunteers' families. It also set a basic pattern for entitlement, which was later used in drawing up criteria in 1914: Of first priority were widows, orphans, and other dependents of officers and men who might be killed in South Africa; second, soldiers who were disabled or wounded and their families; third, wives and children in Canada during the war; and finally, discretionary spending powers for individual cases. The voluntary tradition was maintained once again. The fund remained patriotic in stated intent, charitable in practice. Its unspent balance was later applied to British widows, orphans, and disabled veterans.

The First World War CPF pursued expanded spending priorities, its most immediate the support of poorer wives and children, those with breadwinners overseas and no other means of support. The CPF extended not only the aims of the Boer War fund, but also patterned itself after the much larger plan implemented in Britain as the National Relief Fund. From the beginning the new Fund depended, like recruitment, on exchanges administered between local action and a workable method of national coordination. The CPF's charter was designed to channel the efforts of citizen volunteers into the shared aims of fundraising and distribution, overseen by a national agency. It supported efforts at the local branch level, but did not centralize decision making in most administrative matters, nor did it stipulate uniformity in the benefits it dispensed. 'I sincerely hope,' the governor general, the Duke of Connaught, announced in his role as the Fund's honorary president, 'that in every city and town throughout the Dominion branches of this organization may be formed.' His statement, Morris points out, was reprinted in full in newspapers throughout the country. Morris also claims that this became 'the first shot fired in the campaign to stir up local action.'[6] Endorsement by Canada's head of state emphasized the fact that the CPF functioned primarily on the basis of local initiative.

The formation of the CPF in Ottawa as a body of patrons and executors was matched by decentralized, local organizational efforts to get the Fund up and running quickly. To note, as Morris does, that Connaught's appeal was 'immediately effective' by pointing to the fact that over $2 million was raised across Canada by the end of 1914, with an identical amount pledged, conceals the spatially distributed system quickly set up between municipal and county fundraising organizations and the national body that tried to support, more than coordinate, their efforts.[7] The Fund appealed to donors large and small. Its campaign drives also directly involved business interests across the country that shared concerns of cost and effectiveness in supporting soldiers' families in both urban and rural areas. The CPF's local strategy also highlighted the importance and viable appeal of civic-minded voluntarism, popularized by wartime news and driven by very real needs. Its major campaigns began in late 1914 and continued the following year, then dwindled right when the stress of recruitment on poorer families increased. In the end the CPF's methods alone proved inadequate. Demands for state-run and financed measures ultimately were converted into political action by those most affected and in need after the war – the veterans themselves.

The charter and Connaught's endorsement, of course, gave local organizers a national symbol to rally round. The installation of dignitaries and officials at the CPF's highest governing levels – from the governor general as chairman to the minister of finance, Thomas White, as honorary secretary; the philanthropist, Montreal businessman, and member of Parliament, Herbert Ames, as honorary secretary; and the dozens of local committees headed by town and city notables – itself invoked an authority structure of state sanction without government involvement or, worse, taxation. Reflecting Morris's own insistence that the business at hand was a serious one, Desmond Morton and Glenn Wright conclude that 'it was no game' for those concerned with launching the Fund. 'The alternative would be state intervention at double the cost.' While Fund officials resented branch bumbling and discrepancies that crept into disbursement amounts, and dependent families 'grumbled at Patriotic fund meddling and meanness,' Morris's own account uncovers concerns that some wealthy patrons raised over losing a potentially cheap source of domestic labour, capped by a poignant moment when one official was reported to say that 'he did not see why, when a man donned khaki, his wife should be expected to become a charwoman.'[8] Morris underscores the Fund's intent to redistribute monies, which government could not do as cheaply, and to encourage local control, while redistributing contributions from richer to poorer regions. The CPF organizational tactics, both nationally and locally, point to financially limited but publicly acclaimed efforts to stabilize class, gender, and family relations affected by recruitment and separation. Discretionary powers over home visits and patrolling the use of allowances was assigned largely to women volunteers and agencies.

In Ottawa, the Fund's national executive set a maximum scale that individual branches generally rarely reached: $30.00 per month for a wife; $7.50 for children aged ten to fifteen; $4.50 for those aged five to ten; $3.00 if under five. 'This ensured that in a city a woman with three children would have an income of at least $45 per month and in most cases would receive $60 per month, the additional $15 being provided by an assignment from her husband.'[9] Morris's examples, though, are full of inconsistencies. Allowances varied, sometimes markedly in rural areas with lower family living costs. Morris concedes 'that in the smaller towns and rural communities a reduction of at least 20 per cent [of the maximum amounts] might well be put into force. With but few exceptions the maximum scale was reduced by varying proportions, according to the views of the different local committees. That this did not develop an entirely satisfactory state of affairs will be seen later.' As Morton and Wright point out, using the same report: 'Privately, fund officials fumed at local inefficiency and the gross discrepancies that allowed an average of $24.71 a month to a Saskatchewan Soldier's family while a family on Prince Edward Island made do with $9.70.'[10] Provincial variations, sampled by Morris for May 1915 for the other provinces were: New Brunswick, $15.27; Ontario and Quebec, $16.85; Alberta, $24.00; and British Columbia, $15.27.

Skirting the obvious – that all amounts fell far below the maximum – Morris takes pains to state that maintaining provincial payout differences, allegedly tied to the cost of living (slightly below $60.00 per month based on 1913 estimates), was both justifiable and fiscally responsible. Citing the needs of 61 families in Prince Edward Island, 8,000 in Ontario and Quebec, 800 in New Brunswick, and 1,200 in British Columbia, Morris points out that to 'have adopted a uniform scale of $24, which was considered necessary in Alberta and Saskatchewan' would have eliminated 'the saving effected by the committee's policy,' which 'amounted to at least one million dollars per annum.'[11] The CPF refused to institute a uniformity principle, a system that the federal government would have found impossible to avoid. In short, the plan that business interests, professionals, and municipal leaders so often endorsed at the beginning of the war could not be understood simply through its rhetoric or its stated aims. The self-congratulatory report Morris compiled tends to bury the figures isolated here, which tell a different story.

Decentralized, voluntary fundraising and disbursement under the rubric of the 'Canadian' Patriotic Fund (any imperial reference would have been disastrous in Quebec) began with nominating and appointing local branch executives, disseminating prescriptive pamphlets prepared by the CPF in Ottawa to dependent families, and producing a barrage of local publicity to launch the first of each branch's basic functions – collecting subscriptions. Redistributing monies through local means soon became its second.

Comparing surviving evidence of branch initiatives in the cities considered here with the CPF's own version of its events helps us see these intersecting patterns: fundraising practices indicative of a philanthropic ideal modelled from a differentiated society as construed by the Fund itself; financing mechanisms styled by appeals to civic pride and supported by business interests alarmed by the spectre of wartime taxation; and finally, the use of localized procedures to patrol families dependent on the Fund. Mayors, federal and provincial legislative members, and local businesses typically struck the organizing committees of local branches and called for public support, something Morris claims contributed greatly to their success. City mayors were often contacted in areas that 'remained inactive.' Letters might also be sent from the Fund's national executive to those 'acquainted with some prominent citizen who could be relied upon to take the lead in such a movement. In other places letters were addressed to the Mayor, exhorting him, as the leading citizen, to take the first steps. Members of Parliament were reminded of their responsibility, and local newspapers were asked to use their editorial influence. Public meetings were addressed in many places by the Honorary Secretary. Sometimes immediate action was secured by bringing to the notice of the mayor of a town cases of need in his own community.'[12]

Morris claims that 'every possible means to bring about the establishment of branches was used.' Ontario was, as a result, 'practically completely' organized by the end of 1914, while in Quebec 'large portions remained unorganized.' The explanation that lower response rates in Quebec were the result of a group of nationalistic French Canadian opinion leaders actively agitating a compliant social mass below clearly underscored the CPF's sense that some basic principles of war relief had been unjustly violated. But Morris thought this had taken place through a misuse of social hierarchy, not through the very salient ambivalence to the British Empire felt across the social spectrums of age, class, and gender in French-Catholic Quebec. As Morris puts it, the 'history of the Canadian Patriotic Fund in Quebec can only be read with the most conflicting emotions.' This was a prelude to his condemnation of 'anti-war statements of a leading French-Canadian nationalist' that 'are too well known to need repeating. The effect upon the French-Canadian, living in villages and farms, and relying on instructions in world matters upon these perverted arguments was disastrous.' Of course, his tendency to stress the influence of anti-war nationalists as opinion leaders discounts the broad support their positions received, regardless of their influence, in both rural and urban areas.

In the case of Trois-Rivières, Morris also notes that, 'in fact, wherever an earnest and sincere appeal was made by leading citizens who possessed the confidence of French-Canadians, the response left little to be desired. The city of Three Rivers, almost entirely populated by people of this nationality, is an outstanding example.'[13] Trois-Rivières served as a telling example, he thought, of the best exercise of moral authority. What English Canadians might reasonably expect from French Canadians in this city was realized, thanks to its mayor, or so Morris suggests. While his notions reflect a top-down sense of power, city hall's endorsement of and financial support for the Fund was important in getting local funds going in cities across the country.

Typically, CPF branches received start-up donations from municipal officials. In Lethbridge, Mayor Hardie and City Commissioner A.M. Grace donated 10 percent of their salaries to the Fund, duly publicized, following a similar example set by members of the Alberta legislature. 'The local organization of the fund has not yet been formed,' the *Herald* reported, 'but now that there is a commencement, doubtless it will be promulgated shortly.'[14] Similarly, a $2,000 donation from Guelph's city council topped the patron list for an inaugural $15,000 campaign, which was so successful that organizers extended the drive to top the $25,000 mark by early October 1914.[15] A sum of $5,000 was granted by Trois-Rivières's city council to initiate over $30,000 raised in total, which as Morris later observed was far more, proportionally, than many rural areas in Quebec and an impressive sum for a city overwhelmingly francophone.[16] More was raised in Lethbridge, over $88,000, or about $9.80 per person; and far more in Guelph, over $252,000, with a much higher per capita of $16.80. But as bottom lines these differences need to be compared to variables ranging from disposable incomes to the particular effectiveness of specific drives, since most funds were raised during designated campaigns in late 1914 and periodically in 1915. The obvious contrast between francophone-dominated Trois-Rivières and anglophone-majority cities elsewhere cannot be overlooked. However, the Fund's relative success in Trois-Rivières stemmed from the particular mobilizing strategies of its mayor and organizing committee, and it is these that may be compared to comparable efforts in Guelph and Lethbridge.[17] We can reread accounts of the actual activation and operation of these local funds as cultural practices indicative of how local hierarchies were perceived and valorized. A discourse of civic pride also framed fundraising appeals in all urban centres once locally publicized canvassing drives got underway.

The launch and early campaign of Trois-Rivières's CPF, in fact, stands out as a case of how wartime fundraising efforts could succeed even in a city where recent events had dampened enthusiasm for solidarity with English Canada. It is difficult to gauge the effect on the CPF of the abrupt disbanding, just four months before the war, of the 86th Three Rivers Regiment, quickly followed by Regulation No. 156, discussed in Chapter 1, which certainly insulted Catholics across the province and disabled the city's ability to recruit through an existing militia.[18] This simply added to the resentment already felt over public schools, a contested domain defended by francophones in both Quebec and Ontario who were angered by the Province of Ontario's implementation of Regulation 17, which placed new restrictions on French-language schooling. Depending on the specific problem, English politicians, anglophones in Toronto and Ottawa, or Protestants throughout English Canada came under attack. It seemed that public policies shaped outside of Quebec increasingly served to undermine the preservation of Quebec's dominant language and faith tradition outside the province's constitutional jurisdiction.

These issues received detailed coverage and commentary in the *Bien Public*, the *Courrier*, and the *Nouveau Trois-Rivières*. In the context of such debates, the end of 1914 could easily be cast as a difficult period to launch any cooperation with causes connected to an imperial war effort. The war, nonetheless, brought with it imperatives that could not be ignored by the *Bien Public* or by the Roman Catholic diocese. Emphasis shifted toward endorsement of the CPF, despite the contentious issues of the recent past that were not revisited in any significant way until debates opened over conscription in 1917. The paper, and through it the diocese of Trois-Rivières, appealed for support of the city's CPF branch chapter and endorsed the philanthropy and aims of the Fund, announced both from Ottawa and from local levels throughout Canada.

Trois-Rivières's Presbyterian clergyman, the Rev. J. Aitken Clark, whose son was soon to enlist, was one of the first to air his support. Since the end of August, just four days after the CPF charter was granted, he appears to have used his influence through the *Newcomer* to begin urging fellow citizens to organize their own local fund.[19] As one editorial, probably written by Clark himself, stated: Although only 'a small percentage' could 'actually bear arms' in the present 'life and death struggle for existence,' there remained open 'many other channels through which we may show our loyalty. Perhaps the most practical of these, is the movement begun so successfully, under the name of the Patriotic Fund, for the support of those who through the war have lost their means of support. There would seem to be no reason why a similar movement should not be begun locally; indeed many of our citizens are anxious for just such a chance.'[20] He called for a town meeting to discuss the Fund.

The Fund's local campaign began with a public meeting at Trois-Rivières's city hall as the war entered its sixth week. Mayor Tessier and Reverend Clark joined in an act of shared civic duty to launch the Trois-Rivières fund, as they put it, for the good of all – both French- and English-speaking – citizens. As joint advocates of the aims of the CPF, they affirmed that contributions to this cause were imperative and worthy. Along with other organizers, Tessier and Clark took part in a public event comparable in form to those held in cities and towns across the country. Speeches, resolutions, and the naming of local branch officials took place. Speakers called upon donors, particularly local businesses, to contribute and also asked for volunteer workers sympathetic to the needs of soldiers' families. As well as Tessier and Clark, local MP Jacques Bureau and L.P. Normand, a prominent physician and active local volunteer, addressed the gathering. Each of the speakers referred to the patriotic ideal expressed through charitable donation as something that tied together local communities across the country.[21]

The *Newcomer* described the affair as 'a success in every way' that clearly met its basic aims. As its chair, Tessier delivered what translated simply as 'a strong patriotic speech in French.' Tessier vowed to join his council in voting for a municipal contribution, a move he hoped 'would be loyally supported

8 Military exercises for youths continued after the war. Here students from the De La Salle Academy, staffed by les Frères des Ecoles chrétiennes, are shown in parade formation in June, 1919. The school principal, René Raguin, served as the first secretary-treasurer of Trois-Rivières's branch of the Canadian Patriotic Fund. *Courtesy of Archives du Séminaire de Trois-Rivières, FN-0632*

by the citizens.' Clark 'in English explained the object of the meeting, and thereafter office-bearers and a Committee were appointed with power to add to their number.'[22] René Raguin, principal of Trois-Rivières's De La Salle Academy, agreed to administer the fund as local secretary-treasurer. At the outbreak of the war, Raguin had been vacationing with his family in Switzerland, and the *Newcomer* expressed concern that they might not make it back before the school reopened.[23] Now, safely back from what was described in overblown terms as Europe's veritable 'seat of war,' Raguin 'gave a very stirring account of his experience in French, and made a strong appeal, to support the Fund and make it a success.'[24] Soon active with its first canvass in October 1914, Mayor Tessier served throughout the branch's wartime activities as president. Alexander Houliston, a leading developer, served as vice-president, with Raguin assuming the task of secretary-treasurer, the key administrative post, though he was eventually succeeded by a future Liberal politician, L.G. Balcer. They raised a total of $30,460.64 and dispersed $18,314.80, with the balance dedicated to deficits elsewhere.[25] The amount ultimately raised and redistributed, and the continued coverage CPF activities received in both the *Newcomer* and the more widely circulating francophone papers, consistently indicate a fund that performed very well for an urban setting dominated by francophones.

In sequence, and in form, CPF branches followed much the same pattern throughout the country. 'All over this broad Dominion,' as the *Mercury* put it in grandiloquent terms, 'cities, towns and counties are meeting under the auspices of the Canadian Patriotic Society to devise means for raising funds to care for those dependent on the brave fellows who are defending us who stay at home, so long as the war lasts.'[26] Member of Parliament Hugh Guthrie addressed a public gathering, described in the *Mercury* as an enthusiastic 'mass meeting' held on a Friday evening in late September at the city hall. In his address, Guthrie urged that something be done 'here in the city of Guelph.' Our citizens 'owe much to Great Britain,' he declared, invoking characteristic imperial-nationalistic rhetoric. 'There is no statesman in England at the present time who doubts the value of the colonies, and no colonial who doubts the value of the connection with Great Britain.'[27] Apart from reference to the imperial tie, Guthrie's speech simply echoed the dogmatic formalism politicians from all levels of government used at such moments. He stated simply that it was the 'duty of Canadians to look after the families of those who have gone to the front to fight for them,' a basic humanitarian appeal that could, in different settings, garner the broadest sweep of donations from across the country.[28]

Morris's chronicle notes that Guelph became 'one of the few branches of which the officials have remained unchanged until the present time, J.M. Taylor, L. Goldie, and C.L. Dunbar having held the respective offices of president, treasurer, and secretary continuously. The success of the Fund at Guelph may be said to be due almost entirely to the efforts and ability of these three gentlemen.'[29] Considerable help by volunteer workers and successful drives resulted, but his allusion to their status as 'gentlemen' and their local authority is indicative of the deference constructed by the Fund to legitimize its efforts. By the time Morris wrote his report in 1919, over $252,000 had been subscribed in Guelph, with at least $160,000 dispersed to some 465 soldiers' families.

Lethbridge's organizational efforts moved toward branch status in mid-October, when Lieutenant-Colonel Stewart, in his capacity as a member of the Alberta legislature, asked Commissioner A.M. Grace to put together an organizing committee. By that afternoon the city's public works commissioner had named a group, including Board of Trade president G.R. Marnoch, and Lethbridge's member of Parliament, Herald Publishing owner William A. Buchanan.[30] Stewart assumed the chapter's presidency, while the committee chose L.M. Johnstone, a Lethbridge lawyer, as vice-president, and the omnifarious organizer J.D. Higinbotham as honorary treasurer. Although it was not clear why Higinbotham eventually passed this particular task on, most branches had to replace executive volunteers at some point during the war. Army service overseas took two in this case. Stewart left and was promoted to the rank of brigadier general in Canada's 3rd Division, the highest rank attained by anyone from Alberta. Johnstone joined the 113th Highlanders. Donations for the Lethbridge branch reached $88,000. This was just over half of the amount disbursed ($167,639) to help meet the needs of an inordinately high number of enlistments from the city.

Again, the launch of the fund was framed to present civilian endorsement through civic alliances based on government, merchant, and professional representation. Members of Parliament joined mayors and local businessmen, so crucial to the success of the Fund, as Morris often suggests in his report. Orations drew from narratives of immediate expedience, from MP Hugh Guthrie's endorsement of the Empire in Guelph to the appeal Tessier, Raguin, and Clark made for a 'united' effort in Trois-Rivières. Equally important in interpreting these events, however, is the attention given to their launching ceremonies and many reports for newspaper readers detailing staged, hierarchical displays and collection drives that ultimately signified a corresponding defence of social cohesion.

This was indicated in door-to-door canvasses. Volunteer workers came forward, and though our reports do not give clear breakdowns of gender balances, it appears that more men than women were active in these particular drives. Staged as civic contests, they pitted one town or city's campaign against another. Municipalities across Canada adopted the strategy of dividing their respective cities into neighbourhood districts, covered door-to-door by canvassing teams directed by 'district captains.' Trois-Rivières's Liberal journal, the *Nouveau Trois-Rivières*, entreated its readers to display 'notre patriotisme' in its description of the first major canvass. The city was divided into quarters and a captain and lieutenants were assigned to each neighbourhood to solicit contributions.[31] The funds and moral support that they received proved that Trois-Rivières was as patriotric a town as any: '[les dons] que nous avons déjà reçues aussi bien que l'appui moral qui ne nous fait pas défaut nous prouve qu'à Trois-Rivières on est aussi patriote que n'importe où.' Moreover, the *Nouveau Trois-Rivières* reported that 'le patriotisme aux Trois-Rivières est aussi vivace que partout ailleur ... notre petite population comparée à tant d'autres villes, a su trouver une aide au Fonds Patriotiques, en prélevant chez nous une somme dans les quinze mille dollars.'[32] Citizens were asked to give willingly. When a canvasser arrives at your door, the report implored, 'donnez-la de bon coeur.'[33] Subscriptions raised at this point indicate the kind of successful strategy that for this city produced a surplus of donations over disbursements, compared to many hinterland areas where, as Morris lamented, donations were 'practically negligible.'[34]

In descriptions of CPF campaigns, this paper's readership, primarily francophone Liberals, encountered references to 'patriotism,' a term the

Bien Public also attached to the Fund's activities when it proclaimed that all nationalities, English, French, Irish, and Scottish, had joined to fight 'sous les drapeaux britanniques pour le soutien d'une cause juste et le triomphe de la civilisation actuellement menacée.' The *Bien Public* insisted that donors, whether rich or poor, ought to give in amounts worthy 'de notre générosité et de notre patriotisme.'[35] Again an unclarified use of the term 'patriotisme' appears, one perhaps indicative of French Canada's loyalty to Canada alone. As the local CPF campaign continued, editions of the *Bien Public* featured donor lists, which appear, from the local prominence of many of the contributors, to have been intended to demonstrate support by conspicuous example in a city where broad enthusiasm and donations for wartime causes could not compare to those displayed in our other locales.

In Guelph, preparation for a three-day campaign, with a $15,000 target, began with a meeting at a local restaurant of the 'team committees' that would soon be working their respective 'subdivisions.' The city was divided into twenty-two such districts, to be covered by six- to eight-member canvassing squads. A 'team captain' directed campaigns in each district – tallied the donations, recorded the names and amounts if permission to publish had been given, and otherwise administered the door-to-door canvasses within the district and thus across the city's diverse neighbourhoods. This system was identical to the one in Trois-Rivières. Local firms, which likely shared in the civic pride the campaign inspired, covered incidental expenses. In the process they received recognition by name in the *Mercury*, which even noted the participation of its rival, the Guelph *Herald*. One report itemized the following: the Herald Publishing Co. donated office space; the Guelph Light and Power Co., electricity; free telephone connections were offered by the Bell Telephone Co.; and Hoover and Walker, a local furniture dealer, supplied office equipment. All stationery came with the compliments of the Merchant Bank, and several citizens provided the necessary motor cars. To top it off, the Kandy Kitchen, where the team captains coordinated their three-day blitz, prepared meals.[36]

As the *Mercury* described it, the people of Guelph were 'putting their patriotism in concrete form.' This particular door-to-door strategy solicited subscribers in a drive that collected over $25,000, exceeding the original target by $10,000. This relatively high total led to a decision to extend the canvass. Like other drives of this sort, the Guelph campaign indicated a style of organization, and interactions between canvassers and donors, that can be read as a dynamic engagement of local hierarchies. From the officials appointed at the inception of the Fund to the donations received from larger donors, individuals, businesses, and groups, which often had their names printed in the local paper, such drives served to reinforce an integrated, stratified, and stable model of local community. The same pattern was replicated elsewhere. Funds were tabulated, donors acknowledged, and the 'great success' of many affairs duly broadcast. Fundraising in this way operated within frameworks specific to local settings and local donors, whether individuals or groups – all of whom were loosely assembled under the umbrella of the CPF's office in Ottawa.

Local initiatives were key, as was the face-to-face contact of everyone involved. Reports of such campaigns were often constructed to convey a sense of intense activity, of immediacy, and of individual personalities playing roles. Local action was the driving force, but it remained rooted in broader aims and motivations. While the Kandy Kitchen was 'well filled at noon' with volunteers active on the first day of the campaign, 'when the captains and members of the teams raising the $15,000 in Guelph met to make reports, and encourage each other in the good work they have undertaken,' the focus of their efforts represented local expressions of civic pride, wartime idealism, and voluntarism as a preferred alternative to state intervention.[37]

The interplay of ethnic boundaries also was important in demarcating relationships of difference and stratified distances that Fund organizers themselves worked to create. This is evident both in Morris's report at the end of the war and in the Guelph and Lethbridge canvasses respectively. We might consider this, first, by examining, verbatim, how Morris depicts the contributions of ethnic minorities. This passage casts them amongst a collage of donors, beginning with a particularly large one, a fire insurance company able to dispose of $50,000. From here, Morris proceeds to name individuals and groups. He fashions an impression of the inclusive range of donors that, by identifying them through their social differences, invokes the presence of those very differences. He applauds action taken by specific individuals by region, occupational status, age, wealth, and ethnicity:

> 'Fight or Pay' were the alternatives offered to Canadians during the war. That those who contracted to fight and redeemed their pledge other records than this have told. That those, who by force of circumstance, were obliged to remain at home enthusiastically accepted the obligation of paying is evidenced in these pages. That it was not without sacrifice that many paid can be proven by merely a few instances out of many. In one year a certain fire insurance company in Ontario, at the general meeting of its shareholders, voted the entire profits of the year, $50,000, to the Fund. An old lighthouse keeper near Vancouver, by the cultivation of flowers which he sold to passing tourists, contributed more than $1,000 toward the work. The fisherman of Gaspé, the lumberjack of the Quebec woods, the cheesemakers of Ontario, all gave a share of earnings or profits. Throughout many parts of the west, the farmers set aside a patriotic acre and devoted the proceeds to the work. The North American Indians on the several reserves contributed some thousands of dollars. From Doukhobors and Mennonites, on principle opposed to war, subscriptions were nevertheless received. A gift of $20

> came from the Eskimo of Chikchagolook of Herschel Island within the Arctic Circle. A most touching instance of self-sacrifice was found in Nova Scotia where, following a meeting addressed by Sir Herbert Ames, that aged parents of a soldier gave to the Fund the money they had been saving for a trip to Halifax to say good-bye to their boy, perhaps for ever![38]

As a strategy of representation, Morris depicted diversity in donor sources as a sign of uniform appeal, something echoed in accounts that appeared in both the Guelph and Lethbridge dailies. Insurance company stockholders, fishermen, farmers, and many others, mostly men, from across a varied social spectrum appear in this account. Morris describes them as if they were interrupted in their ordinary daily affairs, knew their duty, and dug deep in their pockets for the cause; everyone, it seemed in his account, stood united in giving to 'the work.' Facile depictions of 'North American Indians' from 'the several' reserves are presented in the array of differences. What Doukhobors and Mennonites gave was highlighted against what they were said to believe. Barriers supposedly transcended through donation were made visible by naming groups and acts of giving: shareholders voted; an old lighthouse keeper contributed, joining fishermen, lumberjacks, and cheesemakers, who from the Pacific shore to the Quebec woods 'all gave.' From the Eskimo of Chikchagolook, 'a gift.' 'The most touching instance of self-sacrifice' closes this passage, a moment said to have followed an address by the Fund's honorary secretary, Sir Herbert Ames, the Montreal MP and philanthropist, whose study of poverty in Montreal had appeared as *The City below the Hill* (1897).[39]

Giving to the Fund, as presented here, framed a model for wartime philanthropy drawn from approaches so often rehearsed in the previous century. The record Morris prepared shortly after the war not only commemorated the Fund's many patrons and volunteers, but in so doing it also portrayed how they saw themselves. It was a system idealized by its promoters, which came embedded in a view of a world of self-evident differences marked by positioned hierarchies: patriarchal, class-based, and ethnocentric. Morris privileged the intentions and roles of white Canadian citizens, English or French speaking, provided that the latter saw the virtue of winning the war. He described war relief as a masculine project, authorized and directed by men and yet applied to soldiers' families who received aid from women in social service roles. Though Morris may have intended to foreground an inclusive range of Fund subscribers, his narrative underscored a hierarchical representation of the CPF.

The Guelph *Mercury* and Lethbridge *Herald* adopted corresponding strategies in depicting ethnic differences among donors. To take us back to Guelph's Kandy Kitchen campaign, round after round of applause greeted announcements of major donations received throughout the city. But one of the smallest corporate donations drew the largest cheer. 'Perhaps the one that appealed most to the assembly,' one *Mercury* dispatch concluded, 'was the amount, some $68, given by the men at the Standard White Lime Co., most of whom are Germans and Italians.'[40] Although non-naturalized Italians were at this time considered neutralists, and would become allies in 1915, the special welcome for this donation from Germans highlighted recognition of minorities soon to be suspected of divided loyalties. This, and the applause their act of giving received, accentuated awareness, however positive, of ethnic difference. The *Mercury*'s coverage reinforced a prescribed view for readers of the Fund's supposedly unifying effects. The special appeal this donation was to have had for those gathered at the Kandy Kitchen that afternoon perhaps marked a brief moment of recognition that sharing in the war effort took place within a society confronting, with ambivalence that would soon turn to suspicion, the presence of enemy aliens. A donation of $1,800 from Lethbridge coal miners, some of whom were enemy aliens, about to be dismissed summarily for 'patriotic' reasons, drew a reference to a demonstration of loyalty that would otherwise have been invisible to many readers. 'The committee is delighted,' the *Herald* reported during its first major canvass, 'not only at the total of the subscription, but also because of the loyalty displayed by the men, many of whom are of foreign birth.'[41]

In Lethbridge, the tribal chiefs of southern Alberta's Blood Nation offered $1,000 'to be used by the empire for whatever purpose it was thought necessary.' In a special 'council of war,' as the *Herald* constructed its report, the outbreak of fighting in Europe was 'fully discussed' by the chiefs and a 'resolution of loyalty to the empire was passed.'[42] Lethbridge's Chinese minority, which stood at 106 men and 2 women in the 1911 census, was noted for its donation to the local CPF and Red Cross branches both individually and through the Chinese National League.[43] Again, contributions from ethnic minorities were highlighted to invoke the presence of difference behind the fictional inclusiveness the Fund was said to foster. Texts like these furnished signs pointing to how strategies of representing a national program intersected with imagined social geographies. Ordinary daily journalism often enhanced stereotypes of war relief campaign enthusiasm and ethnic difference. In the Lethbridge case, simplistic depictions of First Nations living on the Blood reserve outside the city limits, enemy alien coal miners living in company housing near the Oldman River, or Chinese men living in yet another segregated district near the downtown core each became ready figments. All, it seemed, were drawn into the patriotic fundraising drive according to the Fund's imagined kaleidoscope of social cohesion. Fundraising drives, especially, valorized this consensus-based, multicultural image of inclusive contributing.

As a door-to-door canvass throughout the city, Lethbridge's first CPF drive compared closely to Guelph's, though it took place two months later and was combined with a drive for the city's Red Cross branch. At the same time that Commissioner Grace named the CPF steering committee, Mayor Hardie 'called a meeting of about 60 representative members of the various clubs, unions and societies in the city for the purpose of organizing a local branch of the Canadian Red Cross Society.'[44] The Lethbridge Board of Trade reported at the end of 1914: 'It is fitting to mention that our citizens have contributed to the National Patriotic Fund and the Red Cross Fund $10,640.00 in money, besides contributions of supplies and articles knitted and sewn by the women of the city and district, as well as a carload of flour, supplies, and articles of clothing despatched with commendable promptitude for the relief of our Belgian Allies.'[45]

As a joint fundraising effort, Lethbridge's first canvass can easily be compared to Guelph's in terms of its basic organization: the city was divided into seventeen districts, each served by a canvassing squad directed by a district captain. Details for this arrangement were worked out at a combined CPF-Red Cross meeting held in late November 1914. 'The joint committee,' the *Herald* reported, 'has made a comprehensive survey of the city, so that every nook and corner will be covered in the effort to raise money for these splendid causes, and everyone will be offered the opportunity of contributing something that will help in the Empire's struggle.'[46] A single call then was made to residents from a CPF-Red Cross representative in a drive that began later than most others in Canada and that had elected to pool canvassing resources for the two funds. Prospective donors were free to choose their fund. 'When no designation is made, the contribution will be divided between the two.'[47] Lethbridge's combined canvassing efforts seemed practical, as disposable incomes were much lower than those in many parts of central Canada and certainly lower than Guelph's, with a CPF per capita donation total that came out 50 percent higher.

As a fundraising event, certain contexts for social interaction appeared comparable. Lethbridge had its own version of Guelph's 'captain's lunches.' According to the *Herald*: 'At noon today the captains of the campaign had lunch together at the Hudson's Bay and reported the progress they had made in the first day's canvass. Lunch will be taken tomorrow and Friday at the same place.'[48] Fundraising campaigns, in particular, offered participants the things that became important for organized war supporters in general: a chance to socialize, signify their importance, and demonstrate a willingness to contribute. As sites that privileged strategies of social differentiation, expressed through forms of middle-class signification, clubs and associations could be used by groups of local citizens to promote a cause and garner associated publicity. The gestures of goodwill, solicitation, and donation members made may, in fact, have been intended to deflect any criticism of self-indulgence and detachment amid the great trial the war had so obviously become. The Lethbridge Tennis Club, for instance, readily admitted that it had 'done nothing yet in a patriotic way' and that the time had come for 'all members and friends of the club to especially exert themselves' in support of the venture.[49] Their fundraiser slogan, 'Fight or Play,' was even worse than the 'Fight or Pay' motto attributed to Ames. Their mixed-doubles tournament pledged entry fees to the CPF, but more to the point, the club made sure, or someone at the *Herald* made sure a year into the war, that people read about it.

Journalistic styles associated with tag-on reports of local groups contributing to specific causes were very similar to Morris's overall depiction of Canadian peoples from all walks of life doing their bit for the Fund. The point was not to speak about the Fund in terms of its cost-saving strategies; its self-celebrating use of hierarchical signification; its broad, discretionary powers in determining entitlements, which many who had to deal with the Fund directly knew all too well. The point was to tell a story through stories, a narrative about a whole country coming together despite its great diversities to contribute to a noble aim that stood with families behind the lines in Canada. Morris's melodrama of fishermen and lumberjacks, of lighthouse keepers and aged parents all joined in dropping their pennies in the same pot that huge patrons had the foresight to put before them, was a part of a larger script. It was part of a story compiled just after the war ended, and it could have been lifted from the pages of city dailies across Canada, which themselves profited from reporting the practice of fundraising as a great collaboration of rich and poor; young and old; Chinese, Indian, Doukhobor, Mennonite, Italian, or German; women and men from all regions in the country and from all parts of town. One Lethbridge resident, said to have attended a rally at which Ames spoke, was so overwhelmed with a desire to contribute that he went home to procure his most precious possession, a specially bred, prizewinning bulldog, and presented it to the city's CPF committee. 'It was the only thing he had to offer,' the *Herald* reported, 'and he was determined to make his sacrifice, though it meant much to him.'[50] Testimonies upon testimonies were fashioned in the *Herald* and the other papers of Lethbridge and Guelph, and embedded in their appearance was some great revival of will and moral fortitude. While donor lists turned up in each of Trois-Rivières's papers, the gushing style of reporting them was absent.

The *Herald* claimed that Lethbridge schoolteachers' decision to donate 5 percent of their small salaries each month was being considered by teachers and other professional associations across the country. Once such an example was set, the Fund's great proselytizer, the city daily, could apply pressure for others to follow. 'It is understood,' the *Herald* added, 'that teachers throughout the entire inspectorate are considering similar action, and the patriotic fund will benefit greatly thereby.'[51] Of course, most individual donations were small, but as Morris's report later emphasized, the voluntary, self-taxing and, more importantly, self-policing form of relief that poorer families of the men overseas received was a bargain, perhaps half the cost of a uniform rate as the 1919 report put it. During the war, an emphasis was placed on the diversity of the sources of donations – from the police and fire department in Trois-Rivières, which donated $30, to the most modest citizen willing to dig deep – which was presented by local papers as proof that civilians from all walks of life were doing their bit in a great, unifying crusade at home.[52]

During a comparatively large $60,000 CPF campaign staged in Guelph in January 1916, three city residents donated property lots. The three land parcels, located 'in various parts of the city,' were 'turned in to the Patriotic committee with instructions to sell tickets for them, and have a drawing.' Entrepreneurial schemes of all sorts were usually celebrated as signs of local or individual ingenuity. The posture of civic pride such accounts assumed, erased signs of messiness or dissent in the actual job of coordinating subscription drives. 'Selling was brisk,' as the *Mercury* put it, 'and in a short time it was announced that ten gentlemen present had taken ten tickets each, at one dollar per.'[53] The overall campaign for the city was also said to have exceeded its target by $27,000. Although murmurs of infighting crept into its coverage, the *Mercury* matched this with the notion of the Fund's stubborn determination: yes, the Guelph branch had 'growing pains,' but 'it simply refuses to shrivel up and keep small.'[54]

Like the newspapers, Morris did not cast the locally-based fundraising of the CPF across Canada as a great difficulty. The Fund's voluntary strategy championed how much was raised through charitable efforts, making sure to replace the stigma of charity with the dignity of relief – but it was charity nonetheless. On that basis, its economy, its ability to distribute selectively with the lowest possible 'waste' spent on 'undeserving' recipients, and its preference to government measures were also proudly recounted as part of the achievements of the Fund as a national coordinator of local branches. On the Fund's overall financing, Morris stressed the positive: 'The raising of money was rendered a comparatively easy task by the willingness of the people to subscribe. Its distribution for the most part was governed by very simple considerations, and, in any event, it is fair to presume that the dependents would have received adequate financial assistance from the Government had the Fund not been created.'[55] That it did operate, however, stayed that necessity until the war taxes were brought in. The tendency to applaud all who financed the Fund, donors large and small, supported this self-congratulating narrative. The 'willingness of the people' throughout the country to give so that the government did not have to take had become a defining priority. So had the desire to maintain the social hierarchies that preceded the war. That aim, however, led to the policing of the

Fund's benefits distribution system, administered through the gendered and conservative gaze of home front charity.

Patrolling Morality, Guiding the Poor Homemaker: The CPF's 'Third Responsibility'

While men dominated the ranks of CPF branch presidents, secretaries, and treasurers, women dealt most often with the day-to-day affairs of dispensing advice, writing pamphlet material, and visiting every home that received aid. This 'third responsibility,' as designated by the Fund, involved middle-class women with volunteers policing the disbursements of relief. Their home visits and caseload administration reflected the social workers' prerogative, which was influenced by both their class and gender. Highlights of many branch operations throughout Morris's report underscored the varied roles middle-class women fashioned as they supervised how poorer soldiers' wives budgeted their overall monthly incomes, amounts that combined CPF disbursements per family with separation allowances received from husbands in the military.

The monies administered by women volunteers with the CPF often came with dispensing advice concerning its expenditure. They also patrolled the 'moral' behaviour of mothers. As Morris put it, this

> entailed a large measure of personal service. It gave local representatives an opportunity to act, while so many were merely talking. It gave them a chance to teach, while so many were only willing to preach. It enabled them to rectify and ameliorate while others could only criticize and deplore. If the Fund had not voluntarily assumed this responsibility, if the local officials had not readily and freely placed themselves at the service of soldiers' dependents, the condition of many families would have been pitiable indeed.[56]

Morris's view of volunteers given the 'chance to teach,' to 'rectify,' and to 'ameliorate' the conditions of recipient families, many of which 'would have been pitiable indeed,' shows us how the CPF explained the powers that flowed from its class positions. The Fund's conservative functions and its procedures applied to recipients in thousands of home visits across the country.

In gendered and class-based encounters, middle-class women visited the homes of working-class women. Many CPF volunteers belonged to the IODE, the Red Cross, and other women's associations involved with war relief. Their administrative patrols were local and therefore varied considerably with setting and circumstance. The gaps between caseworker and recipients were widest in the poorest urban areas. 'Nowhere was the opportunity for social service more eagerly and profitably seized than in Montreal,' Morris notes:

> In that city several hundred ladies were organized into a volunteer army of social service workers under the leadership of Miss Helen Reid, and these workers regularly visited every family that was in receipt of financial assistance from the Fund. One of their chief endeavours was the prevention of infant mortality which, in Montreal, during the war, reached the heavy rate of 182 per thousand. Miss Reid and her colleagues held the theory that the children of men who were willing to fight for the State were worth saving for the State. To this end there were compiled complete lists of health resources in each district including doctors, nurses, hospitals, dispensaries, milk stations, etc., and with these lists each visitor made herself thoroughly conversant. Every two months, circular letters were addressed to District Heads suggesting means of prevention, the points to be observed when visiting together with constructive plans for improving the home and health conditions. All reports as to dark rooms, improper sanitation and building conditions were forwarded to City Hall and to landlords. For two summers health demonstrations were given in most districts by doctors and nurses co-operating with the Fund. Few monthly cheques were sent to the women unaccompanied by an educational leaflet, and many of these were on health subjects such as care of the baby, milk, flies, infantile paralysis, food, teeth, adenoids, and eyes. Special maternity benefits were given, both of goods and money, and illegitimacy itself was not a bar to service.[57]

In exchange for their monthly CPF allowance, recipients were subject to assessments of housing, nutrition, and child care, made by Miss Reid's volunteer army in the form of reports to municipal authorities. It is not clear how tightly poverty could be policed, but prescriptive leaflets and, for two summers, invitations to certain demonstrations by doctors and nurses 'co-operating with the Fund' were also part of the exchange.

Women on relief who had relationships with men other than their husbands posed a special problem. Morris claims that the Fund still supported them, but efforts made to eliminate 'immoral' relations from the Fund's caseloads could be far-reaching. The statement that 'illegitimacy itself was not a bar to service' requires a closer look. In several cases Morris cites, he notes the 'troubles and anxieties of local relief committees were not inconsiderably increased by the behaviour and attitude of a very small proportion of soldiers' dependents.' A woman's children could be removed as a 'punishment' until she agreed to the Fund's conditions to break off relationships with other men. A subsequent problem arose when the husband returned. Such cases, as Morris put it,

> proved a particularly difficult problem when she had children dependent upon her. To visit the sins of the parent upon the children was no part of the Fund's policy. No matter how much the woman may have erred, the

> Fund's duty to the soldier required that it look after the children. Not infrequently they entailed the separation of the mother from the children and the placing of the latter under the protection of some society. It is rarely, however, that the Fund dropped its interest at this point. Generally the separation from her children proved a sore punishment to the woman and the chance of a reunion seldom failed to act as a spur toward better things. Whatever a local committee could do to assist such a woman to regain her footing, to break away from old influences, was gladly done. Many women, especially those who had escaped the most unfortunate consequences of their indiscretion, were enabled with the Fund's assistance to rehabilitate themselves, while in cases in which the husband became aware of the state of affairs, the Fund has not infrequently induced him to take a tolerant view.[58]

The Fund's policing of 'moral' behaviour, however, is not at issue here as much as the gendered and class bases from which its committees and home visit volunteers operated. Middle-class women fashioned individual roles and interacted in very different local settings and family circumstances while serving their respective recipients. Whether they were dealing with returned soldiers and 'disgraced' wives, dispensing advice on managing the family budget, or insisting that premiums be maintained on a husband's insurance policy, encounters between the CPF volunteer and her cases were informed by a sense of hierarchy and social order held by both parties.

As the volunteers crossed thresholds of privacy they produced reports that offer windows on their perspectives, but it is difficult to know with any precision how recipients responded. In terms of examining the values and ideals of the former, much of what does survive indicates an established reliance on bureaucratic systems, professional expertise, gendered role prescriptions, and class strategies. Each could be used by caseworkers as tools or motivating ideals. The women's efforts, determined largely on the basis of local conditions, had to be negotiated with individual wives and mothers. With far fewer soldiers, Trois-Rivières's branch handled only a fraction of the cases of Guelph's or Lethbridge's, and there is no mention of women in Morris's description of its activities. This probably reflected omissions in the branch report Morris received from Trois-Rivières. Administration duties, in fact, usually fell on women, which reflected how the CPF began as a masculine enterprise in principle and was transformed by women into maternal expressions of class and power.

In Lethbridge, Mrs. Frank Colpman (who is never identified by her given name) appeared as the only regular volunteer in a particularly busy branch. Married to a successful local merchant, one of two brothers who set up several businesses after arriving with the railway in 1885, Colpman is described by Morris as a local secretary. He adds, 'Perhaps the bulk of the work ... fell upon [her].' For this reason, she took on a special position, not found in other branches: 'Dependent's Secretary.' Her caseload of 450 families (see also Chapter 6) was obviously a full-time commitment. She worked with members of the Galt IODE, who helped her carry out family visits.[59]

In Guelph, Morris noted the branch 'perceived the value of the Ladies' Auxiliary.' Their list of duties, 'visiting families, investigating applications and giving to the beneficiaries the advice that was so often needed,' indicates the scale of CPF philanthropy. It also suggests the perspective of class. Morris congratulated the Guelph Ladies' Auxiliary president, P. Savage, who reportedly took the Fund's advice and made arrangements for coal. The fuel shipment served as a supplement in kind, to be delivered to soldiers' dependents in the second and third winters of the war. No mention is made of how grateful recipients were for this, or if they were consulted on how any extra funds might be spent.[60]

The circumstances of recipients, the wives and children of men overseas, who lived on army allowances and CPF relief, posed no threat to the social order. Their husbands comprised a small minority of soldiers at the beginning, but it was a group that expanded proportionally with the war, and eventually the families' needs could no longer be met by charity alone. The CPF saw assisting them, however, as more than a duty; it was a step taken as well to avoid the encroachment of the government and the potential that that would bring even greater burdens to businesses and income earners. Again, this reflected the perspectives of class.

From Voluntary Strategies to State Procedures

The waves of civilian voluntarism associated with the early war may have sustained the kind of approach Colpman executed, but barely so. The Fund's displacement by direct taxation paralleled the state's increased role over the duration of the war. Shifts from voluntary efforts to state control became a significant part of the war's social and economic impact, whether it was the shift from recruitment to conscription or veterans' struggles for increased federal re-establishment programs. Even at the beginning of the war, voluntarism might appear, in certain projects, to be completely out of step with need. For instance, the desire of local donors to supply machine guns was something that the military and federal government acknowledged, but discouraged. Ottawa suggested that money and local war relief efforts be redirected to the CPF, some alternative war relief effort, or to the Military Hospitals Commission. Raising money for guns may have given donors a sense of connection to the real fighting, but it was not a useful one from the army's point of view. A closer look at local involvement in machine-gun funds shows that it is not as interesting to consider the significant and obvious gaps between voluntary efforts and actual needs as it is to contemplate how stridently they could be sustained – how home front civilians could become fixated on doing something for the war to maintain their own sense of relevance, not necessarily to do something tangibly needed or requested by recipients.

Sparked by a series of press reports that stressed a scarcity of machine guns in Canadian battalions, this particular movement crested in the summer of 1915. Donations topped $1.2 million, which we might compare to the $47 million collected by the CPF up to the end of the war. Students and faculty at the Ontario Agricultural College in Guelph raised money for one such machine-gun fund. A preponderance of men donated to this particular fund, though the IODE occasionally raised monies for it as well. Donors regularly forwarded subscriptions to the Receiver General, to be placed at the discretion of the Department of Militia and Defence, and Ottawa faced what one official called the 'embarrassing rapidity' with which donations accumulated. Finally the department decided to 'stem the tide' in early August 1915. A communiqué issued by the department stated that while the 'Department does not wish to influence citizens upon the subject of their donations ... large numbers of guns' have already been ordered, 'most of which cannot be delivered for some time yet.'[61] Nonetheless, faculty and students at Guelph's agricultural college organized a fundraising drive the following month and promptly collected and forwarded $2,500.[62]

Polite refusals continued, even after the militia department's news release. 'Sir Robert Borden has asked me to supplement a letter which he wrote to you,' Maj.-Gen. W.G. Gwatkin, then chief of the general staff, stated in a letter to an IODE Regent from Hamilton. 'I venture to suggest,' Gwatkin urged, 'that instead of saving the Government the price of a machine-gun and waiting indefinitely until it is ready for presentation, you should offer ... the $1,000 which you and your Chapter have collected' to the CPF or the Military Hospitals Commission.[63] As late as November 1915, Ottawa was still issuing press statements to dissuade this particular form of voluntarism.[64]

Apart from voluntary subscriptions for machine guns, Ottawa stood aside and let war relief as a form of organized patriotism, from the CPF to direct donations to the military, run its course, fuelled by its own momentum as Canadian Expeditionary Force regiments trained and shipped out while even darker news of the war circulated. As the fighting escalated, municipal officials and auxiliary aid volunteers gradually perceived limits to their respective resources, and demands grew for organized patriotism to become state-directed. The machine-gun fund was handled differently because it interfered with war materiel procurement, something that required more unified command. Meanwhile, as towns and cities continued to collect CPF subscriptions, and as the costs of war relief climbed, some questioned the relevance of the many war relief causes that had attracted so much attention at the beginning of the war.

As noted at the opening of this chapter, given the many stresses caused by the war's escalation there was no single source for the anxieties and fears growing in cities and towns as ordinary civilians pondered what they should be doing. Signs could crop up anywhere, at points intersecting with other flows of information, local crises, or compelling projects. Two years of war, nonetheless, had shattered many illusions. A somewhat out-of-character letter appeared in the *Newcomer* in July 1916 above the pseudonym 'Common Sense.' It began as just a remark, but the peevishness of the newssheet scribe seemed to spill over into genuine anger. Common Sense described a work gang that had been 'busy picking out and replacing the mortar between the stones on the jail fence.' What ordinarily might be endorsed as a sign of civic pride had become a 'sample of wasted money in War Times.' There was 'absolutely no excuse for this waste at home when thousands are starving in Europe, and at home the Government is asking the people to save all they can: then they set an example of this kind.' Then a more radical shift: 'The writer for one,' Common Sense announced, 'is done with subscribing to the many Funds now being circulated. Why should we deprive ourselves while others are busy spending our money for things that are not necessary?'[65] We cannot be sure, but the writer may have been the Rev. J.A. Clark himself, who had stood less than two years before with Mayor Tessier and others to support the establishment of the Trois-Rivières branch of the CPF. At this point, for Common Sense, government and voluntary approaches stood equally condemned.

Many municipalities, however, were already sharing the financial burden of war relief with private donors. A measure of the increased costs of war borne by local government can be found in a series of special war relief bylaws adopted in Wellington County, in which Guelph was the largest municipality. A hefty sum of $30,000 was initially provided 'for War Relief Funds' in December 1914.[66] This amount was doubled one year later through an increase of 2.0 mils on taxable property.[67] The next year, the same $60,000 sum was designated for war relief by continuing the 2.0 mil supplement.[68] In 1917, however, the allotment was increased to $75,000, covered by a mil rate raised to 2.5.[69] The funds collected through this small tax could be spent on priorities established by the county, not by private individuals, as the war continued unabated and its end remained unforeseeable.

The City of Lethbridge also imposed municipal levies on taxable property to aid the CPF, amid accusations that the voluntary system had collapsed, but these levies were not in place until February 1918, when mounting war relief costs had for some time incited distressed tones in letters to the editor.[70] One concerned citizen, W.D. Lamb, invoked the panacea of a single land tax. 'At last,' Lamb wrote, as if to proclaim it, 'the voluntary method of raising Patriotic Funds in Alberta has broken down.' Direct taxation by the Province of Alberta, he argued, should have been imposed for the CPF much earlier. But if that was not going to happen, he saw 'one fact so plain, so self evident, so simple, that our public men don't seem to be able to grasp.'

Taxes should be paid by anyone holding 'vacant' land, land not under any form of production or useful occupation. 'Just as the Sifton government,' he maintained, 'has raised three quarters of a million dollars revenue, by a one per cent levy on vacant held land, so let them by the very same machinery, collect one or two per cent off vacant land for the Patriotic Fund.' His reference to the 'public men' who should know better implied a stronger sense of frustration than was found in most letters earlier in the war: 'all this is so fair, plain, easy, the chances are that our public men will switch public attention on to something else, maybe propose a tax on house cats, or maybe a tax on dogs in proportion to the length of their tails.'[71]

Less than a month later, the Alberta government effectively declared that the voluntary system for the province's CPF branches had come to an end. In mid-November 1917, the province voted to supply the federal government with $800,000 to cover Alberta's demand for aid to soldiers' dependents. 'This will mean the end of the voluntary system of raising the patriotic fund as far as the province of Alberta is concerned,' the *Herald* noted.[72] A follow-up editorial declared this the 'right course.' In retrospect, 'voluntary giving' had been 'unfair in that the big hearted man gave more than his proportion and oftentimes the man of wealth didn't give anything.' This was the kind of attack that implied disgust at war profiteering or at men and women who simply withheld wealth in time of dire need, and it fuelled calls for the 'conscription of wealth' (see Chapter 5). 'Taxation will remedy that fault,' the *Herald* noted simply.[73]

The province had passed the responsibility on to the municipalities, which were to collect the new patriotic levy through the existing municipal tax system.[74] Predictably, the City of Lethbridge objected to a scheme that would raise municipal rates throughout the province by 1.5 mils. 'The city council,' the *Herald* warned, 'is not enamored over the suggested plan for collecting the Patriotic Fund tax which is now being undertaken by the provincial government.' A formal letter objecting to the method of taxation was drawn up and dispatched to municipalities throughout the province for their endorsement before being sent on to the provincial legislature.[75] As protests from other mayors and municipal officials echoed across the province, Lethbridge's mayor and city commissioners, who three-and-a-half years earlier had helped get their CPF branch up and running, saw the end of the voluntary approach as the sole system. Their lament was really for the waning of war relief as a great national charity, organized at the local level to stave off the costs to business and incomes that direct taxation would bring, a masquerade of patriotism that cloaked a fear, underscored by Morris himself, of even greater burdens in the future.

Collective Action, Local Projects, and Social Difference

Individuals and groups who participated actively in the diverse enterprises of civilian war relief were supported by large numbers of donors and assisted a growing caseload of recipients as the war continued. Boundaries of social difference that structured such encounters were not fixed, and social hierarchies that became models of and models for those connected to these projects were not imposed from above or opposed from below. Led by the CPF, war relief organizers began with a strong sense of their place in the social order. They expressed a corresponding sense of duty to preserve it through philanthropic means. This strategy quickly took root in local settings. It framed numerous activities and exchanges, from fundraising to the soldiers' wives opening their doors for a home visit from a CPF volunteer, in relations of class, gender, and ethnicity. The hometown horizons of local social networks and the convenient campaign territories they contained provided the best contexts in which to raise awareness, money, and volunteers and, ultimately, to provide aid to soldiers' families.

A significant pull from the past, a conservative ethos, and a desire to maintain the status quo seemed to motivate the staunchest agents collecting and redistributing CPF relief. The 'hierarchies' they tried to maintain, however, were not a fundamental system of power that operated from the top down, but the social structures of class-based, gendered, and ethnic differences with which CPF organizers authorized themselves on committees, on speaking platforms, while canvassing, while administering their caseloads, or while writing its history afterwards.

That is not to say that contributors or recipients shared this vision. Rather, we might see many actions taken to preserve social cohesion through a strong sense of patriotic duty – to justify, organize, and distribute war relief – as political positions applied to the very real social demands of home front life. This helps us to understand how contemporaries involved in war relief efforts saw their own projects, themselves, and others.

The CPF's selection of local officials and fundraising practices, its systems of disbursement, and its self-justifying rhetoric reveal efforts geared to maintain, as much as possible, what war relief supporters conceived of as sets of local communities seeking security within a nation coping with disruption. Our readings here correspond to this by focusing on relationships between social differences across the society and local responses within it. From the beginning of the war, when local, voluntary efforts predominated, to its escalation in 1917, when state-directed efforts gained support, the framing of experiences for patriotic organizers, for patrons, or for donors and volunteer administrators had been shaped by their strong sense of duty to preserve the world that the war seemed to have left behind.

4
Demonizations

One of the most neglected questions concerning enemy aliens in Canada during the Great War is how representations of their presence in Canada shaped perceptions of their danger and, on rare occasions, their plight.[1] Since no act of sabotage ever occurred, and since the federal government's coercive actions under the War Measures Act coincided with public demands for state action, considering the signs inhabiting public discourse helps us to locate the origins, if not the logic, of many popular fears. Images of ethnic minorities connected by birth or descent to the enemy were recast by anxieties over their loyalty. Perceiving them as a threat to home front security, local audiences appeared keen to consume reports of enemy alien networks, conspiracies, and sabotage. While a new discourse of fear became pervasive and general, much of the concern over the domestic danger of enemy minorities came into sharp focus on local levels.

Ordinary press reports inverted 'hardworking Germans' into 'militaristic Huns,' or misrepresented other ethnic nationalities by lumping them together as 'Austrians' or as Armenian 'Turks.' As Panikos Panayi argued in reference to both wars, this happens ordinarily as public anxieties over the true loyalties of ethnic minorities circulate and intensify.[2] In many home front contexts, essentialized stereotypes of both 'the enemy' and 'the enemy alien' served to heighten fears and hatreds of the 'other side' and to strengthen resolve for a final victory over forces often unseen directly, often imagined. In many cases, very little meaningful cultural exchange took place between affected peoples before war news circulated, and almost none occurred thereafter.

In our local cases, a study of fabricated images of the enemy and enemy alien as cultural figments helps us understand the power of hometown horizons as a local lens that can capture two related fields: the imagined enemy overseas and local minorities of enemy origin. As a recurrent pattern across histories of enemy aliens in wartime in the modern era, assessments of a 'demonized' foe attract inquiries into how majority cultures construct and act on popular, often grotesque, signs, images, and symbols that justify military action. Taken as a whole, as the Great War intensified and then dragged on, these negative stereotypes came to reside in practices of exclusion and support for state coercion.

Studies of enemy aliens in Canada during the First World War have tended to focus on the consequences of their status – how, in many ways, procedures codified by the War Measures Act affected these newcomers, whether by requiring enemy aliens living within twenty miles of a parole office to register or by creating a national internment system – rather than on the figments through which anxieties were summoned. The lenses majority cultures used to see enemy aliens as objects have remained a secondary issue.

That state actions were connected in some way to 'public fears' of the enemy aliens' subversiveness and suspicions of their 'closely concealed' dangers, is recognized, usually under the rubric of 'public opinion.' As Desmond Morton put it in his study of Sir William Otter, placed in charge of Internment Operations shortly after war broke out, 'obviously, the government was responding to the pressure of day-to-day problems, struggling to keep step with British policy and with Canadian public opinion.' Despite the provisions of the War Measures Act and internment options, he added, 'Canadian opinion was not so easily satisfied.'[3] More recently, William A. Waiser wrote: 'At first, the Conservative government of Robert Borden counselled restraint and toleration, but as public fears about possible enemy alien subversion escalated, there was intense pressure to limit and control the activities of the enemy alien population, especially the eighty thousand who were still unnaturalized.'[4] Between the publication of these two studies, attention has shifted away from government action and toward the lived experiences of enemy aliens, certainly a dominant theme in Waiser's work.[5]

The branch that Otter oversaw created and administered some two dozen internment stations and camps, housing a total of 8,579 men, 81 women, and 156 children. Of these, just 3,138 were classified as military reservists, eligible for duty if they returned to their home country. Ottawa reasoned that since most of these inmates had been used to working in the harsh conditions of mining, railway, and logging camps before the war, putting them to work building highways and roads or other projects near Banff, Lake Louise, Jasper, or Yoho was justified and in the public interest. Many also reasoned that the troops overseas had it far worse. Most enemy aliens processed and confined by Internment Operations – in barbed-wire enclosures in several cities, including the Lethbridge facility, or in isolated work camps in the Rockies, northern Ontario, or Quebec – were detained simply because they could not find work. Destitute, most had sought relief from a municipal office or police station and had been dispatched to the nearest receiving station or detention camp. There, they joined smaller numbers who had violated conditions of parole, firearms possession, or information censorship or had even tried to enlist in the Canadian forces. As Waiser and others have underscored, Ottawa's fear was that young men, in particular, might become dangerous, not because of who they were but because of what they were facing.

Newspaper editorials and depictions of local enemy alien experiences told different stories. In these sources the threat they posed was not seen as rooted simply in their situation, but was in their nature. Demonizing the enemy, ordinarily the 'Germans,' as a people accustomed to living under 'autocracy' brought with it a guilt by association tied to naturalized views of race and culture. And what all enemy aliens faced, either as a state-classified or discursively construed array of newcomers, were relations with the host society mediated through public discourses that conveyed not one kind of message concerning their dangers, but many. The range of interpretations and prescriptions varied, from calls preaching moderation, like Borden's, at the beginning of the war, to the barrage of grotesque forms of deliberate propaganda concerning the enemy that soon followed. In a speech given at the outbreak of fighting, examined below, Mayor Hardie of Lethbridge called upon citizens to sympathize with the enemy aliens' situation. Later, reports of several prisoner escapes from the Lethbridge Internment Camp offered sensationalized images of their cunning and evil intent.

And it is important not to draw too sharp a distinction between enemy aliens and the enemy. That they were imagined by names like 'alien enemies' 'the foreigners,' 'Austrians,' or 'Germans,' and that the enemy overseas with which they were associated was so intensely vilified as the 'monstrous Kaiser,' the 'cruel Huns,' or the product of German 'autocracy,' meant there was an array of fluid signs that could blur distinctions between enemy alien ethnic groups, enemy aliens themselves, and the enemy overseas. How majority cultures constructed images of an enemy overseas, and its potential agents in 'their' midst, as something 'alien' and perhaps dangerous was mediated through the most convenient stereotypical constructions that came to inhabit the calls, addressed briefly by Morton and Waiser as public 'opinion' or 'fears,' for coercive measures.

Representations of the enemy overseas and those of enemy birth at home appeared in diverse spaces and multiple forms, from newspaper texts to public lectures. They worked to distance perceptions from realities, particularly in urban spaces. Accounts of ordinary incidents of arrest and detention often appeared in the press, but in distorted terms. Apart from those detained or forced to work, technically as prisoners of war, over half a million Canadians were associated directly or by descent to enemy states, the nationalities of Central and Eastern Europe that included Germans, Hungarians, Czechs, Slovaks, Croats, Poles, Austrians, Slovenes, Ukrainians,

Bulgarians, Turks, and Armenians. Approximately eighty thousand, as unnaturalized newcomers from an enemy country, were subsequently classified under the War Measures Act as enemy aliens.

The cities examined here give an example of their uneven distribution across the country. Proportionately few lived in Quebec outside of Montreal; Trois-Rivières counted only seven Germans among its nearly fourteen thousand inhabitants. Higher proportions were present in most of Ontario, from Toronto, Hamilton, and Berlin (now Kitchener) to German settlements in rural areas. Guelph claimed only seventy-eight Germans and sixty-six Austro-Hungarians among more than fifteen thousand residents in its last pre-war census. Fears concerning enemy aliens nonetheless circulated in the local newspapers of both cities. Significant concentrations were found in the Prairie provinces, and the situation of close proximity and higher proportions in Lethbridge tended to increase newspaper coverage. A Prairie census completed in 1916 reported 1,069 Austro-Hungarians and 223 Germans living in Lethbridge, figures understated by the reluctance of some respondents at that time to identify their origins.

Hostile reactions toward enemy aliens depended, in many cases, on local patterns of social interaction before the war. In his study of Vulcan, a small service centre between Lethbridge and Calgary, Paul Voisey noted that Germans, like other minorities in the area, 'were too few in number, too dispersed, too assimilated, and too well known personally to invite organized discrimination or arouse mob violence.'[6] While his reference to 'mob violence' that may have been 'aroused' gives us a rather static hypothetical, his general point concerns the important relationship between local reponses and local contexts.

The men and women who worked and settled in the region to establish farms, businesses, families, and local community lives followed pre-war patterns of inter-ethnic exchange that were quite different from one area to another. Most of Lethbridge's population connected to enemy countries did not come to Lethbridge to farm or establish businesses, as was more often the case in Vulcan. A history of segregated ethnic communities began with Hungarian workers who arrived with the CPR and were later joined by other Eastern Europeans arriving to work in the Lethbridge collieries. Many came as younger, unmarried men, some as chain migrants with relatives already in Lethbridge, others as transient workers hoping to settle in Canada or following a sojourner's intention. Although part of the significant influx of newcomers from Eastern and Southern Europe, who joined Americans, northern Europeans, and migrating Canadians during the boom period of western settlement from the mid-1880s to 1914, their experiences were combinations of prior cultures and associations, local conditions, and their own emerging identities. Their work in mining, lumbering, and construction camps coincided with age, gender, and ethnic differences. Their movements remained tied to their search for work, and their lives often remained segregated from Anglo-Canadian communities by their gender, age, language, work, places of residence, leisure, and associational life. That Anglo-Canadians often viewed them through negative ethnic stereotypes was exacerbated by barriers of limited or ambivalent contact.

In Lethbridge, the relocation and low-wage employment of Hungarians, in particular, was part of a pattern in resource-based industries of attracting specific immigrant groups to specific work sites through contract arrangement. The labour used in the Galt-backed collieries on the banks of the Oldman River depended largely on a non-British workforce, employed at low wages. The North-West Coal and Navigation Company relocated and employed Hungarian-born miners from Pennsylvania at its Coalbanks site in the late 1880s and provided company housing on the west edge of what later became Lethbridge. This spatially segregated residential pattern increased when other miners from Central and Eastern Europe settled near the collieries up to the war. In his study of the Galts' role in early resource development in this period, Andy den Otter concluded Galt companies 'introduced the Hungarians into an unstable society, merely to reduce production costs' and did so 'without any regard for the social consequences.'[7]

At the same time, as outlined in Chapter 1, the reconstituting of transplanted Anglo-Canadian institutions, from churches and schools to voluntary associations, in a prairie city that would soon service both the collieries and a growing agricultural hinterland took place across a local population spatially segregated by class and ethnic boundaries.[8] 'The population of early Lethbridge,' Martin L. Kovacs has noted in his study of this pattern, 'was split into two separate and easily distinguishable segments; the more or less permanently settled portion which largely coincided with settlers of British background, and the miners, which after the arrival of the Hungarians and the Slavs, were largely identical with Central and Eastern European immigrants.' Kovacs described a 'profound restlessness, tension and stress' as a 'common denominator' dividing the two. Well into the 1920s, he pointed out, cultural differences reinforced by spatial segregation ensured that relations remained spurious and distant.[9] That young Hungarian men were seen by Anglo-Canadians as 'drinking, brawling and resisting arrest' was connected to their proximity to a 'mining camp' setting. By the turn of century, a more 'settled' Magyar community had developed, but the assumptions used to view these people by the Anglo-Canadian majority were not easily changed.[10] By 1914, more than one-fifth of Lethbridge's population of 8,050 was non-British. Most were from Austria-Hungary and remained spatially and socially ghettoized in neighbourhoods adjacent to the collieries up to the war. Even after the war, according to a 1925 Royal Commission report on the coal industry, 32 percent of mine labour in Lethbridge was 'Slavic,' somewhat higher than that of most other western coal mines, but not unusually so for the industry throughout the region.[11]

Apart from situations where they lived in segregation from the majority culture, which varied between Vulcan, Lethbridge, and other regions across Canada, the histories of Canada's enemy aliens in the First World War point collectively to the problem of misrepresenting ethnic plurality through discourses produced by majority cultures. This opens a wide history of perception, examined in Alberta by Howard Palmer as patterns of prejudice. Anglo-Canadians (and French Canadians as well) structured practices of social differentiation through prejudices that Palmer models as a pecking order, with a person's position determined by proximity to Britain and Northern Europe. This was reflected across the country and in much of the journalistic discourse and relevant events in the cities considered here. During the war, as before, the realities of enemy aliens' varied circumstances were often repressed or screened out altogether in newspaper accounts. Many ironies remained hidden. The loyalties of young men who had left Austria-Hungary to escape compulsory military service became lost in the verbiage of wartime news that either glossed over their ordinary situations and sentiments, or introduced distortions and lies.

Newspapers, lectures, or other signs tended to blur distinctions between peoples of enemy origin and certainly failed to contextualize their actual presence. The host society's general isolation from young men of Central European origin living in ghettoized working and housing conditions, like the coal miners in Lethbridge, combined with the barriers to family and community contact that language and religious differences tended to accentuate, leaving perceptions of many newcomers, particularly if they were not British, Protestant, or English-speaking, confined to a fairly reified set of stereotypes. Shortly after the outbreak of war, images of enemy aliens tended to meld into genres that conveyed a sense of omnipresence, unsubstantiated by their actual numbers, location, and activities. In ordinary press reports, Germans suddenly seemed everywhere in the East; Hungarians, Ruthenians, Bulgarians, and Ukrainians – often lumped together as simply 'Austrians' – quickly gained attention beyond their real numbers in the West. The frequency and form of reports generated in Trois-Rivières, where so few peoples connected to enemy countries could actually be found, is a clear example of the fears of unseen but keenly inferred dangers – an unstable set of perceptions and sensibilities, subject to whim, accusation, or gossip. Such messages proliferated across the country, fed off one another, and had no single source cluster. They were regularly consumed by newspaper readers, lecture audiences, or circulated through everyday conversation. In Lethbridge, with its large proportion of enemy aliens, these impressions were sometimes based on little more than a passing glimpse of the barbed-wire enclosure on the city's exhibition grounds that contained an internment camp, set up by the Department of Militia and Defence in the fall of 1914.

'And Now the War Is Here': Federal Policies, Local Moderates

On an official level, Canada's response to the problem of enemy aliens began from a moderate position that would soon harden as the Royal North-West Mounted Police, Department of Justice parole officials, and local police officers applied the procedures of the War Measures Act. On 8 August, Ottawa stipulated 'that immigrants of German nationality would not be interfered with so long as they 'pursued their ordinary avocations, unless there was reasonable grounds to suppose that they were assisting the enemy in any way.' Five days later, this was extended to include non-naturalized immigrants from Austria-Hungary.[12]

Following Britain's lead, the government also restricted enemy alien movement. Ottawa had been advised by London five days before to prevent only enemy naval reservists, or those who could on reasonable grounds be convicted of espionage, from leaving the country. In effect, army reservists from Germany and Austria-Hungary were given a few days to embark overseas from the United States after the British ultimatum expired. On 7 August, Whitehall cabled Ottawa for an official exit ban for all enemy reservists. But preventing their escape was not yet practical. Close interrogation of railway passengers crossing the border was called off, ostensibly to avoid mistaken arrests of American citizens. The Department of Immigration claimed, with some exaggeration, 'that Germans and Austrians were leaving Canada by every train headed for the United States.' This window of escape, which Ottawa was fully aware of, gave a few loyal German and Austro-Hungarian reservists a fair chance of getting out of the country and served as a useful safety valve. Once Ottawa's final proclamation barring the departure of all enemy reservists was made public on 15 August, Canada-US border areas effectively became off-limits to all aliens who might belong to an enemy force.

As the initial flurry of war enthusiasm settled by mid-August, the full range of enemy alien restrictions was adopted when Parliament passed the War Measures Act during a special session held on 18 August. This new omnibus law placed all enemy aliens on parole and permitted their arrest and detention should any regulation concerning censorship or firearms restriction be broken. In granting the Department of Militia and Defence enforcement authority, the law also gave power 'to the officers and constables of the Dominion and Royal North-West Mounted Police and to such other persons as their respective Commissioners might delegate, to arrest and detain enemy aliens.'[13] Predictably, once the government's unofficial grace period had lapsed, the problem of departing reservists surfaced in Lethbridge. 'AND NOW THE WAR IS HERE,' a *Herald* headline boomed on 17 August to announce the capture of three men, alleged to be Austrian reservists attempting to escape on foot to the United States. Their return to the city by force was said to have brought 'about a realization that military and not civil law prevails.'[14]

This can be compared to other evidence of attempts by enemy alien miners to demonstrate their loyalty to Canada and their unwillingness to support the Central Powers. 'It was reported,' the *Herald* also mentioned, 'that the Austrians were among the enthusiastic purchasers of British flags at No. 3 mine on Saturday, and three Germans, when arrested, thought that they were going to be sent back to Germany to fight, and pleaded for release, which was granted them.'[15] In both Lethbridge and Guelph, enemy alien workers made very public donations to local branches of the Canadian Patriotic Fund to assist Canadian soldiers' families. Reports in the *Herald* and *Mercury* seemed to champion these acts as signs that Anglo-Canadian culture had scored a victory in the men's divided hearts, though these demonstrations of loyalty may well have been inspired by enemy aliens' fears of what lay ahead. Newspaper reports also tended to sensationalize the force of what the *Herald* referred to here as 'military law,' procedures which, in fact, had not yet been codified and passed in full as the War Measures Act.

As the end of August approached, 'nearly a dozen Austrians and Germans' were reported to be 'held at the local barracks' of Lethbridge's Royal North-West Mounted Police detachment 'on suspicion.'[16] A tense interrogation was said to have ended with everyone's release. 'Are you a reservist?' they were asked. 'Do you want to go back and fight for Austria?' Some could have been detained on minor charges, but for now it was thought better simply to clear the barracks and, if possible, approach the general problem with a fresh start. Within two weeks, any enemy alien trying to enter the United States would probably have been interned.[17] They were also required to sign an 'Undertaking,' a document that combined a list of the new War Measures Act restrictions with a pledge of allegiance.[18]

These steps were significant, but in themselves represented only the legal framework that enemy aliens had to contend with. Life for many breadwinners and workers who still had jobs was becoming fraught with frustrations and often significant hardships in rural areas: visiting parole officers, handing over firearms, or enduring circumstances of mutual distrust. Politicians on all levels, ever wary of public opinion taking an excessive turn, spoke from an 'official' position in orations reflecting their responsibility for civil order. They preached moderation and empathy, and as noted above, Borden took the lead as prime minister. He stated in Parliament that Canadians had 'absolutely no quarrel with the German people.' Their fate was not of their making; Germans had simply fallen into the hands of 'a warlike autocracy.'[19] Wilfrid Laurier echoed these remarks. So did J.S. Woodsworth and Frank Oliver.[20]

The effect of such remarks seemed to be to expose the ambivalence between the official views of public leaders and the parochial, hometown horizons of city newspapers. Were enemy aliens innocently trapped by the stupidity and folly of the Kaiser and German militarism? Or were they intrinsically sympathetic to the supposed 'warlike philosophy' that gripped their home countries? Did they really pose a threat to the security of Canada? Signs of fear tended to coincide as well with news of Allied setbacks or German 'barbarism.' Between news of the retreat at Mons and the sinking of the *Lusitania* – the second, of course, a disaster for enemy aliens – negative discourses concerning the enemy and enemy aliens tended to locate fears of the enemy in North America on nearby territories: from reports in Trois-Rivières of a German-American invasion from New England, to those in Lethbridge of enemy aliens 'busy among the threshing rigs.' Local politicians no doubt tried to gauge the opinions of their constituents and respond accordingly.

Mayor Hardie defended a moderate stance toward enemy aliens in Lethbridge during that city's first send-off ritual. When, as seen in Chapter 2, Hardie addressed the large audience at Wesley Methodist's auditorium, he shifted attention to what lay ahead for the high proportion of enemy-born in the city. As the *Herald* put it, he asked the 'huge crowd' to 'consider the foreigner, particularly the wives and families of those of foreign birth, who remain with us, who, though foreign born, are loyal Britishers deep down in their hearts, but who cannot help having strong feelings for their native lands which might be opposed to Britain.' Cheers were said to have met remarks which condemned any 'offensive treatment' enemy aliens might encounter:

> Many of these are British subjects who have taken up the rights of citizenship in our Empire, and again there are many who have not yet done so. But all the same, we should remember that the war is not of their seeking. They may be enemies in name, but it is in name only, and not in reality. If any silent sympathy for the land which gave them birth should be encountered, it is well to remember 'Breathes there the man with soul so dead, Who never to himself has said, This is my own my native land.' We may accord them some forgiveness, provided they themselves do not actively offend.
>
> This, with the bulk who have cast in their lot with us, there is no reason to expect. They have lived long enough amongst us to respect British justice and British institutions. Their eyes, on this side of the water, have, no doubt been open to the true state of things now they are removed from the influences of their political teachers who have instilled in their fellows a false belief.
>
> We have it with us to show these people that we are endowed with the characteristics which have tended to make us a noble nation. Let us put them into practice.[21]

Hardie's comments echoed many elements found in comparable speeches offered at this time. Germany had fallen under the influence of autocracy and militarism; Britain was democratic and peaceful. German citizens were imprisoned by their leaders and a false ideology; Britons were guided by nobler men and aims. That 'we have it with us to show' that Britain and the Empire stood for a higher civilization, a freer society, and the spread of its ideals also served to discursively situate the 'enemies in name' in a negative, subordinate position.

The previous Sunday, a large congregation had gathered at Wesley Methodist to hear a patriotic sermon delivered by the Rev. G.H. Cobbledick. The preacher followed a religious theme, describing the war as a crisis in which human history and divine will were ultimately inseparable. Then he turned to its secular implications. If the 'greatest war of the centuries' had fallen on the Empire, what was the duty of Canada?

> It is to understand the issues. Our quarrel is not with Germany for seeking extension, but because of her method. Instead of seeking it by trade, as Britain does, she is doing so by militarism. This is not a war of the German people, but a quarrel of the military section of the German nation, the Kaiser, his officers, and the big business interests of military armaments. The struggle is between liberty and democracy on one side, and autocratic militarism on the other. The issue will either set back the hands of the clock or will continue the world's progress in democracy.

The congregation was implored 'to believe no false witness even against the enemy until it is verified.'[22] Like Hardie's speech, his sermon lectured caution, but also invoked the spectre of German militarism. Together, their Anglo-conformity reiterated the notion that British institutions and culture stood at the centre of the 'civilized' world. Imperial-nationalists in Canada certainly subscribed to this, but as these texts suggest, ethnicity and even class tended to converge with depictions of Germany as its opposing referent. The interests of the officer class and large-scale German industry rendered the average German, or the 'people,' not only powerless but also captivated by 'false beliefs' imposed by their 'political teachers.' Apart from this, the rhetoric was androcentric in both cases: a war of kings, men, money, and, by extension, male power was foregrounded. Women appear only as the 'wives' of families now bearing the burden of enemy alien status.

If, as a cultural construct, the enemy alien could be cast at the beginning of the war as an innocent subject of circumstance, why did this so quickly change? Some portents appeared in the sermon itself. Hardie said forgiveness should be afforded them, 'provided they do not offend.' As news of the fighting in Belgium and France grew grim, they did offend, due in part to connections between the enemy, catastrophe overseas, and the enemy alien at home, connections routinely drawn by the fluidity of signs city newspapers used to depict enemies overseas and potential enemies at home. Hardie's reference, for instance, to the 'false teachings' enemy aliens had supposedly inculcated set up a transportable stereotype.

The presence of jobless enemy alien men first appeared as a national problem of local consequence about a month after the war began. Summarily fired, with no prospect of alternative paid work, they usually approached municipal offices for relief if unable to turn to family or friends. They were required, by this point, to report regularly to an enemy alien registry and so could not leave their district. As they saw it, this mobility restriction foreclosed any reasonable chance of securing jobs elsewhere. They 'Will Not Starve,' the *Mercury* promised when this situation first surfaced in Guelph. 'It is understood that the city will give the unfortunate natives of Austria, who are out of work in the city, the same chance as the British who are out of work to make a dollar or two this winter.'[23] The 'dollar or two' suggested condescending attitudes toward class and ethnic difference, something later signified when members of Parliament were called upon to defend the forced labour system and argued that hard-earned but scant wages were, after all, the lot of the simple working man that they imagined most enemy aliens were.

In reference to what proved little more than a stopgap measure, the *Mercury* cast a very real problem in convenient figments, unlikely to challenge most readers' sense of social coherence. 'Austrians,' a catch-all term for many non-German enemy aliens, were the demoted 'unfortunates,' a term deflecting responsibility from their previous employers. Of course, many workers during the economic slump of 1913-14 had lost their jobs, but the suggestion that enemy aliens might then compete for work with 'the same chance as the British' was a touchstone lie that could easily be absorbed by those ordinarily comforted by the keywords 'British justice.' Hiring enemy aliens could draw sharp attack from other workers. 'Some of the city labourers' in Guelph, the *Mercury* noted elsewhere, became 'very indignant over the way in which a foreman gave an Austrian the preference of a job to an Englishmen.' Someone alleged 'that he knew for a fact that the foreman discharged a man English by birth and gave an Austrian a job. He also said that the Englishman was considered to be a good worker, and was a British reservist of the South African war.'[24]

Unemployment among enemy alien labourers was already straining the willingness of municipalities to supply further local relief, wherever they had worked in the past. The brutal fact was that scores of transient enemy alien labourers, who risked job-hunting forays while on parole, were homeless. In Guelph, a 'Hungarian, hailing from Toronto asked for and was given shelter at the police court,' just before Canada's internment system began taking in large numbers. 'Chief Randall was suspicious of him and had an interpreter question the man, who stated that he had come here looking for work. He had worked here before, and thought he could strike a job. After the Chief was satisfied that the man was not dangerous, he was allowed to go on his way.'[25]

The animosity this caused was apparent in Guelph, as elsewhere. By the spring of 1915, the situation for some had come to an end as far as municipal relief was concerned. In press reports like this, local settings might be identified by a real place, the city halls or police stations where enemy aliens turned up for work or food, but they offered condescending narratives of enemy alien labourers, untrusted, resented, and without work. After a half dozen men approached the police in Guelph for food and shelter, for example, Chief Randall 'saw that they were given something to eat' and contacted Ottawa. 'All the Austrians, Hungarians, and Austrian-Poles residing in the city,' one report indicated, 'were rounded up this morning and about fifty of them will be sent to Toronto this afternoon to the detention camp, where they will be interned.'[26]

The spectacle of their departure also appeared in the *Mercury*. A large crowd was reported on hand at the Grand Trunk station, perhaps because it happened on a Saturday afternoon. Their departure prompted a notice prefigured by their 'unfortunate' situation. For one, municipal officials and the city police must have been glad to get rid of them. They left under armed guard, one soldier for every two prisoners, a measure that offered onlookers and readers a sign of state endorsement for forced confinement. The report noted that they seemed in good spirits at the prospect of 'getting the meals regularly.'[27] With little to look forward to while the war continued, they may have indeed been glad to quit the city. Identifying these men as 'Austrians, Hungarians and Austrian-Poles' indicates a better than average observation of ethnic difference. But in broadcasting opinion, the *Mercury* also joined other papers in lumping enemy aliens together under signs of resentment. As one Guelph reporter put it, 'Germans know all right that they have become enemies of the British Empire, but the Austrians seem to think that they are still our friends.'[28]

While unemployed enemy alien men did not present a problem for Trois-Rivières, within a year it became politically impossible for Mayor Tessier to continue doing city business with the Shawinigan Quarry Company, managed by a German engineer. After a vitriolic attack by the *Courrier*, a Conservative journal and constant thorn in Tessier's side, city council refused to renew its contract with a firm it now claimed was German in origin and principle.[29] German landlords could find themselves unable to collect rents or take legal action against their tenants.[30] The former secretary of Toronto's disbanded German consular office complained of German-born employees in Ontario not only losing their jobs, but also being denied their wages due.[31] Even local businesses occasionally employed anti-foreign appeals in their advertising. 'We are at War with the Foreigners in the Laundry business in this city,' the Guelph Steam Laundry declared in a classified insert. 'We are all British. Who are you going to support?'[32]

The condemnation of any visible or imagined connection to the enemy in the marketplace, the workplace, or in ordinary business dealings combined with the gaze of newspaper readers of men out of work, in need, and stigmatized. Journalistic reports of local incidents appeared beside fantastic fictions: spies, saboteurs, even invaders from the United States. Most reports of this type subsided by the end of the first year of the war. Their appearance as flashy news items had coincided with the sudden commencement of hostilities and the imposition of the War Measures Act. Both the coming of war and the designation of enemy aliens introduced new conditions, prompting a veritable outpouring of sensational newspaper reports. A history of ethnic minority discrimination and fresh reports of enemy aliens in close proximity framed popular perceptions. Many Canadians developed fears of the foreigner of enemy origin through little else than stereotypes, local gossip, and exaggerated press reports of conspiracies spawned by the most dangerous yet hidden of enemies, those operating close to home.

Local Sites, Imagined Plots, and Violent Incidents

Fears of enemy alien invasions from the United States or sabotage in a given region resided often in a localized sense of place. Rumours of such events involved physical features and were readily imaginable because they were readily recognizable. Much of the reporting of enemy aliens in the first months of the war quickly shifted toward images of imminent danger, of invasion or sabotage plots targeting the most strategic site within the local area, be it the Welland Canal in southern Ontario or the high-level CPR bridge in Lethbridge, or hordes of German Americans crossing the St. Lawrence River from New England.

'Invasion of Canada' appeared as a large-lettered caption for a front-page sensation in the *Mercury* in early November 1914. 'The Dominion Police and local authorities admit that there is more than a mere rumour in the story that German sympathizers have plotted to blow up the Welland Canal and destroy the Hamilton tunnel,' the details ran. Readers were reminded that the canal connecting Lake Erie and Lake Ontario was a 'great grain route, which must be kept open,' and that the CPR tunnel in Hamilton, the closest city to the south, 'is on the direct line of communication between Toronto, where troops are mobilizing, and the Niagara frontier, which would likely be the scene of raids of German sympathizers from the United States.'[33] Two weeks later, another report claimed that 'Guelph had a war scare last evening when word reached the city that Toronto troops were being called out to meet a body of Germans who were crossing the border at Buffalo.'[34]

In Trois-Rivières, both Barnard of the *Bien Public* and Clark of the *Newcomer* used their papers to promote fears of a German-American invasion.

Like the *Mercury*, they speculated in detail on how it might take place and always suggested that something more than rumour lay behind their reports.[35] The actual risk of an invasion, at times, could be cast as an uncertainty Canadians must prepare for: 'La probabilité de l'invasion du Canada par l'armée régulière allemande est fort aléatoire,' Barnard wrote under the caption 'L'invasion du Canada,' also in early November 1914. Such a force, Barnard warned, could easily be raised south of the border. 'Si c'est vrai qu'il y a là cinq cent mille hommes,' he stated in an estimate soon to be inflated by the *Newcomer,* 'tous pour la plupart réservistes retenus aux Etats-Unis n'est-ce que contre leur gré, ou ayant déjà fait le service militaire en Autriche ou en Allemagne, habitués au maniement des armes: nous aurions à faire face à une véritable armée, et les Etats-Unis de même.'[36] Barnard went on to suggest that covert hostile activity was then taking place under the direction of enemy agents on both sides of the border. He wrote in alarming terms:

> Les journaux ont maintes fois révélé des tentatives d'espionnage; des installations de télégraphie sans fil, formellement interdites et supprimées par les autorités, ont été à plusieurs reprises réinstallées, au grand désespoir de la police. Des aéroplanes mystérieux continuent à survoler nos rares points stratégiques et nos principaux centres d'alimentation. Nos ports, nos canaux, nos ponts et voies de chemin de fer sont plus que jamais l'objet d'une étroite surveillance de la part de nos autorités, et cette prudence n'est pas de trop. En effet, toute cette préparation fébrile de la part d'hommes qui nous sont actuellement hostiles, et que nous laissons pourtant jouir dans notre pays d'une liberté relative quoique surveillée, indique au moins une chose.[37]

Reports of ubiquitous spying and intense sabotage planning implied nothing less than a clear and present danger. The near invisibility of the threat of German-American plots gave their phantom presence more power than any true facts could hope to muster. All these developments, as Barnard cast them, pointed to fears of German-Americans rooted in imagined scenarios.[38]

At the same time, anglophone readers of the *Newcomer* were entertained by Malcolm Cargill, a Montreal poet whose doggerel glorified a search for German naval vessels in the English Channel and conjured images of nightfall, a stormy sea, and the tenacity of a certain crew member: 'We were looking for a German, one of the dirty kind.'[39] In the same edition, the *Newcomer* warned of 'an invasion by a German-American host who are backed by plenty of German-American money, whose numbers aggregate about 7,000,000 or nearly the total population of Canada,' and who were 'being constantly urged to invade this country by the representatives of Germany in the States. This is no bogey – it is a possibility which should be seriously faced and provided for.'[40]

Such texts, as public messages, did not generate any stable set of meanings, however, as groups or individuals tend to interpret according to their needs.[41] But their frequency and regularity in newspapers as commercial texts point to expectations of what sold as news. Based on what we may refer to as horizons of desire, as a form of entertainment, they offered interpretations damaging to enemy aliens who were loyal citizens, concerned residents, or fearful and disillusioned transients. When placed behind a series of rumours of sabotage and an imminent invasion that began to circulate in the press, unidentified or misidentified enemy aliens became commodified inventions, conjured at the margins of factual information or through complete fabrications. For any given locale, fears of enemy attack were translated into imagined outcomes based on social geography: proximity to German-American populations, for instance, or the vulnerability of nearby bridges or canals. The cabals and conspiracies readers encountered were often positioned to correspond with how they might predict an attack in their area from a strategic point of view. News of this sort appealed to a parochial sense of place.

In Lethbridge, the most obvious target for sensational journalism was the CPR high-level bridge that spanned the Oldman River. It stood 300 feet above the valley and carried the only rail line through Lethbridge. The first and most dramatic in a series of reports involving plots to dynamite the bridge appeared on 18 August. Its narrative structure, involving discoveries of suspicious characters or events at a bridge that was indeed closely guarded, was repeated in other accounts that ran on until July 1917.[42] What looked like empty casks of dynamite, stolen from the coal mines nearby, were spotted. Guards were increased at either end and below. Finally, someone suspicious was apprehended. The story broke in the *Herald* under a huge headline: 'ATTEMPT TO BLOW UP BIG BRIDGE FRUSTRATED.'

> Just at dusk last night a man, giving the name of Herman Weirmeir, was arrested near the big bridge, and he is suspected of being connected with what looks like a concerted attempt to blow the trestle into smithereens. So strong is the evidence against him, in fact, that if military law prevailed, it is likely that he would have been backed up against a brick wall and shot.[43]

As Weirmeir sat in the police barracks, *Herald* readers learned only that he was carrying 'burglar tools' and was 'a Canadian of German descent.' Within a week the story evaporated as the Royal North-West Mounted Police finally determined that Weirmeir had planned to pry off some window casings for his own use from an abandoned shack on the riverbank. He was carrying a packing-case remover in his pocket, which he intended to use for his ill-fated salvaging venture.[44] The tale of Weirmeir's arrest ended with a description of this noted feature of the local landscape under constant sentry: 'A heavy guard will be maintained hereafter, every hour of the day and night in the vicinity of the high bridge.'[45]

Why did so many stories in local papers describing enemy-based plots in Canada use parochial sites? Deployments of local and regional geographies as strategic targets depended on how local knowledges, as 'experience-near' concepts, intersected with the 'experience-distant' concepts, in this case the imaginary danger of the unseen foe. Reporters readily situated these sensational tales on known landmarks, which allowed readers to picture acts of sabotage taking place, or being planned. Usually depicted as elaborate, often international conspiracies, their destructive tactical missions were typically quite local. Nearby areas and landmarks were, in other words, reconfigured as the targets of 'outside' dangers that might depend on the 'inside' help of enemy aliens, working close to home. Their use depended on transporting experience-distant fears, xenophobias in this case, to known places. The bridges, canals, airspace, ports, pockets of enemy aliens nearby, and concentrations of German Americans on neutral territory materialized as convenient fictions. The ease with which local areas or landmarks could be overrun or destroyed by invisible forces depended on their visibility. Local newspapers deployed them in a variety of ways: to describe the actual presence of enemy aliens, perhaps arrested or deported as new internees, or to speculate on the danger of invasion. The cases here also point to social and physical landscapes that shifted across Canada, but that were used in similar ways because they were readily understood as exposed sites, be they bridges or canals that could not quickly be rebuilt or airspace that could not be immediately controlled.[46]

Boundaries representing the presence of enemy aliens on local spaces also converged with belligerent forms of masculine assertiveness. The *Mercury* valorized its expression as a natural part of 'Scottish' pugnacity, while trivializing the violence it provoked. Just over a month after the outbreak of war, several abusive acts, one of ritualized vandalism, took place in Guelph. They indicated desires to demonstrate power through expressions of hierarchies, not hierarchies that existed as static relations of ethnic difference, but as signs that men sought to impose to position themselves in relation to imagined rivals. As acts of defiance postured against a conjured foe, the parades and send-offs associated with recruitment in the 30th Wellington Rifles or the 11th Field Battery had, among other things, offered rehearsals of this. They, too, exhibited masculine claims to military prowess on a local level. Men eligible for service at this time had certainly been exposed to images of all kinds, local or otherwise, that could spur outbursts in which patriotic sentiments were mimicked in entirely different settings, sometimes involving potent mixtures of pride, manhood, and alcohol.

In the west end of the city in early September, several residents were 'entertained to an active warfare.' A young man, quite drunk apparently, wanted 'to clean up on the Germans,' though it appears he did no damage.[47] The following month a curious act of vandalism was directed against a statue of the Laird of Skibo, donated years before by the Carnegie Trust. A group of 'braw Scots' threw mud at it to signify their indignation at Andrew Carnegie, then rumoured to be a sympathizer of the Kaiser.[48] In several other rows, men did strike others identified as 'Germans.' A slugging match between two 'stalwart men,' a Scotsman and a German, occurred on the floor of one of the local factories. By the time the other workers broke it up, 'the powerful swing of the husky Scot' had done its work.[49] One Saturday night in early November another Scotsman took 'the law into his own hands.' He sent a man 'of German descent' home, fairly badly beaten up 'with a pair of black eyes.' Such incidents rarely reached the papers, and this one probably did only because it served to round off a report of allegedly outspoken Germans in nearby Goderich under the heading 'Germans are Warned.' *Mercury* readers learned of several 'well known' residents 'of German descent' who had been notified by 'government authorities at Ottawa that unless they cease to give expression of their views in favour of Germany, they will be arrested and their property confiscated.'[50]

The Guelph incidents involving 'braw,' 'stalwart,' or 'husky' Scots indicated attempts to impose status, of manhood and loyalty, through violent action, sometimes individually, sometimes collectively. The flare-up in the factory, the mud-throwing affair, and the Saturday night brawl also appeared as transactions of physical force used to draw boundaries, make exclusions, and secure a sense of dominance over the enemy, however illusionary its presence as a target might be.[51]

Press reports also drew on inherited conceptions. The ascribed truculence of Scots, as men, was valorized, their class positions merely implied. Ethnic identity served as a naturalized marker. Some evidence of 'passing,' the strategy of assumed identity, turns up in the *Mercury*. We cannot verify what was claimed in this case, but the assumptions that seem to underlie its reception are clear. A certain Captain Schultz, formerly of Guelph, was acquitted 'of being a German spy' in England. His subsequent decision to change his name to 'Hastings' prompted a letter of complaint. Another pointed out that, in fact, 'Schultz' could be construed as a fine name, not because it sounded 'German' but because it was shared, coincidentally, with the 'popular hero' in Manitoba and Ontario, Dr. John Christian Schultz, who had marched and fought in the first Riel rebellion. The difficulties 'innocent Germans' endured when they faced false accusations of being spies were construed by the *Mercury* as a problem created by their own 'countrymen.' The real blame for victimizing enemy aliens in Canada as potential spies, according to this logic, lay with Germany, not with Canada or its citizens. 'Innocent Germans who suffer must remember that it is largely the result of the German spying system which has spread universal distrust and suspicion.'[52]

This 'we-versus-they' dialectic was often used to represent the enemy in opposition to imperial-nationalistic motifs. The collage of texts that ran parallel across the various sections of newspapers, which simultaneously on any given page offered representations of troop dispatches, battles overseas, casualty lists, and a plethora of other signs that the war was a costly, noble effort, formed the reading backdrop for enemy alien coverage. The local news section often included gossipy items that included incidental references to some 'problem' in the city. Front-page features, on the other hand, might broadcast striking accounts of atrocities overseas or particular threats closer to home. Such relational sequencing could intensify the appearance of negative coverage of the enemy and enemy alien.

The same could be said, as we shall see, for public orations performed locally that paralleled the national and provincial sites of parliamentary debate that were broadcast periodically in the press. That the Empire was a moral, virtuous, and peace-devoted federation was not only central to Hardie's speech or Cobbledick's sermon cited above, but was also taken up in subsequent lectures in Guelph and Lethbridge. That version of Canada as part of 'Greater' Britain could take listeners back to an imagined space and time, when another man called Schultz might prove himself a great Canadian through his ties to 'British values.' But, of course, the deepening crisis of the war, intensified by the German spying system that had spread its 'universal distrust and suspicion,' had changed everything. Modest Canada, chaste but not as sturdy as need be, was portrayed as imminently imperilled in the *Bien Public,* where Barnard conveyed it for his francophone readers as a country with a particularly exposed region along the Quebec-American border. The *Newcomer*'s upward escalation of the German-American population to some 7 million – almost equal to Canada's population – dovetailed with the potential for disaster Bernard foretold. If Canada was small in population and endangered in many ways, the *Mercury* implied to Guelph readers that the country was also magnificent and a vital producer of foodstuffs through that 'great grain route, which must be kept open' – the Welland Canal, inflated in its importance once again in comparable terms.

Gendered representations also served as signs to position anxieties concerning enemy aliens. *Mercury* readers encountered a truculent masculinity, expressed as vandalism and ritualized through mud hurled at the Laird of Skibo statue or as outbursts of physical violence elsewhere, ethnically stereotyped when placed in the overly enthused hands of the 'braw' or 'stalwart' Scot. Against this stood the more ordered practice, as imagined, of a military encounter on the 'Niagara frontier,' perhaps seen through the sign of invasions past and present in that area, reconfigured this time as an American foe of German heritage. When *Herald* readers in Lethbridge were told that military law prevailed, that Weirmeir could have been backed up against a wall and shot, the image was proffered of a desperate saboteur, pinned against the resolute will of military law. As well, a wholly fantastic terrain of espionage was itemized in the *Bien Public* in androcentric terms: the radio waves, ports, canals, bridges, and roads exposed to enemy spies present putative encounters between the police and hostile men.

Barnard's passage above joins other references to an imagined view of authorized violence and force. Would-be invaders or their accomplices in Canada were up against 'the authorities,' a usable image for the state or its apparatus, sometimes preceded by the term 'proper' or 'government' or 'appropriate.' 'The authorities' were the ones who 'knew' what was going on, could 'deal' with matters, or could best 'inform' the public. References to their legitimacy and propriety invoked notions of state-society hierarchies that might be championed for their probity or castigated for their inability to prevent disaster. In Barnard's portrait of the enemy alien menace, 'les autorités' had only been partly successful in intercepting enemy radio communication. In reference to allegedly outspoken Germans in Goderich, the *Mercury* referred, on the other hand, to 'government authorities in Ottawa' that were said to have given them official notice to watch their tongues.

War-related news in general, and representations of the enemy and enemy alien specifically, were sensationalized in newspapers, which circulated partly as an appealing and cheap form of entertainment. By closely examining accounts of how, on the other hand, several well-publicized lectures in Guelph and Trois-Rivières were received, we can begin to examine how certain themes were interpreted at select, hometown gatherings. As signs of active participation at public gatherings, descriptions of audience reactions that survive in the press reports have left us something more than simplistic stereotypes to gauge local perceptions of the enemy 'other.' How crowds reacted to stunning and disturbing 'revelations' concerning the enemy, through public lectures, suggests another powerful avenue of perception.

Local Visits, Revelations, and Clever Discourses

Public speakers often addressed issues concerning the enemy, fashioned for their respective audiences. The speeches and sermons delivered by Lethbridge's mayor or its Methodist preacher at the beginning of the war both set moderate tones for the trajectories that followed. In the cases described below, however, audiences encountered more negative stereotypes. Opinion on the war could be amplified according to the authority speakers held in the view of their audiences. And orations remained at this time an important public vehicle used by home front populations to shape their views on the war.

Public speaking had become a major cultural industry across Western societies during the nineteenth and early twentieth century. It served functions later reconfigured for mass audiences by electronic media, from radio in the 1920s, which removed visual stimuli, to television, which reintroduced it.

Orators of all kinds, who might offer a lecture, sermon, address, recital, or chalk talk, appeared in contexts that varied from the revival meeting to the travelling show, from spokespersons panning panaceas to the chautauquas that appeared first in Canada in Lethbridge in 1917. This important cultural mechanism often presented the latest fashionable notion or solutions to perceived problems that drew variously from religion, philosophy, health, economics, or science. The specific reasons for gathering shaped the social makeup of audiences, from a clandestine union-organizing drive to a public scientific exhibit. Audience context, in other words, tells us much more about the horizon of expectations than can newspaper circulation figures for a city daily. Turning to several speaking events in Guelph and Trois-Rivières helps us consider how images of the enemy were transmitted in particular settings, partially closed to the public at large, but rebroadcast in the public sphere by the newspapers that subsequently summarized each affair.

In November 1914 an archidiaconal conference was held at St. James Anglican Church in Guelph. The Rev. Derwyn Trevor Owen, future primate of the Anglican Church of Canada, and Archdeacon H.J. Cody, future president of the University of Toronto, both rectors from Toronto, each spoke on a theme announced as 'The present distress of nations and its challenge to the church.' Owen referred to the 'spirit of sacrifice' needed to carry on the war. He made no reference to Germany, the 'foe,' or any other enemy. 'One of the good things – if such it might be termed – that would come from the present war would be the breaking down of a too severe provincialism and narrowness,' he stated. 'People are now apt to take a world-wide view of things, because the world is suffering from a common trouble.'[53]

Cody's oration was entirely different. Claiming that the 'hatred of the English had been carefully and persistently instilled into the very souls of the German people for the past forty years,' he pursued three themes: the subverted power of the German state and its intellectual elites; the enduring appeal of warfare in Germany since unification; and its desire to resume war and grab what it could of the British Empire, including Canada. He followed the strategy of constructing a malevolent German nation in relation to the virtue of the other side: 'It was hard for the British people to understand or fathom such a hatred because as a nation the British bear no malice toward any race.' 'Too often,' he added 'have the people of Canada thought of Germany as a place only of art and music. A better conception of the true German ideal is found in the words of Bismarck who referred to the constituent states in the German Empire as being welded together by Iron and Blood.' He singled out the philosopher Friedrich Nietzsche, the nationalist historian Heinrich von Treitschke, and a more recent popularizer, General Friedrich von Bernardi, whose book promoting German militarism, *Germany and the Next War*, had suddenly and not surprisingly gained notoriety in translation.[54] 'Various influences,' Cody claimed, 'had been brought to work by the great national teachers of the Teutons. Back of all these was the one motive and incentive, viz. to wipe forever from the face of the earth, the British people as an empire.' Warning the audience at St. James that there would be 'no short war,' Cody concluded by saying, 'Canadians should not make the mistake of minimizing the danger of the period through which she is now passing. Germany above all else wants colonies, and what could better satisfy this longing than the possession of the Dominion of Canada?'[55]

Cody was a graduate of Toronto's Wycliffe College, a leading institution in the training of evangelical Anglican clergy in Canada since the 1870s.[56] Another alumnus, George M. Wrong, who had already begun his influential tenure as a history professor at the University of Toronto, addressed Guelph's Canadian Club the day after Cody and Owen spoke. The Guelph branch met regularly at the Royal Canadian Café and hosted speakers who addressed the concerns of middle-class English Canada. The Friday night meeting was described as 'largely attended.' Professor Wrong was said to have spoken 'entertainingly concerning the circumstances that led up to the present war, and Germany's reason for the war.' As might be expected, Wrong developed an historical narrative that drew connections between German militarism, the country's unification in 1871, and its subsequent history. This led to speculations that simply echoed Archdeacon Cody's: 'The Germans are in an astonishing degree unanimous. The army is the idol of the German people.' Germany had launched an aggressive war, and was intent on gaining colonies, Wrong concluded.[57]

Cody's and Wrong's talks were singled out for praise by the *Mercury*. 'Guelph has this week heard some remarkably clever discourses on the war, and on the ideals that pulsate through the German people,' ran its editorial.[58] It was quite a shift from Hardie and Cobbledick's pointed exoneration of the German people two months earlier in Lethbridge, but they had spoken when news of war was fresh and enthusiasm highest – when Borden and Laurier could stand up in the Commons and urge compassion for all enemy aliens. Now Cody warned that the war might be a long one, based on the German advance through Belgium and the widely disseminated news of continued fighting.

The interpretations and themes Cody and Wrong pursued were quite derivative. Their views of Germany and Germans employed the usual bipolar oppositions between the essentialized enemy, its nature expressed by history, and a British-centred view of their own society. The interpretations and themes each pursued before their audiences at St. James and the Royal Canadian Café appear equally unoriginal as provocative strategies – that is, they engaged a horizon of beliefs, but probably offered little in terms of new information or logic. The *Mercury*'s casting of these talks as 'clever discourses' suggests, once again, the authority of these speakers seen from the paper's usual perspective when reporting local events: the eye of the middling to lower-brow observer, chatting with its readers.

News flows for the next year presented city daily readers with another juxtaposition – plucky Allies, joined by Canadians, persevering toward certain victory against a despised enemy. Overall, they offered nothing to upset the assumptions Cody and Wrong made near the start of the war. Shocking revelations, however contrived, of German atrocities in Belgium – including the rape of women and children, the cutting off of children's hands and women's breasts, and the use of civilians as human shields – also circulated across Allied home fronts. Worse were yet to come. The findings of a British government inquiry were detailed in and disseminated through the Bryce Report, coincidentally released at the same time as news of the sinking of the *Lusitania* in May 1915. The report's main import was to fuel propaganda; evidence of mass rapes, infanticide, and gruesome mutilations in Belgium were included unquestioned. (Some 1,200 depositions were supplied by Belgian refugees and Allied soldiers but many were not taken under oath.) Attempts to reach a clearer understanding of what took place during the invasion would have to come through other sources.

The German army's stymied advance through Belgium did cause enormous destruction; made prisoners of civilians, some of whom were executed; and created a flood of refugees. During the invasion, the German army killed approximately 5,500 civilians. The rapid retreat of the small Belgian army to Antwerp was standard front-page fare well before the Bryce hearings began in December 1914. After the fall of Antwerp, feisty 'little Belgium' gained heroic stature among war watchers. Branches of the Belgian Relief Fund were quickly set up in Canadian cities and throughout the Empire for those who escaped to England.

The press in Canada played its part, Cornelius Jaenen has observed, in exploiting the alleged atrocities and in stimulating support for the relief fund.[59] Jaenen also notes that Belgian immigrants had long enjoyed favourable press coverage throughout Canada. 'Quebec has been particularly receptive to Belgian immigration not only because Belgians were Catholic, and many were francophone or bilingual, but also because unlike the French they were not perceived as having "imperialistic" or colonizing designs.'[60]

That a refugee came to Trois-Rivières to offer his testimonial, to recount his own experiences to an audience no doubt eager to hear of it, is not, then, all that surprising. Like Owen and Cody in Guelph, this Belgian priest, l'abbé M. Larsimont, spoke at a church, at regular Mass in the 'cathédrale' of Trois-Rivières in January 1915. Given the importance of his visit, he spoke to a mixed audience of laypeople and clerics. He told a long story, the details of which recounted horrors he experienced – what he saw, what he did, what he felt – when German forces invaded the diocese of Tournai in northeast Belgium.

He took his audience back to a day some five months earlier, which began for him like many others. At dawn he had approached the door of his presbytery to prepare the Mass. Suddenly German soldiers accosted him. He ended up in a group of about one hundred other villagers, forced to endure an exhausting march that lasted long into the night. The soldiers insulted Larsimont as he neared collapse from thirst and hunger. Arriving at Malines to the east, the displaced villagers were herded 'like animals' into a city park. Six men were shot without warning. Belgium was now in chaos, Larsimont explained. Schools had been burned; religious buildings ruined. The poor were starving. To make matters worse, socialists controlled the streets and gave nothing to the Roman Catholic Church.

He then appealed for help to relieve the most impoverished, to rebuild school libraries, and to restore damaged Catholic buildings. His plea was placed before a hideous background – the evil 'Prussian regime,' the 'brutal horde,' the bestial intruder who had burned children's books, executed civilians in Belgian cities, or used them as hostages as the fighting escalated. As the *Bien Public* reported, 'en terminant son allocution, l'orateur trace une rapide esquisse de l'invasion de commune de Montigny; la prise des otages que les Allemands placent sur leur ligne de front afin qu'ils servent de cibles aux balles françaises, l'incendie des écoles libres, la consternation du peuple qui fuit.' His listeners were described as profoundly moved and generous in their response. Cast as the 'voice of Belgium,' Larsimont was said to have brought them closer to God and asked them to pray for peace in Europe and protection for Canada.[61]

Larsimont was touring Quebec to raise money, not to speculate on the meaning of the war. His testimony as a victim of 'German' brutality lent authenticity to words designed to provoke sympathy and anger, and ultimately to seek charity. In Trois-Rivières this touring priest succeeded, according to the *Bien Public*. While Owen tried to cast the war in a positive light – it beckoned a 'breaking down of a too severe provincialism and narrowness' – Cody, Wrong, and Larsimont portrayed the enemy as evil, his violence characteristic of his tragic national history and autocractic ruler. Larsimont's account acted to confirm direct outcomes – the brutality of German soldiers – prefigured in the images of Germany that Cody and Wrong presented. Contrasts of good and evil were used. Cody's use, for instance, of a model 'British nation'; Wrong's depiction of Germany's insidious and foreign brand of militarism; or Larsimont's references to the collapse of authority – all were important 'we-versus-they' boundaries employed to present the enemy as a relational archetype. Like the Guelph speeches, too, Larsimont's reached a much larger local audience through the press. The plurality of receptions for each talk, however, was contextual – it was audience specific to the extent that we might contrast the imperial-nationalistic perspectives at St. James or at the Royal Canadian Café with those of

Trifluvien parishioners who were moved to donate money for the Catholic cause in Belgium.

As live, spoken performances, these talks operated very differently from newspapers as written texts. In most settings we find that symbolic boundaries between speaker and audience are established, tested, and manipulated to facilitate communication.[62] Dialogue tends to be continuous. In these cases, both audiences and speakers operated from mutually recognizable sensibilities, conveying information with reverence, whether it was Archdeacon Cody addressing the archidiconal conference; Professor Wrong, the Canadian Club; or l'abbé M. Larsimont, the clerics and congregation at the Trois-Rivières Cathédrale. Each audience was made up of listeners who shared the speaker's perspectives, though reception as a specific process remained individually distinct.

Although this is true for newspapers as well, given an editor's awareness of readers' tastes and interests, or readers' awareness of the paper's stance on issues, orations, as live performances, offer aural information and offer it once only. As sequential ritualizations, speeches, talks, lectures, or sermons oblige audiences to witness, and often respond to, a complete performative cycle. Listeners cannot lay their speaker aside momentarily, nor jump from topic to topic as they might in scanning a newssheet. These talks were each heard by their audiences, as a whole, from beginning to end. Tales of distant lands and peoples were told using familiar languages and themes that each group recognized, though no two people could have 'heard' them exactly the same way.

Cody, Wrong, and Larsimont also dramatized their view of events through rhetorical forms that listeners could appreciate as tragic. A similar thematic interplay in all three talks established idealized notions of a pre-war past, subverted by an evil incarnate, requiring, by the end of each address, some form of new awareness or assertive action. For Cody, 'British people' had lived without any means of conceiving the true evil of German culture, which was hidden by its great artistic works. Quite accurately, and unlike many, he predicted a long war, brought about by Germany's intense hatred for and desire to destroy Great Britain. Canada, he concluded, must recognize and act on what he saw as a very real threat to the security of the Empire. Wrong's themes were similar, with emphasis on the unanimity of militarism in Germany and his warning that hunger for colonies was part of the reason it had 'launched an aggressive war.' Both argued that action must proceed from knowing the full extent of the danger – an imperilment of Canada itself – embedded in German society and history. Larsimont began his story by casting himself as an ordinary priest in Belgium, about to perform the Mass. His injuries at the hands of German soldiers, who did far worse to others, may have increased the horror of his story. Captured without warning by brutes, as he described it, he was forced to witness his country's devastation. Now he needed help to rebuild his diocese and his homeland. Like the others, he wished as much to restore the past as to regenerate the future.

To deal with the past and the uncertain course the war would take was really the challenge everyone faced, from an able-bodied recruit whose background in one way or another had induced him to sign on, to enemy aliens plagued by enemy citizenship. For the proportionally few who were interned, life was lived in limbo. They received little news of war on a daily basis. That it would simply end so they could pick up, if possible, where they had left off was not always their only hope. Many secured early release as labour shortages intensified. A few young men in the camps did not choose to wait for either release or the end of the war. They tried to escape.

The Lethbridge Internment Camp: Military Bureaucracy, Escapes, and the Image of the Internee

'The wrath of Lethbridge citizens, roused to white heat over the horror of Germany's latest piratical act is finding vent in vigorous denunciation of the easy life allowed German internees in the detention camp here. The general opinion is that the internees should be under much stricter regulation, and made to realize that they are prisoners of war ... if regulations permit privileges to be extended to them, the regulations should be changed.'[63] So read the Lethbridge *Herald*'s front page on 10 May 1915, three days after the sinking of the *Lusitania*.

Seven months earlier, on 30 September 1914, the Lethbridge Internment Camp had been set up in the poultry buildings located at the city's exhibition grounds.[64] This barbed-wire enclosure was one of two dozen receiving stations and detention camps set up across Canada. District commanding officers across Canada's six military divisions and three districts were responsible for administering them, a task that began during the first few weeks of war, when US-bound enemy reservists were captured en route. Enemy aliens arrested in Alberta, Military District 13, led by Col. E.A. Cruikshank, were sent to the Lethbridge camp. At first the 25th Field Battery, under Captain Stewart's command, provided guards until permanent squads were assigned by Ottawa. A District Registrar for Enemy Aliens, P.W. Pennefather, was appointed on 4 November 1914 and worked from a Calgary office, which handled most of the Lethbridge cases.[65] Two days later, Maj.-Gen. Otter took charge of Internment Operations, inheriting a system already in the process of expanding.[66]

By the end of 1914, housing in the camp consisted of a series of renovated wooden poultry buildings sheltering bunks for about eighty prisoners. Additional space was also available under the grandstand for another hundred.[67] The first prisoner roll stood at twenty-nine, climbing to 125 by May 1915. Guard assignments usually ran between twenty-five and thirty officers and men.[68] Diet was minimally adequate, though high in starch and low in fresh produce.[69] In January 1915 Stewart wrote to Cruikshank, calling his 'attention to the matter of clothing for Prisoners of War, twelve men being unable to go out for exercise, on account of being without socks.'[70] Underwear, sweaters, caps, and socks were subsequently ordered in lots of one or two hundred.[71] After Stewart left for overseas in the spring, responsibility for the camp was assigned to Capt. J.A. Birney, who took command in May 1916.

The welfare of its inmates was not ignored by civilians. Emily Murphy, then convener of the Committee on Peace and Arbitration for the National Council of Women of Canada, posed a series of questions about the prisoners' welfare by letter, which was passed on to Cruikshank, then to Otter. 'I am making bold to remind you,' she wrote, 'that your position as Commandant is "National service" in the highest sense of the words. The opportunity thus afforded you of lightening the bitterness of the men's incarceration and of showing the true meaning of human brotherhood cannot fail to have its effect on those, who will, in all probability, remain to form the German element in Canada when the war is over.' Seemingly unaware that non-Germans from Austro-Hungarian territories actually formed the majority of the total prisoner population, Murphy's patronizing reference to the camps as an 'opportunity' to demonstrate 'human brotherhood' was used at the close of this letter to justify her intent that humane conditions prevail.[72] She wished to confirm not just that food, shelter, and clothing were adequate, but that educational and other cultural pursuits were encouraged.

Otter had Cruikshank supply, as briefly as possible, affirmative replies.[73] The supply of items like stationery 'to carry on with their School Work' could hardly mitigate a confinement of mostly younger men, validated through both public discourse and state practice. As in other camps and labour gangs, circumstances for the men at Lethbridge fell far short of Murphy's ideal. In reference to the entire system, Otter later admitted that some men suffered emotionally. 'Insanity,' he noted in his *Report on Internment Operations*, tabled in 1921, 'was by no means uncommon among the prisoners, many being interned it was suspected to relieve municipalities of their care, while in others the disease possibly developed from a nervous condition brought about by the confinement and restrictions entailed.'[74]

There is evidence of some abuse at the Lethbridge camp. Such allegations first surfaced in claims made by the Chicago *Tribune*. This American paper reprinted an anonymous letter from a former prisoner of the camp, possibly forwarded by friends or relatives. The statement was introduced as 'purporting to come from one of the German prisoners interned in the Canadian military camp at Lethbridge, Alberta.' It charged that guards routinely abused prisoners verbally and physically, forcing them to stand with their hands above their heads, sometimes with handcuffs.[75] The statement was presented as a 'literal translation' from the German of the former prisoner's letter.

Had the American German counsel not subsequently taken up the allegations, they would probably have been ignored in Canada. Britain's ambassador to the United States was asked for an explanation, and the problem was brought to Otter's attention. The correspondence that followed refers to the punishment system, partly coded in masculinities, for which guards and prisoners might ordinarily negotiate parameters setting out the boundaries of speech, gesture, and transgression by either group that their mutual confinement required. Otter alternatively saw such limits defined by military procedures and 'British custom.' As he put it in his letter to Cruikshank, prompted by the diplomatic exchange: 'Several of the charges made are trivial, and the punishment awarded easily understood as being necessary as well as legitimate, but in four cases recourse was had to inhuman measures, and quite beyond the limits of the Army Act, or British custom.'

He referred to the cases of Prisoner of War 'Makeranko,' who 'was handcuffed' with 'his hands tied above his head for 30 minutes'; 'P. of W. Hans Schultz – stood in Guard Room with his hands tied above his head for 30 minutes.' The same was cited for 'P. of W. Bringewatt' and for 'P. of W. Ewanyczuk,' said to have endured twenty minutes. 'How any palliation can be offered for these punishments I am at a loss to surmise,' Otter concluded, suggesting the practical limits of control he faced as the system's chief official. 'But of this I am certain that a repetition must not occur, and I would trouble you to officially notify Captain Birney – That if a more close supervision cannot be exercised over the Officers, Non. Commissioned Officers and men of his command in their treatment of prisoners, the object of their present duties are rendered valueless, and the good name of Canada brought to the level of the Huns.'[76] His last comment implied the 'we-versus-they' dialectic invoked by Murphy earlier.

Cruikshank passed the warning on to Birney in terms that recognized a gap between measures taken by guards and the boundaries, perhaps idealized, that higher officials preferred: 'This message has already been directed to your attention and it is with great regret that I have again to point out to you that inhumanity must not be exercised by guards over Prisoners of War.'[77] Birney protested that three of the four incidents occurred 'prior to the time that I took over the charge of this Camp and therefore I do not understand how I should be held accountable for this.' Birney regretted 'very much' the case of Makeranko, and conceded that his sergeant 'forgot himself as to mete out this class of punishment. He was however severely reprimanded at the time and given strict instructions that a repetition of this offence would not be tolerated by me.'[78] Nonetheless, in an earlier summary of twelve separate cases of alleged prisoner abuse, Birney reported that the punishments cited by Otter did take place.[79] Responsibility for them, given the change in command at the Lethbridge camp and a high turnover of guard personnel, was difficult to pin down.

The prisoners themselves complained of previous handcuffing incidents to a representative of the American consular official who had visited the camp 'on behalf of the German and Austrian governments' shortly after Birney assumed his duties.[80] Birney responded that the 'charge that Guards have cuffed Prisoners on the slightest provocation is something which I am not aware of, nor have I heard of it being done since being in charge of this Camp.'[81] Life in the camp, by all accounts, was an exercise in endurance. The fact that prisoners suffered winter and summer climate extremes, surrounded by barbed wire and housed in a facility used previously for chickens, no doubt contributed to their resentment.

Camp routines, though site-specific, activated diverse encounters between guards and prisoners throughout the internment system. The range was extreme, from guards being reprimanded for sharing alcohol with prisoners to several cases of prisoners being shot and killed while trying to escape, though this never happened in Lethbridge. The military's official diary from the larger Castle Mountain camp at Banff indicates how guards and prisoners followed strict routines under a regime of forced labour. Other activities were offered, however, from church services to an 'Indian Days' masquerade preserved in a posed photograph.[82] The officers who, in succession, kept this record often began daily reports with details on weather conditions. In our approaches to evidence of prisoner-guard relations, which depend primarily on 'official' records of individual facilities and on the system as a whole, we must consider the fluidity of negotiation and exchange, and the resistances prisoner actions often signified. Bill Waiser's study of enemy alien labour, for instance, underscores the problem guards faced when they tried to induce prisoners to perform at a high level of efficiency. They failed overall because the prisoners did not comply fully. Their refusals appear as inactions that spoke louder than words.[83]

In reference to the Lethbridge camp, where prisoners were only detained, Otter judged the outcomes of contested power relations between prisoners and guards, which he found unsatisfactory on personal inspection, as simply the consequence of having 'undesirable' guards. But like other officials and prisoners, he was well aware that state authority was trying to enforce systematic direction of a diverse group of men who had no interest, beyond survival, in being there. Accomplishing this discipline, Otter judged, depended on how the guards executed, or failed to execute, their roles.

An inspection visit by Otter a year after the consular visit prompted his conclusion, in a handwritten letter to Cruikshank, that 'very undesirable men' were serving as guards. He added, with reference to the problem of maintaining adequate guard personnel when fit men were periodically seconded for overseas training, that this was 'a contingency I can quite understand difficult to control [sic]' But he added: 'One of these men lately deserted under suspicion of being connected with the escape of two prisoners, and two others are evidently useless.'[84] While Cruikshank defended the guards, stating that they had been 'carefully selected' and that 'nothing' had been 'known of them which would affect their character unfavourably,' he reiterated the difficulty of detailing 'good men' for guard duty 'at Internment Camps because if they are found fit for overseas service they are at once drafted in battalions of the Expeditionary Force.'[85]

Besides having little confidence in Lethbridge guards, Otter did not want to entrust district commanders with any authority to release prisoners. He ensured that his office was kept closely informed of any appeals for parole, despite the increase this caused in administrative workload. After Cruikshank inspected the Lethbridge camp in early January 1915, he informed Otter that 'several prisoners were paraded before me who asked for their release. In some cases the Officer in charge stated that he was prepared to recommend their release on parole.' Cruikshank asked if he might approve such cases on his discretion.[86] Otter declined. In each case, separate applications were to be prepared for consideration in Ottawa. 'While not anxious to increase the work now falling upon me in connection with my present responsibilities,' Otter explained, 'I deem it advisable for its proper administration that I should obtain some knowledge of circumstances and conditions throughout the Dominion and it is with this idea in view that for the present I do not ask you to undertake any responsibility arising from the kind assistance which you offer me.'[87] The 'proper administration' Otter insisted upon was often one of delay or refusal.

A Lethbridge case involved a German internee, Ewald Hingst. It began when Hingst appealed directly to Cruikshank in early February 1915. As he put it in a letter, prepared in translation: 'I am a prisoner of war at the Lethbridge Detention Camp and I write this letter to you to explain my case, why I was arrested, so you can decide, whether you would be able to let me out on parole again.' Hingst went on to describe his arrival in Calgary from Germany on 21 May 1914, where he secured employment as a saddle maker for Riley and McCormick Ltd. 'To make my life a little more comfortable,' Hingst continued, 'I have rented 3 rooms and a kitchen at Riverside Center av[e]. 651 and have these rooms furnished. The day I was arrested I've asked the soldiers, what I should do with my rooms, and they've told me, go lock the doors and the government would pay the rent. Yesterday I received a letter asking for the rent and I don't know now what to do.' His explanation of why he was arrested followed: 'I have registered in Calgary on Dec 10, at the police station, and the interpreter did not tell me, that I had to register again on January 10. Now, while I can not read or write English I thought that it was sufficient to register once, and that was the cause of my arrest. If

I had known, that I had to register again, I certainly would have done so.' He also claimed that he was not a German reservist.[88]

This case might be contrasted with group dismissals of labourers without specialized training who were let go by foremen or by employers as a matter of policy, oftentimes at the insistence of other workers. Hingst had quite different relations with his previous employer. After he contacted them, too, the firm replied: 'We have written Inspector Pennefather stating your case, and trust he will see his way clear to release you.' Riley and McCormick Ltd. also promised him his job back, pending a successful appeal.[89] Major Stewart then wrote to Cruikshank, describing Hingst as a 'very quiet character' and saying that, with a job waiting for him, he did 'not see any reason' for further confinement.[90] The appeal reached Otter, who disagreed. His argument seemed based on a particular view of Germans. On Hingst's excuse for failing to report to a parole officer, Otter wrote: 'That "he was not aware of the necessity for reporting" I cannot think is correct as the general run of his nationality are more than ordinarily intelligent and at a time like this do not misconstrue what is said to them unless for a purpose.'[91] A renewed appeal the following month was again blocked as Otter reaffirmed 'the above decision unless informed of mitigating circumstances.'[92]

Some risked escape, particularly from the Lethbridge camp. A total of eight separate escapes involving seventeen internees took place between November 1914 and October 1916.[93] Comparing two sets of evidence helps us address a significant divide between newspaper coverage of these escapes and records produced by the military itself, particularly inquiries afterwards that dealt with causes. In the process, more is revealed about who escaped and how, in contrast to the *Herald*'s penchant for offering more sensational images of the escapees.

The first involved a single man, captured without incident in a nearby town four days afterwards.[94] This story was probably kept out of the *Herald* deliberately, or at least camp officials kept quiet about it. The second, however, received the following description: 'Fritz Rapp, the lusty Hun warrior, who was captured by the city police some months ago and turned over to the military authorities as a prisoner-of-war, was too slippery for the guards at the military prison, and on Friday evening escaped with a pal.' Rapp and his 'pal,' P. Armbruster, managed to elude capture for over forty-eight hours despite a huge deployment of '75 mounted men engaged in the search.'[95]

Following their capture, Stewart sent Cruikshank a letter of explanation that fell short of saving face. He had called out the entire battery to look not only for the escapees, but also for a lone officer, lost somewhere on the prairie and unable to report back. 'The experience,' Stewart rationalized, 'I feel sure will be of much benefit to the Battery and I may say it will be a good lesson for men to always travel at least in twos as we would not have turned the Battery out if he had a companion with him.'[96]

Rapp and Armbruster, as the *Herald* put it, 'were brought back to the city, and are again behind the barbed-wire. Rapp is a lieutenant in the German landwehr, and is considered a prize catch.'[97] If this was true, Rapp would have been one of 3,138 (of the 8,579) interned who Otter later described in his report as actually apprehended 'in arms,' that is, a member of an enemy army or naval reserve captured either trying to escape into the United States or, as 817 were, shipped to Canada after detention in Caribbean ports.[98]

The most notorious breakout occurred at the end of April 1916 when six internees escaped through a tunnel. Subsequently measured at 111 feet (about 34 metres), it led from a bunkhouse, under the wire, and through to a garden outside the compound. 'What military and police authorities all admit to be the smoothest escape pulled off in Canada since the outbreak of the war,' the *Herald* reported at the end of April 1916, 'was successfully consummated in the pitch-dark hours between midnight and daybreak on Wednesday morning of this week.' The *Herald*'s front-page story spoke of 'six full-blooded Germans' who 'made a clean getaway, and have not been seen since though the country has been combed from one end to the other for a trace of the fugitives.' The paper then raised the question of camp security. 'That the whole camp did not get away is a wonder to anyone who has examined the elaborate plans of the plotters.'[99] But the fact that only six escaped suggests the prison population, of just over a hundred at this point, was divided between the half dozen willing to assume the risk of being shot and most who were not, though they were possibly united in keeping preparations, which were indeed 'elaborate,' a secret.

While the search for the half-dozen 'full-blooded Germans' continued, their escape was reconstructed through testimonies gathered by a formal Court of Enquiry ordered by Cruikshank. That they were never captured suggests that they made it across the border. They were probably German reservists, intent on reaching their homeland. Facing a board of three officers headed by Lt.-Col. A.W. Pryce-Jones of the Lethbridge Highlanders, Captain Birney and each of the guards on duty the night of the escape were grilled at length.

'What system of inspection of the Barracks have you?' Birney was asked as the first witness.

'We have,' he replied, 'a daily inspection of the camp, the same as we would inspect a military camp. This inspection is made at 15 minutes to 12, and then [we] go in and have the roll call, and each man answers his name and is counted. Complaints are asked for. I inspect the buildings, but do not say I inspect them minutely every time, but see that everything is right and proper. I inspect the kitchen, latrines. The fences are inspected twice a day by one of the Guards. Once in a while we make an inspection of the bunks to see that nothing is there which they should not have.'[100]

Since the tunnel was dug from an entry hole concealed underneath one of the bunks, attention focused on how the buildings were inspected. The Board of Enquiry asked Birney, 'There is no record of inspection underneath the bunks?'

'No,' he responded. 'Sometimes they put their shoes and valises there. We allow them to put such stuff as prs. of socks, clean change of underwear, comb, brushes, etc. [under their bunks] because they have no cupboards to put them in. General Otter went through the same inspection as we usually do. We do not get down on our hands and knees, and he (General Otter) suggested that cupboards be made for them.'[101]

Testimony from the guards indicated, in hindsight, a restlessness among the prisoners on the night of the escape. A corporal stated that he thought the prisoners were 'getting uneasy' as he watched them staring out their bunkhouse windows. He even claimed that he felt they might attack the guards. When asked why, he recalled: 'My idea was when these men got up at the windows ... they would draw the attention of the sentries ... and I would go out to investigate and they would storm the Guard while I was out.'[102]

Another testified that this same corporal had told him at the time 'to keep my eye on the window. Half an hour after that he again came out and told me to keep on the dark side where the prisoners could not see me. He asked me if I had my rifle loaded and I said yes. He told me to fix my bayonet, as he thought there was something unusual going to happen that night. This would be about 12.30 or 1 A.M.'[103]

Shortly afterwards, the corporal testified. 'I asked the sentry on No. 1 beat if everything was quiet, he did not report that he had seen anything to me, but the sentry on No. 3 beat said he thought there was a bit of noise down below, but he thought it was a Jack rabbit as they were seen there before, and I have seen them myself.'[104]

The escapees, who might have made the noise, were soon long gone. When this was discovered next morning, a search was hastily mounted for their route, which uncovered the tunnel's exit, concealed in the shrubbery of the city's nursery gardens located just outside the compound. The guard who found it was asked to describe the tunnel. 'There was [a] large stone,' he said, 'and I pushed it aside and I took the two boards off, then I took a match and crept a little way into the hole and found overalls, boots and tins of fat then I got most of them out and I crept into the hole again and found little bags with food stuff in them. As I crept through the hole I found 6 loaves of bread, carrots and two small boxes with ropes attached.'[105]

Earlier, Birney reported that 'various tools' were discovered: 'A Butcher's knife with teeth cut into it apparently used as a saw. A wooden maul with tin covering it on one side. A small iron chisel. An old coal shovel with a short handle. A piece of lead pipe with one end flattened out. Two boxes with rope attached. Empty tobacco can and piece of fat ham apparently used for lighting purposes. A crude measuring rod.'[106]

'Did you see the fan?' the guard who first discovered the tunnel was asked. Much of the questioning centred on a crudely fabricated ventilating fan used to supply air to the tunnel. This device, which was also retrieved from the tunnel, had been seen in various states of preparation by many around the camp in the weeks leading up to the escape. Birney reported that the camp's medical officer had noticed the prisoners working on the fan. 'He stopped them and asked them what they were doing, and they told him they were just passing the time away, but he never reported it to me.'[107] Others reported that they 'saw them making something like that about two weeks ago,' or 'I saw them making it, and thought it was an ordinary trinket.'[108] What the prisoners realized was that the best way to hide the most cumbersome necessity was to make no attempt to hide it at all.

No sooner had the examining board uncovered evidence of a poorly guarded camp than the *Herald* got busy providing readers with a series of rumours: 'Is there a nest of German spies working in Lethbridge?' Were the Lethbridge six 'aided by German agents in the city?' This 'suspicion' was 'strongly hinted' at by a 'local police officer.' 'Either they were loaded into a waiting automobile and whisked across the line or they were hidden by friends in some out-of-the-way place close to the city,' the *Herald* claimed. Speculation also led to a theory 'that signals might have been passed by some unsuspected method so that the outside accomplices would know the exact time when the attempt to escape was to be made.' In an effort to place these conjectures on firmer ground, the paper added: 'In fact, it is rumored on good authority that one attempt by an outside party to signal the inmates of the camp had been frustrated.'[109] Nearly two weeks later, a brief notice in the *Herald* reported that the 'country has been combed for clues but none have come to light and it is pretty generally conceded that the Germans got across the line.'[110]

Within six weeks, another two internees had escaped while on supervised exercise leave outside the prison compound.[111] Three days later, Maj. W.D. Date replaced a beleaguered Captain Birney. According to the *Herald*, the new camp commander claimed to be an experienced administrator who 'hopes to be able to handle the situation here.'[112] He had no more success than Birney: two prisoners disappeared that September, another pair in October.[113] Enquiry after enquiry followed, but to no avail. Conclusions that the guards 'signally failed'[114] to carry out their responsibilities or that they 'neglected their duty'[115] revealed perhaps a comedy of errors spawned by the difficulty of retaining capable camp personnel, a fact acknowledged privately by Cruikshank and Otter. It also indicated how tenuous their power was to control these men as prisoners.

The mundane task of housing over one hundred men at a time in secure confinement was fraught with innumerable difficulties, from ensuring there were enough socks to go around to endure the prairie winter, to reassuring area residents that their charges were 'safely' behind barbed wire. Throughout, the *Herald* offered sometimes silly coverage: 'Germans in the Detention Camp Make Zeppelin,' one front-page piece claimed, probably as an eye-catcher. 'The Zeppelins are upon us,' it droned. 'If you don't believe it, get a pass from the military authorities here, and visit the detention camp, where a hundred or more German prisoners of war abide. Suspended from the roof of the building is a fully equipped model of a German Zeppelin. The model raider was built out of pasteboard boxes by some of the prisoners, and is an exact replica of the ones that didn't attack London.'[116]

Absurd accounts of camp life indicate the distances between a local newspaper's perspective and the views of those men who faced everyday life in the camp, prisoners, guards, and officers alike. As rumours began to circulate that the local camp would soon be closed, resentment surfaced in one editorial: 'Canada should have used the labour of every interned alien. They should have been made to build roads and do other work for the benefit of Canada. In some cases they have been used for this purpose but here in Lethbridge, at any rate, they have led a life of idleness. It is true also that they have been given, at times, too much liberty. It is in accordance with the British spirit that they are treated humanely; we would not resort to any other practice. However, since we feed these men, we should get something in return.'[117]

The Lethbridge Internment Camp closed in November 1916, though another one opened near this site for enemy aliens of the Second World War. 'It is thought,' the *Herald* suggested, based on rumour a few weeks before, 'the men will be moved, some to B.C. camps and some more to Spirit Lake, Quebec, where escape is almost impossible and few prisoners will risk it.'[118] On 2 November 1916 the prisoners were dispatched either to serve out further detention as park labourers or to the Spirit Lake Camp. 'Good-bye, Detention Camp,' the *Herald* announced in its brief coverage of this event.[119]

Enemy Aliens: Present at Their Own Making

About one in twelve registered enemy aliens was interned in Canada during the war. However, all enemy aliens lived under shadows others cast, viewed as peoples of divided loyalties and uncertain intentions. Enemy alien representations conveyed new meanings from old distinctions, most obviously with inversions of German-ness, from its positive attributes before the war to the images quickly fabricated at first news of the advance through Belgium. From that point on, rumours of enemy alien conspiracies, sabotage, failed plots, and other horrific tales were commodified, made into highly saleable texts, by newspapers. A few reports of violence surfaced in Guelph and joined a host of new restrictions and barriers posed by the war. Enemy aliens also bore the constant burden of being seen through the enemy overseas. The sinking of the *Lusitania* became a particularly sore flashpoint, but it had been preceded by a barrage of negative images of the enemy and enemy alien, amplified in public lectures sometimes explicit in form, sometimes subtle, from rumours of invasion to invocations to boycott products or services stigmatized by any connection to the enemy.

Enemy aliens, however, were present at their own making. Some began the war by making a donation to the Canadian Patriotic Fund or, as reported in Lethbridge, by actually waving the British flag. The camp evidence clearly points to cases of interned men taking action in many forms: the escapes, the building of the tunnel, the attempts to secure authorized release. These actions, combined with accounts of enemy aliens across the country who tried to signify loyalty to Canada, point to the struggles some engaged in to redefine boundaries many Canadians tried to impose on them. Demonizations of the enemy at home did not operate as uncontested cultural efforts. Specific struggles were often localized. They were also fluid and could appear or dissolve as news of the war shifted, as Ottawa adopted new policies, or as the wartime economy increased labour demands. Very real boundaries of perception, exclusionary practices, and historically constituted social differences produced a home front divided by the presence of enemy aliens as a distinct category of ethnic minorities, but a division that was resisted.

5
Conscription Contested

'Last evening at 9.35 three men in plain clothes, one of whom said he was a Deputy Provost Marshal, called at this house, and demanded that all the members of this community be paraded before him within the delay of five minutes.' This was how Father Henri Bourque, rector of the St. Stanislaus Novitiate, a Jesuit seminary on Bedford farm near Guelph, recalled events in a terse letter of complaint to the Department of Militia and Defence. 'When I asked for his authority for a proceeding so unusual and at such an unseemly hour, he produced from his pocket a brassard with the letters D.P.M., which he said was his authority, and added that if I did not summon the community at once, he would proceed to search the house for deserters and defaulters under the Military Service Act.'[1]

Father Bourque found himself, along with St. Stanislaus's young novices, caught up in a bizarre but telling case, not just of mistaken legal status, but of deciding who had the right to avoid the draft and who did not. The Guelph raid, as it came to be known, was a local fiasco that for a while attracted national press attention, probably because one of the novices suspected of avoiding conscription at St. Stanislaus was none other than Marcus Doherty, son of Charles Doherty, the minister of justice who had helped draft the contentious and divisive Military Service Act of 1917.

The botch-up that caused the Guelph raid is an interesting story in itself. It comes to us through various channels as a process of remaking rumour into fact, from gossip that led to an overzealous military police act and to charges of favouritism raised in the pulpit and the press. But the fact that a Jesuit seminary was raided can take us beyond the surface of this event toward its perception by others in close proximity, with their own views concerning the justifications and authority by which conscription was imposed across Canada. The raid at St. Stanislaus prompted debate on the applicability of a national system of compulsory military service in a plural society, with arguments in this case centred on the law's incapacity to draft men who, otherwise eligible, belonged to a religious order recognized under the act.

Evidence of conscription, contested or supported as a last measure to secure further enlistments for the Canadian Expeditionary Force, survives in many forms across Canada. Oppositional editorial discourse, political campaigns during the 1917 federal election, and a major riot in Quebec City in the spring of 1918 shortly before the Guelph raid accompanied the application of this law, as supporters, largely in English Canada, defended the most divisive step taken by Ottawa on the home front as the war entered its final stages overseas. In each case, perceptions of the legitimacy or the injustice of compulsory military service depended on competing notions of state authority, wartime conditions, and social justice. The problems conscription introduced intersected with local settings, most obviously in Quebec, where the law came into conflict with French Canadian nationalists who felt that their traditional relationship with the rest of the country was being violated.

The editorials that appeared in the *Bien Public* offered detailed recitations of why this particular war measure upset a partnership of dual national identities, using arguments relying heavily on references to political tradition and historical precedent. The newspaper's warnings that the law would promote unrest, and its argument that compulsory military service in a war involving the British Empire defied a very basic relationship between French and English Canada, on the surface appear predictable. And yet the oppositional language its editor, Joseph Barnard, deployed – its symbols, metaphors, and referents – made selective use of cultural narratives and social memories. His commentaries also bore the marks of a cultural conservatism, one that recognized the status quo as a hierarchy of interests expressed by the state, churches, and society in general.

Local conditions also intersected in unique ways in Lethbridge during the 'Khaki' election of 1917. At first glance we find again a foreseeable pattern. W.A. Buchanan, *Herald* owner and Liberal member of Parliament, followed most of his anglophone caucus in crossing the floor in the Commons to join Borden's coalition. His stance was confirmed in the election that followed, as was Union government and conscription as a national law. But he did not run unopposed, nor did he take his constituency by an overwhelming margin. The opposition Buchanan faced unearthed alternative positions on conscription, reflecting a different region with a different sense of social justice than that expressed by Barnard in Trois-Rivières. The terms on which western farmers and labourers opposed the Military Service Act, as proposed, remained anchored in their interests and sense of place in the economic order.

In the cases described here, conscription depended more on how perceptions of history, class relations, and religious freedoms were legitimized than on a simple capacity to exert force. For this reason, it seems particularly apt to approach conscription through public forms used to frame it. Power in these relationships remained fluid, and a core-periphery model of its exercise is misleading. Power to force men into the military did not emanate simply from a central government bureaucracy and legal code to the margins of local circumstance. Rather, each of these cases places us between 'the stream of events that make up political life and the web of beliefs that comprises a culture' to show how power needs to be recognized through matrices of ethnocultural, class, and religious differences that changed from one locale to another.[2] Varied settings and sites in each of our cities served to fix the meaning of state action, but with entirely different outcomes. In this way, compulsory military service can be understood not as a parliamentary act or juridical procedure, but as a consequence of resistances and compliances to the demands of government and the law.

Points of Intersection: From National Law to Editorial Riposte

Addressing contested perceptions of political tradition and of national identity and imposition of conscription takes us first to the origins of the law, then its reception in Quebec, and finally responses in Trois-Rivières. Conscription was Canada's political solution to a military problem. It became a crisis by 1917 because opponents in francophone Quebec felt that their historical relationship with the rest of Canada was being ignored. While in the early weeks of the war some 30,267 volunteers across Canada had scrambled to the recruiter's desk, as each month passed the flow of manpower gradually declined before plummeting in the summer of 1916.[3] By April 1917 the monthly enlistment rate had dropped to a mere 4,761.[4] When Borden informed his cabinet on 17 May, three days after his return from a much-publicized journey overseas that included visiting wounded troops and facing pro-conscription pressure from British leaders, that a change in policy was essential, two francophone ministers from Quebec warned of dire political consequences for themselves and for the Conservative party in their province.

Unmoved, Borden announced his decision in Parliament the next day, where a stunned Wilfrid Laurier sat opposite. 'The responsibility is a serious one,' Borden explained, 'but I do not shrink from it.'[5] His promise of selective conscription, which amounted to a broken one, provoked enormous indignation from French Canada, as he knew it would. Despite the political danger, he considered it a justifiable risk for a larger purpose overseas. With the passage on 29 August of the Military Service Act, his government formally recognized that the voluntary, community-based approach to recruiting was failing and that compulsory service, with administrative authority returned to the federal level, was necessary to force men into the military.

The most serious result was the crisis of national unity dividing French and English Canada, though cleavages between farmers and Ottawa, labour and Ottawa, and a variety of civil libertarians and the federal government were also significant.[6] To complicate matters, a controversial measure implemented by Ontario's Department of Education in 1912, Regulation 17, had become symbolic in the minds of many French Canadians of what lay ahead. This measure restricted francophone public education in Canada's most populous province to the second primary grade.[7] Vehemently opposed in Quebec since its inception, and often tabbed 'Prussianism in Ontario' after the war broke out, Regulation 17 continued to plague relations between French and English Canadians, particularly as debates over conscription surfaced toward the end of 1916.[8]

Yet before Borden's difficult decision, efforts to bridge the gap between French and English had not been completely lost to fights over Ontario's schools or concern over enlistment figures. Entrepreneurs in Ontario and Quebec grew concerned about a possible boycott of English goods called for by some francophones frustrated by the schools issue.[9] The anxieties over political stability and commerce were channelled in a movement called the Bonne Entente, an ephemeral experiment headed by Toronto lawyer John M. Godfrey. Along with an associate, journalist Arthur Hawkes, Godfrey had some success in staging tours in Ontario and Quebec that brought delegates, mostly entrepreneurs, from both provinces face to face to hear speeches, socialize, pass resolutions, and form committees. Their general aim, as one of Godfrey's Bonne Entente pamphlets expressed it, was to try to recapture the spirit of cooperation that had gripped the country at the outbreak of the war.[10]

Support for the Bonne Entente came mostly from manufacturers, boards of trade, chambers of commerce, and municipal leaders rather than from provincial politicians sensitive to the spectre of conscription. Premier Lomer Gouin of Quebec endorsed its aims nonetheless, and though the Bonne Entente could not survive the divisive effects of conscription, its hopes reflected practical concerns shared by middle-class neighbours in Quebec and Ontario. As Brian Cameron put it in his study of its brief history, the Bonne Entente's support in francophone Quebec was strongest among those inspired by 'commercial motives,' who hoped to draw on 'sympathy for English Canadians and the war.'[11] Their aims certainly coincided with self-interest.

After meetings with Sherbrooke's Board of Trade and Montreal's Chamber of Commerce, one of its first travelling delegations was welcomed by representatives of Trois-Rivières' Chamber of Commerce during a goodwill tour Godfrey organized in July 1916.[12] It appears to have been a minor affair and received no coverage in Trois-Rivières' newspapers. If nothing more, it paved the way for a much larger and more prestigious Bonne Entente tour that autumn.

At half past noon on 11 October 1916, a train carrying some fifty Ontario representatives arrived at Trois-Rivières's CPR platform. Though most were presidents, board members, or executives from a cross-section of Ontario firms, the entourage included Queen's University's O.D. Skelton. On the heels of a successful visit to Montreal, news of their arrival had attracted a crowd of onlookers. From there, they were treated to a colourful reception and dinner at city hall. Alderman Robert Ryan introduced them. Acting Mayor Arthur Bettez addressed them. Bettez's speech, delivered in English from a prepared text, amounted to little more than glib platitudes on the virtues of harmony between Ontario and Quebec, a goal he claimed to share with the citizens of Trois-Rivières.[13] This was typical of many of the first receptions and meetings of the Bonne Entente, where ceremonial decorum and genial manners prevailed, while thorny questions over Regulation 17 and conscription were avoided.[14] Bettez did offer one practical suggestion for entrepreneurs – setting up an interprovincial commission to stimulate and coordinate commercial and industrial trade between Ontario and Quebec, though nothing came of this.[15]

From there the delegation moved on to Quebec City and the Eastern Townships. A steamer trip down the St. Lawrence, a banquet at the Château Frontenac, and visits to Thetford's asbestos mines and several educational institutions, including Bishops College in Lennoxville, topped off its publicized swing through the province. At this point, the entire effort was more a movement than an organization. Throughout the meetings and immediately afterwards, committees were formed to promote 'perfect harmony between the races,' however unrealistic this objective might have been as the threat of conscription loomed. A month later, a committee of Quebec supporters met at Montreal's Board of Trade and adopted formally the 'Bonne Entente' label for what had become an interprovincial network of businessmen with a smattering of professionals in search of 'racial harmony' while voluntary recruitment declined across Canada and collapsed in Quebec.[16]

The return of the last of these delegations to Trois-Rivières in May 1917 suffered from disastrous timing. Borden's decision to impose selective conscription had been made public four days before it arrived. Approximately two hundred visitors, calling themselves the National Unity Congress, were greeted by Mayor J.-A. Tessier and local dignitaries, who hosted another city hall banquet. Coincidentally, Lethbridge's mayor, W.D.L. Hardie, was part of this group.[17] While their reception, the largest yet, was described as 'cordial,' the emerging political crisis over Borden's action was no doubt on everyone's mind.[18] In the end, Ottawa's decision to adopt conscription all but extinguished their hopes, though it might be said that the final blow came when Laurier rejected Borden's overture for coalition support.[19] The Bonne Entente simply could not survive, but what can we learn from its efforts at cultural exchange and interaction?

The tours that passed through Trois-Rivières and other local communities were highly ritualized performances, staged by specific groups – entrepreneurs, journalists, and a university professor of political economy – in encounters that served to symbolize national unity outside of government, but within circles of business and intellectual elites: the ceremonial dinner at the Château Frontenac, the special tour of the Thetford mines, inspections of an Anglican college and several other schools, and the city hall reception in Trois-Rivières. As public events, each was situational and strategic. The encounters were formalized. The internal orchestration of activities was structured by shared expectations and interests. Communication, in this sense, was restricted to the dogmatic formalism found, for instance, in Bettez's speech, which saluted cooperation but said nothing of Regulation 17. The *ententistes* comprised a particular constituency, an alliance of mutual benefit with lofty aims propagandized time and again in its pamphlets and public statements: cooperation, goodwill, and support for national unity.

Welcomed visitors and congenial hosts used ceremonial formality to mediate shared interests and avoid intractable problems. Ritualizations that privileged supportive speeches or other affectations of gesture, decorum, or etiquette authorized not the national government but the ideal of national unity. It was possible, despite the rancour over the conscription issue in spring 1917, for the mayor, city council, and local business leaders to meet with their English visitors in essentially private displays for public purposes. If nothing else, the gravity, solemnity, and respect communicated through their encounters served to produce 'cordial' relations between men from comparable social strata in English Ontario and French Quebec who, like Bettez, pledged support for mutual interests defined by trade if not by trust.

By this point, conscription had divided Canadians as no other issue in the war had done. It would divide the Liberal Party along a line of competing nationalisms and lead to coalition government under the Union banner. With newspapers, French and English, reflecting divided opinion and circulating arguments in support of their positions, some evidence of privately expressed bitterness can be found in a letter by a young student from Trois-Rivières, Louis-Georges Godin, sent to the soon to be ordained Albert Tessier, who would later become one of Quebec's most prominent educators, historians, and filmmakers. Godin described his torment at reading pro-conscription press coverage, or as he put it, 'les discours "jingos."'[20] Godin was outraged that he might be forced to fight for 'old England,' or 'la vieille "bitch."' 'Mourir pour "l'Empire" c'est le sort le plus doux!' he stated sarcastically. 'Ah! les animaux!'[21]

Trois-Rivières's member of Parliament, Jacques Bureau, rode a powerful wave of such sentiment as a strident opponent of conscription within Wilfrid Laurier's crumbling Liberal caucus. The year before, Bureau had written to

Laurier to see if his leader had any intention of joining a pro-conscription coalition should such an offer be made, as he put it, by 'les ennemis.'[22] Laurier replied that he had no intention of doing so: 'Je n'ai pas l'intention d'accepter l'invitation de nos ennemis.'[23] Laurier and Bureau remained consistent in their position, though the latter enjoyed overwhelming support in his constituency, while his aging leader watched the Liberal Party's following in English Canada evaporate.

As the 1917 election loomed, Bureau issued a pamphlet, 'Discours et Votes de Jacques Bureau Contre la Conscription en 1917,' which summarized speeches delivered in Parliament against the Military Service Act and tabulated parliamentary voting as the controversial measure became law.[24] At home, no one opposed his candidacy and Bureau regained his seat by acclamation in the autumn of 1917.[25] The ease with which Bureau defended his position, the retreat of local Conservatives, and the absence of alternate challengers reflected Laurier's strength in French Quebec, solidified by his supporter's fervent rejection of conscription.

But something more than party politics emerged. Until conscription was imposed, Quebec's bishops supported the war effort, though some English Canadians complained that their aid was neither wholehearted nor sufficient.[26] The extreme boundary for justifiable support for the war was drawn at conscription. When Borden crossed it, he left French Catholics far behind as they retreated into the camp of Henri Bourassa. Thereafter, French Quebec stood firm, though alienated from most English Canadians. At the end of May 1917, the archbishop of Montreal, Paul Bruchési, wrote to Bourassa and shared his feelings in the wake of Borden's announcement, agreeing with Bourassa and indicating that he stood by his decision to accept Canada's participation in the war: 'Sur la conscription je pense absolument comme vous. Et je ne crois pas manquer de logique parce que j'ai admis la participation du Canada à la guerre actuelle.'[27] He asked Bourassa to consider these remarks confidentially, an indication of the Catholic Church's penchant for veiled, though thinly veiled, opposition to government policy.

The French-language press had no such qualms, despite the fact that many papers had strong connections with the Catholic church. As discussed in Chapter 1, the *Bien Public* was an example of a particular genre of Quebec journalism known as the Catholic press, or '*la bonne presse*,' and it enjoyed a high rate of penetration in the area it served. Editor Joseph Barnard's weekly commentaries were delivered in a format quite different from those in the English press, which normally presented editorials anonymously on an inside page. Under the caption 'Les évènements,' with his name appended below, Barnard's commentaries were a front-page fixture and served to introduce journalistic perspectives from a more personal, if not doctrinal, point of view. On conscription, Barnard could offer a more daring and revealing explanation of why French Catholics should oppose it than could the bishops themselves, at least in public.

Within a week of Borden's announcement, Barnard began by arguing that conscription would destroy the integrity of a constitutional arrangement that recognized Canada's autonomy within the Empire. 'Ce projet de conscription militaire pour le service d'outre-mer,' he maintained, 'est le coup le plus fortement porté contre l'intégrité de notre constitution autonome. La conscription n'existe présentement dans aucune colonie britannique. Il est possible qu'on ait recours à la conscription dans les colonies, mais cette mesure ne sera prise qu'aux seules fins de défendre les frontières locales, et jamais pour lever des troupes pour servir hors de ces frontières.'[28] Barnard reminded readers that Australia had recently rejected compulsory service by referendum, and he argued that Canadians would do the same. The prime minister had no mandate for compulsory service. His *volte face* was a contemptuous act, a mockery of his solemn promise to Canadians, and an insult to the authority vested in the federal government. 'Or nous savons que, depuis, tous les autres Dominions ont eu leurs élections, et qu'ils n'ont pas considéré que l'état de guerre était un motif suffisant pour abandonner tout contrôle du gouvernement.'[29]

The following week, Barnard expanded his argument by drawing on a sense of the past, of tradition, and of precedent. On what basis, he asked, had Canada's Militia Act been amended after the Boer War? Quoting from Hansard and the debate surrounding an important change to the Militia Act in 1904, Barnard related that when Sir Frederick Borden, then minister of militia, was asked if the Militia Act had been revised to protect Canada alone, he had said 'yes.' 'Not for the defence of the Empire?' he was probed specifically. The minister's succinct 'no' was used by Barnard to suggest a limit to the Militia Act that did not in fact exist.[30] Nothing then, or in 1917, prohibited Canadian troops from being dispatched for the Empire. But Barnard believed, or at least hoped his readers would, that Borden was acting on dubious legal grounds, not simply immorally.

Barnard revisited Canada's constitutional and legislative histories in many of his columns to argue that conscription violated the fundamental basis of Confederation. Twice referring to Confederation as a 'pact,' Barnard attacked conscription as an abuse not just of minority rights, but of the legitimacy of the state itself. 'Exactement cinquante ans après la signature du pacte de la Confédération,' he argued, 'premier ministre Borden, chef du gouvernement dont le mandat est expiré, s'apprête à faire voter de force, et contre le gré de la majorité du peuple, la conscription militaire voulue par les impérialistes.'[31] Though the assumption that most Canadians opposed conscription was unfounded, his concern for justice took a high moral tone that rested on constructing notions of something grander than the politics of expediency.

'Le pacte fédératif,' he continued, 'garantissait la justice égale et complète aux races habitant ce pays. Les droits des minorités étaient soigneusement prévus, et leur protection assurée.'[32] Whereas the 'pact' guaranteed equality to all inhabitants and protected minorities, all this, he suggested, was now at stake and threatened by Ottawa.

The *Bien Public* also raised the fear that enforcing the Military Service Act would cause social unrest. Barnard warned that containing public violence against the new law might prove impossible. He sounded this alarm in early June when he reported that 'le peuple gronde et s'agite.' Laurier had just rejected Borden's overture for coalition government, and the House of Commons was consumed daily with angry debate as a political crisis unfolded in Ottawa. Barnard's description of the corresponding public mood in his immediate area did not appear misleading: conscription could be, he argued, a catalyst capable of unleashing an uncontrollable response within a working population already predisposed to strike action in a prevailing climate of public dissent. 'A ses plaintes succêdent aujourd'hui les menaces,' Barnard continued, 'les ouvriers organisés parlent des grèves, de pressions violentes contre les autorités constituées. Le danger de la conscription a amené le peuple à une désapprobation en masse.'[33]

Several incidents outside Trois-Rivières underscored Barnard's warning and sense of apprehension. In Montreal the offices of newspapers daring to print statements in favour of conscription had been attacked in recent weeks. After the Cartierville home of Montreal *Star* owner Sir Hugh Graham was dynamited, and a conspiracy to bomb Montreal's courthouse and city hall was uncovered, Barnard condemned such violence as wholly untenable: 'Il nous paraît de la part des conspirateurs,' he wrote, 'une stupidité qui s'explique assez mal.'[34] But the blame for it rested with Borden and conscription. A government acting without popular support, he argued, had brought on this public sickness.

His remarks following Senate approval of the Military Service Act lamented the apparent violation of a traditional covenant between Ottawa and Quebec, and he foresaw turbulent times ahead. 'Comme on le voit la perspective,' Barnard wrote, 'n'est pas rassurante, et il se peut que nous traversions avant peu des heures mouvementées.'[35] Stricken souls, like those arrested in Montreal, had been pushed beyond the church's guidance. Barnard hoped that reason might prevail if voters had an opportunity to pass judgment on the government. 'Le peuple espère malgré tout que nos gouvernants,' he concluded, 'pris de vertige, se lasseront à la fin d'être dangereux pour revenir dans les droits sentiers de la Constitution, et soumettre au peuple la question que lui seul a le droit de décider.'[36] The people of Quebec, as far as Barnard was concerned, had been pushed too far. He could not condone the violence that had occurred and that would continue to take place, but he put the blame squarely on Borden's government, not French-Catholic Quebecers forced to live under an unjust law.

In late May, *Le Devoir* urged that order be restored, suggesting that anti-conscriptionists follow the advice of their religious leaders to exercise restraint.[37] A mass protest meeting attracting a crowd of some ten thousand had just been held in Quebec City, and the potential for civil disorder grew with each public rally or demonstration. Barnard's warnings were hardly misplaced. Defiance against conscription continued throughout Quebec to the end of the war. The draft evasion rate for the province's two military districts was higher than anywhere else in the country, and 113,291 of the 115,602 Quebec registrants applied for exemption under the act.[38] The most notorious anti-conscription event came a year later in Quebec City, with the riot of Easter 1918. Several thousand demonstrators paraded, the militia was called out to disperse them, and violence ensued. Four civilians were killed, and many others wounded.[39]

Though no incidents of violence surfaced in Trois-Rivières, there were some nearby. In late August, a report from Shawinigan Falls recounted how a large crowd, estimated at well over a thousand, inflicted property damage on a private residence. The same report mentioned an attack against a soldier passing by.[40] In addition, one of the Quebec ministers who had warned Borden against conscription, P.-E. Blondin, resigned from the cabinet, accepted an army commission, and joined a prominent French Canadian militia officer, F.-L. Lessard, to tour the province in search of recruits. Their mission failed miserably, with less than one hundred men signing on during some fifty-eight rallies from May to July. Worth noting with respect to Trois-Rivières, however, was an actual assault made against Colonel Blondin near the city.[41]

The francophone minority, as Barnard pointed out, was by no means alone in rejecting conscription. Canadians everywhere, Barnard argued, were growing accustomed to militarism and the use of force to crush opposition to conscription wherever it appeared. This shift in social attitudes and behaviour was not only abhorrent, but was also fast becoming commonplace. The values of the past, Barnard maintained, had become disconnected from the present. Enforcing the will of the state with brutality brought out all that was ugly about uniformed men. Barnard interpreted recent events in Toronto, Winnipeg, and Vancouver as indicative of peaceable citizenship giving way to a 'régime militaire.' Under the caption 'Singulier héroisme de "nos héros,"' he wrote:

> S'il faut en croire les dépêches, les appels de ce genre tombent à Toronto dans une terre bien préparée. Les soldats de retour du front s'occupent ces jours-ci à disperser à coups de bâton toutes les assemblées anticonscriptionnistes

> tenues dans la ville-reine. Des bagarres sanglantes ont eu lieu, et la police a fort à faire pour protéger les paisibles citoyens qui expriment publiquement leur opinion, comme c'est leur droit, contre les émeutiers. Les villes de Winnipeg, de Vancouver, ont été également le théâtre de semblables attentats contre la liberté de parole; il y a eu là bagarre, violence, scènes disgracieuses, provoquées et perpétrées par les soldats de retour du front.
>
> Nous regrettons vraiment pour nos militaires ces excès intempestifs et injustifiés. Il n'en faut pas plus pour exaspérer la foule contre ceux que tout le pays était d'abord disposé à accueillir avec sympathie et avec fierté.
>
> Ces excès arrivent peut-être à temps pour ouvrir les yeux à notre population. En tolérant de pareils abus, nos pouvoirs publics démontrent abondamment combien notre pays est peu préparé pour le régime militaire vers lequel M. Borden cherche à nous orienter.[42]

In his commentaries on conscription, Barnard consistently maintained that Borden's government was acting illegitimately and that it had broken its promise to the electorate. In the *Bien Public*'s last issue before the election, Barnard expressed faith that a return to legitimate authority in Ottawa would follow a Liberal victory. 'Nous attendons avec confiance,' he stated, 'le résultat final de cette élection qui se fait dans des circonstances tragiques, et nous souhaitons que le verdict suprême marque le retour à la saine tradition de la politique canadienne si malheureusement interrompue.'[43] He offered, in other words, a lament for the traditions as he saw them of a nation's past, interrupted by present circumstances, consumed by malevolent passions. Borden's law, from this editor's viewpoint, was changing the national character. Conscription was portrayed as a measure that had pushed Canadians toward extreme militarism, something extraneous, alien to their collective past.

Barnard's commentaries appeared as politicized responses to particular conceptions of authority, designed to influence public opinion and framed within his sense of values shared within the public sphere of his readers. For Barnard, conscription was a unique and subversive interruption. The violations he referred to, against the constitution, against minority rights, against the Confederation 'pact,' or against a civil society confronted with a régime militaire, were conveyed with references to the people and to the authority of the state as interdependent forces. Borden, he argued, had exercised his power without deference to tradition and without the requisite authorization of the people.

Barnard's rhetoric seemed designed to provoke indignation by exposing an abhorrent transgression. This was the political aspect of his attack. To make these texts effective, though, he had to convey them through what James Fentress and Chris Wickham have described as the 'level of shared meanings and remembered images.'[44] 'The people' as Barnard framed this, need only revisit their collective sense of the past. No reference whatsoever appeared suggesting any division between English and French Canada over conscription, something Godin had not only recognized earlier, but also condemned as the jingoistic discourse of the English press. Barnard's deployments of usable pasts, on the other hand, may have served as sentimental referents for the readers he was addressing, those he thought might respond to an ideal, imagined view of history, that Confederation depended, and always had, on maintaining faith in the kind of alliances and goodwill that the ill-fated Bonne Entente could not sustain.

A charismatic speaker, Barnard delivered arguments that presented Confederation as a pact that had created stability and respect for constituted authority, shared by French and English Canadians alike. His use of history as a social narrative reminds us of the talks delivered by Archdeacon Cody and Father Larsimont (described in Chapter 4), in which the former cast Great Britain within the story of a great country and empire, while the latter spoke of his life as a quiet, Belgian priest: both offered narrational fictions, one collective the other personal, interrupted, in each case as they told them, by Germany's despicable act of aggression. The war became the great crisis of their times, the outcome of which would determine the fate of a civilized past, whether for the freedom of citizens of the Empire or Catholics in Belgium. Borden and conscription, rather than German militarism, appear as the evil construct in Barnard's account, but without interrupting a comparable narrative logic. In Canada's great past, he argued, there had been a constitutional pact. There had been respect for minority rights. There had been a Militia Act. There had been social peace. As referents drawn from his sense of the past, Barnard wrote of a harmonious partnership, lost to compulsory military service, to militarism, to social upheaval.

As a coherent perception of the state and society, Barnard offered a profoundly conservative view of social hierarchy and stability. The authority of the state was depicted as an ideal, framed within a social contract: a consent given by law-abiding citizens to a constitution, a Militia Act, or a federal government in which the rule of law must be respected, not revoked. Borden and conscription, he argued, had made this impossible. Certainly Barnard condemned lawlessness, but his anti-conscription ripostes challenged what he saw as the false use of authority, something that would fail to gain the consent of the populace. Nothing could have been as unfortunate, as he put it, than Ottawa's decision to disrupt a political tradition marked by mutual respect between cultures, which had long held the country together.

The Conscription of Wealth

In Lethbridge, majority opinion favoured selective conscription, though this was only part of the story. Support for conscription was often expressed in the city's two newspapers and was demonstrated in the eventual victory of the Unionist candidate, William A. Buchanan, in the federal election of December 1917. Before joining the Union coalition, Buchanan had represented Lethbridge in Ottawa as a Liberal since 1911. Because he also owned the *Herald,* satirically referred to as 'Buck's Bible,' at a time when popular journalism retained partisan affiliations, his influence on editorial policy, particularly with respect to conscription, was unsurprisingly obvious.[45] Unsurprising, too, was the position taken by the Conservative Lethbridge *Telegram,* a weekly, which championed compulsory military service as avidly as Buchanan's paper did.

Buchanan's move toward Union government, given his stance on conscription, parallelled that of other anglophone Liberals who lined up behind Borden.[46] As party discipline in Wilfrid Laurier's caucus collapsed, Buchanan spoke in favour of the Military Service Act, endorsed it with his parliamentary vote, and was backed by his riding association.[47] Beyond its local significance, however, Buchanan's 1917 victory in Lethbridge unearthed more divisions over conscription than Jacques Bureau's acclamation could possibly have done in Trois-Rivières. What is important is understanding why political debates over conscription split voters in Lethbridge when Bureau could stand for re-election in Trois-Rivières virtually unopposed. In this prairie city, conscription prompted a rethinking of justice and economic distribution and the authority on which it was based.

How subjects in subaltern situations construct authority, in general, is embedded in cultural perceptions: of themselves, of those who exercise authority, of the contested relations that divide them, and of the reciprocities that bind them together. Such relationships under a system of compulsory military service were often challenged outside of Quebec, but in very different terms than those expressed by Joseph Barnard. A significant number of farmers and organized wage earners in Lethbridge argued that conscription had opened a gap between society and the state that could be narrowed constructively, depending on the terms by which it was applied.

Issues concerning compulsory service were interpreted and articulated by a loose alliance of grain growers and urban workers who challenged what they saw as an inequitable economic relationship in Canada, made worse by wartime profiteering and special privileges abused by monied interests: monopolies, a lack of labour legislation, and the advantages they made of regional disparity. In Lethbridge, conscription presented an opportunity to right certain wrongs: not to dispute the authority of the federal government, but to challenge its right to impose conscription without consideration for other issues. These sentiments coalesced under a slogan, and for a time a movement, that called for the 'conscription of wealth.' Across Canada, moderate elements supported the conscription of wealth as a step toward social equality on a national level. In Lethbridge, the campaign against Buchanan and Union government centred on achieving this principle. If the nation's young men were to be called upon to serve, then the nation's affluent should be required to contribute as well, a levy that Buchanan's opponents defined with some precision.

The conscription of wealth has been described as 'a rather vague formula, expressed sometimes by farmers, sometimes by labour, and sometimes even by Liberal politicians.'[48] 'The conscription of wealth is a glib phrase,' the *Telegram*'s editor declared in June 1917. 'It is easily rolled off by individuals and bodies without exactly knowing what it means. Synods, assemblies, and organizations have insisted upon it as part of Canada's programme in prosecuting the war. Parliamentarians and newspapers have echoed the insistence, but none has defined it. For ourselves we are quite as much convinced that conscription of wealth should be a sequel of conscription of men. But what conscription of wealth means should be precisely defined.'[49]

Perhaps the vagueness of the concept contributed to its broad appeal. A wide array of groups and interests endorsed the principle, though they failed, as the *Telegram* in Lethbridge noted, to specify its precise meaning. 'Despite some initial anti-conscription sentiment,' as Thomas Socknat has put it, 'the mainstream of Canada's church, labour, and farm communities accepted conscription, as well as the whole war effort, as compatible with their broad goals of social reform,' goals fashioned from various interpretations of the conscription of wealth proposal.[50] During the summer of 1917, Methodist conferences in Alberta, Hamilton, and one combining Nova Scotia and Prince Edward Island all passed motions advocating some form of wealth conscription. So did Toronto's Methodist Laymen's Association, North Bay's Northern Baptist Association, Toronto's Women's Christian Temperance Union, the directors of the United Farmers of Alberta, the Dominion Board of the Retail Merchants of Canada, and the City of Victoria's municipal council and Board of Trade.[51] On the Prairies and elsewhere, nominally conservative factions comprised of small business, agricultural, social reform, municipal, and religious organizations endorsed legislating into service more than the fighting brawn of young Canadians. But its diverse supporters never agreed upon precisely how this was to be implemented. Such disparate groups, scattered across the country, had little chance to mount an effective campaign to revise how conscription was applied, or even to agree on key objectives.

By the spring of 1917, at the end of a hard year of inflation and a bitter strike in the coal industry throughout the West, organized labour in Lethbridge was able, however, to translate a slogan into a specific list of demands. Unionists drew up a comprehensive set of social and economic reforms that might be gained in exchange for giving Ottawa the authority not just to draft conscripts, but to direct the economy as well. Oddly enough, they managed to put this together at one of a series of staunchly pro-war gatherings that came together under the banner of the 'Win the War' movement, which began holding conventions in cities across Canada, including one in Calgary in May. Representatives from various trades throughout Lethbridge met at that time to elect delegates.

The Win the War movement was yet another patriotic organization spearheaded by John Godfrey and his supporters as a successor to the National Service League established in 1915 to coordinate civilian support for the war.[52] Based in Ontario, Win the War organizers were staging conventions throughout the country. Ostensibly intended to mobilize support for the war, the movement embraced a broad range of interests, from union locals to local boards of trade. This latest venture of Godfrey's, however, was really aimed at whipping up public support for Union government and for some form of conscription.[53]

In Lethbridge, arrangements to send delegates to the Win the War convention prompted discussion among trade unionists in favour of the conscription of wealth. A gathering of trade representatives that met on a Friday night in early May was described by the *Herald* as 'one of the most important labor meetings held in the city for a long time.'[54] A broad cross-section of delegates from the miners, brewery workers, bricklayers, painters, electrical workers, and typographical trades turned out to speak for almost a thousand union members comprising most of Lethbridge's organized workforce.

The meeting was long, and while a list of specific demands concerning the conscription of wealth was drawn up, it was not easily agreed on. Many present had certain 'problems' connected to the entire Win the War movement, which 'were fully discussed until a late hour,' according to the *Herald*. Although on a national level organized labour was divided over conscription, Lethbridge workers reached a compromise as they hammered out priorities for expropriating surplus capital through federal legislation. Their program demanded more than just new taxes on industry and the wealthy. Support for the war effort, as far as labour was concerned, should come with a price tag. 'Conscription of wealth and selective conscription of manhood' introduced their various demands. Next on the list was a call for 'Dominion wide women's suffrage,' spelling out their position on women and the ballot box, an issue dividing organized labour across Canada at this time.[55] Other items in the reform package were:

Income tax on salaries over $2,000 a year.
Graduated Inheritance tax.
Graduated tax on corporation[s.]
National taxation of wild lands [use of Crown reserves].
Free importation of food stuffs, clothing, and industrial machinery from allied countries.
Public ownership and control of all railways, telegraphs, mines, water power systems, banks, mills, elevators etc.

Abolition of child labor under 16 years.
National eight hour law and equal wages for both sexes.
Free lands for returned soldiers.
Equal protection for all soldiers and dependents.
Graduated increase of separation allowance to all soldiers' dependents.[56]

The Lethbridge Trades and Labor Council took this list to the Calgary convention, which attracted, the *Herald* noted, diverse groups from across the region: 'The delegations in Calgary represent a hodge-podge of lawyers, labor men, farmers, women with special and general ideas, reformers, uplifters, autonomists and anti-autonomists.' While a wide range of topics came under discussion, specific reference was made to the convention's support for conscription of wealth.[57] The Win the War gathering had, in short, offered nothing more than conditional support for the most controversial piece of home front legislation Ottawa brought in at any time during the war. As Lethbridge's Trades and Labor Council put it in a dispatch sent home before the whole affair wrapped up:

> At the national unity or win-the-war conference held in Calgary on May 10 the suggestions on how to handle the present situation and following the declaration of peace [sic], contained among others the conscription of wealth first and then conscription along the lines of the present total recruiting of each province throughout Canada, national eight hour day, labor exchanges under provincial control, taxation of all wild lands, government control of the prices of the necessities of life, abolition of child labor, equal suffrage throughout the Dominion on the one-man-one-vote principle. Other suggestions dealt with practically every phase of Canadian welfare, but as space is limited, suffice it to say that every suggestion forwarded by the Alberta conference will require considerable discussion before being disposed of.[58]

Like organized labour, grain growers also favoured selective conscription as a modified approach to compulsory service. As elsewhere, farmers in southern Alberta, with good crops and prices in recent harvests, had a strong interest in seeking exemptions under the new law for those employed as producers of essential goods, wheat as well as coal. When the precise terms of the Military Service Bill were being hotly debated in and out of Parliament, one *Herald* editorial offered the following cautionary remarks: 'The chief industries of this section of Canada are coalmining and agriculture. That it is the aim of conscription to enroll in the army any men who are engaged in these pursuits we cannot believe, and though the bill requires that each man must make application for exemption, it is evident that some arrangement will have to be made for exempting miners and farmers whether or not they apply for exemption.'[59] In the end, the clauses pertaining to exemptions proved, as J.L. Granatstein and J.M. Hitsman put it, 'vague and liberal,' though Lethbridge farmers, tradesmen, and even the Board of Trade had reason to be concerned at this point.[60]

While Lethbridge tradesmen may have been attracted to the conscription of wealth alternative as a bargaining position for other aims, district farmers were also drawn to the challenge it raised against financial power concentrated in central Canada. As John Thompson noted in his study of the regional impact of the war, when 'uttered by a Western farmer,' conscription of wealth 'meant the introduction of an income tax coupled with heavy taxation of the abnormally high profits of Central Canadian manufacturers.' It was, in this sense, a regional protest against what the *Herald* referred to often as the 'Big Interests' in the East.[61]

The *Herald* often cast western grain growers' and local suppliers' sense of commitment to their own interests, whether family owned farms or small businesses throughout southern Alberta, in David-and-Goliath terms. This view was also expressed at the closing of the first chautauqua ever held in Canada in August 1917, just as the conscription bill was making its way through the Commons. Organized as travelling exhibitions of science and pseudoscience, religion and mysticism, political economics and public policy panaceas, chautauquas were an American invention, but as cultural events proved adaptable to Canadian settings.[62] In many ways, chautauquas served to expand the visiting speakers tradition into a kind of festival of touring lecturers, performers, and exhibitors. Dramatic presentations, religious lectures, and musical recitals were included in this kaleidoscope of popular culture, staged in appealing forms that attracted sometimes thousands of visitors and large audiences for featured events.

Most chautauquas ran for an entire week and wound up their programs with a public address concerning some issue or problem likely to draw attention and, most of all, a large audience. Lethbridge's first chautauqua featured the Rev. W.J. Hindley, a war veteran, who spoke about conscription to an audience of three thousand crammed into Lethbridge's Eckstorm auditorium. The talk was said to have attracted 'the largest crowd ever gathered together at one time in a patriotic event in the history of Lethbridge.'[63]

Under the title 'The Test of the West,' Hindley portrayed the Prairie provinces and British Columbia as the backbone of Canada's patriotic war effort. His speech was a highly effective crowd-pleaser, combining a salute to the West's contribution to the war with the grievances of the ordinary income earner, who faced rising prices while, it seemed, others got rich. The 'patriotism' referred to was far more a celebration of regional pride than a call to duty. 'The east,' Hindley claimed, 'has said that the west is materialistic, but when the war broke out, the four western provinces proved themselves by the enlistments of men and by the generosity of their gifts.' Muscular patriotism, as he put it, was a Western virtue.

Having lavished praise on the West and on Lethbridge, Hindley seized upon war profiteering as the central issue in the conscription debate. Conscription, he predicted, 'would affect very little the districts west of the Great Lakes. They have already done their bit in an admirable way.' He went on to speak of conscription as an exchange that should, as he saw it, entail efforts to redress regional disparity between central and western Canada. 'Material goods,' he declared in reference to a rapidly rising cost of living, 'shall not be rated higher on the floor of parliament than the lifeblood of the men who make up the nations.' Excessive wartime gains, he added, must be checked by special taxes placed on commodities exploited by eastern financiers. His speech, reprinted in the *Herald*, seemed to strike a responsive chord:

> 'The spirit of the west,' he continued, 'will not allow the exploiter, the speculator and the profiteer to fatten off the sufferings of the people of Canada and the boys at the front.' He called on the government to apply the same rule to commodities as to men of flesh and blood. 'If men are conscripted, then commodities must too unless dealers will see to it they are delivered to the people without abnormal profits such as some concerns have been making.

Hindley argued 'that if the price of the farmer's wheat is fixed then must the price of flour and other wheat products be fixed.' And finally, attacking railroad earnings on behalf of the West, Hindley declared that 'the railways should pay a pro rate tax on their properties to help pay the cost of the war.' The oration was described as 'a very patriotic and inspiring appeal to the people who are peopling the last great west.'[64]

Events like this contributed to a new political opportunity in Lethbridge to combine the concerns of regional power held by grain growers and the call by organized labour for the conscription of wealth. While support for Buchanan and for conscription remained high, it was not unqualified. By the fall of 1917, as procedures for the new Military Service Act were being implemented, the time had come for some to make their views known through another candidate, one committed, as Buchanan could not be in any explicit way, to support for the conscription of wealth.

On a Saturday night in November 1917, less than a month before the election, some fifty city labourers and local farmers met to choose a candidate to stand against an incumbent who had little chance of being defeated. The nominating meeting was described as 'one of the hottest sessions ever held in Lethbridge, starting at 7:30 and lasting till the early morning hours! Everything from revolution to anti-conscription was talked [sic] and advocated by some of the delegates.' One delegate was to have said, '"I will not be party to any frame-up with either the Liberals or the Conservatives ... They are all tarred with the same stripe. A revolution is coming one of these days against government by party and capitalists ... Let the Union government be returned. A revolution will come all the quicker."'

After some debate among them, and among former Liberals who had broken with Laurier but would not back a Borden candidate, support fell to L. Lambert Pack, a grain grower from the Raymond district, an area situated on a Canadian National spur line about thirty kilometres southeast of Lethbridge. 'He is a young man and a fair platform speaker,' the *Herald* noted, though obviously Pack was in for a rough time as far as Buchanan's own paper could manage. 'As a missionary in the Mormon church,' this brief sketch added, 'he spent three years in Germany.'[65]

Although the *Herald*'s coverage of its owner's opponent cannot be taken at face value, two points may be made. First, the paper never appeared to take Pack's candidacy seriously; and second, because of this, it tended to tone down explicit attacks against Pack during the campaign itself. A negative campaign against a legitmate but unlikely opponent who presented himself as a sincere candidate, launched through the paper Buchanan actually owned, would probably have made Buchanan look worse than the more matter-of-fact reports that appeared. In fact, the paper's concerns about Pack's campaign messages appeared, if anything, rather patronizing. Details concerning how the campaign got off the ground are worth considering, however, in light of his central endorsement of the conscription of wealth.

Pack's selection was based more on compromise than on any firm intention to nominate and promote a clear favourite. Some wanted an out-and-out anti-conscriptionist; Pack favoured selective conscription provided it was accompanied by the conscription of wealth. Others maintained their support for a popular lawyer, H. Ostlund, who was nominated a few days before at the riding's Liberal convention. Sensing that opinion was fast turning against him, Ostlund quickly withdrew his candidacy in favour of Pack's farm-labour constituency. '"The delegates here will not support a lawyer," was the way another candidate viewed the matter,' the *Herald* suggested. '"We decided at the last session that the man nominated by this body must be a producer, and certainly a lawyer is not a producer."'

This concept of a 'producer,' which cropped up several times that evening according to what appears as an eyewitness account, reflected an important aspect of the discourse surrounding the conscription of wealth expressed by Pack's supporters during this campaign. 'Producers,' those who farmed and grew grain, or who applied their skill and their hands in a particular trade, were valorized by it. This suggested that an exploitive political-economic system, run by professionals, managers, and owners, particularly those imagined in the East, accrued gains from the fruits of others' labour. It was as a farmer, or producer, that Pack gained the support of his nominators and backers. He was described as having accepted his nomination 'under pressure,' after many delegates 'had decided that Mr. Pack was the less of the evils [sic] and reluctantly agreed to support him in spite of his stance on conscription,' a reference to the opposition some held for any kind of state compulsion to serve in the military.[66]

At this point, Pack had to deal with the clouded issue of conditional support for conscription in the context of an overwhelmingly pro-war electorate. How could the primary basis of his campaign be cast in 'patriotic' terms, through a rhetoric that signified unequivocal support of the war? While the *Herald* editor soon pressed Pack to choose between running on a Laurier Liberal or a Labour-only ticket, the labour-farm representative held fast to the new alliance he stood for.[67] His candidacy was described as a 'platform of the United Farmers of Alberta together with the platform of the Trades and Labour Congress of Canada.'[68] As Pack put it himself, 'he wore two coats ... the coats of the farmer and of labor,' adding that the 'two horses he drove were going in the same direction.'[69]

Pack's backers quickly renamed themselves the Independent Farmers and Labor Association and set up a 'Press Committee' to clarify their position. Referring to a resolution passed the previous July by the Lethbridge Trades and Labor Council, the committee related that

> in the opinion of the labor men of Lethbridge at a mass meeting held here on July 16th, 1917 to discuss the proposed conscription act, it was the consensus of opinion that the Federal government had not taken sufficiently of the material resources of the country to warrant them at this time enforcing conscription, and whereas the greatest burden and suffering in the war is borne by the working classes, and ... realizing that the working class will not only have the burden of fighting the war, but they and their children will be called upon in purchasing the necessities of life to pay, pay, pay ... therefore be it Resolved [sic] that the Borden government be earnestly requested to enforce the following.

A conscription of wealth proposal followed that was almost as detailed as the one put forward the previous month. It called for new taxes on sizable personal and corporate wealth, along with a radical proposal for public acquisition of railways, telegraph networks, hydro power, and banks.[70] This package, the quid pro quo for sending more men to the front, became the central plank in Pack's campaign.

From the time of his nomination onward, workers and farmers urged Pack and his supporters to see conscription as linked to wealth redistribution, beyond the 1916 Business War Profits Tax and 1917 Income War Tax Ottawa had already imposed as war measures. The novice campaigner for Lethbridge's Independent Farmers and Labor Association spoke and met with voters throughout the riding, and within three weeks the *Herald* observed that 'so much has been said by the opposition in this campaign about conscription of wealth that one would think that there was no such issue as conscription of men.' In defence of its publisher's own campaign, the *Herald* claimed that Borden's new federal income tax already stood as a sound measure, and that failure to implement compulsory military service would entail an enormous risk: possible defeat overseas, with far worse consequences for all in Canada.[71]

From the start, Pack ran his campaign as an outsider, with no direct connection to organized labour or farmers. His Independent Farmers and Labor Association had no direct connection with the powerful United Farmers of Alberta (UFA). While the UFA had been active in the Lethbridge area since its inception in 1909, no local branch had been organized, although branches had been established in nearby Coaldale, Nobleford, Iron Springs, Barons, Raymond, Etzikom, and Cardston.[72] UFA organizers visiting Lethbridge in the hopes of setting up a branch there had argued consistently for the potential of collective action backed by strong organization. When District 18 coal miners gained a war bonus in February 1917 after a bitter strike, one UFA organizer, visiting from Magrath, saw it as a sign of the times. As he put it in an address to grain growers farming near Lethbridge: 'Miners had learned the value of organization, and whenever they made certain demands upon their employers the whole country sat up and took notice. Yet, while the farmer is the strongest man of all workers individually, he was for this very fact the hardest man to organize co-operatively.'[73]

The real problem Pack faced, however, was that conscription was generally well supported. Many men, sons or husbands from the area, had enlisted and seen action, and their families commonly saw conscription as the surest way to bring them home sooner. The problem of taking other men, often younger brothers, had also been dealt with locally. Every one of some twenty-two men called up had been granted exemptions as bona fide farmers in the area.[74] With the election just weeks away, one farmer was reported to have observed that the system was working.[75] To administer this appeal process, Judge J.A. Jackson of the judicial district of Lethbridge appointed a well-known lawyer, Charles F.P. Conybeare, to head up the city's only exemption tribunal.[76] Conybeare was later joined by W. Symonds, a Lethbridge trade unionist named by Ottawa, perhaps as a concession to the organized workforce locally.[77]

By this point support for the Military Service Act appears to have solidified, with the majority of farmers and workers in the riding lining up behind Buchanan and Borden. A pair of political rallies staged by Pack's campaign in its final phase did little more than expose remaining division in Lethbridge over conscription. With his hometown band from Raymond providing a musical interlude and the well-known social gospeller the Rev.

William D. Irvine on hand as a featured guest speaker, Pack addressed a filled Majestic Theatre on the last Monday before voting day. The *Herald*'s account, with its partisan bias, reported:

> Mr. Pack made a hard effort to convince the audience last night for it was very skeptical and its skepticism took the form of a running fire of questions which at times formed a barrage which drowned the voice of the opposition candidate completely. In fact, Mr. Pack did not have a pleasant time at all. Rev. Mr. Irvine was treated somewhat more leniently as was befitting the fact that he was a stranger in a strange land but he ran into a storm of fire which threatened to extinguish him when he told the audience that the conscription act was destined to take all the English speaking and leave the wives and daughters home to the tender mercies of the Germans and Austrians.[78]

The brunt of the audience's heckling was saved for Pack and was confirmed by the city's other paper, a Conservative weekly. 'The candidate was met with many interruptions during his speech, urged by the statements he made,' according to the *Telegram*.[79] Pack tried to defend his position as a dual representative of farm and labour sentiment in the conscription debate. 'Mr. Pack declared,' the *Telegram* noted, 'that the conscription measure was only a device to make the people of Canada forget the mismanagement of the Borden government.' He went on to decry the injustice meted out to any who dared speak against Borden's wartime coalition. 'Many people are afraid to express their attitude against the Union government,' he argued, 'because someone will call them slackers and unpatriotic.' Pack fervently maintained that opponents to Ottawa's current regime were not undermining Canada's war effort: 'We,' he protested, 'are the patriotic people. We are those who are going to win the war.'

Pack railed against what he saw as a privileged, wealthy elite dominating and directing Borden's government and policies. 'The formation of the present government,' he charged, 'was a bringing together of monied interests. Therefore, the common people are afraid of the movement. [Hugh] Guthrie [MP for Wellington South], who spoke against reciprocity, was taken into the government, [Charles Colquhoun] Ballantyne [sic] of the Sherman Paint Co., and it contained fifteen lawyers. Not one farmer. "Is that equitable?" And there was not a single labour representative.' To appeal to farmers as well, Pack attacked existing duties on agricultural implements and concluded that 'the whole burden of the war was being placed on the west.'[80]

A follow-up meeting at the Majestic featured 'fighting Joe' Martin, a Labour MP from the British House of Commons who was then touring the West. The evening reportedly turned into a complete fiasco. The *Telegram* portrayed Martin's platform performance as 'Comic Opera' with 'Drivel,

Abuse and Insult' the 'stock-in-trade' of his oratory. Pack introduced Martin with a warm commendation, stating that it was a 'great honor to be associated with such a great and noble man as Mr. Joseph Martin, a member of the British parliament.' Martin proceeded to lecture, challenge, and cajole his audience, agitating, according to the *Telegram*, numerous hecklers, and provoking heated responses. 'The government,' Martin declared, 'had allied themselves with the big interests so as not to have to look around for election funds. They gave the C.N.R. fifty millions.' To this 'some shouts' retorted, 'No no. Ten millions.' '"All right let it be ten millions," said Joe.' The exchange then shifted to Joseph Flavelle, chair of the Imperial Munitions Board, whom Martin charged had 'stolen millions' with Borden's complicity. And he was 'not the only one.' Flavelle 'says to Borden,' as Martin put it, 'Come on. I shall show others up.' This charge allegedly 'was greeted with shouts of derisive laughter.'

But the *Telegram*'s description of a crowd entirely united against Fighting Joe's 'drivel' appears deliberately slanted. 'As the meeting dispersed,' this report concluded, 'an unseemly brawl was started.' A local physician, sarcastically referred to as an 'apostle of peace' because of his pacifistic opposition to the war, actually got into near fisticuffs with this newspaper's editor. The doctor, according to the *Telegram*'s own account, 'walked up to the editor of this paper and accused him of un-British conduct in disturbing the meeting. The editor hotly resented the unjustified accusation and desired no dealings with a man who had pro-German inclinations. A free fight might have followed with the "apostle of peace" as the aggressor, had not parties stepped in between and the manager of the theatre turned off the lights.'[81]

Whatever was disputed here, this piece of local entertainment seemed to appeal to muscular masculinity in slapstick form, near blows for social justice, violated by either pro-German inclinations or by un-British behaviour. Reports on political struggles invariably appeared in this form, heavily refracted by partisan perspective. Voting results, likewise, appeared in curiously distorted terms.

The *Herald*'s depiction of a 'Huge Majority' for Buchanan interpreted the final poll tallies from each of the neighbourhood booths as 'pronouncedly for aggressive war measures and the provision of immediate re-enforcements.'[82] This simple conclusion, that Buchanan won on the basis of clear-cut support for conscription, overstated the poll results. His challenger was largely unknown and had little to be optimistic about at the outset. Against a seasoned opponent who enjoyed a solid basis of support for selective conscription – the law as it stood – Pack could hardly offer a formidable challenge nor establish a broader following than he did for the conscription of wealth. To add to this, the Conservative *Telegram* rivalled the *Herald* in its partisan coverage of Pack and his alternative position. Buchanan had never sold his paper or himself to voters as anything other than a strong Lethbridge booster. His voters could, without any sense of conflict, have shared the sentiments expressed in Hindley's chautauqua speech.

The young Raymond farmer and newcomer to Lethbridge politics, took 2,468 votes, just under half of Buchanan's total, a surprisingly high proportion compared to his opponent's 5,302 votes. His strength among both farm and wage-earning voters also appeared concentrated in certain areas in the constituency. He took twenty out of fifty-six of the riding's rural polls, posting three draws. His candidacy topped 43 percent of these votes. Support also appeared stronger among urban wage earners. In one city polling station, designated 'Miner's Hall,' fifty-seven ballots went to Pack compared to sixty-three for Buchanan.[83] It might be said that Buchanan's marginal agrarian advantage owed something to military service exemptions that neutralized farm opposition to conscription.[84] During the campaign, Buchanan chose to stay the course, calling on voters in his riding to rally behind Borden's coalition as the best single answer to an end to war. 'The result in the Lethbridge constituency,' Buchanan stated in accepting his win, 'shows that our people are sincerely determined to support every movement that means more effective conduct of the war on our part.'[85]

How accurate was this? Although the Unionist victory in Lethbridge demonstrated Buchanan's ability to steer most voters away from Pack, it did not suggest that conscription had become an uncontested issue throughout his riding: its uneven reception was based partly on perceptions of local and regional conditions. While only a handful of Lethbridge workers and local grain farmers directly contributed their time and effort to Pack's campaign, a significant number, given their candidate's limited political experience and local backing, endorsed his opposition to Borden's coalition with their votes.

The conscription of wealth issue never did proceed beyond the point of reform programs or, across the country as a whole, a slogan that appealed to notions of war profiteering, inequities in wealth distribution, and a desire to redirect an interventionist state toward progressive reforms. When the Lethbridge Trades and Labor Council specified priorities that included women's suffrage, progressive taxation, freer trade, protective labour legislation, and veteran re-establishment benefits, it did not reach agreement on them easily, nor did other groups that supported the conscription of wealth as a general principal necessarily share those priorities. Pack did, nonetheless, help to signify recognition that conscription marked a major departure in Canada's stance toward the war. The shift opened gaps, previously unaddressed, between Canada's expanding wartime state and a home front of ordinary Canadians with other interests besides winning the war, interests that often intersected with relations of gender, class, and region as perceived on a local level.

A Peculiar Social Drama: The Guelph Raid

Occasionally responses to conscription took unexpected turns. In Guelph, hotly contested notions of the fairness of the Military Service Act became a public scandal when a dispute erupted over why young Catholic men undergoing religious training could not be conscripted. A peculiar social drama took place, which became known as the Guelph raid.

Social dramas are public displays that serve to expose an underlying conflict that has divided interacting factions within a given locale or community. As a breach widens and crisis deepens, supporters for each side are recruited; their struggle leads at some point to a search for resolution followed by redressive actions; this, in turn, permits the re-entry of central players into social relations altered by what they have participated in or witnessed.[86] Following this sequence of four phases – breach, crisis, redress, and reintegration – helps us to conceptualize the Guelph raid as a public drama broadcast in newspapers across the country.

The backdrop to the Guelph raid took many months to develop. Local tensions seem to have increased with local gossip, but there is no doubt that when an alderman and several Protestant clergymen in Guelph became aware that Catholic novices and juniors at St. Stanislaus Novitiate appeared unaffected by the new law, they became suspicious, even angry. They demanded action, and this led to the raid. What followed was a prolonged struggle to attach or deflect blame for what proved a botched attempt to arrest the young men, and a prolonged exercise in examining the meaning of conscription and the limits of state authority. But public dramas are more than safety valves for contested issues. They initiate a reordering of perceptions in a given community, and this one certainly did so in Guelph. In functional terms, public dramas like the Guelph raid serve, as Victor Turner argued, to materialize disharmonic phases of the ongoing social process and permit individuals or factions within it to return to the everyday flow of social relations, informed by what has taken place.

The prelude, performance, and aftermath of a surprise military police raid near Guelph were neither accidental nor incidental in their effects on relations between a Jesuit seminary, Protestant clergy in the city, and over two dozen young men of military age who were able to avoid the draft. The novitiate, the raid that took place there, and the controversy that followed did not operate as a stable site of confrontation, but rather as a fluid series of events that tested the limits of the law and allowed the reintegration of disturbed elements as the controversy died down. At the core of the dispute rested conflicting notions of rights, privileges, and obligations. Did the students at St. Stanislaus have the right to avoid military service? Should the military have inspected the novitiate? Did the Jesuits indeed enjoy special privilege, or were their rights abused? Though the central players in this affair may not have been satisfied with the answers the Guelph raid led to, they did come to terms with them through the public process that followed, as did Canadians across the country as they responded to conscription in relation to their immediate circumstances and prior histories.

Considering the intense controversy it provoked, the military police intrusion and interrogation carried out at the St. Stanislaus Novitiate has received little attention from historians.[87] When news of a surprise inspection and near arrests could no longer be contained by Ottawa's censorship bureau, front-page accounts appeared in major newspapers throughout Canada.[88] As well, the *Canadian Annual Review* provided a summary of the controversy in its 1918 volume. The outpouring of commentary concerning the whole affair held the attention of the press across Canada and no doubt fuelled local gossip in Guelph.[89] Prime Minister Borden's mail also reflected the public's preoccupation with the incident: the volume of related letters to his office reached an astounding proportion of one-half to one-third of his daily mail in July and August of 1918.[90] To examine warring sectarian positions, conflicting views of events, and the various roles of those involved, a Royal Commission was summoned at the behest of Sam Hughes and began hearing evidence in the autumn of 1919.[91] Its report contains the testimony of the principal actors and affords a useful source concerning the entire episode. Only one scholarly study of the Guelph raid has appeared, which focused on the sectarian tensions it exposed and, for a time, seemed driven by.[92]

Apart from the raid, however, conscription was not a controversial issue in Guelph. As in Lethbridge and elsewhere in English Canada, the political crisis it provoked prompted Guelph's local member of Parliament, Hugh Guthrie of Wellington South, to abandon Laurier and the Liberals in favour of Borden's coalition. Shortly afterwards, in early October 1917, Guthrie was rewarded with the cabinet portfolio of solicitor general.[93] In the December election he won by a wide vote margin over his lone opponent, Lorne Cunningham, who ran as an Independent Social Democrat but went on to serve several terms as an alderman.[94] Guthrie took almost four of every five ballots cast, with a total of 3,612 votes against only 962 for Cunningham.[95] Cunningham, who did not campaign for the conscription of wealth, appeared to attract little support from Guelph's Trades and Labour Council, which had recently passed a resolution favouring selective conscription.[96]

Ottawa's decision to enforce conscription had also been endorsed by Guelph's Protestant clergy, represented by the local Ministerial Association. As the polling day neared, the association passed a resolution 'heartily endorsing the Union Government.' Its members also complied with a request by the *Mercury* to prepare written statements to explain their position. Two days before the polls opened, the *Mercury* published them, fourteen in all, which took up more than the entire front page.

As the pastor of Guelph's Congregationalist Church, the Rev. W.D. Spence, a prominent prohibitionist and president of the Ministerial Association, stated: 'I am in favour of Union Government because of that for which it stands, "the most thorough administration for win the war purposes." I simply must stand by the men who are pledged to stand by the boys who have gone from my own congregation.' To this, the Rev. Kennedy H. Palmer, pastor of St. Paul's Presbyterian Church, added: 'From my pulpit I, like many others, pleaded with our boys to answer the call of the heroic and preserve unstained on Europe's bloody battle fields the honour of our land. There our word was given that we would not fail at any cost to stand behind them in the fight that no petty politics should turn us aside from giving them every support.' The Rev. Edwin A. Pearson, pastor of Norfolk Street Methodist Church, confessed that 'the principle reason why I support Sir Robert Borden and the Hon. Hugh Guthrie and Union Government is my entire family of three sons are at the front.' One of them was a future prime minister.

Some took swipes at Laurier and Quebec's failure to back the war effort through conscription. As the Rev. I.M. Moyer, pastor of Paisley Memorial Church, put it: 'I am opposed to Quebec with her ideals and her indifference, having a controlling voice in the policies and destiny of Canada in this crisis time in our history.'[97] On the whole, the Guelph Ministerial Association expressed the view that military service was simply the duty of all able men. That young men of eligible age were studying at the St. Stanislaus Novitiate on Bedford farm, four miles north of Guelph, and had not yet enlisted was a situation not likely to go unchallenged by clergymen who had supported the war effort, the formation of Union government under Borden, and the step that seemed necessary to them at this time of legally forcing men into the military.

Conflict over St. Stanislaus

The election campaign in Wellington South seemed to bring suspicions about the Jesuit college to the surface, since immediately afterwards Spence, as president of the Guelph Ministerial Association, lodged a complaint with Military District headquarters in London. He objected to the fact that nothing had been done since conscription became effective to induct students at St. Stanislaus. Spence pointed out that the Protestant colleges had yielded men generously, and he demanded that the novitiate provide its fair share.[98] Rumours circulated, and by all accounts Guelph's Protestant clergy felt that something should be done to rectify the situation. The investigation that followed led to one of the most controversial events related to conscription, not only in Guelph, but anywhere in English Canada.

The primary impetus for the raid itself stemmed from confusion over a particular exception clause in the new conscription law. According to this provision: 'Clergy, including members of any recognized order of an exclusively religious character and ministers of all religious denominations existing in Canada at the date of the passing of our said Military Service Act' could not be conscripted.[99] Subsequent test cases had ruled that this clause did not apply to theological students unless they had joined a religious order prior to the act becoming effective in October 1917.[100]

As it stood, this clause favoured Catholic students because many, as their training required, had joined religious orders prior to the conscription law; students of Protestant denominations, on the other hand, did not receive their training as members of any religious order as specified under the act and thus remained eligible for service, even if their studies began prior to the new legislation. At the time the Military Service Act was proclaimed in August 1917, St. Stanislaus's novices had all been 'tonsured,' a preliminary step in their training that confirmed them to the Jesuit order and thus shielded them from conscription. It seems the ceremony might have been performed in Guelph by the Bishop of Hamilton with this in mind. George Nunan, then a novice at St. Stanislaus, recalled that in September 1917 the bishop 'came to the Novitiate to confer Tonsure on all the Scholastics, both Juniors and Novices. This was done to make doubly sure our title [sic] for military exemption.'[101]

This did not sit well with Henry Westoby, a city alderman who had been active in local recruiting. Westoby wrote to Father Bourque to ask that arrangements be made for the Department of Militia and Defence to carry out medical inspections of all men, novices and juniors, of military age at St. Stanislaus.[102] Westoby later recalled there was 'a very strong feeling in Guelph that these men not being ordained ministers do not come within the clauses of the Act exempting them from service and that they should be required to comply with its provisions.'[103] This brought the students' legal status in question, and their rector, Father Henri Bourque, sought a ruling, which eventually made its way to the cabinet in Ottawa. In response, the minister of justice, Charles Doherty, father of one of the novices, Marcus Doherty, wired Hugh Guthrie to reaffirm that 'members of recognized religious orders ... are not bound to make application for exemption' under the act.[104] This applied to all the students, as all had been tonsured. Nonetheless, Bourque took the precautionary step of having certificates prepared for each resident of the novitiate that identified their membership in the Society of Jesus. He also made it clear to the young men 'that no member should leave the residence without taking his certificate with him.'[105] Both the younger Doherty and a fellow student, George Nunan, recalled feeling that they were looked on with suspicion when visiting Guelph, and they always carried their certificates in town should they be required to produce some proof of who they were.

Conflict existed, but led only to inquiries through official channels. The *Mercury* said nothing at this point. In April 1918, Westoby wrote to Military District headquarters in London to warn: 'Locally the feeling is very bitter against these people, or rather against their practice of harbouring young men of military age, and unless something is soon done there is going to be an explosion, as the Ministerial body have determined to see the thing through.'[106] There matters stood until the spring.

While on a visit to Guelph in late May 1918, Capt. Leslie Burrows from the Military District headquarters in London asked Guthrie if he was aware of rumours concerning St. Stanislaus. Burrows provided the names of three men said to be hidden there to escape conscription. Of these, only George Nunan was actually living at St. Stanislaus at the time, in full compliance with the law.[107] Guthrie passed this information on to the minister of militia and defence, Maj.-Gen. S.C. Mewburn. At this juncture, incidental responsibility for the raid rested with Guthrie. What began as a question from Burrows, possibly prompted by Westoby's letter to Military District headquarters in London, was passed on as a communiqué from Guthrie to Mewburn and taken at face value as information concerning men 'escaping' their duty. Mewburn promptly issued a memorandum of instruction to one of his staff officers in Ottawa, stating that he had been 'informed through a very reliable source' of individuals at Guelph's Jesuit college 'who are escaping military service.' He added: 'Can you have these cases followed up?'[108]

At this time, the staff officer should have issued specific instructions to senior officials at the district headquarters in London. Instead, Mewburn's memorandum was simply passed on to the provost marshal's office there, with a note attached advising that 'every effort be made' to have the novitiate 'cleaned out at your earliest convenience.' The original copy went missing, and considerable effort was later made by the commission examiners to determine whether the precise wording was 'cleaned up' or 'cleaned out.'

To carry out this direction, Capt., A.C. Macaulay was ordered 'to proceed to Guelph and visit the Bedford Farm, and make a thorough investigation as to the young men who are alleged to be residing in that place with a view to evading the Military Service Act.' With a squad of nine men, including a Dominion Police inspector, he headed for St. Stanislaus under the impression that the novitiate might actually be hiding men eligible for the draft. Macaulay had also been instructed to 'exercise the greatest tact and discretion in handling this matter,' and had he done so, the situation, as far as the military was concerned, might have been quietly defused that very evening, though this would not necessarily have satisfied the pastors and ministers in town.[109] But what did take place at the novitiate at Bedford farm served to open the case to public scrutiny, first through the press and later through statements by the clergy themselves, most of them made before their congregations. By this time, what had taken place at the novitiate had already begun to unfold as a public drama.

The breach, the raid itself, really began with Macaulay. He saw himself as an officer representing and enforcing the authority of the Military Service Act. As Victor Turner put it: 'A dramatic breach may be made by an individual, certainly, but he always acts, or believes he acts, on behalf of other parties, whether they are aware of it or not. He sees himself as a representative, not as a lone hand.'[110] Macaulay's duty, as he saw it, was to ensure that the act was obeyed, despite the fact that he seemed unable to recognize a situation in which it simply did not apply.

The Breach

The evening of 7 June 1918 began much like any other at the St. Stanislaus Novitiate. By coincidence, the Rev. William Power, superior-general of the Jesuit Order of Canada, was then visiting the college. Nineteen scholastic novices and eight junior scholastics, along with eleven lay brothers and six faculty were then in residence.[111] Even more coincidental, given what was about to transpire, was the fact that one novice, twenty-year-old Marcus Doherty, was the only son of Canada's minister of justice. The senior Doherty had helped draft the Military Service Act, which included an exemption provision that became, as events ran their course, a matter of dispute.

As the younger Doherty later recalled, the teachers and students at St. Stanislaus had just celebrated the Feast of the Sacred Heart. Doherty and Brother Leo FitzGerald had both served as sacristans. 'We were putting away extra carpets, candles, flowers, decorations used for Benediction of the Blessed Sacrament which had just taken place,' Doherty said. 'Just across the hall, to the right of the entrance was the modest front parlour. It was not surprising then that Bro. FitzGerald and I were the first to hear the bell.'[112] Nunan also recalled an unanticipated turn of events: 'The first inkling that we Novices had that there was anything in store to interrupt the routine of our lives came when shortly after we had retired on the night of the Feast of the Sacred Heart ... we were awakened and told to dress and assemble in the refectory.'[113]

Father Henri Bourque was as startled as his young novices were. The element of surprise simply added insult to injury. Indeed, the entire fiasco occurred on the basis of action preceding careful judgment. Macaulay knocked, entered, and only briefly explained his reason for the intrusion. He interrogated several of the men and was about to demand that several accompany him back to the barracks when the wind was suddenly taken out of his sails.

George Nunan's recollection of events indicated how quickly legal help came for the novitiate: 'Our legal advisor, Mr. Patrick Kerwin, later Chief

Justice of the Supreme Court of Canada, arrived from town with Father Nicholas Quirk, and our neighbor, Mr. Thomas Bedford, Justice of [the] Peace ... In default of proper authorization for the police inspection, recourse was finally had [sic] by telephone to Judge Hayes of the County Court, a member of our parish in town.'[114] In other words, a lawyer, two outside witnesses (one a Justice of the Peace), and a local judge and parishioner were thus alerted or present.

'Judge Hayes,' Nunan continued, 'advised Father Bourque that, despite the irregularity in procedure, he allow the inspection under protest.' Though Bourque had no choice but to do so, the gravity of Macaulay's error in proceeding without investigating the actual legal status of the students was clearly understood by everyone but himself.

Students were ordered to the refectory, where each waited while others looked on. Doherty recalled that the questioning was tense. Macaulay, it seems, held a very real suspicion that the Jesuits might be hiding something, whether facts or people. Doherty described how Brother FitzGerald was the first to face his questions. 'Being a nervous, high strung fellow he was at first rather indefinite in his answers. Finally he blurted out "I am an American Citizen."' He was from Providence, Rhode Island, an unimportant fact to all but his interrogator. Macaulay allegedly 'picked up on this last statement, obviously deeming it a subterfuge, and started putting FitzGerald through a third degree.' The Rev. William Power, head of the Jesuit Order of Canada and a formidable personality, interceded. As Doherty recalled, 'Father Power was undoubtedly a strong character, (sometimes known as Will-Power) and as Mac Auley [sic] discovered to his chagrin, a person to contend with. At the very moment that FitzGerald was protesting his American citizenship, Father Power was ranging up and down the refectory, and seeing FitzGerald in difficulties, cried out in bass stentorian tones that I can still hear – "He is an American citizen."'

Doherty was next. 'Somewhat unnerved by FitzGerald's experience,' he remembered finding it difficult to answer Macaulay's 'rapid-fire' questions and even hesitated when asked his age.[115] Macaulay then ordered Doherty and two other novices to return to their rooms upstairs and get what they needed to accompany him back into town.

Doherty also remembered the turning point that evening. On his way back to the refectory, as he made his way down the stairs, Father Nicholas Quirk, who had just been questioned himself, stopped him for a moment. 'Marcus,' Father Quirk asked, 'does your father know about this?' They asked Bourque about making a telephone call to the justice minister in Ottawa. Bourque cautioned 'that they would need approval from the officer in tweeds,' who seemed anxious to carry out his arrests. Macaulay 'still felt himself cock-of-the-walk,' as Doherty remembered. He gave them ten minutes to get through – otherwise, 'you come to the barracks.' Doherty managed to reach his father and quickly told him what was taking place. The justice minister then got Macaulay on the phone and ordered him to leave the novitiate at once, which he did without taking anyone back with him.[116]

After receiving a formal complaint in writing from Bourque, Militia and Defence Minister Mewburn replied with an apology four days later. 'Words cannot express to you,' Mewburn put it, 'my deep regret of the action taken by the Deputy Provost Marshal, Captain Maculae [sic], on the evening of the 7th instant.' Macaulay was subsequently posted to Winnipeg.[117]

The Crisis

The raid's significance lay in the profound sense of injustice it exposed in Guelph, particularly among the pastors and ministers in town still disturbed over the fact that a group of young men were living at the novitiate, free from conscription. The crisis that erupted after Macaulay's intrusion and retreat widened and ultimately drew them into a process in which they could speak out in public, and many chose to do so.

If a breach can be sealed off, a crisis of contested positions may be avoided, and the process ends there. Efforts at containment appeared in Mewburn's forthright and prompt apology, but word of what happened had spread quickly in Guelph and beyond, and would continue to do so. The immediate concern, from Ottawa's point of view, was to invoke a press ban until an internal investigation could be carried out by the militia department. Charles Doherty consulted with Mewburn, and with the assistance of the chief censor's office a news blackout was ordered, which held for nearly two weeks. In the interim, distorted accounts of the raid circulated as the entire affair aroused intense local speculation.[118]

The most sustained protest came from W.D. Spence and from the Rev. Kennedy H. Palmer. Palmer, in particular, felt that special, unwarranted privileges had been extended to the Catholic Church, its religious orders, and residents of the St. Stanislaus Novitiate. While the publication ban was in effect, Palmer continued to use the pulpit to broadcast what he saw as a moral and legal outrage. A congregation in nearby Preston heard the following statement, which subsequently made its way into the *Orange Sentinel*:

> And now, brethren, I come to what to me is the crowning act of shame on the part of some people in our own district. Outside the city of Guelph, as some of you are aware, is the Novitiate of the Roman Catholic Church governed by the Jesuits. For many months past, in fact ever since the passing of the Military Service Act, persistent rumors were abroad that many young men, whose people were well enough off to pay the price, could be found there in hiding from military service. For a long time, some few of us in

> Guelph who believe in the principles 'Equal rights to all – special privileges to none' have been urging the military authorities to act and find out if there was any foundation for the rumors.[119]

Palmer's reference to 'special privileges' seemed deliberately provocative. 'Men and women,' he continued, 'it is surprising how the influence of the Roman Catholic church dominates.' Then, with a clear reference to Charles Doherty, Palmer stated that the 'military hands were tied by one of the leaders at Ottawa who had much to do with the framing of the law, and who at first had the Dominion Police under his orders.' He then stated, erroneously, that Doherty's son and others were being illegally protected from conscription. 'And, brethren,' Palmer concluded, 'here the matter rests, until you or I, or some one who fears none but Almighty God shall keep on working until public opinion shall demand the same treatment, the same justice, for all our young men, whether they be Roman Catholic, or Protestant, rich or poor' or, as he emphasized, 'THE SON OF THE CABINET MINISTER.'

The press ban posed a short-term obstacle, to which some objected. At this point, one *Mercury* editorial defended its silence against 'much uncalled for criticism.' Its silence had been imposed, the paper pleaded. It was merely complying with 'a special request of the censor that the visit of the police to the Novitiate be not mentioned.' Those who did 'not understand the restrictions governing the publication of news in war time,' the *Mercury* explained, needed to be aware that 'many unkind, and, sometimes, untruthful things' had already been said 'in imputing motives that did not exist.'[120] But when the Toronto *Star* published an explicit account of the raid on 19 June, it set off a flood of news coverage across the country.[121] 'Canada's Government put a fool's cap on its own head in an attempt to put the lid on the activities of the military police at the Jesuit novitiate in Guelph's township,' blasted an editorial in Toronto's *Evening Telegram* as soon as such statements could be printed with impunity.[122] As the news ban requested by Ottawa collapsed, Canada's chief censor, Ernest J. Chambers, was pushed to request broader powers.[123]

Once the gates of press commentary were opened, Palmer and Spence seemed less able to rally public support, since the publication of reliable information served only to weaken their case.[124] On the first Sunday following the *Mercury* and *Herald* reports in Guelph, however, nearly every Protestant clergyman in the city offered some interpretation of the raid, which attracted press coverage across Canada. The Ottawa *Citizen* 'reviewed the Sunday sermons of eight Guelph churches,' noting that all but the Anglican pastor preached on the incident, some at great length and with considerable feeling. The lone Anglican minister, probably A.C. Mackintosh, was castigated by '"Jack Canuck" for failing to censure the Jesuits.'[125] Although the sermons that Sunday were coded to demand fairness and equality before the law, 'some very caustic remarks were uttered and serious charges made,' according to the *Herald*.[126] The *Mercury* reported that the 'charges and rumors' sparked by the novitiate raid had 'been the main topic on the streets and wherever people have congregated for some time.' As gossip circulated, the 'statements most sought after,' according to one report, 'were those of Rev. W.D. Spence and Rev. K.H. Palmer, of St. Paul's church, who has been very active in having the whole Novitiate matter investigated, since the Dominion censor refused permission to the newspaper to make any mention of the raid.' Spence sought to convey an understanding that he and his colleagues were 'not actuated by any sense of religious intolerance.' He also claimed, misleadingly, that the Ministerial Association 'had not made any charges' and was not acting on the basis of 'idle gossip.'[127]

At a special meeting of the Guelph Ministerial Association, held the previous Friday evening, a committee was struck 'to draw up a list of questions in connection with the affair,' which the city's pastors were to use to 'amplify' statements made from their pulpits. Spence, Palmer, and the Rev. J.A. Gordon of Woolwich Street Baptist Church made up this committee. Not everyone endorsed their statements. The Rev. A.C. Mackintosh was absent from the meeting, though he was named to the committee, and no mention was made of Edwin Pearson.[128]

Their 'questions' were not only disseminated from local pulpits, but also appeared as statements published in a pamphlet issued by the Guelph Ministerial Association. The circular charged that the 'Military Authorities have investigated and reported it to be a fact that there were men of military age who were eligible for service under the Military Service Act with the Novitiate.' Most were eligible for service, but they were not compelled to register under the act. Under the caption 'Equal Responsibility,' the Guelph Ministerial Association maintained 'that if the Military Service Act holds any one responsible who shields a defaulter, surely an institution that claims to stand by law-abiding citizenship should not harbor a defaulter, which the report of the Military Authorities implied it did.' No such report, in fact, had yet been produced.

Included in this pamphlet were spicy excerpts from a Toronto *Evening Telegram* editorial featuring statements similar to those of Palmer's recent Preston sermon. 'The alleged utilization of a Jesuit novitiate as a refuge for slackers was a subject for enquiry,' one portion read. 'The attempt to establish a Jesuit novitiate or a Protestant divinity school or any other institution as a place high and lifted up above the activities of the military police was an outrage on the principle of EQUAL RIGHTS FOR ALL AND SPECIAL PRIVILEGES FOR NONE.' Clearly, these snippets, separated by Union Jack logos, were spliced together to attract support locally rather than to supply reliable information.[129]

Similar concerns were then raised by the Guelph *Herald*, which followed the *Orange Sentinel* in reprinting Palmer's Preston sermon under the title 'Astounding Statements.' Directly beneath appeared a call for concerned citizens to attend an 'indignation meeting' to be held on 1 July. 'So strong is the feeling among the Protestant ministers and the people of Guelph,' this message read, 'that an indignation meeting has been arranged for the evening of Monday night next, when this whole affair will be discussed and ventilated.'[130] This event was to have taken place at Norfolk Street Methodist, the home of Edwin Pearson's congregation.

Redressive Action

Palmer and Spence's efforts quickly ground to a halt. Moreover, opinion in the Guelph Ministerial Association did not seem uniform. At St. James Anglican Church, the Rev. Mackintosh maintained, 'I have not yet seen anything that can justify the charges made. The church is no place for stirring up religious strife. That is not the mission of the pulpit.'[131] Edwin Pearson also took a moderate stance on the Guelph raid at this point, preferring to wait for the facts to come in. There is no evidence that an indignation meeting ever took place, and Pearson's own attitude toward the Jesuits' situation may have contributed to its cancellation. As his son's biographer, John English, stated, 'Lester Pearson remembered his father as "a modest minister, not an embattled evangelist," one "who led his flock rather than harried it."'[132] This seems a fair assessment. When the Guelph *Herald* reported that 'some very caustic remarks were uttered and serious charges made' by many Guelph preachers, Edwin Pearson's voice was not among them. He and another pastor, the Rev. I.M. Moyer of Paisley Memorial Church, were reported to have 'dealt only very briefly with the matter in their pulpits.'[133]

Yet some unease persisted, and even Pearson sought confirmation in some form on what had happened and why. As the *Herald* intimated, 'The principal feature of all the sermons was the demand for fair play to both Protestant and Catholic alike as regards the students of their colleges, and this is what the Protestant ministers are taking up and state that is their intention to follow to some end.' Although Pearson conceded 'that the question had been given so much publicity already that it was unnecessary for him to go into the details,' even he suggested 'that the status of the men at the Novitiate should be cleared up at once.'[134] This latter sentiment favoured fair application of a law which, as he saw it, justly maintained support for Britain in the final stages of the war.

As a Methodist minister, Pearson shared the views of his church concerning the war. In his study of Canadian Methodism and the war, Michael Bliss maintained that the 'Methodist Church freely and fully supported the Canadian war effort ... because it believed the cause was just.' The enlistment response of Canadian Methodists had been the target of earlier criticism on the part of some 'Anglican mathematicians' in their calculation of recruiting figures.[135] He added that the 'church was afraid of being labeled disloyal, particularly on the recruiting issue.'[136] But with sons already at the front, Pearson's attitude was hardly a defensive one. 'Anglo Canadians, the Pearsons among them,' John English also pointed out, 'saw the attachment to the British Crown as an indispensable part of Canada's nationhood.'[137] Pearson would likely have preferred to see the men at St. Stanislaus enlisted, but felt further suggestion that they were evading the law was unwarranted and, as everyone soon discovered, had no basis in fact.

Choosing to distance themselves from the more extreme positions taken by Spence and Palmer, Pearson, Moyer, and Mackintosh opened the way for redressive action, which was to consider the Military Service Act, to recognize the legality of the Jesuits' position, and to desist from further criticism or charges of favouritism. They offered advice to their congregations that stood as pragmatic, if not placating. Though Pearson spoke in terms of having the 'matter cleared up,' like Mackintosh he felt that the pulpit was no place to promote an atmosphere of indignation. This approach, as it turned out, seemed to coincide with public opinion generally and set the tone for defusing tensions caused initially by misunderstanding, resentment, and distrust. After the attention given to the sermons of late June, further discussion of the controversy in both papers in Guelph tapered off, then disappeared entirely.

Reintegration

Subsequent coverage in Guelph suggested a new tack, taken by both the *Mercury* and the *Herald*. Perhaps realizing, by the end of June, that the Guelph raid might convey negative impressions to outsiders of sectarian tensions, draft evaders, or a Jesuit college enjoying 'special privileges,' both papers constructed stories emphasizing a return to normalcy for their readers. Less than three weeks after the raid, the Guelph *Herald* reported that 'very little is being heard on the streets today with respect to the controversy and agitation which has been going on for the past week between the Ministerial Association and the Jesuit Novitiate, and it is the general opinion that any further statements regarding the situation and the status of the men at the novitiate, will have to come from the floor of the House of Commons in Ottawa.'[138]

As 'far as Ottawa is concerned,' the *Mercury* suggested two days later, 'there is a lull in the Guelph controversy, and a temporary cessation, at least, in the conflict.' Conjuring images of calmness and almost serene decorum, this report also intimated that the 'Hon. C.J. Doherty was placidly engaged in the consideration of his correspondence by 10 o'clock this morning, and appeared to be thoroughly enjoying his big black morning cigar.' The minister of militia and defence, Maj.-Gen. Mewburn, was portrayed in similar terms as 'having shaken the dust of Ottawa from his feet.' Likewise, one of Charles Doherty's subordinate officials, Col. H.A.C. Machin, who had suggested that the raid was the outcome of a conspiracy against the justice minister, had resumed his duties following speculation that he would be forced to resign over his comments. Two days later, 'Col. Machin did not appear to be worried any more than the Minister [Doherty].' The *Mercury* described him as 'a man of cheerful bluff and philosophical disposition. In fact, it would now appear to be a fairly safe prediction that he will not be removed from his present position.'[139]

By the end of June it was obvious that Palmer and Spence would be unable to mobilize significant opposition to what they charged was an unfair privilege enjoyed by the Jesuits. The raid's aftermath had quickly boiled down to a sense of resentment on the part of some but not all clerics, and the moderates won out in the end. While Spence told his congregation 'that the fight would go on until the M.S.A. was amended to make the obligations alike on Roman Catholic and Protestant students,'[140] others took it upon themselves to restore the situation, not make it worse. The Guelph Raid had, however, caused a split, sometimes expressed with bitterness, between some of Guelph's pastors and ministers and the Jesuits at Bedford farm. The problem of enforcing a law with exceptions that applied only to Catholic seminary students was bound to cause problems. How could special privileges be exercised without causing deep resentment? In this case, within the tight confines of Guelph's clerical community, it was impossible, and contested positions could only be exercised fully through an unusual social drama.

Conscription and Conflict: Local Contexts and the Boundaries of Government Authority

The public aspects of the Guelph raid helped to delineate the boundaries of government authority. Conscription as state-directed imperative became a battleground for competing perceptions of the legitimacy of its application. In all three cities, newspapers framed the law's reception very differently. The *Bien Public* circulated among a large reading audience in and surrounding Trois-Rivières, no doubt as diverse as any reading population in the appropriation of ideas, but within a horizon of perspectives that Barnard tried to connect with in voicing his position – that of a conservative, Catholic news editor mining a powerful vein of French Canadian nationalist sentiment in Quebec.

The *Herald* in Lethbridge also helped to situate debate over conscription, but did so in concert with a series of local events leading up to the constituency campaign of 1917. Union party candidate and *Herald* publisher W.A. Buchanan scored a clear victory in Lethbridge. But as the conscription of wealth ideal entered the political discourse there, a western-based, nascent social democracy appeared to hold sway with voters from this region whose sense of social and economic justice we should not overlook.

A sense of legal justice and the Military Service Act ignited quite different responses in Guelph. There, too, both city papers played their part in framing reports concerning the Guelph raid, but it was several Protestant clergymen who played key roles in directing the course of a peculiar social drama in which strong sentiments concerning fairness and legality found expression. To the extent that sectarian tensions were even acknowledged by the few involved directly in this controversy, preacher- or priest-led animosity between Protestants and Catholics was hardly part of a general or sustained sentiment.

How those differences found expression in the pages of the local press or at a chautauqua or from the pulpits of local churches was also critical in shaping local reaction. Local settings set the parameters for debates over the government's right to impose conscription, from the appeal of French Canadian nationalism in Trois-Rivières, to regional and class-based differences in Lethbridge, to a very particular right based on belonging to a religious order exercised at St. Stanislaus near Guelph. For some voters in 1917, responses took shape within the means and limits of political cultures that had become increasingly fractured across Canada, divided by majority opinion of French Canadians in Quebec, by resentment over wealth distribution expressed by farmers and wage earners in Lethbridge, and by certain members of the Protestant Ministerial Association in Guelph.

Support for conscription obviously depended on attitudes held well beyond a given locale, especially when voters took to the polls in 1917 to vote for Laurier in Quebec or Borden in all regions and overseas. In very different ways our cases suggest that power to induct men into uniform became embedded in the politics of local perception. The varied responses that power prompted from people living beneath the powerful edges of hometown horizons indicate how the conscription crisis of the Great War challenged interests and aims firmly rooted in local and regional histories. They reflected the varied social fabric of a home front deeply divided by 1917.

6
Gendered Fields

By the time Canada had been at war for four months, the first and second contingents of the Canadian Expeditionary Force had been mobilized, and the country had sent its first allotment of troops, mostly British-born, to land in Plymouth, England. While their subsequent training on the rain-soaked fields and rolling slopes of Salisbury Plain garnered occasional press reports through the winter of 1914-15, overly optimistic distortions of 'the Huns taking a beating' or the 'Allies surging forward' circulated daily in the press. Early in this period, two women in Trois-Rivières, H.T. Ham and J.M. Dalton, began to organize the kind of public event still common in towns and cities at this time – the patriotic concert. They secured the help of twelve other women, both English and French. Together, they drew up a program of music and poetry recitals, instrumental numbers from Trois-Rivières's Union Musicale band, and a short comedy, performed in English. When presented, the evening's entertainment drew a crowd of five hundred in a city of less than three hundred anglophones.

During that year in Trois-Rivières, as elsewhere, fears of enemy alien espionage and sabotage were often conveyed in newspaper reports that seemed to reflect and to feed local gossip (see Chapter 4). Such anxieties contributed across Canada to the sudden appearance of home guard units, bands of uniformed, armed men, who drilled, paraded, and patrolled local areas until the ridiculousness of their role became obvious even to them. In the summer of 1915, not long before the movement collapsed in most other places, members of the Lethbridge Board of Trade prodded police chief John Skelton to organize for Lethbridge what many other municipalities already had up and running as a 'safety' measure. After all, there was a much higher proportion of enemy aliens in the surrounding region than in most parts of the country, and rumours were rife of conspiracies to disrupt the harvest or to blow up the high-level CPR bridge. Skelton quickly recruited 125 men. They donned special uniforms, met for weekly drill, posted a guard at the bridge, and at the height of their short-lived notoriety, staged a parade that drew another fifty men into their ranks. A year after the war began, they all marched to the drums, brass, and pipes of the Kilty and Citizen's bands. References in the *Herald* to the 'valor' these men displayed before the 'beauty' that thronged the streets, with so many enemy aliens nearby who might otherwise be 'busy among the threshing rigs,' give us some measure of the smug and androcentric lenses through which such reports appeared.[1]

Skelton eventually quit both his job and his voluntary command post to join the Kilty regiment, the 113th Lethbridge Highlanders, whose band had paraded with the home guard and was still signing up men. He trained with a force that grew during the year to over nine hundred and was soon commissioned as a captain. Shortly before the Kilties set out for further training in Calgary, the president of the Alexander Galt chapter of the IODE, G.W. Robinson, hosted a highly structured, ritualistic presentation of what became this regiment's primary symbol: a set of pipe drums with the inscription 'Presented by the Alexander Galt Chapter, Imperial Order, Daughters of the Empire, to the 113th Overseas Battalion (Lethbridge Highlanders) C.E.F., Lethbridge, Alberta, Canada, May 13, 1916.' To solemnize the moment, Robinson delivered a short speech that offered both conventional and formulaic references to a gendered divide between Lethbridge at home and the fighting overseas. For example, she told the men that local women would '"keep the home fires burning" in anticipation of the time when the enemy shall be vanquished, and you will return covered with glory and honor.'[2] As a double-sided ritualization, the ceremony invoked gendered positions for both the soldiers and the IODE women who looked down at the men from a raised podium. The gilded language deployed here was only resurrected for the fallen men sometime after the war.[3]

Robinson and the IODE used gendered codes to re-present themselves as public volunteers in a public cause. So did Ham and Dalton as patriotic concert organizers and Skelton as home guard commander. This chapter examines how parochial sites for for war-related activities operated as gendered fields, as women relief workers valorized their identities as women and home guardsmen did so as men, and all saw themselves as representatives of their respective social classes. We will consider how class and ethnic boundaries, as well as shifting perceptions of wartime demands, prompted activities empowering to participants, yet culturally conservative in terms of their attachment to traditional notions of the social order. Middle-class women as war relief workers and working-class men as home guardsmen also used local networks, associations, and resources to map out their roles as involved citizens. How did their gendered and class-based differences find expression as fundamentally hometown products? What can local evidence of their actions and discourses tell us about how Canada's part in the fighting was viewed by these groups at home? If, as news of war circulated and anxieties increased, their homebound sense of mission – aiding soldiers overseas or protecting civilians at home – took shape within gendered fields of practice and self-representation, how did they use traditional models of femininity and masculinity to empower *themselves*, as much as to fulfil the 'wider' purposes their 'local' efforts seemed to them to be directed toward?

Gendering Civilian Service through Hometown Settings

During the war, hundreds of thousands of civilians assumed new public roles as citizens on a profoundly gendered home front. Mostly working-class men filled the home guard, while predominantly middle-class women boosted memberships in the IODE and the Red Cross. Ethnocultural pluralities and the prolonged prosecution of the war influenced how Canadians understood and responded to changing home front conditions across the country, but so did the local settings their responses took shape within. Local rituals and practices drew from widely circulating discourses on a national level that addressed why victory was imperative and how civilians could either protect their local community as men or aid the troops overseas as women. In both cases, the experiences of civilian service were felt most profoundly within one's gender and class. From civil defence to making bandages or purchasing and presenting a set of regimental pipe drums, gendered fields were mapped out rapidly, strategically, and as contests for power waged first and foremost at home in communities of friends, associates, pals, and companies.

Volunteers for pro-war effort causes from both sexes came forward in large numbers in Lethbridge and Guelph, especially in the early war. As shown in Chapter 3, support in Trois-Rivières for its Canadian Patriotic Fund (CPF) campaign, while much lower than in the other two cities, intersected with the view that Canada needed the support of all citizens. Whether by staging cultural events such as a patriotic concert, or by marching in home guard units, the gendered fields home-based volunteers created joined a sense of national affiliation that empowered both masculine and maternal forms of military support.

Some men sought a vicarious sense of connection to the fighting overseas, guarding bridges or railway stations, while women promoted ties between home and fighting fronts through a variety of initiatives, from patriotic essay-writing contests in local public schools to visiting thousands of families of men receiving aid from the CPF. In different ways, both sexes responded to imagined views of the dangers at home or of the war overseas.

Sensational news of the fighting overseas prompted many causes that seemed most immediate and pressing, from recruiting to policing enemy aliens. The chronology of the war, from the outbreak to its horrific battles, to the armistice, framed the rationale for sustained local organizing. The formation, for instance, of a new IODE or Women's Institute chapter (the Jack Ross Imperial Daughters in Lethbridge, the Speedwell Women's Institute in Guelph) or the rise and fall of the Lethbridge home guard, occurred in each case as part of a homefront in transition, but one constituted through local efforts.

Particularly in the early war, civilian activities, whether in the form of weekly meetings, parade rehearsals, target-shooting drills, or charitable events, proliferated as primarily local causes: a Red Cross table at a local rally, an IODE section of a review stand at an exhibition park, the patrolled zones of local bridges and railway stations. They gave civilians the opportunity to apply perceptions of themselves as men and women to wartime duties, to participate in a national enterprise of 'protection' or 'service' through the immediacy of local settings. The effects on gendered boundaries, however, are difficult to assess in general terms.

There is no stable consensus in the literature regarding the impact of war on gender systems, but by examining civilians' use of local spaces we can attempt to assess its effects.[4] In their respective historiographical reviews of gender and war, Joan Scott, Angela Woollacott, and Billie Melman have each emphasized how wartime patterns in the relations and systems that differentiated men from women varied enormously in different geographical and social contexts. They have argued that attending to localized outcomes and intersecting gendered identities brings us closer to understanding how contemporaries experienced and expressed their wartime lives and underscores the salience of differences across both home and fighting fronts. Groups of men and women, divided too by class and ethnicity, experienced the war in divergent ways that both shaped and were shaped by their gendered identities. In reference to both world wars, Scott has suggested that searching for a single interpretation of wartime effects on gendered boundaries can lead to debates that 'seem ultimately unresolvable.'[5] Even studies that examine the roles women constructed that were closest to those of men in combat – for example, military nurses, munitions workers, and women's auxiliary corps – arrive at competing claims concerning their short- and long-term consequences.

In southern Ontario, for instance, some women briefly assumed an armed guard's posture when at least two ladies' rifle clubs were formed in Toronto and a women's home guard was mustered in Hamilton. But this proved exceptional and was trivialized by the press as deviant.[6] In England, Vera Brittain complained of women's 'enforced inactivity in the military part of war.'[7] The multiplicity of women's roles and experiences, from front-line volunteer ambulance drivers to home front fundraisers, challenges this notion to the extent that such fields acted to reposition conventional relationships of gender, power, and discourse.

To contrast the experiences of men as soldiers with women in a variety of roles is also problematic. George L. Mosse's thesis that, for European countries, the war 'remasculinized' society tends to subsume a growing historiography on women's experiences completed by Woollacott and others.[8] To equate soldiers, their ethos, and their cultural impact with entire societies or nations during the war might point too far in one direction, conflating militaristic images of manhood with nationalism in the post-war era while overlooking a more nuanced and inclusive approach to gender relations. Studies of change evident in masculine and feminine significations and behaviours, either based on the home front or the front lines, increasingly recognize the contingency of lived experience, the relevance of local context, and the fluidity of gender as a boundary of social difference.

The literature on women alone has passed through three conceptual phases. Initially in the 1960s and early 1970s, the war was seen by historians of British women as sets of opportunities for women simply to expand the range of their experiences – as munitions workers, nurses, or patriotic war relief workers. Women at work, whether at home or at the front, obviously demonstrated competencies their male counterparts had traditionally ignored. Against this optimistic view, however, a second and much less sanguine theme developed in the literature of the late 1980s. Feminist studies that emphasized reversals in women's social status in the 1920s, such as the reversions from paid work in war industries to domestic service for working-class women or the persistence of maternalistic policies endorsed by middle-class women after the franchise, developed a longer-term picture of women and war to suggest that patriarchal systems either recovered or perhaps had never really been shaken by the events of 1914-18.

As a consequence of competing claims, what Melman has termed aptly the 'change conundrum,' debate has not closed on the question of whether the war fundamentally altered gendered identities. Instead, a recognizable third phase in more recent work seeks conclusions grounded in specific geographical and social contexts. From looking at wartime responses optimistically as an emancipation for women to seeing obvious signs that many of its discourses stagnated or re-embraced patriarchal models, the question of if and how shifts took place has been examined either through sets of evidence from local case study or through specific groups of women defined by class, military, or work histories. How gendered boundaries shifted within a web of political, economic, and social relations, pushes us toward questions of context and setting, some focusing on localized sites, others cutting across broadly shared discourses and experiences.

In terms of women activists in Canada during the war, Linda Kealey, Barbara Roberts, Veronica Strong-Boag, and Thomas Socknat have taken the lead in studies of socialists, suffragists, and pacifists. Each has pointed to cleavages within these movements that the war introduced or exacerbated. On pacifism, Socknat dissects the general collapse of its progressive, liberal strains in the early war by noting, first, that supporters of both sexes responded in different ways to the war's outbreak and prosecution, from moderates seeking some elusive middle ground to radicals who maintained their anti-war stance on religious, moral, or reformist grounds. Social gospellers, labour activists, social workers, and women suffragists were prominent among the latter group.[9] Laura Hughes, Alice Chown, and the Women's Peace Party receive close attention in Socknat's review of their ensuing anti-war activism, as they famously broke ties with the new moderates, whose rise in the wave of pro-war sentiment in August 1914 spelled the demise of the liberal pacifist tradition. Radical feminists, he points out, along with Quakers, 'were among the first to make this shift.'[10]

Strong-Boag notes that women pacifists like Marion Beynon and Chown faced hostile receptions from both sexes.[11] They also represented a surprisingly diverse group. Anti-war feminists, Roberts concludes, embraced a wide spectrum of women and 'cannot simply be labeled urban, middle-class progressives.'[12] And many feminists supported the war. Both women suffragists and socialists, according to Kealey, divided between anti- and pro-war positions.[13] Kealey is also sensitive to the fracturing of maternalistic positions among women in general, noting that many redirected their deep-seated antipathy to warfare in principle toward supporting the war in order to break the stalemate and end the slaughter.[14]

On the other hand, maternal feminist support for a final victory – for a hard-fought and 'just vanquishing of the foe' overseas – was upheld most stridently by Canada's IODE women. As a set of intersecting war relief projects, from supporting recruitment drives to providing aid for veteran re-establishment, IODE activities provided new opportunities for middle-class Anglo-Canadian women to fashion motherly roles for themselves as matriarchal community leaders, as self-empowered imperial-nationalists capable of mobilizing gendered differences in support of the cause. Katie Pickles's close reading of an expanding and gendered field of IODE projects, that significantly augmented home front support for the Empire at war, underscored this point: the 'power of the maternal was clearly important,' Pickles notes. IODE women deployed their gendered status to their considerable advantage, 'providing new opportunities' for IODE women at a time when, 'gendered identities are accentuated' across society and when the 'maternal identity was of particular significance to the IODE's place during the First World War.'[15]

On the pro-war side, the National Council of Women of Canada joined with the IODE, Red Cross, YWCA, women's auxiliaries of the CPF, and women's recruiting leagues to promote recruiting, contribute to war relief, and stage a diverse array of public exhibitions on the local level, from concerts to horticultural displays. Symbolic endorsements fused with material aid and were arguably as important. Thus, across the fractured, contested terrain of Canadian women and the war, we find the 'change conundrum,' the difficulty of determining useful generalizations, indeed applies. The riddles of diversity once again remain embedded in the contingencies of individual and group choices made during the war. Feminisms and femininities, even in the form of maternalistic opposition to the war, as Kealey indicates, shifted in accordance with other social relations, values, and beliefs in smaller currents, favouring case-study approaches in lieu of broad-pattern assessments.

The same is true of masculinities. In her study of men's bodies in Britain, for example, Joanna Bourke examines how the violence on men's bodies wrought by the front-line experience led to more 'domesticated' masculinities, a nuanced and insightful counterpoint to Mosse.[16] The point is that both Mosse's emphasis on representations of manful assertiveness and Bourke's on the moderating influences of death, injury, and disease contribute to useful understandings of wartime masculinities. If they are not taken out of context, such competing claims can co-exist. Their very different forms of evidence simply point in different directions. Of real importance to future work is the fact that the 'change conundrum' opens possibilities for departures; solutions to its paradoxes are partial, contingent, and site-specific. For Melman and contributors to her recent volume, examining gender on the borderlines of place, class, ethnicity, and wartime contexts promises more nuanced conclusions, ones reflecting the actual experiences and perceptions of contemporaries in a given setting.[17]

Apart from the succession of interpretive positions – from the war as an emancipating experience, to its supposed stagnating effect on feminist advances, both of which run the risk of essentialism, to finally the borderline encounters Melman favours – Joan Scott identified three subject clusters that cut across both older and recent work: studies of militaristic rhetoric and representations of gender; consideration of state policy and family welfare, especially post-war 'stabilization' programs; and recovery of hidden portraits of lived experience.[18] Scott insists that by interrogating how contemporaries encountered and remade their situations, and how their experiences were constituted through discourse, we can move beyond the pitfalls of essentialism and avoid the tendency to suppress the distinctive subjectivities of men and women in dissimilar circumstances. Whether they were working-class men, many too old to enlist, patrolling the streets in special uniforms, or middle-class women supporting the causes they selected or the cultural events they chose, little attention has been given in the Canadian literature to the gendered aspects of their activities on a local level.

Using the evidence of local experience in hometown settings, representations of gender and evidence of gendered practices can be examined from a wide array of sources, most of which circulated in the public sphere. By investigating the actions of local communities as well as how they represented their actions, Scott's advice can be taken a step further. Distinct sets of voluntary activities evident across the country, from the efforts of middle-class women volunteers to those of working-class home guardsmen, offer useful points of entry. How both groups made and used public spaces as sites of gendered activity takes us to the meeting grounds of gendered histories across Canada and the contingencies of community life on hometown horizons.

Middle-Class Women, Patriotic Idealism, and Gendered Practice

The outbreak of fighting and early mobilization as represented in the popular press tended to privilege the celebration of militaristic masculinities in the public sphere. Public events, from enlistee parades and patriotic concerts to the send-off ceremonials considered in Chapter 1, mirrored a style of manful assertion made popular by the war. As recruitment drives proliferated, a new patriotic discourse that implored women to encourage their loved ones to enlist appeared first in editorials in the late autumn of 1914 and intensified as enlistments started to drop off.

Such rhetoric was cast against claims that 'selfish' women might hold men back from signing on during these campaigns, which had become carefully staged affairs. In Guelph, as seen in Chapter 1, a recruiting organizer for the 71st Battalion not only called upon 'whole-hearted' men to heed the call to the colours, but appealed to 'whole-souled women ... who will place no obstacle in the way of their sons, lovers or sweethearts and try to stop them from enlisting.'[19] Ritualized in many war-related public events and echoed in the discourses of the popular press, these signs skewed representations of women's actual wartime activities and repressed signs of their actual experiences.

While most recruiting discourse exploited the appeal of militaristic masculinities, some depended in part on a specious relegation of women's roles to those who were 'left behind.' Embedded in patriarchal models of society, messages like this, widely broadcasted on recruiting posters, in editorials, in sermons, even in women's speeches, shed light on the kinds of representations contemporaries deployed that acted to obscure the lives of home front women. They were patriarchal messages employed to empower the ideal soldier, certainly not the real one. Women's images could be idealized as well, as hundreds of thousands on the home front in Canada, as elsewhere, applied themselves to a variety of war relief projects. They activated gendered spaces on the borderlines of their age, class, and ethnicity, and though sometimes divided on other issues, pro-war supporters vastly outnumbered anti-war activists. Many left their original homes or domestic work in pursuit of other paid work, or volunteered to serve overseas as ambulance drivers or nurses. Their experiences, overseas or at home, point to extended domains of action and power.[20]

9 Not all women war relief workers were drawn from the middle class. While the older women seen here in this staged portrait probably did not work in paid employment in war industries, they did work for the cause as volunteers. This 1916 photograph of Guelph's Salvation Army Red Shield Auxiliary portrays a maternal patriotic effort in which knitting in organized groups became an activity of extended gender power rather than a sign of passive roles in a patriarchal society. It also made possible the crossing of class boundaries. It is clear from their facial expressions and the special Red Cross kits worn on their wrist that the women were proud to participate as relief workers. *Courtesy of Guelph Museums, 985.31.2*

At the same time, middle-class women activated established social hierarchies in their respective locales through a variety of voluntary associations. They created larger or new chapters and locals that expanded pre-existing networks to support the war effort: a new Jack Ross chapter of the IODE in Lethbridge, for example, or a new branch of the Red Cross in the same city. In Guelph, the Speedside Women's Institute and the College Heights Relief Association made their appearance.

As a social movement, war relief engaged gendered fields in the public sphere to coordinate efforts to dispatch the first group of local volunteers and to mount cultural displays that, in turn, brought out 'patriotic' sentiment embedded in concepts of wartime nationalism for didactic purposes. From the first troop send-offs, women's participation in the Red Cross, the CPF, and various relief campaigns was contextualized as a set of maternal, gendered practices.

Newspaper coverage and masculine projections of the purposes and ideals of the soldiers enlisting and fighting overseas brought little of this to the foreground. Instead, parades, concerts, orations, and many other public displays privileged the myth of the volunteer and the valour of active serviceman as a male ideal, particularly in the early phases of the war. 'The

First World War,' Mosse wrote in reference to European evidence, 'tied nationalism and masculinity together more closely than ever before and, as it did so, brought to a climax all those facets of masculinity that had been latent and that now got their due.'[21] But his thesis, quite deliberately, navigates in the realm of stereotypical signs, not lived realities. In Canada, public discourses placed a premium not only on constructions of masculinity in uniform, but also on patriarchal images of femininity behind the lines, the gendered myth through which women's contributions as home front volunteers were often fashioned.

Despite the increased presence of women in new markets in the paid labour force and their active mapping of new fields of voluntary, organized patriotism, the press rarely presented examples of these gender slippages or the departures from conventional norms that actually took place on these sites. Moreover, in the city presses, where their intentions could be masked behind patriarchal metaphors, women received far more coverage as voluntary patriotic organizers than they did as wartime replacement workers. This distortion reflected the androcentric lenses through which many popular texts, including newspapers, were produced.[22] Editors tended to cast women's war work in terms that suited them, if not a fair portion of their readers, and this was no less true when it came to occasional coverage of women entering non-traditional areas in the workforce.

By 1916, the number of women in paid employment had increased significantly, but this was construed as temporary and necessary, and their work was of little consequence to their gendered positions. Whether as middle-class, patriotic organizers or as working-class factory hands, women on the home front were discursively situated both in explicit propaganda and in a variety of editorial and event coverage newspaper texts as standing behind the fighting men. It helped to sustain, as a screening discourse, a pervasive mythology nurtured both by contemporaries and by social memories of the war.

The *Herald*, for example, carried an editorial on the Alexander Galt IODE captioned 'Where Womanhood Shows Itself.' The 'Daughters of the Empire of Lethbridge, representing the motherhood and the sisterhood of the city,' as this paper put it, 'have done the woman's part in the active and practical interest they have shown in helping towards a send-off' of the city's first volunteer contingent, adding that such stories were being 'read throughout our Dominion and Empire.'[23]

But what of this 'woman's part'? Activities of mostly middle-class women in a variety of patriotic causes had activated networks that privileged class- and ethnic-based forms of social interaction on local levels and engaged tens of thousands of mostly white, Christian women across the country, who came forward as civilian volunteers. As J. Castell Hopkins put it in the *Canadian Annual Review* of 1915: 'Women's organizations of every kind had been at work in every corner of Canada and of them the most conspicuous was the Imperial Order, Daughters of the Empire, with its 500 chapters and 30,000 members.'[24] While a plethora of other local women's groups, active alongside the IODE with significant membership overlaps, created new, site-specific wartime roles for themselves in local projects and causes, essentialized notions of the 'woman's part' they supposedly played within them operated as a patriarchal figment and contributed to a myth that concealed how these gendered fields were actually being mapped out.[25]

Formal interactions between IODE women and uniformed troops, whether special visits, formal parade reviews, hosted dinners, or gift distributions, were also configured by class boundaries and gendered significations. To cite one example that integrated these elements, a painstakingly itemized description of a dinner given for the 25th Battery by the Galt chapter women suggests how carefully charted these affairs could be. Local hierarchies and the gendered boundaries produced the following decorative display, seating arrangement, and performative sequence, at the Wesley Methodist church hall in April 1915:

> Wesley Hall was aglow with life and color with flags of Allied nations and bunting, added to by the kaleidoscopic red, white and blue caps and aprons worn by the amateur waitresses. These were relieved by the drab of the khaki of the men along the long lines of tables. Gaskell's orchestra enlivened the proceedings, and the whole scene was one of animation and good cheer. Not only in the selection of viands for the spread but in the capable manner in which the items were served by the voluntary attendants and dispensed by those in charge, every want of the guests being anticipated, the entertainment was a triumph to the organizing capabilities of the Daughters of the Empire.[26]

The order in which the list of guests present appeared, with heed to those absent but invited, gives us some measure of how a social hierarchy was construed. It also provides a model of a local community as perceived by those hosting and reporting this affair, as well as a prescriptive model for it, a kind of ideal template for local community for those who might read about it. As the *Herald* described:

> Owing to the lack of space the invitations were limited and were confined to representatives of public bodies. The following is a list of those sent out. Father Rosenthal and Mr. Donald Duff were unavoidably prevented from being present.
>
> Officers of the 20th Battery including Rev. Canon McMillan, Non-Com. Officers and men.

The officers attending were Lieut.-Col. Stewart, Capt. Ripley, Lieuts. Mewburn and McLelland.

Guests of the officers: Dr. D.A. Taylor, Mr. H. Boyd, Mr. R.R. Davidson, Mr. Donald Duff, Mr. A. Hayr, Mr. C. Raley.

I.O.D.E. guests – supt. of R.N.W.M.P. Supt. Pennefather, Mayor Hardie, Commissioner Grace, Commissioner Reid, Senator DeVeber, Mr. W.A. Buchanan, M.P., Mr. W.S. Ball, Conservative Candidate.

The Board of Trade (appointed by the Board): Mr. S.J. Sheered, Mr. R.T. Brymner, Mr. F.W. Downer, Mr. D.J. Hay, Mr. S. Dunham, Mr. A.W. Williamson.

The Clergy: Rev. Canon Murrel-Wright, Rev. G.H. Cobbledick, Rev. A.H. Denoon, Rev. A.C. Bryan, Rev. D. Ross, Rev. Father Rosenthal.

The Y.M.C.A. – Mr. Carson.

The Red Cross Society – Judge Jackson.

The Veterans – Mr. L.L. Asquith.

The Press – Mr. C. Groff (Herald), Mr. WA. R. Cocq (Telegram).

Those who associated with the training of contingents leaving Lethbridge: Mr. J.E. Hodson, Major Burnett, Mr. Filmer.

Also Dr. Thomson, Capt. Birnie, Lt. P. Bawden, Mr. G.W. Robinson.

The report begins by mentioning that meals arrived for twelve men posted at the Henderson Park barracks and three in hospital, then goes on upward through the list, from the men who helped train the soldiers, through the press and local voluntary associations, to the clergy, local business, IODE guests, and the officers themselves. The invitation scheme and dinner rituals occasioned a sense of connection between the world as lived, hierarchically, and the world as imagined through symbolic display. That no women were listed as guests is noted, but only as a sign of how the IODE chose to present a head-table – how they elected, in other words, to re-present their organizational powers within a site-specific version of maternal public power, one they sought to foreground on this occasion.

Maj. J.S. Stewart and Mayor Hardie addressed the gathering, the mayor launching into a pronounced xenophobic attack, to cheers, based on encounters he claimed to have had 'amongst the young Germans' some years before. His hawkish rant served to remind those present of what they should think of when they think of the enemy. Stewart's speech, which followed, shifted the focus back to the troops themselves and, in formulaic pleasantries, spoke of ties between the IODE women and the men in uniform:

> Lt.-Col. Stewart on rising was the occasion for an outburst of cheers in the way of ovation from the battery boys and the assembled guests. On behalf of the battery boys he thanked the Daughters of the Empire for not only

> providing the entertainment but the kindly thought which had at all times been given to the soldier boys. They would carry away with them a happy recollection of the occasion, and the memory of the 'pies' so often provided will dwell long with them. He was proud to have the command of such men, and could fearlessly say that no woman who had a son or a brother, or anyone related to the unit had or would have any occasion to be ashamed of him.

A baseball game and dance at the YMCA, with 'a very large crowd taxing the capacity of the building,' followed, with refreshments donated by local businesses.[27]

As strategic interactions, these affairs could also signify sentimental ties, structured by maternal gestures. This was evident when this same IODE chapter presented gifts to the 39th Battery just before its departure. A.B. Stafford, an executive member, was married to the regiment's commanding officer, Maj. Alexander Stafford, a hardware merchant who was later killed in action in June 1917. Sergeant-Major Holyoak's chronicle of the 39th Battery's final hours in town suggests a tightly interwoven connection between departure, organized patriotism, and gender. These rituals, exclusively the domain of these women, provide some measure of their desire to use powers conferred by class, ethnocultural privileges, and the authority of their organizations, to participate in ceremonies enmeshed with military procedure.

The battery received its marching orders and paraded on a Sunday morning, 20 February 1916. Members cleared out and cleaned their barracks and had photographs taken of each sub-section. Then the IODE presented personally assigned gifts 'to each man of the Battery.' After the Kilty and Citizen's bands played them to the station, as 'crowds thronged the streets,' gift packages and drinks, which this report makes a point of noting were non-alcoholic, were waiting for them on their seats.[28]

The appreciation of the troops was noted by Galt chapter members at their next annual meeting, when they congratulated themselves for providing a year and a half of voluntary home front service. Executive member A.B. Stafford listened, along with some seventy-five other women present, while a letter from her husband was read. Major Stafford thanked 'the chapter on behalf of the 39th for their kindness.' His letter was followed by another from a sergeant of the battalion, 'signed by every member of the battery, expressing their gratitude for the kindness of the I.O.D.E.' Since the outbreak, the Galt chapter had kept busy, visiting soldiers' families, organizing schoolchildren in sock-knitting drives, compiling scrapbooks for convalescent soldiers overseas, and, most recently, aiding the re-establishment of returned soldiers.[29]

In many cases IODE women expanded their volunteer activities through association with other patriotic organizations. 'One of the most important works of the Chapter,' as the *Herald* put it, 'is that undertaken by Mrs. Colpman as I.O.D.E. representative on the Patriotic Fund committee. The work of investigating cases that come under the fund, filling out papers, taking part in and supervising the visiting, demands practically all her time.' In her report to the CPF, Colpman claimed to have had 199 soldiers' families 'on her list,' which was then 'being increased every week' as recruits signed on with Lethbridge's new Kilty battalion. She also 'appealed for more visitors as the soldiers' wives and families look forward with so much pleasure to visits' from women volunteers.[30]

In these gendered fields of activity, the salience of maternal sensibilities and intentions seemed self-evident. But were such feelings uniformly held, or a defining aspect of their motivations? The ideal of maternalism as a gendered response connected to motherhood, which was contested among feminists before the war, could take on many forms and expressions. The need to expand our notions of maternalism for both pro- and anti-war advocates seems equally clear. As Kealey put it in the case of socialist women, 'motherhood was viewed as predisposing women to a critical view of war. To be sure, maternal ideology was also shared by supporters of the war effort, but the conclusions reached were quite different ... While maternal feminist arguments stressed the importance of women's support for public activities geared to support the war, maternal feminism also shored up the arguments of socialist-pacifist women who appealed to women as mothers to stop the carnage on the battlefield.'[31] Such multiple sentiments, as we have seen across the literature on women, gender, and the war, were not surprising.

It is, therefore, speculation to assume that an idealized predisposition toward motherhood roles, or even a common consciousness coherent enough to form a maternalistic ideology, is self-evident in the practices identified here. Such an interpretation attempts to read contemporaries' thinking patterns solely through their actions. What is more clearly defined is their active role in delineating specific fields of action and securing specific sites where women's power could be expressed. This was especially true if their aims entailed an incursion into spaces traditionally coveted by men: the regimental dinner, troop movements, barracks routine, and the supplementing of family incomes through the CPF – which were seen as intrusions into the gendered territories of breadwinning, armed service, and comparable forms of 'manful' citizenship. Clearly, notions of motherhood circulated in much of what took place, but maternalism did not act as a stable ideology behind a unified goal, as shown by its support of and opposition to the war effort.

What seems clearer is that many women, as maternal pro-war organizers, were greatly expanding their numbers, spatial practices, and propensities to configure public events and exert control over public welfare and material aid delivered directly to the troops, from bandages to the front to care packages for troop send-offs. They also secured privileged access to the soldiers and used it to signify their endorsement, as women, of the men's training and departure. Whatever individual attitudes they held, from jingoistic to maternal sensibilities, it was through these organized and empowered 'patriotic' groups and associations, configured by class and ethnocultural boundaries, that these women secured and defended cultural zones as signified responses to sexual difference. On occasion, they took it upon themselves to defend the spaces they secured in these fields – even if it meant limiting the participation of men working alongside them.

The advent of war led directly to the formation of a local branch of the Red Cross in Lethbridge in October 1914. The process began officially with an inaugural meeting, chaired by Mayor Hardie and addressed by a physician visiting from Banff, who spoke of how the 'present war has made formation of new branches and the revival of old ones an apparent necessity.'[32] What seems most significant about the politics of this process, however, was that the women present acted to ensure that its constitution secured for women majority representation on its planning committee. After resolutions to establish a Lethbridge branch and to install its executive had been passed, a motion was carried to set up a steering committee, initially comprised of seven members, with an upper limit of twenty. 'Four of the seven' from the initial committee were 'to be ladies,' to which was added 'the majority of the twenty' of any expanded steering committee must also 'be ladies.'[33] These conditions certainly seemed to signify that the concerned women recognized the need to defend their territory, especially at a time when both men and women were actively creating new domains of organized patriotism and war relief. In this case they inscribed gendered power procedurally, locating their presence in the more powerful zone of actual decision making, rather than in the nominal authority of a figurehead. As demands for the Red Cross increased, women volunteers also staked out particular fields of activity, wartime 'service,' as they saw it, securing medical supplies, prisoner of war packages, and other forms of material aid. In the process, they engaged in struggles of coordination and control with civilians and military authorities, invariably waged at the local level as branches across Canada snowballed in size and activity.

As their lists indicate, group memberships overlapped. This suggests, particularly in terms of executive member networks, multiple instruments of control. Organizations were often able to coordinate efforts. No sooner was the preliminary work of establishing Guelph's CPF branch underway in September 1914 when the city's Victoria chapter of the IODE, along with

Guelph's Horticultural Society, began arrangements for a city hall show. Collections from the exhibition, which ran for several weeks, were pledged to the CPF campaign. The *Mercury* helped to publicize the affair, stating that the 'ladies of the Victoria chapter' would be 'in charge of the decoration of the hall' and had announced their 'intention to charge a small admission to the show, the proceeds to be handed over to the Patriotic fund.'[34] Dozens of donors visiting the foyer that month contributed to a drive that surpassed $30,000 by Christmas.[35] Events like these stressed certain interactions between middle-class women, patriotic edification, and public spaces that succeeded on the basis of their genteel associations. Such silent and visual exhibits, distinguished by the refined, leisured pastimes they represented, were yet another communicative strategy, simple in form but assigned to legitimize a designated pro-war cause through associations with class-based manners and codes. For some it displaced the aural and visual stimuli of that first, fervid week of war in August, when Guelph, like other cities, witnessed its jingoistic festivals of crowds, cheering, and loud, booming bands. The quiet, decorated corners of a public building that likewise endorsed Canada's sudden war footing signified different class and gendered practices.

But for the most part, a frenetic drive to organize, speak, delegate, and direct took hold of both sexes, with many women soon concentrating their efforts in clubs and associations. The outbreak of the war boosted Guelph's Red Cross membership. During a special public meeting held at the city's YMCA, some ninety new members signed on, most of them women. Like many such meetings held at this time, the affair was described as highly enthusiastic, almost festive, drawing about three hundred members and pledged volunteers in total. After yet another rendition of 'God Save the King,' so frequently sung at such gatherings, the meeting was called to order. Member of Parliament Hugh Guthrie 'spoke on the conditions existing through the war' and of its present requirements. His brief address preceded appeals by several women to assist in voluntary war work, all in the context of a membership influx repeated in towns and cities throughout Canada. Though purportedly disinterested in social distinctions, with reports describing how these affairs attracted the interest of 'all' local citizens, specific practices at such gatherings, cloaked in formulaic expressions of pro-war sentiments, were embedded in pre-existing class and gender systems. For middle-class women attending these meetings or hearing patriotic orations before breaking off to carry out specific activities like bandage making or knitting bees, techniques of feminine sociability were coopted into wartime service. The Guelph women, for example, pledged to begin a major project of knitting headgear. Bundles of grey, beehive yarn, dozens of knitting needles were collected, and special classes were scheduled at the YMCA for the following day to prepare volunteers for a marathon knitting bee to be held in the basement of St. George's Anglican church in early September 1914.[36]

Women also took the lead in organizing charities, like the Belgian Relief Fund, as soon as news of war refugees circulated. Nearly two years later, as the stalemate in Europe dragged on, a war that took prisoners as well as lives soon presented another cause for the Galt IODE. In early May 1916 it established a Prisoners of War in Germany Fund. Thirty-three women donated gift parcels of foodstuffs, tobacco, socks, and candy, and nine donated money. In addition, the Lethbridge Teachers Patriotic and Relief Association presented a $100 cheque to the new POW fund.[37] Donations were channelled through the Canadian Prisoner of War Department of the national Red Cross, which at one point administered some 4,500 cases.[38]

Such efforts helped to integrate existing social networks engaged in patriotic work, to enlarge the scope of women's voluntary work, and to sustain larger memberships in imperial-nationalist organizations, led by the IODE, whose members, by the spring of 1916, realized that the fighting might not end soon. At its sixteenth annual meeting, convened shortly afterwards in Toronto, which drew delegates from 387 chapters across the country, its president noted that the 'growth of the Order in the past two years has been phenomenal. It is now immeasurably the largest Women's organization in the Empire, and its leadership in patriotic work is everywhere recognized.'[39] Such self-congratulating satisfaction was not misplaced, given its new membership rolls, greater regional penetration and density, and multiple activities. Yet even as the largest single charter organization of its kind, it remained an important but constituent part of associational networks at local levels that included small, interest-specific groups. Many had formed some time before the war, and then chose to direct their attention to war-related activities.

One such group, the Mathesis Club, a literary and music circle of some sixty members, had formed in Lethbridge a year before the war. Largely middle aged, middle class, and Anglo-Canadian, its membership lists, minutes, and club activities were indicative of certain techniques of sociability and strategies of social differentiation that structured members' social space and interactions. Through music and poetry recitals, or plays staged by and for members, or special teas and hosted lectures, they created performative discourses that edified and privileged a range of cultural behaviours, from language and gesture to dexterity, knowledge, and skill. Their mimicry of classical texts and orientations, of 'high' cultural sensibilities and traditions, appealed to the age, class, and ethnocultural preferences of a confined network of women. 'The object of this Club,' according to its constitution, 'shall be self-improvement and united effort toward the highest development of the home and community.'[40]

Although many of its members were married to men of established social rank, it would be misleading to assume their pro-war effort sensibilities went hand in hand with non-oppositional stances on women's suffrage, social welfare, or social reform, as some members had been active in these areas in other contexts. But progressive causes were not explicitly evident in club activities at this time. From the outset, members struck committees to host visiting speakers, stage music recitals and plays, and present panel discussions on current events. Their subsequent interest in war-related activities offered new pretexts for monthly meetings as encounters of bourgeois respectability and gendered social interaction. These fields of organizational procedure and display, from patriotic recitals to fundraising lectures, transported the Otherness of a distant war that at times fictionalized the experience of those overseas, offered lectures and discussions to imagine its consequences, or promoted the appropriateness and necessity of certain causes. As with the IODE, social encounters were structured to interpret wartime conditions and gendered obligations through select practices and discourses, which often served to locate foreign images through the accessible screens of familiar domain. In this way, participating women gathered in groups to experience visions of a community order – for instance, their responsibilities as middle-class women in Lethbridge witnessing a 'horrific act of tyranny' against Belgium that became personally empowering.

Germany's march through Belgium, a typical example reiterated in local settings across Canada, prompted members to form a special collection for the Belgium Relief Fund.[41] Two months later, a volunteer from the club's History Section delivered a talk, recorded in the minutes as 'exceedingly interesting and instructive,' on the 'Wars of Germany leading up to the present War,' then a common lecture theme across Canada.[42] The following spring, another 'gave a splendid talk on Belgium to which nearly sixty ladies listened with much interest, including a goodly number of the Daughters of the Empire who were guests.'[43]

Reciprocal attendance at each other's events is indicative of how members mapped out multiple domains, networks of overlapping encounter, and potentially synergistic effects. As one item from a general meeting of October 1915 recorded, the Galt IODE requested that 'as many as possible' from the Mathesis Club 'avail themselves' of the opportunity to hear a local missionary, returned from India, deliver an address entitled 'India, Her Part in the War.'[44] In keeping with the integrated approach to local fundraising often used in Lethbridge, as elsewhere, proceeds would be donated to the local CPF branch.[45] A 'farcical comedy,' staged by the Mathesis Club's Dramatic Art Department, also raised money for the city's CPF, as well as for a locally supported Red Cross nursing station.[46] Such events, often meticulously planned and staged, created contexts of sociability and forms of cultural expression on sites that activated certain horizons of expectation. Their effects, gradually and at discrete moments, introduced new visions of overseas combat or home front imperatives, but they used recognizable modes of behaviour and communication in gendered, class, and ethnocultural terms, further authorized by the familiarity of local setting and social milieu.

Turning to Trois-Rivières, we find far fewer examples of women engaged in organized pro-war activities, reflecting very different predispositions toward the war across francophone Quebec.[47] Although francophone Trifluviens greatly outnumbered local anglophones, women of either language often worked together for the local Red Cross branch and the CPF (see Chapter 3). While the scope and scale of their activities does not compare to that of Lethbridge or Guelph, surviving evidence points to sites of special significance, to moments of cooperation. These are in contrast to differences between francophones and the small anglophone minority that were constantly reinforced in other settings by barriers dividing men in the public sphere, whether these barriers were their roles in separate clubs, associations, and churches; their differentiated occupational categories at local mills and factories; and, after the outbreak of war, their enlistment into either English or French regiments through separate recruitment channels.

Against this background, the case of Mrs. H.T. Ham and Mrs. J.M. Dalton stands out. They shared the task of staging a 'Grand Concert' in aid of Trois-Rivières's CPF, with a program in both 'English and French Provided By Local Talents.' On this night, and in the planning that led up to it, differences that acted to divide men did not stop women from transcending barriers of tradition and association when they had the chance to make a joint effort.[48] The evening's musical program featured selections by the city's popular Union Musicale band, followed by local vocalists and instrumentalists, mostly women, bearing both French and English surnames. The affair was described as a great success, attracting a turnout of 'about five hundred people' according to the *Newcomer*, with proceeds pledged toward families of recent volunteers. Such events were rarer in Trois-Rivières than in Guelph or Lethbridge. But this particular evening, of poetry and of music provided by the city's largest band and by soloists performing in both languages, indicates how a sense of wartime unity was nonetheless evident there as well.[49] The majority, both in the crowd and on stage, may not have shared a sense of ties to Britain, but they endorsed an Allied victory and signified consensus on the aims, if not the imperial basis, of Canada's participation in the war.

Acting against the tensions created by the closing of the 86th Three Rivers Regiment, the imposition of Regulation No. 156, and the absence of any local centre of francophone recruitment, the significance of a small group of women taking the lead in staging a successful bilingual public event may be overstated, but should not be overlooked. Certainly their efforts were comparable to those of women's organizations across English Canada, which often hosted public events for patriotic purposes. Alternatively, women in Trois-Rivières turned their attention to furnishing send-off packages or first aid supplies from the city, though on a lesser scale compared to English Canadian cities.

Established voluntary organizations were often rejuvenated by war relief work that drew on existing social networks, which varied across local regions. In Guelph the Fireside Circle, a thirty-member association of women, 'chiefly composed of ladies and staff' at the Macdonald Institute, a prominent Ontario school of domestic science, found an activating aim in using the Institute's facilities.[50] The women renamed themselves the College Heights Relief Association in October 1915. Their president, G.E. Day, suggested that the group dedicate all voluntary 'time, energy and funds to war relief works, including Red Cross, sewing, etc.,' an effort said to have been 'enthusiastically upheld by every member.'[51] Three weeks later, 'the work of sewing and bandage rolling' was reported underway, soon furnishing hospital supplies 'to the Guelph Branch of the Red Cross Society.' Finished supplies were sent on to Shorncliffe's Queen's Hospital, a British army hospital connected to Guelph through a local physician and nurse stationed there.[52] As the fighting dragged on and Canadian casualties mounted, the demand obviously increased. To reflect their new dedication to war relief, the group changed its name in November 1915 to the College Heights Relief Workers Association, joining many such groups active at that time.[53]

Rural women in Wellington County surrounding Guelph had organized several Women's Institute branches in the years leading up to the war, but the appeal of organized patriotism broadened their range of activities. The Speedside WI, launched in 1915 in Eramosa township, was formed directly in response to the war. Like other women's groups, WI branches often organized visiting speakers' addresses, fundraising drives, and boosted attendance at meetings with speakers on the war. They also promoted household management to conform with wartime food control regulations.[54] Thus, women's groups like the IODE and WI introduced new discourses of structured practices through the gendered and local systems then proliferating. Power to redirect practices through voluntary compliance, from contributing a portion of disposable income to patriotic funds to rationing household consumption, was often controlled by women who chose to prescribe self-governing conduct rather than resort to state imperatives. Cooperative effort and voluntary compliance fuelled initiatives typified by the Speedside WI and take us beyond simplistic models of social control that fail to see the relevance of cultural mediation between ideal and actual behaviours.

This leads us to consider certain techniques IODE women legitimized to inculcate home front mythologies among children. The essay-writing contest, a common ritual introduced in many public school systems, presented fairly systematic prescriptions for children to fabricate discourses related to the war. In the spring of 1916, the Galt IODE organized a patriotic essay-writing contest, open to participating classes throughout the school district. Pupils competed for prizes 'for the best essays on patriotic subjects.'[55] The exercise not only served to extract expressions of loyalty from children, but also often moved parents, teachers, and civic leaders to offer parallel messages to their captive audiences. As the *Telegram* pointed out, the 'teaching of patriotism as an important subject in the school curriculum has in these days been strongly urged.' In 'days gone by ... in the absence of such a startling event as the war, patriotism, though in the hearts of the people, did not occupy the pedestal which it now holds.'[56]

But the real task of inculcating an imagined sense of the war was carried out in the context of classroom rituals accessible to children's experiences and level of understanding. The *Telegram* said that children could best 'sense the importance of events' under the guidance of the IODE. 'To appreciate their bearing, and to be acquainted with facts which otherwise might, possibly, have remained unknown was the scheme of the essays.' In terms drawn from a metaphorical diction generic to such editorials, the paper suggested that the 'torch in this respect has been kept flaming by the good offices of the local Daughters of the Empire in the offering of prizes for patriotic essays ... From the subjects given out to be written on by the pupils of our schools there cannot but arise a love of Country and Empire. The essay writing was a splendid stimulus to the young mind for gathering information, and thereby reaping knowledge [sic] of the things that do concern the individual and the nation.'[57]

Exercises like the essay-writing contest could easily reproduce collective memories and an ethnocultural sense of mission during the war, although, as Fentress and Wickham suggest in their approach to social memories as a transmitted practice, histories cannot be imparted as pure and reliable information.[58] As instruments of the state, public school classrooms in English Canada sought to promote a unifying sense of wartime nationalism, and could reach out to the wider community to do so. The essay-writing contest offered one means to forge uplifting, citizenship-based affiliations with the war effort for school boards, teachers, parents, and children, and few spoke out against it.[59] Such contests by the IODE valorized the gendered place of 'outside' women in the classroom who selected the project, enjoyed the cooperation of the schools, and were conspicuously endorsed for their efforts in Lethbridge by both the *Herald* and the *Telegram*.

Intersections of gender and patriotism remained an important part of the IODE as it structured the sentimental education of various audiences, onlookers, and newspaper readers through public events organized, staged, and re-presented through city press reports. At about the same time that these essays were being read, the Galt chapter hosted the strikingly elaborate send-off ceremony, including the presentation of regimental pipe drums, for the 113th Highlanders, the city's community-based regiment considered in Chapter 2.

The presentation began at 2:00 p.m. on a Saturday afternoon at Henderson Park, an expansive facility of some 296 acres that encompassed a small lake and agricultural exhibition grounds with a permanent bandstand.[60] The battalion marched into the main exhibition field and formed a hollow square in front of the bandstand. The IODE executive, including President G.W. Robinson, was seated. Before the drummers of the regimental pipe band stood the pipe drums, each engraved with full identification of the IODE, the battalion, and the date of presentation. 'The youngest member of the pipe band then stepped forward to present Mrs. Robinson with a large bouquet of red roses tied with the battalion colors, yellow, black, and green.' Lieutenant-Colonel Pryce-Jones 'thanked the members of the order for their interest in the Highlanders.' Robinson replied:

> We feel confident that the men of the Lethbridge Highlanders will worthily uphold the reputation for bravery won long ago by other Highlanders, and which gives you the proud distinction of being allowed to take your pipe band to the firing line.
>
> When your turn comes to face the enemy, may the beat of these drums serve to remind you that the people at home, in Alberta, are thinking of you and expecting to hear that you have added your share to the countless deeds of bravery already to the credit of Canadians....
>
> We regret that military necessity may soon remove you to other training quarters. Our opportunities of seeing the regiment on parade have been very few, but may I congratulate you on the splendid appearance of the battalion on Thursday, when we had the pleasure of seeing it on a route march.
>
> To those of you in the ranks leaving families behind, I can safely promise for the Order, which I have the honor and pleasure to represent, that we will at all times and in all ways do our best to help them and 'keep the home fires burning' in anticipation of the time when the enemy shall be vanquished, and you will return covered with glory and honor.

Robinson's oration was reprinted in full in both the *Herald* and the *Telegram*.[61] The affair formalized a transaction partly as a gendered encounter between the IODE and the troops. Symbolically, the Galt chapter presented itself as 'the women of the home front' through social narrative, retold in its president's dedication speech, that appealed to misrecognition. It re-presented the men by locating them in the myth of a chivalric, heroic masculinity that hearkened back to an imagined tradition, in this case by an allusion to the Highland warrior of long ago. As a communicative, didactic exercise designed to introduce or amplify certain sentiments, the ceremony was structured, solemn, and tactical. Events of this sort may have impressed onlookers, family and friends, far more than the troops. That was often their intent. Here, the elevated review stand put up by the IODE may also have helped to signify the organizers' sense of self-importance in a social hierarchy that endorsed the causes for which the war was purportedly being fought.

While Robinson's reference to a 'military necessity' that would 'soon remove you to other training quarters' referred to something very real and immediate, the gendered forms of this exchange proffered a vision of war quite removed from anything the men might actually come to experience. The presentation of roses by the youngest member of the battalion to Robinson, as an idealized portrait of maternal connection, hardly seems an accidental gesture. Although unreflective of the trenches, the hospitals, the munitions works, or other actual wartime situations, such interpretations helped create a vicarious notion of gender and virtue, and underlined the fact that women often played prominent roles in ritualizing signs and symbols.

Much of the wartime-inspired volunteer activity – from raising funds for hospital and clothing supplies for the families left behind to organizing programs, projects, and special events – seemed to privilege gendered modes of behaviour that, at first glance, seemed to do little more than to valorize the 'women's part.' In practice, however, many activities served to legitimize incursions into the war effort at home that expanded women's power. The wide variety of activities performed by middle-class volunteers were also structured by their sense of feminine power. In Lethbridge, Red Cross women sought to preserve this through the branch constitution's quorum for women.

Women's voluntary activities also offered pretexts for sociability, structured as a select encounter, even when men were present, to express support for the war on their own terms. Through a host of encounters and transactions, whether staging a dinner, organizing a fundraising drive, or presenting a regimental mascot, middle-class women organized group efforts that deployed gender differences to decide what was to be done, by whom, and to what end. Organized patriotism may have acted to strengthen rather than relax perceptions of sexual difference, but it was part of shifting configurations of gendered practices that established new fields of power. Despite the fact that gendered experiences as well as perceptions were far from consistent across class and ethnocultural boundaries throughout the war, women's participation in organized patriotism suggests that middle-class women actively mapped out territories and prerogatives that proved significant in scale and scope. Although their longer-term effects on gender differences were ambivalent, these fields offer historians localized and specific sites in which to examine gender power.

The Home Guards, Escapism, and Masculine Adventure

The home guard units that sprang up across the country are also useful sites on which to examine gender. Their histories were ephemeral, but provide points of entry for examining masculine experiences and expressions. In terms of an aesthetic ideal, men in soldiering roles, even as civilians far removed from the fighting overseas, had a popular appeal, embedded in pre-war associations of masculinity with marksmanship. For some men, opportunities to display manhood through the handling of firearms surfaced through a few weeks of drill, target practice, and parading in cities on a home front still uncertain of where the war would lead.

Across many sites and varied activities, civilian men handled their responses to wartime demands in cultural ways that expressed and reaffirmed pre-existing patterns of class relations and popular representations of wartime manhood.[62] Our consideration of militarized forms of masculinity, an important part of constructing identity for the departing men in Chapter 1, can be extended to these civilian men, who often could not enlist, but donned uniforms as civilian security officers nonetheless. After the outbreak of war, there was interest across the country in home front security. This concern was also shaped by the chronology of the war, and it increased with sensationalized newspaper coverage of the war, fuelled by rumour and gossip, of an enemy alien menace in every local community. Stories of German-American conspiracies, of spies and saboteurs infiltrating parts of Canada, circulated widely in the press, with most reports concentrated in the first year of the war. Civilian defence efforts grew on the fears such discourse inspired, as discussed in Chapter 3. As Duguid stated in his official history of the Canadian forces: A 'patriotic desire to do something urged many who could not volunteer for overseas service, and who did not belong to the Militia, to form independent organizations, collectively termed "Home Guards."' Members were 'largely over military age,' and while they 'drilled enthusiastically after business hours' in towns and cities across Canada, they lacked a 'well defined purpose.' The Department of Militia and Defence did spare a few rifles for these groups, but gave no substantial support to their cause. On a local level, hundreds of mostly middle-aged war supporters across the country felt, as Duguid put it, a strong urge to demonstrate their military prowess, to participate in what they saw as the business of war, however vicarious and tangential their role was. With no direct threat to Canadian territory, the movement largely evaporated by 1916.[63]

Histories of the height of its popularity, which in some cities was striking, take us into the cultures of working-class and, at the organizational level, middle-class men. Embedded in local settings in the early war, their efforts conveyed ambivalence between a self-serving show of power and pride, and claims of selfless endeavour. As a national movement, shaped by perspectives of hometown horizons, they carved out an explicitly gendered field. In purporting to activate manful home service to protect surrounding communities, they also featured displays of manhood on parade or at the rifle range that held some allure for the would-be marksman, the pseudo-soldier, and the semi-authorized official serving weekends or the occasional evening.

One aspect of the guardsmen's activities appeared as a curious appropriation of rifle shooting, a sport traditionally reserved for the upper classes, which middle-class men on both sides of the Atlantic popularized in the Victorian period. After the outbreak of the war, an eager influx of working-class men rushed to take up rifle shooting at local ranges and shooting galleries in both Guelph and Trois-Rivières. The appeal of rifle-shooting across Canada was, like the Militia movement, more connected to fraternal masculinity than to the mimicking of upper-class pursuits. Rifle shooting in organized men's clubs flourished across Canada in the late nineteenth century. The sport combined patriotism, citizenship, and manhood with local community participation, feelings participants experienced most intensely on the evenings and weekends when they met to practise and to display their skills. 'What made these meanings even more powerful,' K.B. Wamsley argued, 'was the potential for individual internalization of interpretation and experience, but within the range of constituted boundaries of political activity.' It promoted, in short, a series of imagined, nationalizing moments across different regions for well over a generation. For the men who participated in it, as Wamsley put it, 'shooting practice and competition became valorized cultural signifiers of patriotism, duty, contribution to collective purposes, and protection of territory and society. Yet, simultaneously, it served to reproduce hegemonic masculinity, assigning distinct roles for men as participants and women as supportive spectators – a separation of leisure practices based on gender alone.'[64]

Ottawa spent over $1.5 million from 1868 to 1908 to establish and maintain local shooting ranges under the auspices of the Dominion of Canada Rifle Association, Canada's first state-supported sport body. A common and powerful cultural site of masculine leisure in Victorian Canada, organized rifle shooting helped to construct a cultural sense of male power through firearm skill and masculine fraternity. Its popularity increased into the early twentieth century and intersected with the growth of the militia movement, also a site for masculine cultures, in the same period.[65] The appeal of rifle shooting, and the close attention guardsmen gave it, suggests ties in local areas between its pre-war connection to manhood and its extended manifestations after August 1914. During the early war, Canada's home guard, with its emphasis on target training and a high level of marksmanship, was partly a branch of this more broadly based tradition of a 'hegemonic' masculinity, with its symbolic sense of protecting a local territory.

This suggests how these men construed their world, even if their sport had no profound effect on gender systems or relations generally. Its relevance as a gendered practice concerns the ways in which rifle shooting drew on popular forms of masculine self-identification as men learned to handle firearms in groups and competed with each other. Of course, before the war, acquiring skills in marksmanship and knowledge of firearms through rifle-shooting clubs and associations was but one sport among many that drew on an appeal to masculine association and power signified through athletic competence. But the fact that home guardsmen across Canada quickly enlisted men through this sport and frequently made use of facilities, weapons, and amateur expertise supplied by existing rifle clubs suggests a ready-made tradition. Rifle shooting and marksmanship as an established leisure pursuit was easily coopted as a necessary skill for civilian defence, falling neatly into the hands of home guard organizers looking for something that might attract weekend warriors.

Evidence of this surfaced in Guelph when the local rifle club drew a large crowd on the first 'pleasant Sunday' following the outbreak of war. The Guelph Rifle Association had opened its range to the public and loaned firearms, free ammunition, and advice to would-be marksmen. About sixty men turned out, 'anxious to learn something about the military rifle.' On hand to instruct were club officials as well as several recruits temporarily stationed at the armoury in town.[66] Two days later, the rifle association led another target drill, this time at the armoury and under the auspices of a full-fledged 'home guard' organization.

Calling themselves 'Clark Rifles' in honour of Capt. Walter Clark, who had formed the Highland Cadet Corps a generation before, they obtained permission from the school board to use the gymnasium and target facilities of the Guelph Collegiate Institute. At first, they were quite successful in attracting participants. Within a month, Clark's Rifles boasted three forty-five-man companies, decked out in special uniforms, and had secured the services of a militia officer, stationed at the armoury, who drilled them in marching as well as in target shooting. Their uniforms were said to 'give a finished appearance to the drill, and the men looked as though they were ready for the front.'[67] With memories of recruitment for the real fighting front still fresh, it seemed likely that many men, as Duguid put it, would be eager to take part in some form of military exercise.[68] Within a few weeks, however, the novelty seemed to wear thin. Practices became less frequent and by the following spring, Clark's Rifles had quietly suspended its activities.[69]

Rumours of a home guard association forming in Trois-Rivières first circulated at the end of October 1914, when the Liberal press reported that plans were underway to reinstate the 86th Regiment.[70] Ultimately, the endeavour succeeded, though the process unfolded in much the same way as had recruitment locally, with little association between francophones and anglophones. The *Bien Public* downplayed the home guard as a 'private initiative' within a larger statement issued in December 1914, which called for the reinstatement of a local regiment.[71] The *Newcomer* saw home guard drills as a useful exercise, something that could very well 'teach a man all he requires to learn' of military preparedness.[72] What became the Three Rivers Rifle Association began modestly, with little more than a few backers, a licence from the city to operate a shooting gallery, and less than forty men. Trois-Rivières's federal parliamentarian, Jacques Bureau, declined to serve as its vice-president, though a local judge, Alfred Désy, did stand.[73] All other surnames listed on the executive, with the exception of the club's treasurer, were English.[74] Charles Whitehead, a Wabasso Cotton Company official, donated firearms to the fledgling association.[75] Nonetheless, having this club up and running enabled him to forward a formal request to the militia department to reinstitute the 86th. Whitehead presented an all-English slate of officers, from himself as commander to the Rev. J. Aitken Clark as regimental chaplain.[76]

While the home guard's appeal may have varied, from simple curiosity about military practices to a lingering envy of those who had enlisted, the same blend of militarism and masculinity expressed in English Canada could be found in the promotional style its sponsors adopted. 'The organisation will exist for the defence of the City,' the *Newcomer* claimed at its inception, to 'affor[d] the men of Three Rivers a chance to show their patriotism in a concrete fashion.'[77] Their brief presence offered a structure for manful recreation that drew on a perceived need, perhaps in this case more the product of middle-class organizers than rank-and-file members, to signify commitment to the war overseas. Practices were held at a makeshift shooting gallery set up at the Market Hall on Tuesday evenings. Most of the thirty-seven members who turned up to fire the .22 calibre rifles that Whitehead supplied were identified explicitly in the *Newcomer* as 'working class' men who either could not or had not enlisted to date.[78] As elsewhere, after several weeks of target practice, attendance dropped off.

Meanwhile, the club's executive continued to push for a new regiment, which was finally approved in January 1916. Once a revamped 86th was reinstated, its new officers quickly organized a series of events to install a unit that, after the war, would eventually draw interested men, both French and English, back into the fold of an official militia unit. Although the opening of the non-commissioned officers' mess, which took place with considerable ceremony in February 1916, or the first public 'march out' followed by a special 'Whist and Dance,' both held that spring, appear to have been all-English affairs, their efforts did mark the resurgence of military traditions in the city.[79] In effect, the home guard movement had been successfully coopted by supporters of a reorganized militia.

Typically a site of masculinity and militarism, the revival of a regiment in this case appeared confined to certain ethnic (anglophone) and class (middle and upper-middle) pretensions as well. It began as an appeal to what R.W. Connell refers to as 'gentry masculinity' – marked by a 'code of honour' defining culturally appropriate manly behaviour – which organizers used to attract local anglophones to 'defend' their city in wartime. While their efforts led to the creation of a new regiment to replace the one that Hughes had seen turned out some two years earlier, it would be some time before its membership would come to reflect the overwhelming presence of francophone men in the city.[80]

Civil defence mobilization did not become widespread in southern Alberta until near the end of the first year of the war. In the case of Lethbridge, high levels of enlistment in the Canadian Expeditionary Force had pre-empted interest in home defence until the fall of 1915. But just as the last of the city's volunteer units were being recruited, a persistent stream of rumours concerning enemy alien sabotage began to raise concerns, particularly among local grain growers, that the security of their property and local community might be at risk. In contrast to the 'sporting' traditions expressed in the rifle-shooting drills in Guelph and Trois-Rivières, Lethbridge raised the largest and most active home guard corps of the three cities, due largely to the presence of significant numbers of enemy aliens in the area.

An appeal to manhood to 'protect' the city of Lethbridge was first raised by that city's chief of police, John Skelton, who was joined, if not pushed, by local businessmen to ensure that private property was protected. While support for the home guard was collapsing elsewhere, the police chief acted in response to escalating fears of spies, saboteurs, and rumoured plots to disrupt railway transportation. While such perceptions had no basis in fact, the unusually high enemy alien population contributed to a series of reports in the *Herald*, describing everything from imagined plots to dynamite the CPR high trestle to alleged attempts to disable machinery needed to harvest the bumper crop of that year. Allegations that nearby Magrath had become a gateway for enemy aliens escaping to the United States, the discovery of firearms on a German farm in the area, or reports that saboteurs were 'busy among the threshing rigs' seemed to fuel concerns that enemy aliens were more dangerous than benign.[81] 'I might point out,' one member of the Lethbridge Home Guard's organizing committee wrote in a failed attempt to secure official authorization from Ottawa, 'that we have cause to fear for the safety of our crops, owing to the fact that we are practically a border town, and are surrounded by coal mines, the miners in which are almost entirely of Austrian and Slav citizenship. We have a large number of interned prisoners here also, and at this time a great many harvest hands are coming into this country, and we do not know anything about their nationality. As we have been warned constantly to protect the crops, it looks imperative that the citizens should join together for that purpose and assist the Government by doing their part.'[82]

In more sedate terms, the *Herald* stated: 'The people of Lethbridge have too much at stake to neglect to take steps to guard their property and persons from possible danger, and that consequently an organization of citizens should be formed so that in case of developments the situation could be handled with promptness and efficiency.'[83]

While no significant 'developments' ever took place, local home guard organizers meticulously planned for any contingency that some feared might arise. In mid-July 1915, a committee, dominated by Lethbridge businessmen, appointed Skelton commander-in-chief of the new civilian defence force. Members of the Lethbridge Home Guard soon enjoyed greater powers than most civilians across the country. As the *Herald* revealed, placing Chief Skelton in command had solved the 'vexing problem' of obtaining official status from the federal government because he was able to swear in all 'members as special police,' which legally enabled guardsmen 'to do ordinary police work with the powers of a policeman.' Granting special constable status to a civilian defence force, the paper added, had been successfully employed in Britain. In London alone, some twelve thousand guardsmen wielded this authority.[84]

In addition, what was termed a 'Flying Squadron' of motorcyles and automobiles was placed in Skelton's command. 'Every speed demon in town has expressed his intention to become a member of the motorcycle brigade,' the *Herald* boasted. An 'arms and ammunition committee' was also set up, which advertised for citizens to donate any firearms or ammunition they might possess.[85] A city-wide 'census of firearms and munitions' was initiated and was reported to be 'progressing satisfactorily,' with the city police station serving as a temporary armoury. 'The matter of uniforms' was also considered. The *Herald* reported that 'prices have been obtained from the Peabody Co. who [sic] are manufacturing uniforms specially designed for Home Guard Corps.'[86] With 'four high-powered motor cars,' motorcylists 'armed with revolvers,' and the new Peabody uniforms on the way, it came as no surprise when the *Herald* intimated that '[r]ecruiting for the guards has received an impetus lately.'[87] One hundred and sixty men had signed on by that point.

What did come as a surprise was Chief Skelton's 'denouncement' three weeks later of a 'lack of interest' in the city's new defence corps. 'It is a shame that a city the size of Lethbridge,' Skelton stated, 'cannot turn out more than 125 men for the Home Guard drill ... The citizens of this city are not patriotic enough.' While a lack of support for the war was clearly not evident in Lethbridge in general terms, sustained participation in home guard units was a rarity across the country. Participation simply could not be maintained in these organizations, which failed to serve any demonstrated purpose. For most units, the redundancy of their weekly drills supplemented by the odd parade or guard detail in search of a non-existent enemy became painfully obvious to all but the most quixotic. Despite Skelton's complaint, a 125-man turnout was not, comparatively speaking, a particularly poor one. Nevertheless, the home guard commander felt that some overt display of support for his movement was needed. He then 'announced that on Friday next the Guard will be marched through the streets of the city headed by one or more bands, and he especially wishe[d] a full turnout.'[88]

The parade went off as a 'big success,' according to the *Herald*'s detailed description of a public display that connected manhood to militarism. 'The valor and beauty of the city were there: the valor marched in the ranks and the beauty thronged the line of march, which presented an animated scene for the whole distance.' Led by the 'skirling pipes' of the Kilty and Citizen's bands, the guardsmen marched '175 strong' and 'four abreast, arms at the slope.' While this report concluded that it was 'evident that the movement has come to stay,' a note of realism was added with the remark 'at least as long as it is needed.'[89]

Like other units across the country, the Lethbridge Home Guard failed to carve out any viable role as a civilian defence force, and participation dissipated as the weeks went by. After five months of effort to keep it going, a general meeting was held to elect new officers. It was described as 'a most enthusiastic though not largely attended' affair.[90] But those who remained found a new purpose for it in supporting local recruitment. 'One of the biggest recruiting campaigns ever undertaken in Western Canada,' the *Herald* announced, 'was launched at the annual meeting of the Lethbridge home guard last evening ... a huge committee of the home guard and other citizens was elected to act with the local military authorities in a big effort to complete the recruiting of the Lethbridge Highlanders in as short a space of time as possible.'[91] Local support for raising a Kilty Battalion succeeded, and in the spring of 1916 the 113th Lethbridge Highlanders left, 'about 900 strong,' for further training before heading for the front.[92] Among them was Chief Skelton, who had assumed the rank of captain.[93] As the 113th prepared to depart, the guard's remaining members petitioned Ottawa to grant militia reserve status for their association, as had been done in Trois-Rivières. The proposed unit would 'be open not only to Home Guard members but also to the cadets of the schools so that all might receive more advanced training than is possible under present conditions.' To follow up, arrangements were made for upgrading target drill exercises as well as 'increasing the membership' through the informal men's gathering, the 'smoker,' at which the 'larger plans' of forming a reserve unit could be presented.[94]

News that the Department of Militia and Defence was about to authorize a fourth depot battery in Lethbridge was made public the following month.[95]

But what became the 78th Battery had no direct association with local guardsmen, nor is there any evidence of the guards endorsing the new depot battery. This sudden turn against support for another unit might be explained by the fact that many guardsmen were either businessmen or farmers, and both groups were beginning to feel the pinch on the local labour supply caused by recruitment.[96] Lethbridge Board of Trade president G.R. Marnoch went so far as to state in late July 1916 that 'it behooves us now to consider whether it might not be well to recommend that active recruiting should be halted until harvesting is over and the crop movement well underway.'

Marnoch's concern over further recruiting stemmed not only from fears that it would drastically reduce agricultural labour, but also that it would draw needed labour from the city's collieries. The negative effect, he argued, could become acute: 'Coal will be required for the threshing machines, for transportation and for farm and household use during the winter.'[97] The *Herald* echoed his sentiment. 'When filling up a battalion,' an editorial suggested two weeks later, 'a big husky farmer is a mighty pleasing recruit to the recruiting agent who displays no hesitation in accepting him. But such action is wrong. We have pointed out before that it is poor policy. President Marnoch of the Board of Trade has lifted his voice against the practice.'[98]

At this point, the home guard in Lethbridge had virtually disappeared. While the movement across the country had proved a short-lived experiment, its initial appeal suggests how masculinities among relatively small groups of civilian men could be channelled into a special form of collective action during the first year and a half of fighting overseas.

Class, Gender, and Voluntary Action

Manhood signified through home guard activities and displays was valorized largely through an interplay of practice and fantasy, of masculine assertions expressed in parades, drills, and, in Lethbridge, occasional patrols of the CPR bridge that held little purpose beyond symbolism and the allure of military action. The effort was shaped by notions of militarism as a manful pursuit and duty, an association of manliness with marksmanship, military drill, and the ideals of uniformed service that seemed to blur distinctions between sacrifice and camaraderie. During their public displays and activities, guardsmen tried to make their purpose conform to popular representations of war shaped by idealized images of the fighting overseas. When mostly middle-aged, working-class men lined up to try their hand on the firing range or paraded in uniform or took part in guarding bridges and rail lines, their sense of wartime nationalism was partly defined by popular perceptions of masculine ideals reiterated constantly from the voluntary phases of the war onward. As Mosse put it, in many ways the war 'tied nationalism and masculinity together more closely than ever before.' For the men who generally could not enlist, 'the urge to serve in a cause higher than the individual, to put manliness in the service of an ideal' seemed to make this movement a nominally attractive alternative to enlistment for active service.[99] Its local histories reveal activities framed by popular notions of what should constitute masculinity in wartime.[100]

For both men and women who sought direct involvement with the war effort, whether as war relief workers or as home guardsmen, gender and class combined and encoded the specific practices and fields of activity they pursued. In each case, their efforts served as a pretext for encounters that communicated feminine or masculine ideals through particular techniques of sociability as well as home service. In the case of the guardsmen, local organizers sought to appropriate enthusiasm for military participation into formal authorizations for additional militia units. Their initial appeal depended on cultural norms concerning the social use of the male body.

As mostly middle-class women prepared care packages and mostly working-class guardsmen drilled, a massive assault was taking place on millions of male bodies that would have dramatic consequences in the post-war years. The return of the soldiers, whether wounded or deemed fit for work, needs to be placed against the backdrop described here of gendered fields mapped out in the specific areas of war relief and home guard service. 'Although the range of "masculinities" remained extremely wide,' as Joanna Bourke contends, 'military experiences led to a greater sharing of gender identities between men of different classes, ages and localities.' The real experience of war, in part, led to an increased yearning for domesticity 'far from oppressive statist and military interventions,' as Bourke suggests.[101] As the fighting dragged on, this served to relegate the idealism of civilian volunteers, who never saw the fighting front, to popular but fading notions of how loyalty could be communicated through gendered practices, all of which bore little relationship to the challenges soon to come.

7
Men Like Us

'When the scribe arrived at the College, the Lance Corp. could not be found, and the reporter had about given up hopes of locating him when he spied a man in khaki crossing the campus.' The soldier was reluctant to speak. Though recovered physically, he had suffered a bullet wound in France that spring, near Ypres. It was now October 1915. He was somewhere on the Ontario Agricultural College grounds in Guelph, strolling around. He had been a student there before enlisting with Princess Patricia's Light Infantry, a privately sponsored regiment from Montreal that had joined other Canadian units in their first major battle. Now Tubby Nourse was a special guest at President Creelman's invitation.

'"Yes I'm Nourse," he said, when the *Mercury* man caught up with him, "but I haven't much of a story to tell."' Of his regiment he said only: '"There are just a few left."' As his interview progressed, it seemed obvious that Nourse's priorities were connected to his re-establishment, while the reporter seemed primed to extract as much as possible from him about his so-called 'adventures' at the front.[1]

This chapter examines boundaries between returned soldiers and civilians. How, through local encounters, did veterans, who began filtering back in 1915, portray themselves and how were they in turn portrayed by others as they attempted to adapt to life out of uniform or 'back to mufti'? Becoming a civilian again was easier said than done, as efforts by the men and by others operating within the local civilian networks and the military bureaucracy often made clear. We turn, then, to consider how civilians and veterans in local circumstances came to negotiate the distances between each other, detachments of perception and circumstance that were perceived through localized texts and settings, from city newspapers that offered transfiguring images of soldiers overseas to struggles at Guelph's Speedwell Military Hospital waged by men who wanted former soldiers rather than civilians placed in charge of their care.

We will also consider the ambivalence of voluntary efforts to assist returning men in Lethbridge during the war, before the federal government had adopted measures through, most notably, the Department of Soldiers' Civil Re-establishment. The *Herald* featured frequent and detailed coverage of efforts that uncover underlying anxieties some civilians held concerning veteran relief and re-establishment. When faced with the actual rather than the ideal ex-soldier, civic stakeholders like Mayor Hardie might respond to fears quite distant from any glorified image of the fighting man returned. They often saw unemployed veterans not as heroes, but as potentially idle, restless, and unproductive, and they engaged in charitable activities and rhetoric indicative of the perceptions one might encounter at any city hall, chamber of commerce, or local board of trade. They engaged, in other words, in efforts to protect themselves from what they feared might prove to be a destabilizing post-war phenomenon.

So often home seemed changed to the men, and the men had been profoundly altered by their experiences, even more than their illnesses, disabilities, or nightmares made obvious. They certainly confronted an enormous distance between their memories of civilian life and the realities of post-war adjustments faced by former soldiers across individual circumstances. Many had been on the margins of adolescence when they enlisted, and the challenge of trying to reshape their new lives in a changed country rested on the unstable footings of uncharted courses and uncertainty. To add to this, home front civilians had difficulty reconciling the actual experiences of the soldiers who returned with their own sense of what had taken place overseas.[2]

Veteran re-establishment took place within a still-powerful and persuasive parallel discourse that spoke of the ideal combat hero, then nearly finished in uniform or on his way back home. Since the fighting had begun, writers and orators of all kinds had translated casualty lists, letters home, and newspaper reports into speeches, sermons, editorials, and poems that justified and glorified the sacrifice. In the dogmatic formalism of such rhetoric, prevailing narratives fused religion, civilization, democracy, and a host of other ideals with the toll for victory. It could even be heard overseas. Sir Arthur Currie's appeal to the Canadian Corps during Germany's devastating spring offensive in the spring of 1918, for example, implored the troops to look 'back with pride on the unbroken record of your glorious achievements.' God's grace, earned through the duty and sacrifice of Canadian soldiers, he implied, would save the British Empire: 'In this fateful hour, I command you and I trust you to fight as you have never fought, with all your strength, with all your determination, with all your tranquil courage. On many a hard-fought field of battle you have overcome this enemy, and with God's help you shall achieve victory once more.'[3] Words like this did not themselves motivate the fighting men, concerned primarily for their own safety and for those closest to them, but they echoed how the slaughter might be converted into terms that justified it, whether in the field or at home.

Home front patriots, in turn, produced countless variations of the God and triumph myth, often through projected masculinities conveyed in terms of 'our gallant fighting men' or 'our boys overseas.' As one of Lethbridge's most ardent war-effort supporters, J.D. Higinbotham conjured an imagined sense of manful bravado in 'Canadians at Lille,' a simplistic poem that he had privately printed a month before the Armistice, decorated with Alberta's Coat of Arms.[4] In ornate terms, the pharmacist fancied Canadian infantry making their way to the French town of Lille during the collapse of the Hindenburg Line in September 1918: 'So eager were our daring lads / To reach the fleeing Huns / That into No-Man's Land they went / To bring up heavy guns.' Ignoring the warnings of a British sergeant-major, the Canadians charged over the top and fought to free some three thousand townspeople. When the fighting was done, the locals poured out their affections: 'They cheered us and they beered us; / They shouted, laughed, and cried; / They wined us, and they dined us / Till we very nearly died.'[5]

Yet many veterans felt that the kind of gratitude expressed by civilian romantics, like Higinbotham, too often failed to translate directly into policies and programs that met their needs. Even if they had escaped debilitating injury, they faced irritating delays and administrative processing on their return. Their efforts to re-establish themselves have been documented on a national level, most notably by Desmond Morton and Glenn Wright. In their collective struggles in the interwar period, particularly those of the Great War Veterans Association (GWVA), they sought solutions that incrementally expanded Canada's interventionist state, setting relatively early precedents for government, rather than voluntary and local, responses to the problems of veteran re-establishment.[6]

As the fighting continued into its second year and casualty lists appeared more often in local papers, municipal governments grew anxious over the anticipated costs of unemployed or disabled men, a burden many feared would be left to them. Municipal officials and civilian volunteers faced a growing and difficult task with limited financial resources. At the same time, towns and cities staged often subdued public ceremonies before demobilization to welcome returned soldiers home, symbolizing gratitude and local embrace for those who came back first. Many well-intentioned citizens tried to help the men re-establish themselves. But they seldom understood the real needs of their returning heroes. Injury, disease, or demobilization itself eventually brought veterans face to face with the problem of communicating what they had become, the things they wanted and needed, and how they wished the dead or dying men close to them to be remembered.

To deal with this problem, we turn first to press reports early in the war that often served to distort popular images of trench warfare. Addressing how a local newspaper depicted men's bodies against modern weaponry at Ypres sets a backdrop for what took place when the returned soldiers began to make their way back home in significant numbers. These perceptions should be situated where they were most often exchanged, from everyday reports circulating in the press to local encounters between veterans and civilians that occurred across a deep, cultural divide. Considering how newspapers portrayed the battles overseas, and how local incidents took place, helps us to retrace how notions of the common soldier underwent inversion, how reverence for 'our boys' at the front became dramatically displaced once civilians began to imagine them in proximity as dangerous men – diseased, drunken, and generally unfit.

Men's Bodies, Images of Destruction, and the Ordinary Local Boy

Whether home front civilians embraced romantic notions of the war or faced shattering news of family or friends killed in action, their understanding of the overseas experience was indirect and often shaped by information gleaned from newspapers. First reports of Canada's participation in a major battle reached home with revelations, couched in horrific terms, of German gas attacks on Belgium's Ypres salient in late April 1915.

Coverage in the Guelph *Mercury* was typical of the popular press: 'HELL TURNED LOOSE ON THE WESTERN FRONT' was served up as a front-page sensation following the Second Battle of Ypres. As this and countless other reports indicated, it was not just the German army, but also its brutal machinery, that introduced chlorine gas to trench warfare. 'Standing on a hill, five miles from Ypres,' one United Press reporter related, 'I saw reflected along a fifteen-mile panorama, filled with smoke, the gigantic opposition which General French's army is making against the weight of the reinforced German war machine.'[7] At month's end, *Mercury* readers learned that Canadian casualties had surpassed 9,000.[8] Less than two weeks later, *Mercury* readers saw total Allied casualties approach 300,000, a figure estimated by the British government.[9] Of those, 50,000 troops had been killed before the first year of fighting was over. Newspapers across Canada made a special effort to publish casualty lists and to highlight coverage of local men killed or wounded overseas.[10]

The *Mercury*, for instance, reported that an officer from the city's 30th Wellington Rifles, Lieut. Peter W. Pick, had been wounded on the Canadian lines. 'When he left with the expeditionary force from this city some months ago he was known to Guelphites as Captain Pick,' the *Mercury* related in describing a young man 'very popular in this city and district.' Ypres had taken soldiers like Pick into a new kind of mechanized combat, and papers like the *Mercury* framed trench warfare with vivid depictions of exploding shells or chlorine gas. Loved ones or close friends appeared often under signs of easily imagined figures, whether local 'boys' or 'fighting men' or simply 'Canadian soldiers.' Even as clichés, the imagined presence overseas of individual men to whom many readers were closely attached could be read into each of these categories. And yet these faces, beings, or struggling bodies, mere glimpses snatched of men like Pick, came also through the fire and haze of trench combat, imagined as horrific, cruel, and machine-driven. Such juxtapositions served as powerful, and officially non-directed, forms of propaganda. 'ALL SORTS OF WAR MACHINERY USED,' one headline in the same issue blared above a text furnishing horrid descriptions of machine guns and heavy artillery. The scene was cast in terms of the 'roar of these great pieces of artillery, the latest product of the Krupp factories,' which could 'be heard for thirty miles.' Against this backdrop, the narrative returned to Guelph's Peter Pick, injured by a single bullet: 'It is hoped his wounds are not serious, and that he will be spared to return with his men, many of whom are Guelph boys.'[11]

For Canadians across the country who knew or loved men like Pick, the desperate wait for news, official or otherwise, became an anxious vigil that newspaper coverage only made worse. To feed public fascination, mixed with genuine fear, city papers often published letters from overseas. For the *Mercury*, the genre took the form of a column called 'At the Front,' which printed letters from the men for over a year. In one of the earliest, Pick's description of Ypres revealed a pathetic carnage, conveyed through the conventional language of bravery against barbarism. 'Just a line,' he began in his letter home, 'to say that we of the 30th are still to the fore.' His injury was manfully cast aside as 'a tap on the head' in a brief account of his regiment that included the names of three officers killed and five wounded: 'This left me the only officer. We had to advance across about fifteen hundred yards of open ground with out a foot of cover in the face of rifle, machine gun and artillery fire, and when within about 500 yards of the enemy we were ordered to dig ourselves in. We of the 1st [Battalion] lost heavily in wounded, and the usual barbarism was used by [the] enemy. They shot at anyone seen to be still moving.'[12]

Pick's depiction appealed to a romantic sense of masculine pluckiness against a disordered and dangerous killing ground. Though the 'boys did splendidly,' he related at one point, they 'were terribly handicapped at this point through lack of artillery support.' He closed with regrets for 'not mentioning places. It is forbidden, but you will be able to get this from the papers.'[13] Meanwhile, the *Mercury* joined papers across Canada that continued to portray the disaster as an imminent victory, being won step-by-step through stubborn, 'splendid' determination.

There was no shortage of sensational losses capturing the attention of the press. Just when reports of the Ypres nightmare were being digested, news of a disastrous attempt to break through Turkish defences guarding the Dardanelles straits reached the *Mercury*. 'ALLIES DETERMINED THAT

DARDANELLES SHALL BE OPENED UP,' one headline boomed on 4 May, with the sub-caption 'British Casualty List Is Heavy.'[14]

Four days later, coverage shifted from Ypres and the Dardanelles to the North Atlantic. This sudden pivot chased one of the hottest stories produced by the war. Not far from Liverpool, with nearly 1,400 passengers aboard, the *Lusitania*, part of Britain's Cunard passenger fleet, was torpedoed by a German submarine. The fact that 128 of the 1,195 drowned were Americans, neutralists at this time, became the most notorious aspect of this disaster. Reported slaughters on land or sinkings at sea also fuelled speculations in many editorials that the costs of war were mounting and would be far greater than anticipated at the outbreak.[15] 'War cost is computed from various points of view,' as the *Mercury* put it, 'the financial obligations it imposed, the industrial and commercial impairment, moral laxity and vice that train after the disbandment of armies and the time consumed in the recovery of normal adjournments, and losses in men killed and disabled.'[16]

The use of new weapons – machine guns, exploding shells, chlorine gas, and submarines – indicated physical capacities for mass destruction that lent an entirely new meaning to the war. 'German barbarism,' as the press often demonized such signs, had been moulded by the industrial might of a rapidly developed enemy nation into a wholly unprecedented system of warfare. As the *Mercury*'s editor put it in the wake of the *Lusitania* sinking: 'Today the world stands aghast at the latest horror of the hellish German system of warfare ... When the use of poisonous gases became established, the world could not doubt the offence, and now with the sinking of the Lusitania the record is so complete as to leave no doubt that the Allies are engaged in a fight not with a nation but with a mad dog.'[17]

Papers also shaped perceptions of the fighting through a fresh series of statistics and commentaries that accumulated in the wake of setbacks in the spring of 1915. 'Canadian casualties sustained in the fighting at Langemarck ... are rapidly reaching the 5,000 mark,' the *Mercury* noted under the headline 'CANADIAN LIST IS MOUNTING UP.' Periodically placing such eyecatchers above ominous details like 'There is no abatement in the numbers coming in each day to the official record office' seemed to place an authorized gaze over an accelerating horror.[18] Two days later, the five thousand casualties level was exceeded, and Langemarck took its place among the bloodiest of battles.[19]

As news of fresh casualties circulated across Canada, the *Bien Public*'s editor, Joseph Barnard, noted that French Canadians had paid heavily as well: 'Parmi les morts et les blessés, il y a un bon nombre de canadiens-français.' He even wondered how French and English Canadians could remain divided at home when young men of both races were, as he put it, united in immortal glory in France.[20]

The anglophone *Newcomer* frequently echoed these views as the fighting intensified during the next year. On the first anniversary of the Battle of St. Julien, for example, a front-page commentary drew attention to the coincidental feast day of England's patron saint, St. George. The paper cast killing, or 'the task' of confronting 'the foe,' and imagined ideals and places, like 'freedom' or 'England,' as reciprocal necessities. Derived meanings attached to real casualties, often carefully catalogued elsewhere in the paper, leaned heavily on figures of social memories and imagined national community. Renewed fighting at St. Julien was depicted as a revival of the 'spirit of an age when men could say as they went out to meet the foe: There is but one task for all – / For each one life to give. / Who stands if freedom falls? / Who dies if England lives?'[21]

Shortly afterwards, the *Newcomer* joined papers across Canada in releasing official numbers of six thousand Canadian casualties in resumed fighting on the Ypres salient during the first week of June 1916.[22] Though the disastrous Somme campaign was less than a month away, depictions of slaughter following slaughter relied consistently on terms of spiritual revival, battles for freedom, or taking up arms in a righteous cause. Discourses of stark juxtaposition, of horrific realities and sublime interpretations, had become fixed, not just as a convenient genre but as a conventional one, hardly open to revision or critique. Such reality/meaning disjunctures often appeared inseparably, closely integrated and mutually reinforcing in a single text. Ordinary battle reports placed horrific outcomes in metaphysical domains, not so much to screen out realism as to embed it simultaneously in the politic of a grander language, one of optimism and purpose. Identified battles, heavy casualties, and attempts to convey a sense of trench-war tactics were punctuated by keywords drawn from eschatological, gendered, or national narrations that added a religious meaning, an expression of military masculinities, or a defence of democratic institutions. These imagined, cultural recitations worked to validate the fascinations and fears home front civilians held as they tried to imagine an overseas war.

News of casualties, particularly after the Somme catastrophe, that reached families at home often brought private anguish into public view. City newspapers certainly had much to gain by constructing scenes at which news of death reached parents. Such lurid rebroadcasts beyond the family threshold became part of an ordinary day's news, especially if they referred to the son of a prominent citizen. We cannot know how local reading audiences appropriated such accounts, but the range of uses certainly embraced a wide spectrum. Though they were usually little more than convenient inventions, the reporter's best guess at what happened, such stories could serve to collectivize grief, as much as to cheapen it as a horror/pleasure. For example, news of the death of Stuart Hayes, son of Judge Hayes, who later helped to mediate the dispute over the St. Stanislaus raid, reached his father by telegram first, before appearing in the *Mercury*: 'The Judge had scanned casualty lists very carefully, thinking the name of his son may have been amongst the wounded or killed. Nothing turned up, however, until the dreadful news came to the family [by telegram] last night.'[23]

Apart from this, ordinary readers were often left with little more than anonymous illusions through which they might interpret, even justify, the overall scale of casualties, both present and anticipated. But not always. Local papers like the *Mercury* occasionally worked people like Pick into their battle reports. Metaphorical and realistic signs of both glory and gas, for instance, could be in this way authorized and located through the presence of someone actually known. As with fears of the enemy and of enemy aliens (see Chapter 4), intersections of experience-near and experience-distant referents located perceptions of the distant, imagined battles overseas, construed in ordinary press reports as impersonal, mechanized carnage, with the parallel presence of a nearby, knowable, perhaps intimately known figure, a local soldier caught up in it. The mere appearance of detailed battle reports on one section of the page or paper and casualty lists, which included local soldiers, on another could resituate anonymous killing locally.

Lieutenant Pick, who returned to the front after recovering from his head injury at Ypres, would soon be killed in France. Like young Hayes, his fate was rebroadcast by the *Mercury,* with first word coming through a letter to his father from an officer in the 30th Wellington Rifles. This letter described how Pick, with another man in his regiment, not identified, 'were putting on their equipment at the door of a dug-out, preparatory to going into the charge, which cost us so many men. Just as they were ready to move a shell came over and burst between them, killing them both instantly.'[24]

In their letters to family members, officers came to use a standard set of phrases to describe death in battle to shield recipients from what was perhaps a worse end. Their form became regularized, a rhetoric used by the military to reinvent death in the trenches. But even the officers' tendency to describe such deaths as 'instant' depended on locating fallen men in the clutches of a horrific, if mercifully swift, war machine. In similar terms, the ordinary use by the front-line soldier of an array of specialized equipment, be it gas masks or trench periscopes, coupled with the anonymous threat of exploding shells and stray bullets, were constantly rehearsed in papers like the *Mercury* as an integral part of the new warfare.

The countless images of new weaponry contributed far more to readers' sense of stubborn determination than to any significant challenge to end the war. The human cost of the weapons' use was no mystery and was often, as with Judge Hayes or Peter Pick's parents, too clearly felt. Large dailies routinely practised self-censorship and circulated state-directed (sponsored, promotional images) and self-generated (editorials, routine reports) propaganda. As far as Ottawa was concerned, tragic news often helped to focus attention in a useful way on an enemy not yet defeated. As Jeffrey Keshen has determined in detail, state censorship seldom came into play directly in the form of a close policing of texts like those produced by the *Mercury*.[25] City dailies most often sought to sanitize images of Canadian soldiers through quixotic motifs that redirected attention from the realities of high casualties. Ottawa's interests were best served by their continued circulation.

As the end of the first year of fighting neared, one *Mercury* editorial reminded readers that the 'the whole thing was done so fast that the world could hardly grasp that the signals for a world war were being run up.' The paper then freely admitted what could hardly be said at the war's outbreak almost a year before: 'The end is not in sight.' It noted, too, that the 'task of making an unprepared Britain ready for the struggle, and of carrying on war at the same time has been a gigantic one.'[26] Also gigantic was the number of casualties, and so had to be the preparations to follow.

At the beginning of July 1915, Ottawa created the Military Hospitals Commission (MHC), the first national body established to coordinate primary care for returned soldiers. The *Canadian Annual Review* of that year alluded to a variety of complaints that 'had come to the Government as to the treatment or alleged neglect of individual cases amongst returned soldiers.' Its observation that 'hundreds were returning, and there soon would be thousands of wounded,' understated the unprecedented scale anticipated. The CAR also noted, optimistically, that rehabilitated soldiers might help to alleviate an impending labour shortage. It invoked a centralized-planning rhetoric, noting the role governments at all levels faced given the simple fact that 'workers were in demand and many recovered and partly recovered soldiers soon would need employment.' While ex-soldiers and industrial demands hardly presented a smooth exchange at this point, for Ottawa as much as for municipalities and provincial governments the 'problem was obvious and it was important.'[27]

The language of the CAR had shifted by this point, with the war into its second year. It combined with the new explicitness of the patriotic press to foreground an industrialized war. Both the CAR and city dailies offered blends of heroic idealism and enormous casualties, with technical references to anticipated costs that privileged the role of state planning, present and future. The discourse of sacrifice, which often couched the starker language of bureaucratic procedure, was a tactic that could celebrate both the efficiency and the foresight of the state. When the CAR said that 'every need for care and recuperation and understanding treatment' would be available to returned soldiers, it implied a capacity to act that masked the real problem of scale at that point. To add that such measures were aimed at men 'broken in health or maimed in body and spirits' worked to dichotomize the same body/mind split found in battle reports in the press, where plucky, spirited troops seemed to charge directly into shells and bullets.[28] The patriotic press and the imperial-nationalist CAR cast the war in a tactical discourse, aimed at public screenings for public purposes. To discount as mere cannon fodder the soldiers chewed up by the German 'war machine' transgressed, and would continue to transgress after the war, public attachments to notions of purpose and sacrifice. Placing fabricated details of death under the sign of its 'instant' occurrence for family grieving repressed little out of the ordinary, yet frequent references to scale and to therapeutics introduced a language almost unseen in ordinary reports before the spring of 1915.

Movements from allusion to specification, from reports of battles to casualty lists, did take place from late 1915 onward. Like papers across Canada, those of each city considered here generated increased coverage of the problems and costs of veteran re-establishment. At the same time, there appeared to be no diminishment in the frequency or form of references to the artificial war of ideal purpose, or its great warriors. Sensationalism and a sanitized version of the war continued to appear. The ideal fighting man appeared, in a parallel discourse, as a noble spirit, not a body wounded by the war or ill from its sojourn overseas. The rhetoric of the heroic soldier surfaced, for example, in the *Mercury*'s depiction of the return of Tubby Nourse from Ypres in October 1915.

The Ontario Agricultural College (OAC) graduate and Princess Pat veteran was one of the first troops to arrive back in Guelph. Nourse had suffered a single bullet wound to his neck on 8 May 1915 in the Vallewarde woods near Ypres. He lay in the trenches waiting for medical attention for some fifteen hours. After passing through a series of treatment facilities, he ended up at the Shorncliffe hospital in England, which, coincidentally, soon would be receiving supplies donated by Guelph's Red Cross. Following two months of convalescence, he was invalided home and steamed for Canada aboard a vessel sunk by a torpedo attack. Most were saved in this particular sinking, but few could count themselves luckier than this Guelph soldier had been to make it back. Nourse was originally from South Africa, where his family probably still lived. Dr. G.E. Creelman, president at OAC, invited him to stay on as his personal guest. Nourse accepted and apparently wanted nothing more than a quiet respite, surrounded by the places he had known at his alma mater. 'A reporter from the *Mercury* interviewed him at the O.A.C. this morning,' ran the story, which appeared on the paper's front page.[29]

Under a sub-caption 'Has Little to Say,' the reporter admitted that Nourse 'was so reserved that the story of his adventures in the trenches on the battle line in Belgium had to be fairly dragged out of him.' He did offer a brief outline of his 'adventures' as a scout under another section entitled 'Is Very Reticent.' Nourse made a point, however, of referring several times to the severe losses suffered by his regiment. '"I was engaged in scouting, and many times was within 'listening distance' of the German lines,"' he related. After noting that Norse was awarded the Distinguished Service Order, the reporter also noted the Princess Patricia insignia on his cap, 'an emblem that can only be worn by the members of a regiment of heroes,' as he put it.[30] 'There are only a few of them left,' he then noted, echoing Nourse's lament. His conclusion that 'wherever they go they are heralded as heroes pure and simple,' reiterated the ennobling discourse. When asked how he liked trench life in the winter, Nourse replied laconically: '"I don't want to say anything about that ... I would sooner face the shot and shelling at night, when it comes to a winter in the trenches."'

Despite this, Nourse was described as 'anxious to get back to the front.' Not yet demobilized, he seemed to have no immediate intention to leave the army. 'He may be asked to help in the recruiting,' the *Mercury* added, 'until his arm is once more in shape to allow of him going back on the fighting line.' Recruiting campaigns often counted on public appeals voiced by returned soldiers. This so-called 'personal appeal method' was used in Guelph when Cpl. Joe Fitzgerald, also wounded by a bullet, promoted enlistment for the 71st Battalion (Chapter 2). It hardly seemed a good choice for Nourse, at least yet. While still in uniform, Nourse was now situated as a returned soldier in limbo, probably concerned about little more than his immediate future, though the *Mercury*'s reporter was obviously more interested in highlighting his past. For Nourse, all that belonged in the past. Heroism meant little for this soldier on recuperative leave. What Ottawa had in store for him came first. Dealing with practical problems – his physical recovery, his next job, even his clothing – seemed to occupy his attention. The reporter mentioned that he was wearing his third uniform since departing for England. As Nourse stated, '"Yes, I was wounded all right ... but it didn't amount to much, and I will be all right again and back on the job again before long, if I continue to improve the way I have been doing."'[31]

Civic Voluntarism, Local Interests, and Perceptions of the Soldier's Return

Getting soldiers back 'on the job' as civilians became the central focus for re-establishing veterans in local communities across the country. The challenge, on a national level, would prove immense. It developed in stages as demobilization intensified. Veteran re-establishment was also shaped by the returned soldiers' own specific demands, put forward by newly formed organizations led by the Great War Veterans Association. In the fall of 1915, however, the brunt of this national task still fell on the more limited resources of local areas: municipalities, voluntary soldiers' hospitals, civilian groups, and of course the veterans themselves.

Mayor Hardie was well aware that Lethbridge, with about twelve hundred men from the area enlisted, would bear a heavy burden. He called a public meeting at the end of October 1915 to form an independent citizens group that might assume responsibility for handling problems surrounding the anticipated influx. 'Soldiers will be returning with increasing frequency henceforth,' the *Herald* noted, 'and many communities have already taken steps to establish a permanent society for dealing with these men, and seeing that they are re-instated in their former positions, or that some proper provision is made for their future.'[32]

Like other mayors and municipal officials, Hardie felt that, ultimately, the federal government must take responsibility for soldiers' re-establishment. 'Mayor Hardie's opinion,' the *Herald* added, 'is that if an independent body of citizens handles this, a better opportunity is given for an independent appeal to the government, if such an appeal becomes necessary on behalf of any returned soldier.'[33] Apart from the Military Hospitals Commission, jobs, job training, and interim support were also needed. It was obvious that the thousands of young men on their way back home to places like Lethbridge would demand no less. Hardie quite clearly sought to deflect the caseload away from city hall. Still, local volunteers could help. The citizens' committee Hardie had called for was set up. 'The Khaki league is to be the name of the organization in Lethbridge that will look after the returned soldiers,' the *Herald* reported in its coverage of its inaugural meeting.[34] This new civic organization, however, by name and by affiliation, was not an entirely local initiative.

The original Khaki League had made a recreational room available for volunteers in Montreal back in December 1914. The first soldiers' convalescent homes supported by the league were set up in central and eastern Canada. Affiliated Khaki Clubs formed first in Quebec City, Saint John, and Halifax before others began to appear in the West toward the end of 1915.[35] In November 1915, Lethbridge joined that growing list. Before the end of the war, these associations arranged for temporary housing for veterans and assistance in securing work.

Within a month, the Lethbridge group was formally recognized by the Alberta branch of the MHC, with which it began coordinating arrangements to greet discharged men in search of housing and employment. CPR conductors were to notify Khaki Clubs by telegraph of the arrival of soldiers en route to Alberta who might need their help. The soldiers were to receive their official discharge at Calgary; only then would they be free to move on to their chosen resettlement location.[36]

Lethbridge's club was put together by locally prominent individuals, many already actively involved in war relief work, from Mayor Hardie, who was elected president, and city commissioner A.M. Grace, to city solicitor W.S. Ball, who was at that time in the process of securing approval from Ottawa for the 113th Lethbridge Highlanders Battalion.[37] Sub-committees were named and assigned a schedule to meet returned soldiers as they arrived. Hardie, Grace, and Ball served on these, along with E. McKillop, executive officer of the Lethbridge Red Cross; G.W. Robinson, regent of the Alexander

Galt IODE chapter; C.F.P. Conybeare, a city lawyer who would also serve on the local Military Service Act exemption board; John Skelton, city police chief; and, W.A. Buchanan, Lethbridge's MP and owner of the *Herald*.

First they secured space to house the men in facilities of the local YMCA. 'The benefits and privileges of the Y.M.C.A., with the additional privileges of smoking and a card room will be extended to all returned soldiers at the usual membership rates,' the *Herald* announced. Memberships would be provided by the Khaki League with the understanding, as the Herald put it, that 'the "Y" will throw open the building for the benefit of returned soldiers. They have gone to the extent of agreeing to waive the former rules of the institution and permit smoking in the lounge room downstairs, save on the two days a week during the time in which the ladies are in attendance.'[38]

Coordinating this voluntary effort with the Department of Militia and Defence was not without its problems. 'Bungling of the grossest kind,' league secretary J.R. Oliver charged in early December 1915, 'is being exhibited somewhere along the line in the matter of the treatment of returned soldiers.'[39] Most of the problems seemed to be connected to communication between himself, the Alberta MHC in Calgary, and the army.

A case involving a returned soldier identified only as Private Waller serves as an example. Though Waller was still entitled to full army pay, since his discharge had not yet been completed, Oliver claimed that he had arrived in Lethbridge with just two dollars in his pocket and no documentation authorizing further pay. Furthermore, he had been sent to a convalescent hospital in Calgary when he should have been ordered directly to Lethbridge. Oliver complained to the MHC in Calgary, but learned only that arrangements between that body and the Department of Militia and Defence to coordinate discharges were still being worked out. Returned soldiers like Waller were often caught in the middle.[40]

As far as the Lethbridge Khaki League was concerned, however, loose ends like this were not supposed to fall on the municipality. By the end of 1915, when veterans began returning in larger numbers, the Lethbridge Khaki League realized that while it may have secured smoking privileges and a card room for local veterans at the city's YMCA, its real task was to lobby hard to see that the federal government, not the City of Lethbridge, assumed primary responsibility for veteran re-establishment.[41]

Mayor Hardie would soon take the lead among Canadian mayors in pushing for comprehensive, equitable, and substantial veterans' pensions. Speaking to the annual Union of Municipalities convention held at Montreal in August 1916, Hardie proposed a resolution from members, city mayors and officials from across Canada, calling for equal pensions for all veterans, regardless of rank. 'Whereas, the Canadian overseas army is purely a citizen army,' his statement read, 'the Union of Canadian Municipalities put on record its opinion that the Dominion government should amend the pension act so that all soldiers, officers and privates alike be on an equality in all pensions.'[42] The convention endorsed Hardie's position fully. Military pensions, however, remained linked to rank during and after the war, although Ottawa would eventually adopt far more comprehensive support for veteran re-establishment, a move the municipalities really wanted.[43]

When Hardie first raised the equality issue, rank-and-file privates were entitled to a maximum of $264 annually, while colonels received $1,400 and brigadier-generals $2,100.[44] Efforts by Maj. John L. Todd, who spearheaded reform of Canada's Pension and Claims Board, led to an increase in a private's maximum pension from $264 to $480 per year. 'In this war,' the secretary of the Great War Veterans Association later testified before a special House of Commons committee on pensions, 'the old idea of one man being worth more than another is being wiped away.'[45] Although challenged and subsequently modified, the pension hierarchy remained.[46]

After Montreal, Hardie approached organized labour for support. In September 1916 he joined the executive of the Lethbridge Trades and Labor Council in calling for a revised scheme. The local trades council, at its next meeting, 'voted unanimously in favor of a resolution condemning the present schedule, and urging that a change be made making equal pensions for all Canada's soldiers.' For the City of Lethbridge and the TLC it was a matter of mutual concern, but not necessarily shared interests. Municipalities worried about the social burden they might face, whereas labour saw it primarily as a moral issue. Calgary's TLC soon joined Lethbridge in passing its own resolution in favour of pension equity, and other branches were said to be considering the same. The *Herald* noted as well the possibility of organizing a national petition. As the Lethbridge trades council put it, 'The difference between the pensions for a private and a lieutenant colonel is altogether too extreme and is not in keeping with the democratic principle for which Canada is fighting.'[47]

Whatever might be said of the principles guiding the war effort, concrete action regarding veterans' pensions, employment, and reintegration required the efforts of full-time, paid administrators, not volunteers. By the beginning of 1917, it was becoming painfully obvious in Lethbridge that voluntary, civic efforts alone could not deal adequately with an alarming lack of jobs. Although only twelve men were said to have returned as of January 1917, 'it is also true,' the *Herald* noted, 'that those who have come back are still unable to secure satisfactory employment.' Meanwhile, the city's Khaki League, which the paper reminded readers had been 'organized expressly for the benefit of the returned soldier,' had, in its opinion, 'almost been forgotten.'[48]

The league's concerns reflected the class interests of those who came together to form it: get ex-soldiers and wage-earners back on the job and off the streets. The *Herald* certainly shared that view, and at one point prodded the group to stay on course to this end. Is the 'Khaki League Dead or Only Sleeping?' the *Herald* asked. 'In Lethbridge,' one editorial ran, 'the problem is already developing serious proportions, and upon the citizens of the city devolves a duty that must not be shirked.'[49] In fact, the time had come, as far as the city was concerned, to appoint a full-time administrator for the Lethbridge branch, even if it meant establishing a precedent of direct support from the City of Lethbridge.

That step was taken three weeks later at a public meeting, chaired by Hardie, held in one of the city's Board of Trade Building conference rooms. The most significant matter resolved was to convert Oliver's voluntary secretarial position into a paid one. He was to receive $50 per month from the city and thereafter assumed responsibility for operating what was essentially an employment exchange with a new name: the Returned Soldiers' Bureau. 'Don't Forget the War Veteran When You Have A Job To Offer,' this new municipal office declared through advertisements Oliver then placed in the *Herald*.

The MHC's Provincial Central Committee in Alberta, operating from Edmonton, and the local Khaki League urged prospective employers through an advertisement printed in the *Herald* to 'find out what jobs are vacant in your community. Make it a matter of pride for employers to give the first chance to a returned soldier.' Or, more pointedly: 'Encourage the men to get back to work. Loafing is bad for them, as it is for any of us.'[50] Such ads broadcast the problem of jobless men, back from the front, in terms entirely unconnected to the heroic volunteer myth of the early war. The idle returned soldier was, in short, a danger that employers and concerned citizens everywhere should work to eliminate. Oliver, through the Returned Soldiers' Bureau, also lobbied Ottawa for improvements in pension administration.[51] In terms of regional administration, this new municipal agency wanted to work through a separate pension board for Alberta 'with full powers so that local conditions will be better understood and unnecessary delays in payment' could be avoided.[52]

Oliver's appointment to a paid position and the committee's decision to set aside 'suitable quarters' for him to administer his task marked a step toward more direct involvement by the city. As far as Hardie was concerned, however, this was merely a stopgap measure in lieu of state intervention at the federal level. The next step, and a far more significant one, would be for the men themselves to organize and lobby, locally and nationally. That would come later, when larger numbers and acute problems were no longer just on the horizon. From then on, Lethbridge veterans, which at this point stood somewhere between thirty and forty, could meet at the west room of the Board of Trade Building as well as at the YMCA, where some, in fact, were already being housed. 'At last,' the *Herald* cheered simplistically, the community 'has taken action which should put the organization in a position to do something tangible in the way of aiding returned soldiers. The appointment of a permanent secretary, part of whose salary the city is asked to pay, was the step needed to place the organization on a firm business footing.' But this same editorial maintained that Ottawa, not the City of Lethbridge or any other municipality, should bear full responsibility for the huge task ahead: 'It would seem, however, that the time will have to come when all expenses in connection of [sic] the returned soldier will have to be met by the Dominion of Canada, and small municipalities should not be compelled to foot the bill.'[53]

Towns, cities, and counties across Canada were saying much the same thing at this time, including Trois-Rivières, where a comparatively low number of men would be returning. In late 1916 the *Nouveau Trois-Rivières* applauded the aims of the MHC, soon to be replaced by the more extensive Department of Soldiers' Civil Re-establishment.[54] The real point in praising what had been done by Ottawa, however, was to point out where the burden of Canada's social responsibility was being taken up effectively, and where it must remain. Ottawa and its programs, not local initiatives, were seen, once again, as necessary and most effective.[55]

This view was reiterated at the 1917 convention of the Union of Canadian Municipalities (UCM), held in London that year. Hardie was elected president and, coincidentally, alderman Robert Ryan of Trois-Rivières was elected first vice-president. At the gathering, Hardie renewed the call for what municipalities throughout Canada had a uniform interest in endorsing: increased federal responsibility for veteran care. The first step was to see that the largest segment of veterans, discharged privates and corporals that is, got more money. A resolution calling for 'equal pensions irrespective of rank' was then put before the members.

A Toronto alderman took the initiative, advocating a twofold pay increase for privates. It carried unanimously.[56] The implication was as clear in London as it had been in Montreal a year before. Higher pay scales, separation allowances, and greater pension equality offered the best solutions for helping veterans adjust to civilian life, not dipping further into municipal coffers. No one really disagreed with this as a general direction. The question was where Ottawa would draw the line.

As UCM president, Hardie repeated such messages into the following year, just as the government was preparing for its largest demobilization. Speaking twice in Lethbridge in December 1918, for instance, he also emphasized that the federal government should pay far more attention to securing employment for veterans.

By this point, a group of Lethbridge professionals and businesspersons, headed by Board of Trade president G.R. Marnoch, had launched another coordinating body, known as the Reconstruction Committee, during a special meeting held in the mayor's office.[57] Its appearance seemed reactive. As

Hardie stated: 'It was eminently unfair that the government should bring the men to Lethbridge, discharge them and dump them on the community to find employment for themselves.'[58] It is not clear, at this point, how many men had arrived, though by 1919 over a thousand were expected.

The number of Lethbridge veterans who returned mentally or physically disabled cannot be determined precisely from sources uncovered in this study; however, nothing indicates that this city's proportion of veterans suffering permanent disability varied significantly from the national average at this time of approximately 9.7 percent.[59] Given the *Herald*'s estimate of 2,000 total enlistments from Lethbridge, from which some 146 fatalities are subtracted, there were probably about 180 disabled ex-soldiers returned to the city once demobilization was completed.[60]

Securing employment for some of these men in public service at any level could be difficult.[61] The case of one veteran, who served in a British engineering corps and was thus ineligible for a Canadian pension, demonstrated a tendency to speak about jobs for returned soldiers as a kind of duty, 'our professed duty,' as the Lethbridge *Telegram* put it. This veteran was identified only as Sergeant Gobelle, but his plight, as 1917 approached, drew the attention of both city papers. 'A returned soldier is in our midst today,' the *Herald* related on learning of his difficulties,

> in the person of Sergeant Gobelle. He left his home and occupation in Lethbridge to join an engineers' corps in the Old Country, feeling his qualifications would be of use in the Empire's need. He did his duty well, was wounded and incapacitated for further service. After spending some time in hospital he returned to his home in Lethbridge, and has been in receipt of a temporary British army pension of some six dollars a week. He was a weak man when he returned and, though his wounds were healed, had not recovered from the shock in receiving them. This was last June.

Since then, Gobelle had managed to supplement his paltry pension with casual work obtained from the city as groundskeeper of a municipal park.[62] Married with three children, he desperately needed a steady job. When his custodial position was about to become redundant as winter approached, and with his pension discontinued, the treatment of this veteran, who was probably shell-shocked, gave the *Herald* an opportunity to offer a running critique of an ordinary soldier's plight, though his case presented a special problem.

The paper charged that Hardie, in his capacity as chairman of the local hospital board, had denied Gobelle an available position as engineer at the Galt hospital. The offer, instead, of another casual outdoor job failed to impress the *Herald*, which in one editorial stated: 'Sergt. Gobelle apparently was physically fit to shovel snow from Henderson lake in 20 below zero weather at $1.60 per day, scarcely a sufficient wage to keep himself and his family in clothing and food.'[63]

Gobelle was then offered a job at the hospital as an assistant engineer, helping to maintain the boiler room. But in a letter of protest reprinted by the *Herald,* his former supervisor at Royal Collieries claimed the job demanded seventeen-hour shifts at twelve and a half cents per hour. He also commended Gobelle's pre-war employment record as an engineer in the mechanical department. Referring to the treatment of ex-soldiers in general, he added: 'It is too bad there is not more effort put forth for the welfare of the returned veterans. They give up their all to fight for king, country and homes and we derive the benefit while they return wounded and unfit.'[64] The *Herald* added its voice in presenting this letter to push for something better for Gobelle and condemned Hardie for failing to come up with it. Probably because of his condition, Royal Collieries did not seem to have anything to offer Gobelle. There is no further mention of his fate in the pages of the city's newspapers, but it seems the real controversy stemmed from the fact that Gobelle's mental health presented a barrier to a better job and life.

Shell-shock victims received ambivalent, sometimes contradictory diagnosis and treatment in the military, and then faced a public that often saw such conditions only through preconceived notions of mental disabilities.[65] One *Herald* contributor invoked such prejudices in a letter to the editor, although he did urge support for all disabled veterans, regardless of illness. 'He may appear to the most of us [sic] as a "huskie," but inwardly he is "all shot to pieces,"' this self-appointed expert explained. Many such men were predisposed, he warned, to unpredictable, even dangerous behaviour: 'He will have trouble re-entering civilian life; he will need employment which his disability will permit him to perform. [He is] maybe a neurotic, nerves all gone from shell shock or the strain of excitement he has been through, is likely to "blow up" at any moment, commit [sic] some depredation or crime.'

The preceding examples – from this letter, which appeared at the end of the war, back to Hardie's positions as UCM president in 1916, and finally to the formation of the Lethbridge branch of the Khaki League in 1915 with which we began – make it clear that anxieties concerning returned soldiers stemmed from two notions. The first was that soldiers themselves, particularly the ordinary man of the ranks, would come back to Canada poorly equipped to get back to life in mufti, to adjust to civilian routine and expectations. The second was that there might be, at any rate, little available for them. Economic downturn might well accompany conversions to a peacetime economy, and employers could hardly be expected to assume the burden. Neither could municipalities.

This situation was perceived by Hardie and many others in Lethbridge as particularly acute, given the much higher proportion of local men that were then being demobilized. What the men themselves thought seemed irrelevant. This was, in a sense, the gaze of settled civilians, local stakeholders, and municipal officials who spoke for the existing social order, especially its limited capacity to absorb, at the municipal level, the social aftermath of this war.

Voluntary approaches organized at this level were seen as necessary first steps, but little more than that. Like the soldiers themselves, the City of Lethbridge, the Returned Soldiers Bureau, and the Reconstruction Committee, looked to Ottawa. But nothing in their actions suggests that civilians saw the ex-soldiers or their circumstances in the same light that the men themselves did.

The *Herald* published a series of letters, reports, editorials, and statements from local officials and volunteers that seemed rooted in these two overlapping fears that civilian stakeholders held: that soldiers were unable to look after themselves, and that they faced a grim situation given anticipated economic conditions. Just over a month after the armistice, there were calls in the paper to rally as many volunteers as possible around reconstruction efforts that might at least mitigate disaster. 'There is plenty of work in this movement for all,' one editorial put it, optimistically. Existing clubs and associations might make themselves available to do their part. A suggestion, for instance, that the Lethbridge Rotary Club might 'take this subject up as part of their business discussion' during its next meeting typified editorial opinion at this point, which seemed unwavering in its support for voluntarism, barring anything definite and further from Ottawa.

This same editorial then turned to promote the idea of a special returned soldiers fund, an open invitation for local networks, the same ones presumably that had campaigned for the Canadian Patriotic Fund earlier, to take part in supporting demobilization. A veteran re-establishment fund, which never got off the ground, was touted by the *Herald* as 'a nation-wide movement; why not make the fund a nation-wide movement also, and show the world that Canadians do not forget.'[66] This boosterist discourse seemed to reflect the parochial outlook expressed by the organizers of the CPF at the start of the war, one that sought to signify what they were contributing as civilian war relief workers as a mark of local strength and power. No such work was undertaken by the city's Rotarians, an effort that in any meaningful way was far beyond their resources as a civic club.

Ottawa was pressed to act quickly to get more money into the hands of men in the ranks. The Borden government began by announcing that it would grant what it called the War Service Gratuity. This significant increase could, depending on length of service, double the basic pay rate for a six-month period for soldiers who had seen active service.[67] Hardie conceded that it 'will tend to relieve the cities of a great burden in earning for the men who are returning.' But he continued to push for 'a great series of public works' to engage job-seeking veterans.[68]

As far as the *Herald* was concerned, the plan marked a 'very generous' approach to smoother post-war adjustments for the men and for the localities that received them. 'After hearing many schemes advanced for demobilization of the Canadian army,' its lead editorial stated, 'the announcement of the definite plan adopted on Saturday should convince the public that the Dominion Government has taken a very wise and generous step. The plan is to discharge soldiers as rapidly as they can be brought home, and to provide for them for a period of six months by giving them double pay for six months after discharge, to be paid in monthly installments.'

Mayor Hardie's views on the need for Ottawa to take primary responsibility for veteran re-establishment, partly through public works projects, were mirrored at this time by the paper. 'What remains to do now,' the *Herald* professed, 'is for us all to urge upon the government the need of undertaking great works, so that when demobilization is over we shall have passed through that trying period with a minimum of unrest, and be in a better position than ever as a nation to take the place in world affairs the boys of the Canadian army have won for us on the field of battle.'[69]

The ambivalence expressed earlier, of the soldier as hero and the soldier as public burden, quickly shifted at the end of 1918 into a stark dichotomy. The 'boys of the Canadian army' may have won a 'place in world affairs' on the 'field of battle,' but some wondered if, on their return in large numbers, they might in fact become radicalized.

Fears that civil unrest across the country would accompany the veterans' return had already been expressed in the *Herald*. 'The aftermath of the war is bringing its own troubles in the form of social discontent' was how one report on national politics was cast shortly before Christmas 1918. 'One of the most prominent Montreal bankers,' it added, 'recently lamented the manifestations of Bolshevism in the West.'[70] How the great mass of veterans would respond to a homecoming of perceived political unrest, unemployment, and, to make matters worse, a sudden influenza epidemic, fuelled considerable unease in Lethbridge and elsewhere.

Suggestions of interning discharged soldiers in military camps to handle the large influx, though an extreme notion, pointed not to a wavering position, but to one that inverted heroic soldiers into nothing more than a public menace. It was put forward by one contributor to the *Herald*'s 'People's Forum':

> A number of well-organized and comfortable military camps throughout the country would take care of the returning soldier for the time being better than any other method. The boy returning from France on one of the

> troop trains and set adrift on the station platform without a home to go to would be a very lonesome individual indeed, no matter how much the community appreciated the great service rendered and done by the army. Let us remember that these boys have been picked up from civilians and converted into soldiers, and that is what they are now. Let us take care of them as such until they are in a position to properly take care of themselves.[71]

The images of returning soldiers conveyed by this contributor, and his concern that local communities were simply not equipped to deal with their arrival, suggests a considerable distance, of perception if not of politics, between civilians and veterans. Regardless of 'how much the community appreciated the great service rendered,' his letter suggested, the 'boys,' who went to war had been transformed into something quite different from home front civilians – 'picked up from civilians and converted into soldiers,' as it was expressed here. And so many men 'set adrift' in places like Lethbridge would immediately create an insurmountable problem.

As Lethbridge joined other areas, urban and rural, bracing for demobilization during Christmas 1918, it seemed accepted that charity in the form of veteran re-establishment should begin some distance from home. The eclipse of voluntary, charitable efforts toward the end of the war coincided with a new and negative image of the common soldier back on the streets, adjusting to civilian life. Against the earlier discourse of the heroic volunteer, a pure and virtuous figment, a profoundly negative discourse accompanied the actual process of reintegrating fighting men back into society. Our focus on local evidence also points, as it did in Lethbridge, to the ways in which perceptions were generated from both an imagined view of the war, this time a war of battle-damaged men, and an awareness of local circumstances, this time cast in terms of their limits and the means local volunteers might deploy to defend the status quo. Much of this intersected with fears of what the soldiers had become as fighting men, to which we now turn.

Demobilization and a Fearful Public

The westward transport of troops by rail, which became a common sight in cities along the CPR line throughout 1919, drew far more journalistic commentary in Trois-Rivières than in our English Canadian cities. Demobilization was occurring in a completely different context there, which helps to explain why. Where stakeholders in Guelph and Lethbridge were concerned about the local impact of re-establishment efforts, Trois-Rivières received far fewer veterans and tended to encounter the men only at a distance or through reports of disturbances in other cities. Those seen en route tended to be recognized only as uniformed men, not as local soldiers returning with a regiment that townspeople had perhaps followed in the city papers or knew firsthand from its enlistment, training, and departure.

In Trois-Rivières, situated along the CPR line running north of the St. Lawrence, both the English and French press tended to see soldiers as anonymous groups on the move, a faceless mass of troublesome transients. Often they were cast as social pariahs, a potential threat to public health or even social stability. On the whole, Trois-Rivières both served, and represented itself in its newspapers, as a transit point through which many thousands of disabled, diseased, and allegedly dangerous veterans passed. Its role as a troop train whistle stop appeared to change little throughout the war. As well, national programs for veteran re-establishment, here as elsewhere, were viewed as a federal responsibility; more particularly, they were considered an undertaking that served Canadians best when returned soldiers were separated from direct contact with the public.

Since the onset of hostilities, the city's railway station and port had been the scene of ordinary flows of fresh enlistments eastward and returned soldiers westward, which drew a fair amount of local press coverage, based largely on an imagined view of uniformed men. As the war entered its last year, however, city newspapers hardened their interpretations, often markedly. Unfavourable depictions of troops from other parts of Canada passing through the city began to appear, stories of boisterous rank-and-filers, of men infected by tuberculosis, or of hardened men back from Europe supposedly corrupted by radical politics. They did not, however, displace earlier representations of the noble volunteer, the soldier as hero. They co-existed and were deployed alternately to fit the situation described, whether to revere the supreme sacrifice of fallen men or to revile the drunken private sleeping it off in the local lock-up.

The new images did share something important with the older ones: they offered representations distanced from the actual histories and experiences of what were often very different groups of men, some perhaps troublesome, most not, who saw their worlds quite differently as well. As myths, such negative images displayed the durability of half-truths. They emerged partly on the basis of fact, but largely on the basis of how civilians had been prepared to see the condition of returned soldiers, simplistic portraits of disease, alcohol use, political radicalism, and immorality.

In late February 1917, the *Nouveau Trois-Rivières* commented on conditions at the front promoting the onset of tuberculosis among troops. Readers were informed that many of these soldiers were infected but asymptomatic before they enlisted. A connection was suggested, not inaccurately, between soldiers, soldiering, and the onset of 'peste blanche,' as tuberculosis was known in Quebec.[72] Later that spring, the same paper described a special system organized to transport tubercular as well as wounded men in special

10 Trois-Rivières's CPR station, pictured here shortly after the war, was never the site of crowded, enthusiastic send-offs. In fact, with 'unruly' soldiers detraining while the fighting dragged on, the *Newcomer* described the station as a new public menace for a city that should be grateful that a military police guard had been posted there. *Courtesy of Archives du Séminaire de Trois-Rivières, FN-0064-51-4*

hospital trains, many of which passed through Trois-Rivières.[73] Obviously, transporting military personnel was part of the business of a nation at war, and local communities were only indirectly involved. While Trifluviens witnessed this exercise, they did not participate in it, which was just as well as far as local papers, from the *Newcomer* to the *Bien Public*, were concerned.

Many returning soldiers were portrayed not only as tubercular and contagious, but also as prone to drunken rowdiness. 'The other day,' the *Newcomer* reported at the end of May 1917, 'there was a fight on a train bearing returned soldiers and men going to the West to help with seeding. A couple of them were arrested and brought up before the recorder of this city.'[74] In this case, civilians were mixed in with veterans, a practice that the *Newcomer* had already warned would only bring trouble. 'We are pleased to see that the Military Authorities have a Military Guard on duty at the C.P.R. Station here,' the paper had noted the previous September. Allegedly, the guard had 'plenty of work keeping the unruly soldiers on the trains in order and looking after deserters.'

Encounters between civilian men, most of whom locally, of course, were francophones, and soldiers, who may have resented others their age not in uniform, could spark more than bitter feelings. Arrangements should be made, the *Newcomer* cautioned, to keep the 'unruly' men in khaki away from any contact with the community: 'All that is lacking now is a special coach on all trains for the exclusive use of the private soldiers, because sometimes it's really disgusting the way some of the privates conduct themselves. One day last week the train had to be held here while a couple of drunks were forcibly hauled out of the first class coaches and put in the second class.'[75]

Such images of soldiers in the ranks in transit as volatile, even disgusting, not only departed from the model of 1914 – when they were heroic boys becoming men as they defended so many of the ideals used to justify the war – but also reconfigured experience-distant notions of what these men had encountered overseas. As a result, the men returning had become a liability, even a potentially destabilizing menace politically.

The clerical and conservative *Bien Public*, particularly as the end of war approached, offered figments of the soldier as a radicalized political subject, prone to violence. This was consistent with the paper's conservative opposition to conscription and wartime militarism generally (see Chapter 5). It saw the increased presence of uniformed men as a potential threat to public security if appropriate means of restraint from within the military itself were not exercised. This argument appeared in the paper's coverage of the Toronto riots, perhaps the most violent incident involving veterans anywhere in the country during the war.

On 8 August 1918 the *Bien Public* joined papers across the country in reporting the week-long disturbances that broke out in Toronto when veterans vented their frustrations against the local Greek community. Beginning on 2 August, following an incident that sparked rumours a veteran had been mistreated at a College Street café, Greek restaurants were targeted for violent attacks, which subsided only after Mayor Tommy Church read the riot act five days later.[76] Damage purported to total some $80,000 was partly compensated for not by Ottawa but by the City of Toronto. According to the *Bien Public*, such violence justified precautions against the menace posed by returned soldiers: 'les soldats vétérans qui pratiquent l'émeute ou le pillage méritent le mépris public et deviennent un danger contre lequel la société fait bien de prendre ses précautions.'[77]

For the *Bien Public*, the real danger of returned soldiers lay not in their alleged predisposition to violence, but in their political radicalism. The fiction that many soldiers had become socialists was indicative of the *Bien Public*'s parochial outlook in suggesting that veterans would place a strain, politically, on the country's social and moral fabric at a difficult time in its history.

Shortly after the armistice, Barnard issued a statement in his weekly commentary entitled 'Les dangers du socialisme.' He warned readers of revolutionary violence sweeping the country. In a thinly disguised reference to veterans, Barnard urged disarming 'turbulent groups.' Mobs like those that had wreaked havoc on Toronto streets, he argued, had to be countered with vigilance, even force, particularly in the atmosphere of growing unrest as the war ended. For many like Barnard, Canada no longer stood sheltered from the upheavals of Europe. 'Il nous semble,' he suggested, 'que les pays alliés qui viennent de connaître la victoire ... devront être épargnés, du moins pour un temps, de bouleversement social qui désole le centre de l'Europe.'[78]

Such alarmism, and the fact that the city served as a transportation node for veterans heading to central or western Canada, underscores the contrasts often present in newspaper coverage between the returned soldier as threat to society, whether as a rioter, a radical, or a jobless newcomer, and the soldier as returned hero. The city, for instance, hosted a colourful veterans' parade to mark the end of war in November, as 'les Légionnaires défilèrent par nos principales rues précédés de la fanfare des cadets et de l'Union Musicale.' Nonetheless, while local veterans were honoured with a civic festival featuring an air show, speeches by city dignitaries, and an evening banquet, throughout which 'toute notre population trifluvienne n'a cessé de manifester la joie la plus enthousiaste,' they remained a segment in society subject to an ambivalent gaze.[79] That many were diseased, that they might brawl in public, or that they might even become an armed vanguard for a general insurrection had appeared as signs in the city's newspapers through which Trifluviens might imagine soldiers, whether watching from the docks downtown as a troopship passed on the St. Lawrence toward Quebec City or encountering soldiers passing through at the CPR station during the westward flows of troops bound for home.

Comparable signs, of course, appeared in other cities. The *Herald*'s 'People's Forum,' for instance, became the site of a heated exchange between the Lethbridge branch of GWVA and civilian correspondents over the controversial issue of veterans and venereal disease. It began less than a month before the armistice, when the paper published a lengthy letter from a reader concerning the problem of venereal disease in the city's red-light district, proportionally one of the most active in western Canada.[80] The writer referred to the high incidence of venereal disease among soldiers. H.P. Maddison, secretary of Lethbridge's GWVA, was disgusted with the claim and sent a heated response to the paper. The original letter's author, perhaps recognizing the significance and continued currency of the former ideal, apologized. Maddison refused to accept the apology.[81]

But the real concern was hard to overlook. Another city resident, John Seymour, maintained that recognizing problems with prostitution, venereal disease, and returned soldiers was simply facing 'the facts as they exist.'[82] As Jay Cassel suggested in his study of venereal disease in Canada, public awareness of sexually transmitted diseases was greatly heightened by the war. The federal government and provincial health authorities launched a series of anti-VD campaigns at this time to accompany the return of soldiers, many of whom were indeed infected.[83] The exchange of letters in the *Herald* highlighted, again, the durability of fears that circulated on fluid planes between fact and fiction. The image of the returned soldier inhabited an ambivalent position, half hero, half menace.

Of the returned soldiers themselves we learn nothing, apart from the fact that Maddison was outraged. Once they began organizing themselves through both local and national networks led by the GWVA, however, they produced signs of dissent that signified, above all, their desire to direct their own futures. As the Speedwell case in Guelph, described below, suggests, they preferred to see other ex-soldiers, or those still serving, placed in charge of administering their re-establishment, rather than civilians.

The Fight for Speedwell Jobs

Sources generated during a dispute between the Guelph branch of the GWVA and officials responsible for a newly designated military hospital in Guelph indicate the perspectives and language of dissent of demobilized men, organized on a local level. In 1917 the city's provincial reformatory became a military hospital known as the Speedwell, the second largest tubercular care facility established by the MHC for Canada's veterans.

The military hospital in Guelph was part of a national system that tried to cope with multiple needs dispersed across diverse regions in the country. Tubercular care became a particularly challenging category given its high frequency and the demands it placed on long-term convalescence. Many soldiers requiring hospitalization, however, suffered multiple ailments, and while strict breakdowns in types of illnesses and wounds offer us some measure of the scale and range of disabilities Ottawa faced, the real challenge was to coordinate state and charitable approaches for a national system that tried to respond to the individuality of cases, regional resource disparities, and a new dynamic: that of returned soldiers themselves initiating demands as they made their way into civilian life and began to challenge the discipline codes of active service. In the spring of 1917, MHC president James A. Loughheed stated the obvious when he said that the 'work and responsibility' of his commission were 'developing very rapidly.' Lougheed estimated then that the rate of invalided men returned to Canada had reached 1,600 per month.[84] Much higher figures were in sight, and hospitals like the Speedwell had to be ready quickly.

On 8 April 1917, the MHC and the Ontario provincial secretary's office, responsible for Ontario's prisons, hastily negotiated a lease for the Ontario Reformatory in Guelph. Although never mentioned in the press, it became an open secret that such deals between governments for housing and vocational prison facilities were possible during the war because, in absolute numbers, young men who might otherwise have committed jailable offences were overseas; provincial prisons simply had fewer prisoners at this time. Guelph, then, became the location for one of seventeen military hospitals set up under the MHC.[85]

Their agreement, reached on 19 April 1917, was initially for eighteen months at $25,000 per annum.[86] Many complications ensued: apart from refurbishing buildings and securing supplies to meet the needs of an eight-hundred-bed hospital, prisoners had to be transferred to other locations. What later proved of most importance to the veterans were the decisions that needed to be made about staffing. Civilians were available and were hired at all levels, from the hospital's assistant director to kitchen staff. As well, the province insisted that, wherever possible, existing prison staff in custodial positions be kept on by the military.

The *Mercury*'s focus on contractors and purveyors, many of whom were locally based and delighted with new work orders, reflected the enduring boosterist mentality of city papers. In early May 1917, for example, it reported that painters had already begun applying fresh coats, 'getting the institution ready for the reception of the returned soldiers which is expected to take place in a short time.'[87] 'This work will have to be done immediately,' the paper added the next day, 'and one of the biggest rush jobs that was ever undertaken or completed is what the commission [the MHC] is looking for.' While a Montreal firm was awarded the largest contract to construct additional buildings, their needs were met locally.[88] One editorial offered an example of the way in which a complicated and contested process could be simplified for ordinary readers' perspectives: 'Guelph is pleased with the distinction of being one of the great centres where these returned men will be nursed back to health and taught to follow such industrial pursuits as their physical condition will stand.'[89] The anticipated arrival of visitors and perhaps even recovered men who might choose to stay on in the city was contained in coverage that gave brief mention to the hospital as a 'great centre' where men would be 'nursed back to health,' before devoting far more space to the boost it promised the local economy, from its renovations to possible longer-term spinoffs.

When the facility reverted back to Ontario in January 1921, however, the federal and provincial governments disputed the original terms. The Department of Soldiers' Civil Re-establishment (the DSCR, which replaced the MHC in February 1918) and the Ontario government both objected to bearing amortized costs for numerous maintenance and restoration expenses not contained in the provisional settlement negotiated at the Speedwell's inception.[90] Apart from disagreements over long-term liabilities, the province argued that it was owed an additional sum for the basic use of the facility and for two other provincial properties.[91] The provincial secretary of Ontario launched a total claim of nearly half a million dollars that dragged on for over a decade before a negotiated settlement was reached.[92]

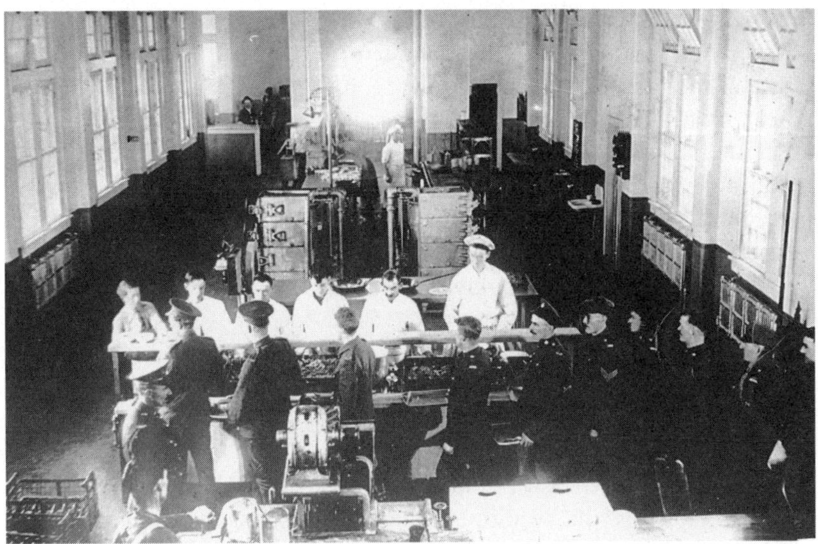

11 Regimented routine remained part of many soldiers' experiences as military hospital patients. Although this photograph, taken at the Speedwell Hospital, seems to reflect an 'efficiency' theme underscored in many photographs produced by the military, it does give us a rare glimpse of an ordinary cafeteria lineup at the hospital. As patients and as former active duty soldiers, these men were represented by the Guelph branch of the Great War Veterans Association. Most of them resented the fact that civilians, pictured here as servers, held paid positions in the hospital, jobs that they felt only veterans should have filled. *Courtesy of Guelph Museums, 978.6.1*

But that was an accountant's battle. From the veterans' standpoint, voiced by the Guelph branch of the GWVA, who ran the hospital was more important than who paid for it. Like the dispute over financial liability, the problem with personnel can be traced back to the original contract governing the transfer of the institution for military use. This agreement stipulated that Ontario's provincial secretary's office could retain, and even increase, reformatory staff without interference from the military.[93] Civilians without military experience were kept on, and others were hired. When the Speedwell was in full operation two years later, one tally listed 174 civilians, never in the CEF, on the payroll compared to 95 veterans.[94]

The veterans' objections were significant for two reasons: first, they signalled a boundary between themselves and other men who had not served but were otherwise qualified and capable of taking 'their' jobs. As they gave their reasons, veterans adopted a language of solidarity rooted in a sense of entitlement: only those who had been overseas could be employed by the government to care for convalescent soldiers. It was not just a matter of jobs, but of cultural identity and power. Second, they were able at this point to organize themselves as men in the ranks to work through the local branch of the GWVA to demand an official hearing. Their demands, taken up by Guelph's member of Parliament, did prompt a visit to Guelph from the DSCR's most senior officials. While some officers may have shared the men's point of view, and a former overseas chaplain helped to voice it, the initiative and the language of dissent deployed came largely from ordinary men in the ranks, represented by the secretary of the Guelph branch of the GWVA.

Tensions first surfaced on paper when the Guelph GWVA petitioned for 'special consideration' in employing returned soldiers at the hospital. The men had already tabbed civilian workers at the Speedwell the 'prison gang.'[95] They were on solid ground as far as precedent and policy were concerned. The DSCR ordinarily employed veterans with overseas experience whenever possible.[96] Unfortunately, the strings attached to the Ontario deal trapped the DSCR between ordinary practice and its contract with the province. The Guelph GWVA was told that replacing all non-military staff with returned soldiers would needlessly disrupt the hospital's efficient operation.

Through their organization, the men were able to maintain lobbying efforts that gave ordinary veterans a secure avenue through which to speak. In September 1919 the Guelph GWVA passed a resolution demanding a dramatic increase in jobs for veterans at the Speedwell, even if this meant a disruptive layoff of existing staff. As William D. Robertson, secretary of the Guelph GWVA, put it during a subsequent Commission of Government investigation, his members were getting less than a 'square deal.' He added that 'a square deal for every returned man and his dependents' had become the new motto for Guelph veterans.[97] While the problem for the DSCR lay in determining what was fair and what was obtainable, for the men the notion of fairness was clearest in terms they invoked and took as their own: the 'square deal' that Robinson implied might be more broadly applied to 'every returned man and his dependents.'

The language used to voice further complaints during the investigation, held the following month, helps us to address certain attitudes and values that men from the ranks held regarding not just civilian men who had not served, but officers as well. Their grievance gained momentum when the president of the Guelph GWVA, Archdeacon A.C. Mackintosh of St. James Anglican, sent a copy of a resolution demanding significant adjustments in civilian staff to the local member of Parliament, Hugh Guthrie, who was then solicitor general. The resolution opposed 'several appointments,' including that of the Speedwell's assistant director, G.E. Black. As far as the men were concerned, returned officers and other ranks currently residing in Guelph 'should receive every consideration in that respect,' as opposed to those 'who have not had Overseas service in the Great War.'[98]

Guthrie received this with a cover letter from the archdeacon expressing 'the hope that you will be able to give me the assurance that you will personally look into the matter.' Mackintosh nudged Guthrie toward seeing this as a matter of shared interests. 'I need hardly tell you,' he added, 'that should you be able to accomplish this, that you will make yourself solid with the Guelph boys.' Mackintosh also claimed that the present situation at the hospital was 'having a very unsettling effect upon the men in the city.'[99]

Guthrie passed the forwarded resolution to the DSCR, and within ten days F.G. Robinson, the deputy minister, told him that an investigation was already underway.[100] At the end of October, Robertson, as secretary of the city's GWVA, sent an urgent telegram to Guthrie requesting that all administrative positions at the Speedwell 'be declared vacant and the same to be filled by qualified returned men li[v]ing within the district.' This led Guthrie to write directly to James Lougheed, minister responsible for the DSCR. Lougheed informed Guthrie that his department was already investigating the complaint and that plans for an inquiry were underway. Senior officials from his department, he told Guthrie, would be sent to Guelph immediately after the current Commons session to, as he put it, 'investigate the whole situation.'[101] Lougheed then set up a Commission of Government fact-finding panel.

The hearing convened on 25 November, with the panel meeting at the Speedwell. As Lougheed promised, senior officials were involved. The DSCR's deputy minister, its chief inspector, its director of vocational training, and its director of medical services were all present. The panel was chaired by the DSCR's parliamentary secretary, Col. Hugh Clark. The Guelph's GWVA, on the other hand, was represented by its president, Mackintosh, and secretary, Robertson, both of whom spoke. Robertson had more to say in specific terms about the day-to-day concerns of running a hospital with mostly civilian staff, and he noted grievances over the issue of rank and privilege.

The proceedings recorded positions articulated clearly by Mackintosh and Robertson in terms that Robertson, in particular, claimed reflected his members' views. But given the thorny contract problem and given that the hospital was up and running, the DSCR chose to stay the course on civilians at the hospital, maintaining support for departmental employees without military experience on staff at the Speedwell. What Mackintosh and Robertson were unable to do, however, is not nearly as important for us here as what they were able to say, how specific grievances were voiced, articulating signs of perception we can often only guess at in other sources.

Mackintosh had been a chaplain overseas and later, on a temporary basis, at the Speedwell, and he did not speak as a man from the ranks. His statements indicated a distinction he wished to draw explicitly between his 'personal feeling' and his duty to represent the views of the Guelph GWVA. Robertson, on the other hand, spoke directly for the men from the ranks and as a former patient at the Speedwell.

The archdeacon began by claiming to represent an association of about 950 men. He claimed that the concerns of the Speedwell's patients were shared by veterans in the city who met Tuesday evenings at the Guelph Museum. Mackintosh noted that he had served for a period as the Speedwell's chaplain and that Robertson had been a patient there. As he put it: 'I have no personal feeling in the matter, but am simply a representative of 940 or 950 men, who are interested in the patients in [the] Speedwell Hospital, who come up every Tuesday night to the meetings, registering their grouches. As members of the Association, stock has to be taken in what is being said.'

Robertson then spoke, stating: 'As Secretary of the Guelph branch of the G.W.V.A., I have had a great deal of ins and outs amongst the Hospital. I was a patient there myself.' Robertson stressed that since its inception in 1917 his local association, like GWVA branches across Canada, had worked 'for the betterment of the conditions and the welfare of the returned men.' Veterans outside the Speedwell, he also claimed, felt a comradeship and close connection with those inside the hospital.[102]

For Robertson, it was also an issue of military rank. 'Why is it,' he asked at one point as he listed a number of concerns, 'that the best positions on the administrative staff are given to officers? In the administrative positions of the Department [the DSCR] there are very few men from the rank and file.'[103] As he faced the department's top officials, Robertson charged, 'this Department is being administered, to a great extent by civilians, who are just as capable of serving overseas as any man who went. These men stayed behind, got good positions, and being in the position while the returned men were overseas, got accustomed to the positions, and when the returned men came back, held them; with the result that while these men were fighting the battles and came back, these others stayed behind and got positions in Institutions which could be filled by returned men. These men draw good pay, and it is not a square deal.'[104] Robertson went on to raise a series of grievances, some trivial, others more substantive, from the way the linen was changed to allegations that Speedwell's assistant director had interfered with military medical officers.

Much of it, however, was hearsay, which annoyed the panel. Deputy Minister Robinson wanted to see specific complaints documented. 'If a man is in the right,' the director of medical services, E.G. Davis, added, 'he should not mind his name being mentioned.' The director of vocational training, N.F. Parkinson, added that any veteran with a legitimate grievance should 'fight his own battles. If he cannot get adjusted by going to the proper person,' responsible for a particular program, 'he should be man enough to get out.'[105] At this point the hearing's chair, Hugh Clark, called a halt. 'I think this covers the ground' he interjected. 'I think this Conference has cleared the air.'[106]

12 This is what any veteran-patient, entering or departing from the Speedwell Hospital in Guelph, would have seen as the postwar period approached – the sight of buildings that had been the core of an Ontario reformatory prison, temporarily converted into a military hospital. Complaining veterans sometimes used the fact that the facility had been a prison to suggest that it still operated like one. *Courtesy of Guelph Museums, 978.6.2*

Obviously it had not. Some indication of the discord that lingered surfaced in correspondence following the inquiry from G.E. Black, whose assistant directorship at the Speedwell had been challenged by veterans galled by his lack of military experience. Black wrote to Deputy Minister Robinson, claiming that Mackintosh had telephoned him after the conference to voice his personal satisfaction and that of Robertson with the investigation's findings. This seems dubious. 'He ended up by saying,' Black claimed, 'that he supposed people would call it a coat of whitewash but I assured him that no matter what the findings were, half the [Guelph GWVA members] ... would be dissatisfied.'[107] This very likely understated his opinion.

At the outset of the hearing, Mackintosh had gone so far as to accuse Black and other civilians running the Speedwell of being unable to empathize with the veteran patients. He charged that the 'present Assistant Director and most of the men holding administrative positions are not men who are able to understand the men.' Mackintosh referred to it as a 'want of understanding' between the patients and civilian staff working at the hospital. He saw it as 'a source of unnecessary friction, as well as creating in the minds of returned soldiers, – I am just giving what is expressed by a number of men – "Now that the war is over, nothing matters what happens to us."'[108]

For Returned Heroes? Commemoration Collapses

On 9 December 1918, a group of Lethbridge soldiers boarded ship in Southhampton, England, for Canada and their southern Alberta home. One of them, Jack Murray, originally with the 20th Field Artillery, had left with the CEF's First Contingent amid general expectations that the war would be over probably before his unit saw action. Though his subsequent infirmity was not explained, Murray was hospitalized after reaching England and never reached any fighting front. He finally made it home for this Christmas, four arduous years later. After travelling to Lethbridge aboard two vessels and a troop train to the West, all within what the *Herald* called, probably in truth, 'a record' twelve days, Murray and other Albertan men pulled into the city's CPR station. He was said to be wearing 'the same smiling face as when he went away.'

But the crowd waiting for his train appeared subdued, in no way comparable to the station platform gatherings of 1914. Friends and relatives were there. So were representatives of the Lethbridge branch of the GWVA, with its secretary doing 'everything in his power to make the homecoming boys comfortable.' As the *Herald* described, the city had become 'so accustomed to having her heroes return during the night without any reception of a public nature, that the crowd hardly knew how to react yesterday when given the opportunity, but citizens who were heard to express themselves are determined that in future Lethbridge will organize to give the boys a welcome home such as is their due and such that they will know their risks of the past four years will be appreciated.'[109]

Since news of the armistice, a variety of citizens and voluntary associations had already begun considering how Lethbridge would commemorate such appreciation in the form of a civic memorial to the Great War. We turn finally to look at how a cross-section of citizens and the veterans themselves wished to memorialize the war. What forms of commemoration appealed to them? What happened to a movement to erect some monument, library, garden, hospital, or statue in the city of Lethbridge that would be a physical sign of how some of its citizens had chosen to remember the war and the men who fought in it?

It was not, in other words, so much a case of war-hardened veterans returning home only to be shunted aside or ignored. In the flesh, whether jobless, wounded, or eagerly trying to re-establish themselves, they encountered ambivalent, sometimes contradictory reactions. But their image offered something entirely different and grew in stature in the interwar period. Across Canada, veterans were revered for their sacrifices in commemorative forms that responded to the myth of the noble volunteer who had made the supreme sacrifice: poems; plays; novels; monuments; naming practices for public buildings, geographical features, and newborns; prize names; commercial advertising. The memory of war became in the interwar period a persistent, mutable, and ubiquitous set of narratives and symbols of national identity. Commemorative practices coincided with the country's development, in the 1920s, of new institutions, art forms, and political discourses. These served as vehicles to imagine a new, post-war nation of greater economic and political autonomy within imperial and global systems also altered by the war.

During Armistice and, later, Remembrance Day ceremonies, veterans joined with local civilian communities to commemorate publicly memories of the fallen soldier and the meaning of a victory that brought such loss. 'In Flanders Fields,' written by Col. John McCrae, a soldier who had grown up in Guelph, became the single most recited set of stanzas anywhere in Canada, the Empire, and later the Commonwealth each year on 11 November.[110] First published anonymously in December 1915 by the English magazine *Punch,* McCrae's famous fifteen lines were written after the Ypres disaster, when so many of Pick's 'splendid boys' faced chlorine gas for the first time. Recited annually, amid poppy boutonnieres and cenotaph displays first used by the British Legion as a symbol for remembrance, the poem's imagery has become synonymous with wartime commemoration.[111] Its versatility as a memorial anthem in verse for the annual observances of that day derived from the multiple frames it offered through which to see the myth of the fallen soldier and his comrades. A voice from the grave beseeched his comrades to keep faith, 'to take up our quarrel with the foe.' Through the metaphor of a torch passed on, the poem invoked a mythic chain between death and life, between sacrifice and survival, victory, and the invented purposes of the war that came to be commemorated. A poignant eulogy, then, that served to 'mark our place,' shifted its message in its final verse, sounding more like a recruiting poster, but without a hollow ring for many.

The inventions we associate with the memory of the war were not crafted from the experiences of real men, training, departing, fighting, and returning as survivors, but from the motivations and aims of a society in transition, as Canada was in the interwar period. Social memories, in general, reflect the interests and social intentions of their inventors. To establish their position in a social context conceived through a usable past, the prime architects of an ideal past typically seek to meld selected events, actions, and aspirations into grand narratives. This is done to secure their own, often privileged, place in history, whether to construct or reinforce a sense of proud identity, identify enemies, explain the present, or glorify noted figures in the past to which they claim connection. It is a way of social imagining that depends on appropriating, through a claim on past events, a place in history. What social memories constitute depends very much on who is making them, who is inventing the poems, stories, rituals, and symbols that can bring such imagining into the present.

Historical work on social memory and the Great War, studies of literature, popular culture, or remembrance ceremonies, generally selects objects of study about a decade into the interwar period, when clusters of evidence, whether works of fiction or cenotaph unveilings, first appeared. But the social memory of the war in Canada, which offered such a useful myth for the nation builders of the 1920s and 1930s, as Jonathan Vance suggests, often had uncertain beginnings in forms that McCrae's poem helped to direct. Our evidence from Lethbridge suggests why.

Immediately after the war, some citizens felt that commemoration should begin as soon as possible. We can sample, widely enough to establish a general pattern, a variety of opinions as to how the war might be remembered, collected and summarized by the *Herald* less than two weeks after the armistice. Municipal leaders, schoolteachers, and local business, labour and service groups from women's voluntary organizations to the Rotarians all held different views of how the war should be commemorated locally, reflected by the particular project each proposed. As the number and variety of suggestions expanded, a post-armistice community portrait emerged. Lethbridge veterans were part of this scene, but they posed as just a group of demobilized men etched into a larger canvas. While coming home for them meant establishing their places within this wider social setting in real terms, for the time being it also meant searching for some site of memory, a search that was not completed in the form of a cenotaph until the early years of the Great Depression.

Toward the end of November, the *Herald* began to solicit ideas. They multiplied, but generally according to the specific interests of each person the paper asked for her or his opinion. One officer, Capt. E.C. McKenzie, who was said to be 'in close touch with the needs of returned men,' suggested a veterans' convalescent hospital. Ottawa's support was anticipated, he explained, and the reasons for his choice may well have reflected the preferences of men at the beginning of a long struggle across Canada to lobby for better facilities, programs, and policies connected to veteran re-establishment.[112]

But while they may have wanted a hospital, the veterans also had considered a statue. After 'considerable discussion,' as the *Herald* put it, the city's GWVA spoke of a statue of British prime minister David Lloyd George. They imagined engraved under it the names, serial numbers, and battalions of all district soldiers who served. Their choice of Lloyd George atop an honour roll remains open to interpretation, but suggested they felt some connection not only to Britain, but also to this prime minister. Lloyd George, after all, had manoeuvred his way into the prime minister's office on the basis of a strong pro-war policy. Class, too, influenced how he could be perceived differently by ordinary men than by a more privileged elite. British commanders like Field Marshal Sir Douglas Haig or Field Marshal Sir William Robertson, the European war historian Marc Ferro has noted, 'had difficulty in imagining a plebeian directing the affairs of Empire.'[113] Apparently, Lethbridge veterans did not. Any proposal to commemorate a British war general instead would certainly have been more surprising, as might have been suggestions for a monument honouring Prime Minister Borden, or even Gen. Sir Arthur Currie. The city's GWVA also thought that the inscription should commemorate the war service of the living as well as the dead; in other words, they wanted themselves recognized not just as survivors but as men who served. And identifying all by their serial number and battalion may have signified the close bond soldiers often felt toward their regiment or battalion, often the fighting man's most enduring site of face-to-face relations, companionship, and loss.[114]

What the men themselves wanted was quickly eclipsed by what civilians wanted. For some time, J.D. Higinbotham, 'one of the leaders for years of public movements in Lethbridge,' as the *Herald* cast him, had tried without success to establish a public library in the city, a ready sign of stability and culture that the political architects of urban spaces before the war had eagerly sought, often through the Carnegie public library trust. Lethbridge had not yet made this step, and that Higinbotham might speak in favour of it at this moment was hardly surprising. He was not alone, but was one of the first to tender support for a public or 'free' library as a memorial edifice. Within it, he suggested, there might be a museum display of war memorabilia on a separate floor somewhere in the building, as well as a gallery, a venue for a public gaze at the material traces through which, for schoolchildren and adults alike, anyone might imagine what had taken place. His preference may have also reflected the fact that he had twice served as a trustee for the local school board.[115]

The educational purposes of a war memorial library received support from another school board member, H.P. Wallace.[116] Principal R. Howard Dobson of the Lethbridge Collegiate Institute added his voice in favour of Higinbotham's 'public library museum idea.' 'A monument,' he suggested, 'is a very fine thing to look at, but it fills very little further purpose than filling the eye with architectural beauty.'[117]

Building a war memorial library was the single most popular idea among opinions canvassed. But its supporters were not agreed on why. Their differences seemed rooted in particular views of the world that was coming as they saw it, not the one that had been. President Marnoch of the Lethbridge Board of Trade, for instance, knew that a 'considerable sum' of $35,600 might be obtained from Carnegie's public library trust.[118] He mentioned as well that the project would put unemployed veterans to work. Fred Smeed, president of the Lethbridge Trades and Labor Council, wanted nothing to do with a plan involving Carnegie money. Smeed endorsed a public library if and only if it was supported by the City of Lethbridge alone, and he rejected flatly the GWVA's proposal for a Lloyd George statue. On the other hand, William Symonds of the International Brotherhood of Electrical Workers conceded that a suitable statue might be erected with 'support from some wealthy citizen who desires to show his appreciation of the sacrifices made.' But nothing, Symonds added, could equal a public library for promoting democratic ideals, something he thought the war had been fought over.[119] 'What better idea,' the Rev. J.E. Murrel-Wright of St. Cyprian's Anglican church asked, 'than that the people go to a building associated with the memory of our fallen heroes in order to keep abreast with the civilization which they fought to maintain?'[120]

The Lloyd George notion, which in fact bore the weight of a branch resolution passed by members of Lethbridge's GWVA, was buried in a chorus of possible projects endorsed for a variety of ends, from the didactic to the aesthetic. Other proposals reflected contrasting values. Public Works Commissioner W.H. Meech, described as having a great deal of 'architectural experience,' favoured an ornate monument, but did not specify its form. Fred W. Downer, a former recruiting campaign speaker, wanted a monument too, but one with a large pedestal for public addresses.[121] J.F. Simpson of the Women's Civic Club suggested a memorial fountain placed at the centre of Galt Gardens.[122] The only citizen's proposal responsive to veterans' actual needs came from the Lethbridge Great War Next-of-Kin Association, an organization established in many parts of Canada in 1917 by soldiers' families and dependents. They suggested a children's home for sons and daughters of veterans who died in service or who had returned unable to support their families.[123] As various ideas circulated, one worried ratepayer, identified as Louis Moore, cautioned that a memorial edifice of any kind might become a perennial tax burden.[124] Very few recognized that many returned soldiers might feel little personal interest in a city library. At any rate, former Kilty regiment and city Khaki League organizer W.S. Ball favoured a war memorial library. School board secretary J.H. Fleetwood, a longtime library booster, echoed his view.[125]

Finally, as it continued to gather opinion, the *Herald* offered its own suggestion beneath the editorial caption 'Why Not a War Museum for Lethbridge?' It suggested a permanent local exhibit of war trophies brought home by the men. This notion was probably prompted by a recent announcement to municipalities by the Department of Militia and Defence that

13 Towns and cities in every region in Canada erected monuments for the fallen during the interwar period. This is Trois-Rivières's cenotaph. Located in front of the city's post office, its honour roll lists the war dead on the shaded plaque, and the alternate face states: 'A nos soldats morts/To our dead soldiers.' *Courtesy of Archives du Séminaire de Trois-Rivières, FN-0064-65-28*

captured war trophies, mostly field guns, were available for public display.[126] Mayor Hardie forwarded a request the following year, and in July 1920 two German cannons arrived and were placed in front of city hall, where they remained for almost a decade.

After the *Herald*'s survey, public discussion of war monuments and newspaper coverage of war-related issues quickly dissipated in Lethbridge and, generally, throughout Canada.[127] The Rotarians had set aside $500 as a first step toward a memorial, but they were entirely neutral concerning its composition. They simply resolved that city council take the initiative in striking a citizens' committee to decide what should be done.[128] A 'start has been made in the right direction,' the *Herald* noted on the last day of 1918, 'and it remains now for the citizens of Lethbridge and district to organize without delay to carry the project to completion.'[129] The newspaper's attention on local and regional affairs, however, soon focused on the immediate crisis of the influenza epidemic and on increasing incidents of labour activism. Nothing further was done to launch a war memorial fund during that time.

Some four years later, however, a committee formed by the Alexander Galt IODE began quietly taking donations for a war monument. By the summer of 1927, when cenotaph unveilings had become a common event in many towns and cities in Canada, they were just $1,500 short of an estimated $10,250 needed for a monument. The committee had also obtained permission from the CPR to erect the memorial at the centre of Galt Gardens on land still held by the railway. A Montreal sculptor had already been commissioned to begin work on a statue and pedestal. In October 1930, city council loaned the committee the balance needed and expressed concern over repeated setbacks in completing the project. An unveiling on Armistice Day of that year was anticipated, and disappointment was expressed when it passed. Securing a suitable bronze wreath for the cenotaph delayed the ceremony until the summer of 1931.[130]

By then, southern Alberta, hit hard by the Depression, was struggling through a period of regional out-migration that began with the droughts of the 1920s. War remembrance remained, however, a growing part of local culture, demonstrated in actively publicized and well-attended ceremonies subsequently held each year at the new cenotaph. In Lethbridge, the myth of the Great War as a heroic sacrifice had as much a local focus as a national one: Armistice Day and later Remembrance Day both came to foster an enduring view of Canada as a nation forged through world wars. More recently, in 1986, the German field guns that Mayor Hardie secured were moved to the east end of Henderson Lake, where over seventy years earlier Sergeant Gobelle had been employed by the city to shovel ice, presumably for public skating and undoubtedly to keep his family fed while he and other veterans looked for steady jobs.[131]

Men Overseas and at Home: Intersections of Canada at War, the Local Press, and City Politics

Localized studies of the men who returned and the perceptions they encountered help to clarify relationships between soldiers and civilians. Such approaches also help to situate the figures each used to express their interests, anxieties, and memories of what had taken place. Patterns of battle reporting became regularized in the press, as demonstrated in the *Mercury*'s overriding tendency to embed the carnage it depicted within larger narratives of the war as a justifiable and noble sacrifice. The tactic of including, whenever possible, a familiar soldier or regiment in battle reports was also regularized and supplemented by news and letters from the front in its 'With the Troops' columns. Images of horror worked largely to demonize the enemy, as it autographed an imagined war with the presence of known men and their units.

Across the country, municipal leaders pointed to a looming gap between federal and municipal jurisdictions, marginally reduced by voluntary efforts, as the first returned soldiers made their way back. Ottawa's responses, from the War Service Gratuity to the replacement of the Military Hospitals Commission with the larger Department of Soldiers' Civil Re-Establishment, which came to run military hospitals like the Speedwell, did not address it entirely, but did represent unprecedented state involvement in a war of unprecedented scale. News coverage of bureaucratic machineries, refitted from afar, seldom found much of a place in city dailies. In the newspapers of our three cities we find no critiques of large systems of veteran re-establishment unfolding, but rather ordinary fears of the men gleaned largely from ordinary incidents and an imaginary view of the menace they posed.

For the men, places like the Speedwell became their most immediate encounter with post-war illness and recovery. In this case it also became a site for an exchange of views cast in the language of men with 'grouches' about their treatment perhaps, but with very real concerns about their place in the post-war economic order. In general terms, from first reports of local boys killed overseas to a debate about a possible war memorial project, boundaries of perception between veterans and civilians were constituted through the intersections of local circumstances and discourses and those of the country as a whole, as each changed. As returned soldiers fell under the civilian gaze while passing through cities like Trois-Rivières, entered convalescent care, or simply sought work or further training, they came to be seen through superficial knowledges and constantly reinforced fears of what the war hero might constitute in close proximity. The stereotyped veteran generated inverted images: from selfless hero to social hazard. That he had no job, in cities with little extra work; that he was also 'changed,' a victim of multiple conditions and predispositions: shell-shock, tuberculosis, venereal disease, alcohol abuse, and 'dangerous' political ideas – these notions accompanied efforts to deal with the reality of some 400,000 men coming home.

Canada's home front, considered through the signs of ordinary city life, remained divided by interests, by fears, and occasionally by mutual distrust between veterans and civilians. At the very end of the war, Lethbridge citizens seemed without a focus for developing symbols of remembrance. The image of the soldier, however, was much easier to honour and to celebrate than the reality of his return. In the years that followed, cultural practices connected to the memory and meaning of the fallen soldier would become one of the war's most enduring legacies.

8
Beyond Hometown Horizons

When we consider patterns of social interaction and signs of difference during the war we run the risk of remaining fixed in our use of illusionary dichotomies: the individual and society, local and national, subjects and objects, or consciousness and the external world. Ideals concerning personal freedom and autonomy can present figments of modernity that separate individual experiences from the interrelationships of communication and action from which any person's sense of connection to 'great' events are derived, whether formed by common history, shared aims, or hometown horizons. Here, our attention has been on the local, though each of Trois-Rivières, Guelph, and Lethbridge has presented varied and complex sites of communication and community constructed by civilian-military relations – soldiers, war relief workers, enemy aliens, government officials, clerics, and many others, bound to wartime demands shaped by the collective responses of millions. Few could remain islands unto themselves, especially during the war years, and I have argued that approaches to their fashioning of experience can be misled by notions of a split between the immediacy of local settings and the distance of an outside world.

In work overlooked until recently, Norbert Elias argued that two long-term processes have contributed to the idea of the individual-versus-society rather than a society of interconnected individuals: the state's monopoly of the use of 'authorized' violence and the increased differentiation of social roles in industrializing societies. Together, they have established in Western histories over the long run regularities in social boundaries that contribute to an imagined presence of self, individuality, and autonomy set against the surrounding social world construed as an organic whole. For Elias, this notion effaces the socially configured construction of experience, a point he makes for historians concerned with the formation of multiple identities and boundaries through relational encounters. The various groups, factions, collectivities we have considered neither made themselves nor were made by others, but established their differences through relationships activated on different levels spatially, from local to global domains. This underscores the hazards of separating individual and group identities, whether recruits, enemy aliens, war relief workers, or veterans, however fluid and contingent they were, from the social and cultural forces that shaped them. The complex interdependency within which subjects operate explains their place in the world, not independent claims to freedom, volition, or adherence to some extrinsic reality. Connections between the external world and local situations operated as a tightly woven net, structured through interdependencies in variable states of flux. They shaped the social habitus of period and place, the norms and functions evident on local levels, though not determined by localized relationships alone.[1]

The separations created between civilians and soldiers, between civilian men and women, between enemy aliens and the host society, or between conscription's supporters and opponents made collective action possible, but only through exclusionary practices that engendered distinct roles, patterns of social interaction, and modes of signifying social difference that linked past identities with present engagements. 'Let us imagine as a symbol of society,' Elias suggested, 'a group of dancers performing court dances, such as the *française* or *quadrille*, or a country round dance. The steps and bows, gestures and movements made by the individual dancer are all entirely meshed and synchronized with those of other dancers. If any of the dancing individuals were contemplated in isolation, the functions of his or her movements could not be understood.' Relationships of social memory, of gendered norms, of imagined ethnocultural affiliations, coded in recognizable patterns, established social parameters for individual action from which the movements we examined proceeded. As Elias put it, the 'way the individual behaves in this situation is determined by the relations of the dancers to each other. It is similar with the behaviour of individuals in general. Whether they meet as friends or enemies, parents or children, man and wife or knight and bondsmen, king and subjects, manager and employees, however individuals behave is determined by past or present relations to other people.'[2] From recruitment to veteran re-establishment, a continuous sequence of prior relationships and subsequent actions shaped the patterns and boundaries of civilian-military relations wherever local circumstances and war-related linkages intersected. This was as true for civilians who had spent the war at home as it was for the men, cast often as 'battle hardened heroes,' who returned to the mundane and often merciless realities of the post-war period.

Toasts over Dinner: Romantic Horizons of Memory

At the end of the war, before the large-scale demobilizations of 1919, returned soldiers, depending on their discharge circumstances, often made their way back home singly or in small groups. Local initiatives, like the

Next-of-Kin Association or even the veterans' own GWVA chapter, might be caught unaware by their arrival, and the men would simply slip back into their home destination with no public fanfare of any kind. Despite the fact that this might have been what many preferred, city council in Lethbridge expressed concern that not enough was being done to welcome ex-soldiers back home. In January 1919, two returning men from a group of thirty-five got off at the CPR platform and planned to stay. No mention was made of any greeting by family or friends. 'Those going through were met' by the wives of the mayor and of a long-established Anglican clergyman, 'but owing to lack of organization there were no cigarettes or coffee, for both of which the boys asked.'[3]

Often across Canada, veterans publicly and politely thanked civilians who made some effort to recognize their return or their passage toward home, whether by providing coffee and cigarettes or through the formalities of a special rally or parade. Formally, that is, they tended to express gratitude for gestures that were usually voluntary local offerings. Frank and open discussion, on the other hand, marking a contrary discourse of protest regarding federal initiatives, was something quite different. Dissent, demands, and debates over political questions concerning civil re-establishment were often situated, as the previous chapter considered, within their own advocacy bodies, led by the GWVA.[4]

However, the men did use many special occasions in towns and cities across the country to consider what had just happened overseas and what the war might come to symbolize at home through an emergent discourse of valour and sacrifice. The more ordinary language of protest, a potent and significant force in itself, might be punctuated by commemorative rites of many types, often localized and vernacular in form, and often more appealing to the public at large than the contrasting rhetoric of veterans' rights. How could this catastrophe – of fallen comrades, of cherished ideals, of hopes, and of costly victory – be spoken of? Far from complaints, demands, or lobbying efforts that Ottawa faced from veterans' organizations, the men at home often took part in rituals, created in local settings, which idealized their place in society. Such sites, to take a final look at Lethbridge, appeared quite early, just seven weeks after the fighting ceased.

At the end of 1918, the Lethbridge branch of the GWVA staged a banquet on New Year's Eve in its club room, perhaps fearing that some members might be without a festive circle at a time of year when loneliness could haunt anyone without friends or family. Some one hundred returned men turned out for the second such affair ever held in the city.[5] As social gatherings, banquets since the early Victorian period had acquired the formalities of privileged affairs of conspicuous consumption that by design deployed restrictive practices.[6] As an exclusionary ritual, such dinners established particular domains, separated from daily routine, of convivial activity. As

14 The return of war in Europe in September 1939 set the stage for this respectful viewing by a pair of Guelph soldiers of a commemorative plaque set in a corner of the McCrae residence on Water Street. Their retrospective glance at the home of Canada's famous war poet is shown here at a time when war enthusiasm anywhere in Canada could scarcely match that of August 1914. *Courtesy of Guelph Museums, 979.75.48*

for any banquet, the Lethbridge veterans and their guests drew from traditional rituals and gestures, but they also infused their formalities of speeches, toasts, and responses with war-related references. In this case, organizers and participants alike seemed intent on instilling sentimental attachments to all – whether army or navy, men or women – who served for Canada on this, the first New Year's Eve since the Armistice. The eyewitness account that survives also describes how the GWVA branch arranged officers and civic dignitaries hierarchically to deliver, in turn, a round of head-table toasts and speeches before the men of the ranks. Included among them were Mayor Hardie, Judge J.O. Jackson, C.F.P Conybeare, MP and *Herald* publisher W.A. Buchanan, and D.H. Elton, the city magistrate who had delivered the firehall parade speech in August 1914 (see Chapter 1).

Each of their speeches recognized, endorsed, and affirmed social boundaries as well as bonds of imperial-nationalism and gives us some idea of the lens through which the war came to be seen only weeks after the actual carnage had finally ended. The banquet served to promote sanitized images, communicated by a cross-section of civic leaders and veterans who, as Elias put it, signified and performed their encounters with others through mutually understood gestures and within designated social roles. While the civilian guests that evening tended to cast their remarks in the dogmatic formalism they had used time and again since the outbreak of hostilities, some of the most obvious expressions of high diction and ennobling discourse came from the ex-soldiers themselves. Their remarks reinforced a new, emergent war mythology, one that replaced a negative, backward-looking sense of horror overseas with a positive, future-oriented vision that honoured the men for what they had made possible. 'After the toast to the King,' and after a telegram of best wishes had been read from the chapter's former secretary, 'Capt. Beeman proposed a toast to the army and navy conveying the tribute of the army man to the great power of the navy.' Following brief responses to this gesture of comradeship among the land and sea forces, Capt. the Rev. A.H. Dennon proposed a toast to 'Our Country' in a speech said to have 'thrilled all present.'[7]

In his talk, Dennon introduced a subtle shift from the Anglocentric colonialism that often had relegated Canada to the margins of the Empire, with a claim, about to be echoed across English Canada, that the Dominion itself had intrinsic greatness and worth, something that imperialists in Britain might well take notice of. In reference to Dominion Day observances held overseas six months earlier, he recalled that 'the last time he had spoken on this subject had been in France on July 1st.' Dennon's speech, as he remembered it, had 'dealt with the great resources and possibilities of the country.' At that point, a British officer was to have 'remarked that he must have drawn on his imagination for his facts.' In recalling the moment, Dennon claimed to have pushed his homeland boosting a bit. He recalled noting that Canada remained part of the Empire to be sure, but his skeptic need only take a geographical and historical look at this young country 'to see that what he had said was true.' Paying heed to the traditional bonds of imperial-nationalism, this former army chaplain pointed as well to a new maturity and confidence that many Canadians would choose to underscore more publicly than in the past, four long years ago. Dennon then moved on to the rhetoric we might associate with a cleric in the armed service. In the end it was the 'spirit of the men,' their 'God-given moral courage that drove them forward to almost impossible tasks.'[8]

His short speech and toast were a fairly early rehearsal of the discourse and rites of noble sacrifice that would shape so much of what became the social memory of the Great War. These men, Dennon claimed, 'must not have been sacrificed in vain. They died for ideals, let us live that those ideals might be fulfilled.' The *Herald* reporter also noted that 'during the silent toast which was drunk to the memory of "Our Fallen Comrades," Mr. Elton also recited "In Flanders Fields."' In a small but comprehensive way, then, the heroic-making discourse, the commemorative silence, and the recitation of John McCrae's anthem to the lost generation in France, three key elements in the Armistice and later Remembrance day rites, were observed in turn at the Lethbridge banquet.

The dinner was not entirely an all-male affair, as Conybeare's daughter was present, identified as Nursing Sister Brander. Gestures of masculinity and femininity, nonetheless, seemed to conform to fairly traditional patterns associated with the banquet form. After Judge Jackson proposed a toast to 'Our Nursing Sisters,' Brander, who had 'just been admitted to membership of the Veterans, responded to the toast, and on behalf of the Red Cross Nurses thanked the soldiers for their great appreciation of the work of the nurses. Sister Brander also pleased the gathering with a very fine rendition on the piano. She received an ovation when she rose.' Later, 'Comrade Morrow spoke of the part women had played in the war. "God Himself only knows," he said in a reverent tone, "What we men would have done many a time, had it not been for our women."' Despite the honorary induction that evening of Nurse Brander into the veterans' group, the terms 'we men' and 'our women' are indicative of gendered language and perspective.[9]

The report tailed off with a sense of the aftermath of the banquet's more formal moments: 'During the evening, very enjoyable songs were rendered by Comrade Stott, Leo Coombs and D.H. Elton, while Mr. Arnold presided at the piano. Robt. Barrowman introduced a unique form of entertainment in the series of rapid sketches he drew, some of them depicting the guests present.'[10]

Such moments soon began to contribute to a new hometown horizon, one that inspired an imagined sense of war as noble sacrifice. In this first local veterans' banquet, as in comparable events staged across the country, organizers and participants alike structured many encounters through rituals set apart from everyday routine. While the descriptions here of the toasts, speeches, performances, and camaraderie reflected regularized patterns of social discourse and interaction in such contexts, those gathered also performed and experienced this event in uniquely situated ways of hometown peculiarities through which a national narrative of war remembrance could be told. From the presence of Lethbridge notables and returned men of past associations in this Prairie city, to the specifics of the club room and its history, to the incidental appearance of a sketch artist, interactions were both localized and shaped by prior relations for those present. The banquet activated the kind of ritualized contexts in which both general histories connected to wartime experiences of Canadian men and women, and a localized space connected to immediate surroundings of familiar faces, established roles, and public personas came together.

The whole affair unfolded as a continuous exchanges between cultural signs of the social past – imagined nationality, masculine fraternity, and a venerated vision of wartime sacrifice – and those of the immediate present in the form of the setting and circumstances of the dinner gathering experienced by those present. Analyzing everyday exchanges, complicated by the varied levels of perception they activate, can help us understand how 'nation' and 'home' often intersected across Canada's home front and postwar society. Such cultural encounters – the sweeping or 'exterior' contours of a national story taking shape within the site-specific 'interior' particulars of place – could be found across the hometown horizons of Canada's diverse populations. The war overseas, just ceased, remained a reality of horror and gruesome loss, still distanced by the tangential way in which myths arose whenever and wherever national narrative was perceived through local places and sites. Their meeting grounds appeared and disappeared – in newspapers, in the streets, in the long series of formalized events connected to the war – not as distinct separations between home and country, but as interconnected communicated exchanges. Elias's court and country dancers model helps to explain these patterns, which people conformed to, or challenged, on local levels. Remembrance rituals, however, conformed to the roles assigned for soldiers as valiant volunteers, for their fallen comrades, and for the supreme sacrifice that the entire nation bore witness to and was now destined to prosper from.

The 'National' and the 'Local': Reciprocal Linkages and Structured Sentiments

Home front life in our three cities cannot, then, be sealed into units of solely city-based relationships between individuals and groups in close spatial contact that operated apart from the complex and reciprocal ties extending throughout and beyond Canada. As a country at war, Canada's military procedures, backed by the authority and force of the state, attracted the support of broad elements across local populations and raised ordinary expectations that coercive measures would be applied: of arrest, censorship, or confinement for specific acts of transgression or non-compliance. Relationships between Ottawa's directives and city life, to use another illustration from Elias, could be placed on a social chessboard:

> The fact that each act of a ruler, while perhaps closest to the ideal picture of an individual act based on free decision, makes the ruler dependent on the ruled through being directed at other people who could either oppose it or at least not respond in the expected way. This is exactly what the concept of interdependence expresses. As in a game of chess, each relatively independent act by an individual represents a move on the social chessboard which produces a counter-move by another individual – or frequently in reality, by many other individuals – which limits the independence of the first and demonstrates his dependence.[11]

Neither equivalent nor balanced, reciprocal ties nevertheless constrained numerous parties in ways seldom apparent to contemporaries. Oftentimes they simply saw themselves acting on the basis of 'proper' conduct, 'duty-bound' imperatives, or to further interests that intersected with their naturalized sense of ethnocultural, class-based, or gendered being. This approach to home front boundaries is more useful in conceptualizing how local populations understood and reacted to shifting configurations of power and identity than are simplistic dichotomies between local life and national conditions, between individual lives set against the supposedly anonymous, supra-individual forces operating under the sign of 'Canada,' the 'Empire,' or 'the war' itself.

In local settings, people used the most available and convenient sites to construct experiences and to develop interpretations of the war overseas and the one at home. Public rallies, parades, city newspapers, schools, churches, exhibition parks, or railway station platforms, to note some common ones, were appropriated in purposive ways to convey particular meanings at particular moments. Through exchanges of discourse and action, hometown experiences of the Great War produced a synchronic sense of local events and distant struggles. Many strands of memory and experience came together. Their liminal potential derived from the power they held to change people's sense of history and their place within it. The send-off ritualizations, fundraising drives, press rumours of German-American invasion, editorials for and against conscription, war relief meetings and rallies, and government inquiries that this book considers each served to situate contemporaries in local contexts of communicative exchange that exercised their orientations toward an imaginary view of the war, the surrounding social world, and history itself.

Social boundaries, both new and reconfigured, appeared wherever and whenever Canadians came to believe that their collective and individual responses mattered and were transforming their local lives. In turn, heroic ideals of military masculinity, hierarchical views of charitable duty, demonized views of the enemy, gendered views of civilian war relief, conflicting views of the authority of the state to impose conscription, or veterans' views of their rights took shape in situations that deployed, through local means, broader signs of social difference. Few Canadians could escape their influences entirely, effects that often, in terms of immediate sensation and understanding, overlapped and reinforced each other. 'One does not,' as Elias puts it, 'understand a melody by considering each of its notes in isolation, unrelated to the other notes.'[12] The structuring of both feelings and perceptions took place through symbol systems used on sites formed by generalized horizons of expectation and locally integrated means of comprehension. 'Its structure too is nothing other than the structure *between* different notes'

– between, in our cases, the contrapuntal interplay of wartime signs and practices that circulated across the country, but converged at focal points that were local, parochial in style, and often intense as displays of aural and visual stimuli.

In Lethbridge, for instance, the scene of the departure of the 25th Field Battery soon after the outbreak of hostilities prompted a rite-of-passage ritualization, where visible and audible signs – the red, white, and blue bunting put up by the Overseas Club, the music of the Citizen's Band, Major Stewart's laudatory introductions of each recruit – engaged the expectations and cheering of the assembled audience. As the recruits marched to the CPR platform, the 'band played several musical selections and escorted the party to the station, where the largest crowd ever assembled out-of-doors in Lethbridge waited to say the good-byes and God-speeds. Members of the battery were carried aloft on the shoulders of their comrades, and cheer after cheer followed them down the platform. The reservists were also the property of their friends and relatives during the last few moments. When the train pulled in the special coach was ready, and the crowd prepared for the final wrench that would take their heroes away.'[13]

Such encounters between civilian families and well-wishers and the officers and men, recast in comparable forms across Canada at this time, initiated patterns of exchange that structured the liminality of civilian-to-soldier transitions as a 'dance' staged for the hometown crowds as much as for the troops themselves. They contributed to the myth of volunteer, and they proffered a sentimental education for civilians and soldiers through displays that served to blur distinctions between the real and the imaginary in what was taking place on these and on similar sites across the country. And yet the lenses used to see wartime conditions through or with, in many cases, offered little more than fictions, however potent, pervasive, and enduring. Appealing or grotesque stereotypes of armed conflict, from the 'heroes' who left for the front to the enemy they were to have faced, did not merely circulate in the public domain, they were constructed on its many surfaces. Actual events elsewhere, especially overseas, could not be understood apart from eagerly sought news of war; information and images that moved through local populations as communicating currencies, though their value, authority, or meanings could not be fixed, especially by veterans who saw such different wars from such different places.

Nonetheless, sensational signs and stories dominated almost all others at home. In functionally distinct yet corresponding ways, the demonizations of the enemy signalled by the 'clever discourses' of Archdeacon Cody at St. James Anglican in Guelph or Professor Wrong at a Canadian Club gathering, also in Guelph, conformed to the patterned expectations of audiences predisposed to respond to certain cues, to stereotypes of the German 'character,' for instance, delivered through what the *Mercury* depicted as the compelling presence and logic of these speakers. Similarly, the donations l'abbé Larsimont received in response to his sensational narrative of captivity in the hands of the Germans invading the diocèse de Tournai reflected how the flexible genre of public oration meshed effectively with the vernacular context of a Mass held before a congregation at the Cathédrale of Trois-Rivières in January 1915.

Sometimes stark lines of conflict could be construed, displayed, attacked, or defended. The public drama of the Guelph raid unfolded as a sequence of events that, at their climax, prompted a defence of conscription on the part of Protestant clerics, obviously concerned with how loopholes or the 'fine print' of the Military Service Act might be exploited against what they saw as the fundamental intent of this law. To cite other examples, advocates of the conscription of wealth in Lethbridge, veteran-patients at the Speedwell hospital in Guelph, or the editor Joseph Barnard commenting in Trois-Rivières on conscription each presented claims in relation to certain reciprocities they imagined between themselves and others that impinged on their social identities as wage-earners, as westerners, as veterans, or as a French-Catholic voice against compulsory military service.

Fluid Spaces: The Double Character of Wartime Discourses

Crucial to these claims were the exclusionary practices themselves, operations that proceeded as cultural trajectories from prior differences 'external to discourse,' as Roger Chartier has framed it, 'that characterize the various groups, communities, and classes making up the social world.'[14] What Elias modelled as the configurations between dancers and their dances, we approach here as pluralities of military-civilian relations expressed within particular social spheres made, re-made, and challenged on hometown sites. In the confines of hometown experience, common interests, histories, and expectations were expressed through localized vehicles, social networks, or texts. From recruits to enemy aliens, from middle-class, female, war relief workers to working-class, male, home guardsmen, from veterans to civilians, each group was present at its own making and deployed cultural modes to separate its fields of activity in order to structure its experiences accordingly. Given the departures from routine the war accentuated, these efforts often led to stark boundaries and differences. As Chartier observed: 'What any history must think about is thus the *difference* that all societies bring into play (using various figures) to separate a particular domain of human activity from daily routine.'[15] The cultural making of groups set apart from others, of recruits, of fundraising hierarchies, of enemy aliens, of civilian masculinities and femininities, or of compliances and resistances to state authority, each brought differences of history and identity into play.

Volunteers, enemy aliens, war relief organizers, home guardsmen, and veterans were produced by an international war, but their appearances were constantly communicated on vernacular sites that operated as capillaries connecting the signs and forces of external events to the immediacy of local social networks and cultural vehicles, from city newspapers to public events staged on familiar spaces. Each group used locally displayed configurations borrowed from pre-existing repertoires of structured communication, from street parades and patriotic concerts to lectures and organizational meetings. Local groups, alliances, and interests created and applied these modes in urban contexts to display particular affiliations and commonalities as an assertion of contrasts, distinctiveness, and power. As exclusionary practices, each depended on the presence of outsiders. Recruits were separated from civilians; signs of the enemy alien introduced new cleavages between affected 'foreigners' and the 'host' society; middle-class volunteers and many war relief donors proffered a sense of duty through efforts that intersected with gendered, ethnocentric, and class-based ideals of social hierarchy and power; positions on compulsory military service divided Canadians, sometimes acrimoniously, given loyalties or ambivalences to an imperial war, class positions, regional alienation, or religious affiliation; veterans vented their frustrations in actions that often reinforced their sense of solidarity and distinctiveness. Contrasts and conflicts caused or accentuated by the war engendered locally displayed signs of separation that made social differences visible, tangible, and immediate, though in different forms and for different purposes throughout the war's changing chronology.

As fresh troops paraded, as speeches warning of the dangers of the enemy were delivered, or as ex-soldiers encountered an anxious public at war's end, onlookers, audiences, and readers frequently used experience-near concepts and referents to apprehend the experience-distant terrains of an imagined war. Through these windows, patriotic campaigns took shape as thinly veiled auto-representations of social hierarchies; fears of enemy aliens circulated through referents of geographical proximities to invasion, sabotage, or espionage; a public drama in Guelph prompted debates over the legitimate boundaries of state authority; and city newspapers routinely circulated negative images of the returned soldier just when ex-troops began returning home in larger numbers. The power of such proximate modes of communication flowed from their effects, their capacities to invoke perceptions of dissimilarities and conflict in civilian-military relations across the series of encounters this book has considered.

During the fighting itself, control over the use of violence acquired new legitimacies in the hands of soldiers overseas or in the coercive practices that enemy aliens became subject to at home. Throughout the war, the broader contexts of external events and processes remained in a constant state of flux and re-presentation. Whether considering distances invoked by gender, ethnic, class, or age differences, we cannot disengage communication exchanges and social differentiation from the war's changing chro-

15 The war has ended. This photograph captures a passing trade union's float, 'Local 34' of the Bell Piano and Organ Company in Guelph. This first Armistice Day parade in Guelph helped start a long tradition. Victory celebrations – like this one in November 1918 and like the exuberant Peace Day that marked the Treaty of Versailles nearly a year later – soon gave way to new, more subdued annual rites: of assembled veterans, of somber buglers playing 'The Last Post,' and of recitations of John McCrae's 'In Flanders Fields.' *Courtesy of Guelph Museums, 990.2.2*

nology. It quickly became impossible, after August 1914, for there to be any stability and regularity in how the war was perceived or how specific segments in society might respond to it. Its duration itself was a daunting revelation: the short campaigns and swift victories expected at the outset escalated into the protracted carnage that dragged on for over fifty months. What many had thought a justifiable war at its beginning eventually became, for some, a senseless slaughter. A voluntary war became a war of compulsory military service and of increased state intervention. A manful war of movement and action became a fundamentally static, defensive war as entire divisions remained pinned down for months under barrages of industrially manufactured shells, bullets, and chlorine gas canisters. What many hoped would prove a cleansing struggle of social, moral, religious, and political redemption was followed by a significant period of social dislocation, from the challenging scale of veteran re-establishment to conflicts between labour and capital that intensified in 1919 at a time when almost as many lives were being lost to influenza (50,000 across Canada) as the trenches had consumed (some 51,678 Canadians were killed in action or died of wounds throughout the war).

These broad and often disillusioning gaps between battle reports, casualty lists, and collapsing expectations of a swift victory served as backdrops that constantly reset the local frames through which fresh news from the front were viewed. Hometown horizons frequently confined how the fighting overseas came to be imagined at different stages: the *Mercury's* coverage, for example, of the first use of chlorine gas at Ypres established a series of shifting images that circulated locally, situated within actual contextual shifts in Ottawa or overseas of anticipated victory giving way to heavy losses, of volunteerism giving way to state intervention. Support for Canada's participation in a British and European-centred war was soon undermined as home front populations beat a hasty retreat to the competing affiliations of region, class, and nationality.

Redirecting our reading of war toward the local helps us understand how it was experienced, not how it was caused. While the assassination at Sarajevo in June 1914 can be understood as a catalytic incident that set off the chain reaction ushering in Germany's march through Belgium – the result of the system of diplomatic alliances and coexistent histories of militarism, nationalism, and imperialism – it is equally true that the responses that followed cannot be blocked out simply as a story of various empires entering the war. As Jay Winter has put it, the 'human dimension' of the war was something 'expressed through collective life at the local level.'[16] The experience of being part of a national home front always occurs, in part, as localized, individualized, and particular sentiments and knowledge formations. The complex junctures between personal and pervasive forces are framed in unique ways, as recent approaches to life-writing make clear. But their meanings –how in larger terms local populations use hometown horizons to make sense of a distant war – are necessarily derived in relation to contexts that move backward in time or stretch across much wider places.

Communicative exchanges that deployed particular symbols as models of and models for popular perceptions on the home front seldom operated in our cases as simple two-way mirrors, producing and reproducing interpretations of reality in identical ways across contrasting social domains. Such ruptures often proved significant. Local patterns, for instance, of voluntary recruitment, of fundraising projects, of reactions by or against enemy aliens, of attitudes toward compulsory military service, or of efforts to re-establish returned soldiers varied according to local conditions and the indeterminate responses of active subjects. Historical change, in such cases, can be located in cleavages that developed within particular groups, gatherings, or communities as perceptions shifted and rearranged themselves through the agency of their members.

The double character of such communication was not a closed system but an open one, a force for change rather than for stability. Pronounced

16 Peace Day, 19 July 1919, which marked the signing of the Treaty of Versailles, inspired a series of parades and other victory demonstrations across Canada. This photograph foregrounds a float, jointly constructed by the Sons of England and Kentish Men's Society of Lethbridge as a victory ship, celebrating imperial Germany's final and unconditional surrender. *Courtesy of Sir Alexander Galt Museum and Archives, P19760209061*

gaps and transformations often flowed from disjunctures between efforts to explain realities external to local life and attempts to impose such interpretations on others. As we have seen, the Canadian Patriotic Fund, as a voluntary, charitable fundraising organization, secured its endorsements, waged its campaigns, and policed its disbursements through its own particular auto-representations of social hierarchy – its own model of society that served as its own template for an ideal world. It was, however, a view of social relations and class-based obligations by no means shared by families that actually received allowances. Conscription, too, became a contested issue in localized domains, where pre-existing social networks appropriated particular vehicles – a constituency contest, a series of forceful editorials, an unusual public drama – within their own sense of broader, national movements either to endorse or to oppose government authority and legislated action. Top-down, core-periphery approaches to the imposition of state authority tend to override and oversimplify the actual processes by which different social settings and sites configured contrasting reactions to state procedures. Instead, as Elias has described it, long-term processes by which modern state procedures have been contained, if not regularized, within nation-state and international relations of conflict or cooperation depend crucially on activating local populations in communicative exchanges whose instruments are symbolic in form and cultural in force.

Public Spaces: From Send-Offs to Remembering the War Dead

During send-off ceremonies of countless and varied forms across Canada, large crowds gathered in Guelph and Lethbridge to witness their units at patriotic rallies or on parade in motions of departure, both dramatic and significantly large. And yet, when a group of fellow office workers from the Wayagamack Pulp and Paper Company, after commandeering a company tugboat, unfurled a banner for R.A. Gillis, believed to be abroad the SS *Missanabie,* then moving downstream toward the Gulf of St. Lawrence, their much smaller local ritual very likely held comparable significance for this small group as they shouted and waved to a man they did not even appear to see that afternoon.[17] Whether a concert in support of Belgian refugees in Trois-Rivières or a rummage sale in Guelph in support of the Red Cross, public events large and small helped to inscribe a shifting sense of the imperatives and consequences of a war that few anticipated would last so long or cost so much.[18] When, as late as January 1915, the *Bien Public* in Trois-Rivières continued to print reports of escalating German-American militarism south of the border, this paper simply reinforced what other city dailies across the country were also actively doing – demonizing the enemy through sensationalized reports that helped to sell papers while fuelling local anxieties.

At stake, then, were attempts to configure the cultural norms and social habitus of home front populations through horizons of experience and expectation that drew connections between their objective, immediate situations and the wider contexts of a war seen largely through public domain representations. At stake, also, were symbolic efforts to affirm, or to negate, the social identities of various social groups affected by wartime realities, efforts that depended on localized signs of the divisions of a wider social world affected by the prosecution of the war. Recruits, civilian men and women, enemy aliens, conscription supporters and opponents, and veterans each appeared through their capacities on local levels to ensure recognition of their own histories and identities. Affirmations of any particular group's social being depended on the credence given to its messages, often strategically developed images or symbols. What was sensed and what was believed circulated first through the most usable, local vehicles, the most understood and thus vernacular of situations or cultural spaces, from city dailies to public events. From the call to the colours in August 1914 to the Armistice, localized modes of representing wartime signs were appropriated in multiple contexts to do their most political work: to delineate identities and boundaries constituted as a result of wartime conditions.

By the end of the war, as early as December 1918 as the case of the Lethbridge veterans' banquet suggests, local ritualizations that commemorated the war dead and the returned were staged to displace the realities of the carnage overseas with the narratives of an ideal past, stories of the war as a great and noble sacrifice. The veterans themselves participated in such myth-memory making quite publicly during the annual rites of 11 November. In the process, an awareness of the past as actually lived, as suffered in the toll either at the front or through the lives of returned men, began its silent disappearance. Gradually, war's harshest realities became eclipsed by the effects of the cyclical production and consumption of its most persuasive symbols and usable commemorations. At such points, as when the Rev. Dennon spoke of a greater and more independent Canada in which 'those ideals might be fulfilled,' new sites were being created for future dreams. Set apart from the everyday flow of peacetime lives and, eventually, the return of war, their signs and languages framed narratives in which remembering and forgetting the Great War could become one and the same.

Notes

Introduction

1 Eric Hobsbawm, *Age of Extremes: The Short Twentieth Century, 1914-1918* (London: Abacus, 1994). See also Hobsbawm, *The Age of Empire, 1870-1914* (New York: Pantheon Books, 1987).

2 Hobsbawm, *Age of Extremes*, 23.

3 Guelph *Evening Mercury*, 25 December 1917, 1 and 2.

4 Lethbridge *Daily Herald*, 13 August 1917, 1.

5 Roger Chartier, *On the Edge of the Cliff: History, Language, and Practices*, trans. Lydia G. Cochrane (Baltimore and London: Johns Hopkins University Press, 1997), 5. Joan Scott's seminal essay first appeared in 1991 and has stimulated a wide range of reponses, particularly from post-structuralists, their critics, and feminist scholars. A recent critique appears in Michael Pickering, *History, Experience and Cultural Studies* (New York: St. Martin's Press, 1997), esp. ch. 7. See Joan Scott, 'The Evidence of Experience,' *Critical Inquiry* 17 (1991): 773-97.

6 Desmond Morton and J.L. Granatstein, *Marching to Armageddon: Canadians and the Great War, 1914-1919* (Toronto: Lester and Orpen Dennys, 1989); J.L. Granatstein and J.M. Hitsman, *Broken Promises: A History of Conscription in Canada* (Oxford: Oxford University Press, 1977); Desmond Morton, *A Peculiar Kind of Politics: Canada's Overseas Ministry in the First World War* (Toronto: University of Toronto Press, 1982); Desmond Morton and Glenn Wright, *Winning the Second Battle: Canadian Veterans and the Return to Civilian Life, 1915-1930* (Toronto: University of Toronto Press, 1987); Desmond Morton, *When Your Number's Up: The Canadian Soldier in the First World War* (Toronto: Random House, 1993).

7 John Herd Thompson, *The Harvests of War: The Prairie West, 1914-1918* (Toronto: McClelland and Stewart, 1974); Elizabeth Armstrong, *The Crisis of Quebec, 1914-1918* (1937; reprint, Toronto: McClelland and Stewart, 1974); Donald Avery, *'Dangerous Foreigners': European Immigrant Workers and Labour Radicalism in Canada, 1896-1932* (Toronto: McClelland and Stewart, 1979); Howard Palmer, *Patterns of Prejudice: A History of Nativism in Alberta* (Toronto: McClelland and Stewart, 1982); Bill Waiser, *Park Prisoners: The Untold Story of Western Canada's National Parks, 1915-1946* (Saskatoon: Fifth House, 1995); Jean-Pierre Gagnon, *Le 22e Bataillon (canadien-français), 1914-1919: Étude socio-militaire* (Quebec: Presses de l'Université Laval, 1986); Paul Maroney, '"The Great Adventure": The Context and Ideology of Recruiting in Ontario, 1914-17,' *Canadian Historical Review* 77 (1996): 62-98.

8 A.F. Duguid, *Official History of the Canadian Forces in the Great War, 1914–1919*, vol. 1 (Ottawa: King's Printer, 1938); G.W.L. Nicholson, *Canadian Expeditionary Force, 1914-1919: The Official History of the Canadian Army in the First World War* (Ottawa: Queen's Printer, 1962); C.P. Stacey, *Canada and the Age of Conflict*, vol. 1, *1867-1921* (Toronto: Macmillan, 1977); Stephen J. Harris, *Canadian Brass: The Making of a Professional Army, 1860-1939* (Toronto: University of Toronto Press, 1988); Desmond Morton, *A Military History of Canada* (1985; reprint, Toronto: McClelland and Stewart, 1992).

9 Morton and Granatstein, *Marching to Armageddon*, 1.

10 Jonathan F. Vance, *Death So Noble: Memory, Meaning and the First World War* (Vancouver: UBC Press, 1997), 266.

11 Ibid. On the uses of wartime social memories of the war in Europe see also George L. Mosse, *Fallen Soldiers: Reshaping the Memory of the World Wars* (Oxford: Oxford University Press, 1990), and Jay Winter, *Sites of Memory, Sites of Mourning: The Great War in European Cultural History* (Cambridge: Cambridge University Press, 1995).

12 Eric J. Leed, *No Man's Land: Combat and Identity in World War I* (Cambridge: Cambridge University Press, 1979); Paul Fussell, *The Great War and Modern Memory* (New York: Oxford University Press, 1975). On home front propaganda see Peter Buitenhuis, *The Great War of Words: British, American, and Canadian Propaganda and Fiction, 1914-1933* (Vancouver: UBC Press, 1987), and Jeffrey A. Keshen, *Propaganda and Censorship in Canada's Great War* (Edmonton: University of Alberta Press, 1996). Margaret R. Higonnet et al., eds., *Behind the Lines: Gender and the Two World Wars* (New Haven: Yale University Press, 1987); Miriam Cooke and Angela Woollacott, eds., *Gendering War Talk* (Princeton: Princeton University Press, 1993), and Billie Melman, ed., *Borderlines: Genders and Identities in War and Peace, 1870-1930* (New York: Routledge, 1998) each present useful collections on women, gender, and the war. In *Dismembering the Male: Men's Bodies, Britain, and the Great War* (Chicago: University of Chicago Press, 1996), Joanna Bourke offered an innovative approach by locating shifts in gender boundaries in a cultural history of men's bodies in Britain during and after the war.

13 Richard Wall and Jay Winter, eds., *The Upheaval of War: Family, War and Welfare in Europe, 1914-1918* (Cambridge: Cambridge University Press. 1988), and Jay Winter and Jean-Louis Robert, eds., *Capital Cities at War: Paris, London, Berlin, 1914-1919* (Cambridge: Cambridge University Press, 1997).

14 Winter and Robert, eds., *Capital Cities at War*, 3-4.

15 Ibid., 4-5.

16 Ibid., 5.

17 Ibid., 3-5.

18 Clifford Geertz, *The Interpretation of Cultures: Selected Essays* (New York: Basic Books, 1973), 22.

19 *Newcomer*, 23 June 1915, 2.

Chapter 1: Places and Sites

1 Ringuet, *Trente Arpents* (1938; reprint, Montreal: Fides, 1969), 154. '"I'll have to go, Mr. Moisan," he realized that what was happening over there, so far away from them, had reached out to a quiet Quebec parish and there touched a peaceable man who, seemingly, had never wanted to harm anybody, who had never coveted either his neighbour's land or his house. He understood then that war meant going away. His own sons wouldn't have to go, since it had nothing to do with them. But things might be different in the case of this fellow here, who had never been altogether one of them – and that in spite of the twelve years he had lived with them on this thirty-acre strip of farmland.' Ringuet, *Thirty Acres*, with an Afterword by Antoine Sirois (Toronto: McClelland and Stewart, 1989), 150.

For a recent collection of studies on Philippe Panneton's (Ringuet's) life and work see Jean-Paul Lamy and Guildo Rousseau, eds., *Ringuet en mémoire: 50 ans après* Trente Arpents (Quebec: Pélican/Septentrion, 1989).

2 For a comparative study of agricultural and economic development in the two regions see John McCallum, *Unequal Beginnings: Agriculture and Economic Development in Quebec and Ontario until 1870* (Toronto: University of Toronto Press, 1980).

3 Réne Hardy and Normand Séguin, *Forêt et société en Mauricie: la formation de la région de Trois-Rivières 1830-1930* (Montreal: Boréal Express, 1984), 204. See also Jacques Belleau, 'L'industrialisation de Trois-Rivières, 1905-1925' (Master's thesis, Université du Québec à Trois-Rivières, 1979); Normand Brouillette, 'Le développement industriel d'une région du proche hinterland québécois: la Mauricie, 1900-1975' (PhD thesis, McGill University, 1983); and Alain Dion, 'L'industrie des pâtes et papiers en Mauricie, 1887-1929' (Master's thesis, Université du Québec à Trois-Rivières, 1981). For useful introductions to *Annales* approaches,

see Traian Stoianovich, *French Historical Method: The Annales Paradigm* (Ithaca, NY: Cornell University Press, 1976); and Guy Bourdé and Hervé Martin, *Les Ecoles historiques* (Paris: Editions du Seuil, 1983).

4 *Fifth Census of Canada 1911* (Ottawa: King's Printer, 1913), vol. 3, Table 11, 354.

5 Ibid., vol. 2, Table 2, 130 and 146.

6 Trois-Rivières's Roman Catholic parishes before 1914 were Immaculée Conception (est. 1678), St-Phillipe (1909), Notre-Dame-des Sept-Allégresses (1911), and Ste-Cécile (1912).

7 A useful introductory text on urban history in Trois-Rivières, which includes useful maps and numerous historical illustrations and photographs, is Alain Gamelin et al., *Trois-Rivières illustrée* (Trois-Rivières: La Corporation des fêtes du 350e anniversaire de Trois-Rivières, 1984). For more specialized studies see also Hélène Desnoyers, 'Le Logement ouvrier à Trois-Rivières 1845-1945: l'exemple du secteur Hertel' (Master's thesis, Université du Québec à Trois-Rivières, 1988).

8 See André Beaulieu and Jean Hamelin, *La presse québécoise: des origines à nos jours*, tome quatrième, *1896-1910* (Quebec: Les Presses de l'Université Laval, 1979), 310-11. Beaulieu and Hamelin incorrectly cite 4 November 1902 as the termination date for the *Courrier*. On the *Bien Public* see also William F. Ryan, *The Clergy and Economic Growth in Quebec, 1896-1914* (Quebec: Les Presses de l'Université Laval, 1966), 99.

9 Jean Hamelin and Nicole Gagnon, *Histoire du catholicisme québécois*, vol. 1, *1898-1940* (Montreal: Boréal, 1984), 209-12. Hamelin and Gagnon cite *La Vérité*, *L'Action sociale* (*L'action catholique* after 1915), *Bien Public*, *Le Droit*, *L'Action populaire*, *Le Progrès du Saguenay*, and *Le Messager du Sherbrooke* as leading Catholic newspapers. In their general survey of Quebec's history from Confederation to the Great Depression, Paul-André Linteau, René Durocher, and Jean-Claude Robert underscore the importance of the 'Catholic press' or 'la bonne presse' as a major disseminator of clerical-nationalism. 'The best known of these newspapers,' they observe, 'was undoubtedly *Le Devoir* of Montreal, founded in 1910 by Henri Bourassa.' See Paul-André Linteau, René Durocher, and Jean-Claude Robert, *Quebec: A History, 1867-1929*, trans. Robert Chodos (Toronto: Lorimer, 1983), 538.

10 Hamelin and Gagnon, *Histoire du catholicisme québécois*, vol. 1, 211.

11 Beaulieu and Hamelin, *La presse québécoise*, vol. 4, 310-11.

12 Ryan, *Clergy and Economic Growth in Quebec*, 99.

13 L.-J.-A. Derome, *Le Canada ecclésiastique: almanach annuaire du clergé canadien, 1917* (Montreal: Librairie Beauchemin, 1917), 87.

14 On the history of militia units in Trois-Rivières see Hélène Desnoyers, *12e régiment blindé du Canada: la milice canadienne et le 12e régiment blindé du Canada* (Trois-Rivières: Le 12e Régiment Blindé du Canada, 1988). On the cadet movement at this time see Desmond Morton, 'The Cadet Movement in the Moment of Canadian Militarism, 1909-1914,' *Journal of Canadian Studies* 13 (1978): 56-68, and Mike O'Brien, 'Manhood and the Militia Myth: Masculinity, Class, and Militarism in Ontario, 1902-1914,' *Labour/Le Travail* 42 (1998): 115-41.

15 See the *Bien Public*, 4 June 1914, 8, and 11 June 1914, 1; and the *Nouveau Trois-Rivières*, 3 July 1914, 4, and 10 July 1914, 3.

16 *Bien Public*, 18 June 1914, 1.

17 *Nouveau Trois-Rivières*, 3 July 1914, 8; *Courrier*, 3 July 1914, 8.

18 The command 'a causé une vive sensation parmi les soldats et les officiers catholiques du camp des Trois-Rivières.' *Nouveau Trois-Rivières*, 10 July 1914, 3.

19 *Courrier*, 17 July 1914, 1.

20 Ibid., 26 June 1914, 1.

21 *Bien Public*, 26 June 1914, 1.

22 *Newcomer*, 16 September 1914, 1.

23 Population for 1840 is cited in Leo A. Johnson, *History of Guelph 1827-1927* (Guelph: Guelph Historical Society, 1977), 30. Canada's national census of 1911 provided the later figure. See *Fifth Census of Canada, 1911*, vol. 2, 431.

24 As quoted in Johnson, *History of Guelph*, 13.

25 The proportions for Ontario as a whole in 1911 stood at: Methodist (26.6 percent), Presbyterian (20.8 percent), Anglican (19.4 percent), and Roman Catholic (19.2 percent).

26 Higinbotham's romantic account of growing up in Guelph and making an adult life as a pharmacist in Lethbridge is found in *When the West Was Young: Historical Reminiscences of the Early Canadian West* (Toronto: Ryerson Press, 1933). This excerpt appears on p. 20.
27 On the role of the Galt family in economic development in this region see Andrew A. den Otter, *Civilizing the West: The Galts and the Development of Western Canada* (Edmonton: University of Alberta Press, 1982).
28 On the social consequence of drought and setbacks in the failed experiment in dryland farming in this period see David C. Jones, *Empire of Dust: Settling and Abandoning the Prairie Dry Belt* (Edmonton: University of Alberta Press, 1987).
29 See J.R. Miller, *Skyscrapers Hide the Heavens: A History of Indian-White Relations in Canada* (Toronto: University of Toronto Press, 1991), ch. 9, for an overview of Canada's numbered treaties from 1871 to 1921. Treaty 7, covering most of present-day southern Alberta, was made effective in 1877. On the region's ethnohistory in the fur trade era see Theodore Binnema, 'Old Swan, Big Man, and Siksika Bands, 1784-1815,' *Canadian Historical Review* 77 (1996): 1-32.
30 Cited in Alex Johnston and Andy A. den Otter, *Lethbridge: A Centennial History* (Lethbridge: City of Lethbridge and Fort Whoop-Up County Chapter, Historical Society of Lethbridge, 1985), 25.
31 Ibid., 40.
32 Higinbotham, *When the West Was Young*, 113.
33 See Alan F.J. Artibise, 'Boosterism and the Development of Prairie Cities,' in *The Prairie West: Historical Readings*, ed. R. Douglas Francis and Howard Palmer (Edmonton: University of Alberta Press, 1992), 511-543.
34 In absolute terms, male-to-female totals stood as follows: Trois-Rivières, 6,493 to 7,198; Guelph, 7,408 to 7,767; Lethbridge, 4,462 to 3,588.
35 Howard Palmer, *Patterns of Prejudice: A History of Nativism in Alberta* (Toronto: McClelland and Stewart, 1982).
36 W.L. Morton, 'A Century of Plain and Parkland,' in *The Prairie West: Historical Readings*, ed. R. Douglas Francis and Howard Palmer (Edmonton: University of Alberta Press, 1992), 28.
37 Higinbotham, *When the West Was Young*, 76.
38 See, for example, Elizabeth Vibert, *Trader's Tales: Narratives of Cultural Encounters on the Columbian Plateau, 1807-1846* (Norman: University of Oklahoma Press, 1987).
39 Higinbotham, *When the West Was Young*, 180.
40 Johnston and den Otter, *Lethbridge: A Centennial History*, 95.
41 Ibid., 82 and 97.
42 Cited in ibid., 84.
43 Cited in ibid., 85.
44 Cited in ibid., 86.
45 On race and recruitment, for instance, see James W. St. G. Walker, 'Race and Recruitment in World War I: Enlistment of Visible Minorities in the Canadian Expeditionary Force,' *Canadian Historical Review* 70 (1989): 1-26.
46 *Lethbridge Daily Herald*, 3 August 1914, 7.
47 J. Castell Hopkins, *Canada at War: A Record of Heroism and Achievement, 1914-1918* (Toronto: Canadian Annual Review, 1919), 33.
48 *Guelph Evening Mercury*, 5 August 1914, 1.
49 Hopkins, *Canada at War*, 33-4.
50 *Newcomer*, 12 August 1914, 1.
51 *Bien Public*, 13 August 1914, 8. Jacques Bureau served as a member of Parliament. A Rev. M.R. Clark is identified, though this was likely Rev. J. Aitken Clark of St. Andrew's Presbyterian church.
52 Gordon A. Craig, *Europe Since 1914* (1961; rev. ed., New York: Holt, Rinehart and Winston, 1966), 509.
53 *Lethbridge Daily Herald*, 5 August 1914, 1 and 6.
54 Roger Chartier, 'Text, Symbols and Frenchness,' *Journal of Modern History* 57 (1985): 685.

55 Robert Darnton, 'The Symbolic Element in History,' *Journal of Modern History* 58 (1986): 227-28. See also Darnton's *The Great Cat Massacre and Other Episodes in French Cultural History* (New York: Basic Books, 1984).

56 Along with the French, English, and Irish said to have marched together in Quebec City above, the *Manitoba Free Press* reported from Winnipeg that 'the patriotism was so contagious it inspired everyone on the streets whether or not they were British subjects. Americans, Swedes, Norwegians, Chinese, marched with the rest and joined their voices in the cheering. Even the ladies were represented, many marching with their escorts and some even joining in the singing and cheering.' See *Manitoba Free Press*, 5 August 1914, 3. The *Toronto Star* referred to 'many ladies that watched the bulletins.' See *Toronto Star*, 5 August 1914, 5.

57 References to young and older men together on the streets were quite common. 'Amongst the crowd' in Ottawa, ran one report, 'were a number of old soldiers with whom young men seemed to take a special delight in talking war.' See *Ottawa Citizen*, 4 August 1914, 10.

58 *Lethbridge Daily Herald*, 5 August 1914, 6.

59 Victor Turner's many writings on liminality, ritual, and social change began, most notably, with the publication of *The Ritual Process: Structure and Anti-Structure* (Chicago: Aldine Publishing, 1969). See also Turner's 'Variations on a Theme of Liminality,' in *Blazing the Trail: Way Marks in the Exploration of Symbols*, ed. Edith Turner (Tucson: University of Arizona Press, 1992), 48-65.

60 James Fentress and Chris Wickham, *Social Memory* (Oxford: Blackwell, 1992).

61 John Bodnar, *Remaking America: Pulic Memory, Commemoration, and Patriotism in the Twentieth Century* (Princeton, NJ: Princeton University Press, 1992).

62 Robert Bocock, *Rituals in Industrial England: A Sociological Analysis of Ritualism in Modern England* (London: George Allen and Unwin, 1974), 9.

63 See Edmund Leach, *Culture and Communication: The Logic By Which Symbols Are Connected* (Cambridge: Cambridge University Press, 1976).

64 Catherine Bell, *Ritual Theory, Ritual Practice* (New York: Oxford University Press, 1992), 197.

Chapter 2: Dancing before Death

1 For a synchronic approach to Berlin at this time see Modris Eksteins, *Rites of Spring: The Great War and the Birth of the Modern Age* (Toronto: Lester and Orpen Dennys, 1989), 55-64.

2 Frederick George Scott, *The Great War As I Saw It* (Vancouver: Clarke and Stuart, 1934), 15-6.

3 See, for example, Desmond Morton, *When Your Number's Up: The Canadian Soldier in the First World War* (Toronto: Random House of Canada 1993), 9. Ilana R. Bet-El underscores the point for Britain in 'Men and Soldiers: British Conscripts, Concepts of Masculinity, and the Great War,' in *Borderlines: Genders and Identities in War and Peace, 1870-1930*, ed. Billie Melman (New York: Routledge, 1998), 75.

4 Guelph *Evening Mercury*, 25 September 1914, 8.

5 Lethbridge *Daily Herald*, 18 August 1914, 6.

6 *Nouveau Trois-Rivières*, 27 November 1914, 7.

7 Two mobilization plans were available at the outbreak of the war. The first, completed in 1912 by Col. W.G. Gwatkin, a British general staff officer serving in Canada, called for the organization of regional battalions in each of the nine military divisions and districts across the country. Decentralization and delegating responsibility to divisional and district commanders were key aspects of this plan, with 'each divisional and district area contributing a quota proportionate to its military resources.' See A.F. Duguid, *Official History of the Canadian Forces in the Great War, 1914-1919*, vol. 1 (Ottawa: King's Printer, 1938), app. 11, 'Note on the Overseas Mobilization Scheme 1911-1912.' The second plan, drafted in the spring of 1914 by Lt.-Col. G.C.W. Gordon-Hall, involved even more decentralization, employing existing militia units for the initial concentration and training locations. See Stephen J. Harris, *Canadian Brass: The Making of a Professional Army, 1860-1939* (Toronto: University of Toronto Press, 1988), 93.

8 G.W.L. Nicholson, *Canadian Expeditionary Force, 1914-1919: The Official History of the Canadian Army in the First World War* (Ottawa: Queen's Printer, 1962), 20.

9 Ibid., 18.

10 National Archives of Canada (hereafter NAC), RG 24, Militia and Defence Records, Central Registry Files, vol. 1220, HQ 593-1-5, Instructions for Mobilization War 1914, '9 Night Lettergrams,' 6 August 1914.
11 Ibid., 'Militia Headquarters to All Officers Company Infantry Regiments,' 8 August 1914.
12 Canada's official offer of a second contingent was contained in a telegram dated 6 October 1914 from Canada's governor general to Britain's secretary of state for the colonies, which stated in part: 'The Dominion government offers to place and maintain in the field a second over-sea contingent of twenty thousand men.' See Duguid, *Official History*, 109.
13 Robert Craig Brown and Donald Loveridge suggest that Maj.-Gen. W.G. Gwatkin and Maj.-Gen. Eugene Fiset administered recruitment more competently in Hughes's absence. See Robert Craig Brown and Donald Loveridge, 'Unrequited Faith: Recruiting the C.E.F., 1914-1918,' *Revue Internationale d'Histoire Militaire* 51 (1982): 57.
14 According to the *Official History*, 'The recruiting and mobilization of the First Contingent by mass methods had convinced the Minister of Militia that local preliminary mobilization and training would, for the future, yield more satisfactory results.' See Duguid, *Official History*, 424. Brown and Loveridge have subsequently suggested, 'Perhaps the chaos at Valcartier convinced Hughes that a more systematic approach was necessary.' See Brown and Loveridge, 'Unrequited Faith,' 57.
15 In 'Unrequited Faith,' Brown and Loveridge present an analysis of infantry recruitment that incorporates these phases, though not in the terms used here.
16 Desmond Morton, *When Your Number's Up*, 8-9.
17 Guelph *Evening Mercury*, 8 August 1914, 1.
18 Ilana R. Bet-El, 'Men and Soldiers,' 73.
19 Lethbridge *Daily Herald*, 8 August 1914, 1.
20 Guelph *Evening Mercury*, 8 August 1914, 1.
21 Ibid., 15 August 1914, 1 and 4.
22 Ibid.
23 The use of the militia in parades to symbolize local associations with a military past had become a well-established, frequently rehearsed, invented tradition by the end of the nineteenth century in many countries. See, for instance, from a large literature, Mary Ryan, 'The American Parade: Representations of the Nineteenth-Century Social Order,' in *The New Cultural History*, ed. Lynn Hunt (Berkeley: University of California Press, 1989), 131-53, and Susan G. Davis, *Parades and Power: Street Theatre in Nineteenth-Century Philadelphia* (Philadelphia: Temple University Press, 1986), esp. 49-72.
24 Guelph *Evening Mercury*, 20 August 1914, 1.
25 Ibid., 28 August 1914, 1.
26 Ibid., 20 August 1914, 6.
27 Ibid., 15 August 1914, 1.
28 Of Victor Turner's many writings derived from applications of Arnold Van Gennep's approach to threshold enactments, his 'Variations on a Theme of Liminality' in *Blazing the Trail: Way Marks in the Exploration of Symbols,* ed. Edith Turner, 48-65 (Tucson: University of Arizona Press, 1992), offers a useful indication of different contexts for liminal transformations.
29 Guelph *Evening Mercury*, 20 August 1914, 1.
30 Wellington County Museum-Archives, A983.43, Cliff Allan to Mrs. A.S. Allan, undated, postmarked 21 June 1915.
31 Lethbridge *Daily Herald*, 14 August 1914, 1.
32 Public Archives of Alberta, *The Alberta Club Woman's Blue Book* (n.p.: Calgary Branch of the Canadian Women's Press Club, 1917), 89-91. See also Sir Alexander Galt Archives (hereafter GA), Jack Ross Chapter, IODE, *Forty Years History of Major Jack Ross Chapter, Imperial Order Daughters of the Empire, 1917-1957* (n.p., n.d.), P19800046001.
33 GA, Dr. Alex Johnston, 'Lethbridge and the Militia' (unpublished manuscript). Johnston noted that the battery's first public appearance was on 10 May 1910 when it fired a sixty-eight-gun salute to mark the funeral of King Edward VII.
34 John Bodnar, *Remaking America: Public Memory, Commemoration, and Patriotism in the Twentieth Century* (Princeton: Princeton University Press, 1992), esp. 13-20.

35 NAC, RG 24, Militia and Defence Records, Central Registry Files, vol. 1220, HQ 593-1-5, 'Preliminary Instructions for Mobilization War 1914,' telegram dated 8 August 1914 from Lt.-Col. L.P. Mercier to Adjutant General.
36 *Newcomer*, 19 August 1914, 2. An annual inspection completed by the Department of Militia and Defence in 1913 indicates that, in addition to the officers, the 86th Regiment had 181 non-commissioned officers and newly qualified riflers as well as 12 signalers. See Archives Musée Militaire du 12e Régiment Blindé du Canada, FR KA 2.7, 'Report of the Annual Inspection 1913 of the 86th Regiment (Three Rivers),' 8 September 1913.
37 NAC, RG 24, Militia and Defence Records, Central Registry Files, vol. 1220, HQ 593-1-5, 'Preliminary Instructions for Mobilization War 1914,' telegram dated 8 August 1914 from Lt.-Col. L.P. Mercier to Adjutant General.
38 Lethbridge *Daily Herald*, 14 August 1914, 4.
39 F.H.H. Mewburn, 'The 25 Battery, Canadian Field Artillery' (n.p., 1938).
40 Desmond Morton, *A Military History of Canada* (Edmonton: Hurtig, 1990), 127.
41 Lethbridge *Daily Herald*, 19 August 1914, 4.
42 Eric J. Leed, *No Man's Land: Combat and Identity in World War I* (Cambridge: Cambridge University Press, 1979), 37-72.
43 For a brief history of Gédéon Désilets' exploits in Italy see an account written by his son, Georges, entitled 'Un cinquantenaire mémorable: les zouaves Canadiens et le régiment des zouaves pontificaux,' dated 18 January 1918, in Archives du Séminaire de Trois-Rivières, FN-0356, Fonds Gédéon Désilets, famille.
44 Ibid., Gédéon Désilets à Georges Désilets (son fils), 8 August 1914, 1.
45 See the *Bien Public*, 6 August 1914, 1, and the *Mandements, lettres pastorales et circulaires de S.G. Mgr F.-X. Cloutier*, 3ième Evêque de Trois-Rivières, 1914-1923, vol. 4, (Trois-Rivières, 1923), 38.
46 Archives du Séminaire de Trois-Rivières, FN 0011, Fonds Nérée Beauchemin, unedited manuscript in file 109, calepin no. 16.
47 *Newcomer*, 26 May 1915, 1.
48 *Bien Public*, 26 June 1914, 1.
49 *Nouveau Trois-Rivières*, 10 July 1914, 3. See also ibid., 3 July 1914, 4.
50 Cited in Duguid, *Official History*, 425.
51 An exhaustive historical and statistical analysis of the creation of the 22nd Battalion appears in Chapters 1 and 2 of Jean-Pierre Gagnon's *Le 22e bataillon (canadien-français), 1914-1919: étude socio-militaire* (Quebec: Les Presses de l'Université Laval, 1986), 19-88.
52 Ibid., 33-6.
53 *Newcomer*, 21 October 1914, 4.
54 Gagnon, *Le 22e bataillon*, 356.
55 *Newcomer*, 19 August 1914, 2.
56 Ibid., 30 June 1914, 2.
57 Ibid., 14 July 1915, 2.
58 Ibid., 22 September 1915, 5.
59 Ibid., 23 June 1915, 2.
60 Ibid., 15 September 1915, 5.
61 Ibid., 22 September 1915, 2; 2 November 1915, 3; and 24 November 1915, 3.
62 Ibid., 8 September 1915, 6.
63 Ibid., 24 March 1915, 1, and 1 September 1915, 3.
64 For a concise history of the demise of the 41st Battalion see Desmond Morton, 'The Short, Unhappy Life of the 41st Battalion, CEF,' *Queen's Quarterly* 81 (1974): 70-80.
65 Ibid., 74.
66 *Newcomer*, 5 May 1915, 1.
67 Ibid., 7 July 1915, 2.
68 Ibid., 23 June 1915, 2.
69 Ibid., 1 September 1914, 5.
70 Ibid., 8 September 1915, 1-2.
71 Ibid., 2.
72 Lethbridge *Daily Herald*, 2 November 1914, 1.

73 Ibid., 28 November 1914, 1, and 2 January 1915, 1.
74 Ibid., 19 December 1914, 1, and 11 January 1915, 1.
75 Ibid., 19 February 1915, 1.
76 See GA, World War, 1914-1918, Collections and Documents, P16941307000. Reports of the mock battle exercise and the send-off for the 20th appear in the Lethbridge *Telegram,* 22 April 1915, 1, and 29 April 1915, 1, respectively.
77 Lethbridge *Daily Herald,* 22 May 1914, 1.
78 Lethbridge *Telegram,* 22 April 1915, 1.
79 Guelph *Evening Mercury,* 14 May 1915, 1.
80 Lethbridge *Daily Herald,* 13 October 1915, 1.
81 GA, F.G. Holyoak, *The History of the 39th Battery, Canadian Field Artillery* (1919; reprint, n.p., 1947). Holyoak chronicles the progress of the 39th Battalion from its inception to the honours it received after the war, complete with lists of men promoted, wounded, killed, or struck by illness. He prepared a chapter for its part in each major battle, from Ypres to Cambrai.
82 Ibid., 'In Canada,' 12.
83 Brown and Loveridge, 'Unrequited Faith,' 57.
84 As of 15 February 1916, 62 percent of recruits in the CEF were officially designated as 'British-born in the United Kingdom.' Only 30 percent were classified as 'Native-born Canadians,' with the remaining 8 percent listed as 'Others.' See J. Castell Hopkins, *Canadian Annual Review, 1915,* (Toronto: Canadian Annual Review Company, 1916), 219.
85 Guelph *Evening Mercury,* 20 January 1915, 1.
86 Ibid., 21 June 1915, 1.
87 Ibid., 31 August 1915, 1.
88 Ibid., 1 September 1915, 1.
89 Paul Maroney, '"The Great Adventure": The Context and Ideology of Recruitment in Ontario, 1914-1917,' *Canadian Historical Review* 77 (1996), 78.
90 Guelph *Evening Mercury,* 4 September 1915, 1.
91 Ibid., 7 September 1915, 1.
92 Ibid., 9 September 1915, 1. Women were frequently criticized for discouraging their loved ones from enlisting. In early 1916, for example, the Lethbridge *Daily Herald* placed a special notice in its women's section under the caption 'An Appeal to Young Women.' 'How many young men who should be in khaki are hiding behind skirts?' it asked. 'In other words, how many men are there whose only excuse for not enlisting is that their lady friends do not want them to go?' While women often promoted recruitment through their participation in enlistment campaigns and related organized patriotic efforts, they were still perceived as a potential barrier to manpower mobilization. See Lethbridge *Daily Herald,* 3 February 1916, 5.
93 Guelph *Evening Mercury,* 13 September 1915, 1.
94 The last pre-war census, completed in 1911, reports that 35 percent of Lethbridge's 8,050 inhabitants were born in the British Isles. The corresponding proportion for Guelph is 18.6 percent of 15,175 residents. *Fifth Census of Canada, 1911,* vol. 2 (Ottawa: King's Printer, 1913), 431 (Guelph) and 438 (Lethbridge). Recent poor grain harvests in southern Alberta, combined with a regional recession, prompted the Lethbridge Board of Trade to state in its annual report that 'our development as a city is in many respects farther advanced than the present development of our agricultural resources warrants.' See GA, *Lethbridge Board of Trade, Annual Report 1914,* 5.
95 Enlistments nationally were as follows during this period: August 1915: 17,867; September 1915: 16,722 (down 8 percent from August level); October: 12,877 (down 23 percent from September level). From Nicholson, *Canadian Expeditionary Force, 1914-1919,* Table 1, 546.
96 Of the many published sources that include assessment of recruiting figures on a national level, C.A. Sharpe's 'Enlistment in the Canadian Expeditionary Force, 1914-1918: A Regional Analysis,' *Journal of Canadian Studies/Revue d'études canadiennes* 18 (1983/84) offers the advantage of demonstrating regional variation throughout the war, including the post-conscription period.

97 Ron Haycock, *Sam Hughes: The Public Career of a Controversial Canadian* (Waterloo and Ottawa: Wilfrid Laurier University Press and the Canadian War Museum, 1986), 205.
98 Brown and Loveridge, 'Unrequited Faith,' 59.
99 A fine description of this diversity appears in Desmond Morton and J.L. Granatstein, *Marching to Armageddon: Canadians and the Great War 1914-1919* (Toronto: Lester and Orpen Dennys, 1989), 31-2.
100 Lethbridge *Daily Herald*, 27 November 1915, 1.
101 On Hughes's supportive attitude toward local initiatives see Haycock, *Sam Hughes*, 213.
102 Reprinted in full, Lethbridge *Telegram*, 4 May 1916, 1.
103 Lethbridge *Daily Herald*, 17 November 1915, 1.
104 These front-page articles appeared in the Lethbridge *Daily Herald* from 18 to 29 November 1915.
105 Ibid., 4 December 1915, 1.
106 Ibid., 6 January 1916, 1.
107 Lethbridge *Telegram*, 18 May 1916, 1.
108 Ibid., 4 May 1916, 4.
109 Wellington County Archives, A984.12, R.T. Pritchard, *The 153rd Battalion, Canadian Expeditionary Force* (n.p., 1938), 7.
110 Ibid.
111 Ibid.
112 Brown and Loveridge, 'Unrequited Faith,' 60.
113 Lethbridge *Telegram*, 10 June 1915, 1.
114 See Guelph *Evening Mercury*, 15 August 1914, 1.

Chapter 3: Hierarchies

1 Cleo Melzer, 'Puslinch Past,' *Puslinch Pioneer* 6 (1981), 9.
2 Archives du Séminaire de Trois-Rivières, FN-0356, Fonds Gédéon Désilets, famille. Gédéon Désilets à Georges Désilets (son fils), 8 August 1914, 1.
3 *Bien Public*, 6 August 1914, 1.
4 *Mandements, lettres pastorales et circulaires de S.G. Mgr F.-X. Cloutier*, 3ième Evêque des Trois-Rivières, 1914-1923, vol. 4 (Trois-Rivières, 1923), 38.
5 The *Herald*, for instance, ran an editorial entitled 'This Is a Duty Not a Charity' to encourage support for a special fund for the local Kilty Battalion. See 31 January 1916, 4.
6 Philip H. Morris, *The Canadian Patriotic Fund: A Record of Its Activities From 1914 to 1919* (n.p., 1920), 15.
7 Ibid., 21.
8 Ibid., 36. Cited also in Desmond Morton and Glenn Wright, *Winning the Second Battle: Canadian Veterans and the Return to Civilian Life, 1915-1930* (Toronto: University of Toronto Press, 1987), 6.
9 Morris, *The Canadian Patriotic Fund*, 30.
10 Morton and Wright, *Winning the Second Battle*, 5-6.
11 Morris, *The Canadian Patriotic Fund*, 32.
12 Ibid., 32-3.
13 Ibid., 235-6.
14 Lethbridge *Daily Herald*, 11 September 1914, 1.
15 Guelph *Evening Mercury*, 28 September 1914, 1, and 1 October 1914.
16 Archives municipales de Trois-Rivières, Procédés du Conseil. A proposal to donate a sum of $5,000 to the Canadian Patriotic Fund was made by Alderman Robert Ryan and seconded by Alderman O. Beaulac, 5 October, 1914. This motion was executed by the city clerk, who dispatched a letter to René Raguin dated 7 October 1914, of which a copy is retained in the Procédés du Conseil. By the end of the war, subscriptions for the CPF from Trois-Rivières totaled $30,460.64. See Morris, *The Canadian Patriotic Fund*, 252.
17 Canadian Patriotic Fund contributions for Lethbridge and Guelph appear in Morris, *The Canadian Patriotic Fund*, pp. 84 and 219 respectively. Lethbridge's population is cited in a police census report dated 29 November 1916. See GA, Police Census, 1916, Chief Constable William Hardy to W.D.L. Hardie, report dated 29 November 1916. The police

department's survey indicates a marked rise from the 1911 census, which lists 8,050 inhabitants for Lethbridge. See *Fifth Census of Canada, 1911* (Ottawa: King's Printer, 1913), vol. 2, 438. Guelph reported a total population of 15,174 during this census. See ibid., 431.

18 NAC, RG 24, Militia and Defence Records, *Militia Orders*, 1914, No. 156. For a brief description of the damaging effect of Militia Order No. 156 see Desmond Morton, *A Peculiar Kind of Politics: Canada's Overseas Ministry in the First World War* (Toronto: University of Toronto Press, 1982), 18.

19 Rev. J. Aitken Clark was one of four founders of this weekly, which commenced publication in March 1914 (others listed are René-Émile Raguin, J.L. Williams, and J.W. Briten). See André Beaulieu and Jean Hamelin, *Les journaux du Québec de 1764 à 1964* (Quebec: Presses de l'Université Laval, 1965), 279. Much of the *Newcomer*'s editorial opinion and local news coverage reflected Clark's influence.

20 *Newcomer*, 26 August 1914, 1.

21 *Nouveau Trois-Rivières*, 27 November 1914, 7.

22 *Newcomer*, 16 September 1914, 3.

23 Ibid., 5 September 1914, 4.

24 Ibid., 16 September 1914, 3.

25 Morris, *The Canadian Patriotic Fund*, 252.

26 Guelph *Evening Mercury*, 24 September 1914, 1.

27 Ibid., 25 September 1914, 8.

28 Ibid., 1.

29 Morris, *The Canadian Patriotic Fund*, 219.

30 Lethbridge *Daily Herald*, 15 October 1914, 1.

31 'La ville a été divisée en quartiers et dans chaque quartier un capitaine et des lieutenants ont été nommés pour solliciter les contributions.' *Nouveau Trois-Rivières*, 25 September 1914, 1.

32 Ibid., 25 September 1914, 1.

33 Ibid., 6 November 1914, 1.

34 Morris, *The Canadian Patriotic Fund*, 235.

35 *Bien Public*, 1 October 1914, 1.

36 Guelph *Evening Mercury*, 26 September 1914, 1 and 6.

37 Ibid.

38 Morris, *The Canadian Patriotic Fund*, 26.

39 See Paul Rutherford's introduction to Herbert Ames, *The City below the Hill: A Sociological Study of a Portion of the City of Montreal, Canada* (1897; reprint, Toronto: University of Toronto Press, 1972).

40 Guelph *Evening Mercury*, 28 September 1914, 1.

41 Lethbridge *Daily Herald*, 10 December 1914, 1.

42 Ibid., 11 August 1914, 1.

43 Ibid., 30 November 1915, 3.

44 Ibid., 15 October 1914, 1.

45 GA, *Lethbridge Board of Trade, Annual Report 1914*, 22.

46 Lethbridge *Daily Herald*, 30 November 1914, 1.

47 Ibid., 1.

48 Ibid., 2 December 1914, 1.

49 Ibid., 20 September 1915, 3.

50 Ibid., 6.

51 Ibid., 3 November 1915, 1.

52 This $30.00 donation from the 'Police & Fire Dept.,' listed in the *Nouveau Trois-Rivières*, 27 November 1914, 3, was part of another early publicity tactic of local funds to use city newspapers to draw up lists of donors, by name and often by affiliation, either as an individual or as a business or associational group. See also NAC, RG 24, Militia and Defence Records, vol. 1858, file 17, 'Gifts,' 2. For a similar contemporary account of organized patriotism see J. Castell Hopkins, *Canada at War: A Record of Heroism and Achievement, 1914-1918* (Toronto: Canadian Annual Review, 1919), 260-62.

53 Guelph *Evening Mercury*, 19 January 1916, 1.

54 Ibid., 21 January 1916, 1.
55 Morris, *The Canadian Patriotic Fund,* 48.
56 Ibid.
57 Ibid., 41.
58 Ibid., 37.
59 Ibid., 83.
60 Ibid., 219.
61 NAC, RG 24, Militia and Defence Records, vol. 1858, file 17, 'Gifts,' 3.
62 *Guelph Mercury: Centennial Issue,* 20 July 1927, 128.
63 NAC, RG 24, Militia and Defence Records, vol. 1858, file 17, 'Letter – C.G.S. to "Regent" of I.O.D.E. desirous of donating a machine gun.'
64 One such statement appeared in the *Newcomer,* 17 November 1915, 5.
65 Ibid., 5 July 1916, 3.
66 County of Wellington, Records and Bylaws, Bylaw No. 820 Effective 12 December 1914.
67 Ibid., Bylaw No. 853 Effective 29 January 1915.
68 Ibid., Bylaw No. 883 Effective 27 January 1916.
69 Ibid., Bylaw No. 895 Effective 24 January 1917.
70 The *Herald* reported that allotments to soldiers' dependents in Alberta had exceeded voluntary subscriptions the previous year by $800,000. See Lethbridge *Daily Herald,* 15 November 1917, 1.
71 Ibid., 20 October 1917, 9.
72 Ibid., 15 November 1917, 1.
73 Ibid., 16 November 1917, 4.
74 Ibid., 23 February 1918, 13.
75 Ibid., 25 February 1918, 7.

Chapter 4: Demonizations

1 For a thorough study of the limited extent of German conspiracies against Canada see Martin Kitchen, 'The German Invasion of Canada in the First World War,' *The International History Review* 7 (1985): 245-60.
2 For a comparative assessment see Panikos Panayi, ed., *Minorities in Wartime: National and Racial Groupings in Europe, North America and Australia during the Two World Wars* (Oxford and Providence: Berg Publishers, 1993). Panikos Panayi, *The Enemy in Our Midst: Germans in Britain during the First World War* (Oxford and Providence: Berg Publishers, 1991) is the standard study of the British experience, which also receives specialized treatment in David Cesarani and Tony Kushner, eds., *The Internment of Aliens in Twentieth Century Britain* (London: Frank Cass, 1993).
3 Desmond Morton, 'Sir William Otter and Internment Operations in Canada during the First World War,' *Canadian Historical Review* 55 (1974): 35.
4 Bill Waiser, *Park Prisoners: The Untold Story of Western Canada's National Parks, 1915-1946* (Saskatoon and Calgary: Fifth House Publishers, 1995), 3.
5 See also Howard Palmer, *Patterns of Prejudice: A History of Nativism in Alberta* (Toronto: McClelland and Stewart 1982); Donald Avery, *'Dangerous Foreigners': European Immigrant Workers and Labour Radicalism in Canada, 1836-1932* (Toronto: McClelland and Stewart, 1979); John Herd Thompson, *The Harvests of War: The Prairie West, 1914-1918* (Toronto: McClelland and Stewart, 1978); Morton, 'Sir William Otter and Internment Operations,' 32-58; Lubomyr Y. Luciuk, *Internment Operations: The Role of Old Fort Henry in World War I* (Kingston: Delta Educational Consultants, 1980); and Frances Swyripa and John Herd Thompson, eds., *Loyalties in Conflict: Ukrainians in Canada during the Great War* (Edmonton: Canadian Institute of Ukrainian Studies, 1983). An assessment from a Ukrainian perspective of the war years also appears in Orest T. Martynowych, *Ukrainians in Canada: The Formative Period, 1891-1924* (Edmonton: Canadian Institute of Ukrainian Studies, 1991), 309-449. See also Lubomyr Luciuk, *A Time for Atonement: Canada's First National Internment Operations and the Ukrainian Canadians* (Kingston: The Limestone Press, 1988); John Herd Thompson, *Ethnic Minorities during Two World Wars* (Ottawa: Canadian Historical Association, 1991); Bohdan S. Kordan and Peter Melnycky, eds., *In the Shadow of the Rockies: Diary of the Castle*

Mountain Internment Camp 1915-1917 (Edmonton: Canadian Institute of Ukrainian Studies, 1991); and Gerhard P. Bassler, 'The Enemy Alien Experience in Newfoundland 1914-1918,' *Canadian Ethnic Studies* 20 (1988): 42-62. For a comparative assessment of Canada's prisoners of war see Desmond Morton, *Silent Battle: Canadian Prisoners of War in Germany, 1914-1918* (Toronto: Lester Publishing, 1992), and Jonathan F. Vance, *Objects of Concern: Canadian Prisoners of War Through the Twentieth Century* (Vancouver: UBC Press, 1994).

6 Paul Voisey, *Vulcan: The Making of a Prairie Community* (Toronto: University of Toronto Press, 1988), 228.

7 Cited in Martin L. Kovacs, 'Hungarian Communities in Early Alberta and Saskatchewan,' in *The New Provinces: Alberta and Saskatchewan, 1905-1980*, ed. Howard Palmer and Donald Smith (Vancouver: Tantalus Research, 1980), 106.

8 Raymond Williams, 'Base and Superstructure in Marxist Cultural Theory,' in *Rethinking Popular Culture: Contemporary Perspectives in Cultural Studies*, ed. Chandra Mukerji and Michael Schudson (Berkeley: University of California Press, 1991), 416. Williams's critique of Marxist theory and cultural formation compares 'residual' and 'emergent' cultures in the formation of either alternative or oppositional forms. Emergent cultures create anew shared meanings and values to incorporate new practices and experiences. The rise of regional exceptionalism in the West might be placed in this framework, but not increased tolerance between Anglo-Canadians and ethnic minorities at this time.

9 Kovacs, 'Hungarian Communities,' 106-8.

10 Ibid., 107-8.

11 Avery, *'Dangerous Foreigners,'* 31.

12 A.F. Duguid, *Official History of the Canadian Forces in the Great War, 1914-1919*, vol. 1 (Ottawa: King's Printer, 1938), 235.

13 Ibid.

14 They were identified as George Miszkosky, Dmytras Lucak, and R. Twaroski in the Lethbridge *Daily Herald*, 17 August 1914, 1.

15 Ibid.

16 Ibid., 24 August 1914, 6.

17 Ibid., 25 August 1914, 6.

18 NAC, RG 24, Militia and Defence Records, vol. 1755, D.H.S. 10-10-C. Reprinted in Duguid, *Official History*, 235.

19 Cited in Thompson, *The Harvests of War*, 75.

20 Ibid., 74-5.

21 Lethbridge *Daily Herald*, 19 August 1914, 4.

22 Ibid., 18 August 1914, 6.

23 Guelph *Evening Mercury*, 9 September 1914, 4.

24 Ibid., 13 October 1914, 4.

25 Ibid., 6 November 1914, 3.

26 Ibid., 15 May 1915, 1.

27 Ibid. See also ibid., 14 May 1914, 1 and 4.

28 Ibid., 27 November 1914, 1.

29 *Le Courrier*, 8 October 1915, 1. On Tessier and the Shawinigan Quarry Company see François Roy, 'Le crépuscule d'un rouge: J.-A. Tessier, maire de Trois-Rivières, et l'enquête Désy de 1920' (Master's thesis, Université du Québec à Trois-Rivières, 1988), 38.

30 Guelph *Evening Mercury*, 11 September 1914, 4.

31 Ibid., 12 September 1914, 2.

32 Ibid., 8 September 1914, 7.

33 Ibid., 2 November 1914, 1.

34 Ibid., 17 November 1914, 1.

35 Martin Kitchen's study of the only case of pro-German espionage in North America uncovers both the limits of the threat, which ended with the arrest of a hazardous dreamer, Werner Horn, after he damaged the CPR bridge in Vanceboro, Maine, and the ineptitude of key officials in Berlin. Their 'idiocies and failures,' Kitchen concluded, were somewhat indicative of Germany's political future. Ottawa, however, was not swept up by 'unfounded fears.' See Kitchen, 'The German Invasion of Canada,' 260.

36 *Bien Public*, 5 November 1914, 1. 'If there truly are five thousand men, for the most part reservists, in the United States, possibly being held against their will, or having already done military service in Austria or Germany, and used to handling weapons, then we will have a veritable army to face, and so will the US.' (Author's translation.)
37 Ibid. 'The newspapers have, numerous times, revealed spying attempts; installations of wireless telegraphy that were officially banned and removed by the authorities, have on many occasions been reinstalled, much to the dismay of police. Mysterious airplanes continue to fly over our rare strategic points and main food supply centres. Our ports, canals, bridges, and railway tracks are more than ever before subject to surveillance by our own authorities, and this prudence is warranted. In fact, this feverish preparation by men who are presently hostile, and yet who are allowed to enjoy relative freedom in our country, albeit under surveillance, indicates at least one thing.' (Author's translation.)
38 *Bien Public*, 5 November 1914, 1.
39 *Newcomer*, 18 November 1914, 2.
40 Ibid., 5.
41 See, for example, John Fiske, 'Television: Polysemy and Popularity,' *Critical Studies in Mass Communication* 3 (1986), 392.
42 See Lethbridge *Daily Herald*, 16 December 1915, 1; 23 December 1916, 13; and 25 July 1917.
43 Ibid., 18 August 1914, 1.
44 Ibid., 25 August 1914, 6, and 23 September 1914, 5.
45 Ibid., 18 August 1914, 1.
46 Clifford Geertz, *Local Knowledge: Further Essays in Interpretive Anthropology* (New York: Basic Books, 1983), 57. As Geertz put it, such intersections of experience-near and experience-distant concepts, a bridge and a fear of attack, offer useful currencies in the generation of local knowledges. Someone like an editor or reporter might present them as potent figments, 'might naturally and effortlessly use [them] to define what he or his fellows see, feel, think, imagine, and so on, and which he would readily understand when similarly applied by others.'
47 Guelph *Evening Mercury*, 10 September 1914, 4.
48 Ibid., 2 November 1914, 2.
49 Ibid., 6 November 1914, 4.
50 Ibid., 2 November 1914, 4.
51 On violence and the social organization of masculinity see R.W. Connell, *Masculinities* (Berkeley and Los Angeles: University of California Press, 1995), 83.
52 Guelph *Evening Mercury*, 10 November 1914, 2.
53 Ibid., 6 November 1914, 5.
54 This work was made famous by anti-German propagandists, but had no influence on German military policy. See Peter Buitenhuis, *The Great War of Words: British, American, and Canadian Propaganda and Fiction, 1914-1933* (Vancouver: UBC Press, 1987), 3, 31-32, 40. See also Gerhard Ritter, *The Sword and the Sceptre: The Problem of Militarism in Germany* (Coral Gables, FL: University of Florida Press, 1972), 113.
55 Guelph *Evening Mercury*, 6 November 1914, 5.
56 For a primary account of the founding and activities of Wycliffe College see D. Hague, S. Gould, H.J. Cody, et al., *The Jubilee Volume of Wycliffe College* (Toronto: Toronto Wycliffe College, 1927).
57 Guelph *Evening Mercury*, 7 November 1914, 5.
58 Ibid., 2.
59 Cornelius J. Jaenan, *The Belgians in Canada* (Ottawa: Canadian Historical Association, 1991), 14.
60 Ibid., 4-5.
61 *Bien Public*, 14 January 1915, 1.
62 On approaches to public dramas and perception see Victor Turner, *The Anthropology of Performance* (New York: PAJ Publications, 1986), esp. 72-98.
63 Lethbridge *Daily Herald*, 10 May 1915, 1.

64 NAC, RG 24, Militia and Defence Records, vol. 1502, HQ 683-1-30-3, 'List of Internment Stations or Camps.'
65 Ibid., 'Registration Centres of Names of Registrars.'
66 In addition to Desmond Morton's study of Sir William Otter's role in Internment Operations, cited above, see Morton's biography of Otter, *The Canadian General: Sir William Otter* (Toronto: Hakkert Press, 1974), esp. ch 9.
67 NAC, RG 24, Militia and Defence Records, vol. 4696, 448-14-20, vol. 7, Cruikshank to Otter, 17 December 1914.
68 A series of weekly reports were prepared on prisoners interned in Military District 13. See ibid., Weekly Reports.
69 A typical daily diet, from a list submitted by Commander Stewart to Cruikshank, consisted of breakfast: porridge, butter, coffee, bacon, bread, and milk; dinner: beef, soup, beans, and bread; and supper: stewed beef, jam, tea, and bread. See ibid., Stewart to Cruikshank, 29 January 1915.
70 Ibid., Stewart to Cruikshank, 5 January 1915.
71 Ibid., Stewart to Cruikshank, 26 March 1915.
72 1,192 were of German origin; 5,954 were from Austro-Hungarian territories. See Kordan and Melnycky, eds., *In the Shadow of the Rockies*, 12.
73 NAC, RG 24, Militia and Defence Records, vol. 4696, 448-14-20, vol. 2, 'Enemy Aliens.'
74 William Otter, 'Report on Internment Operations, 1914-1920,' reprinted in V.J. Kaye, *Ukrainian Canadians in Canada's Wars* (Toronto: Ukrainian Canadian Research Foundation, 1983), 82.
75 NAC, RG 24, Militia and Defence Records, vol. 6595, 48-14-20, file 4, clipping from Chicago *Tribune*, 29 November 1915.
76 Ibid., vol. 4695, 48-14-20, file 4, Otter to Cruikshank, 16 December, 1915.
77 Ibid., Cruikshank to Birney, 20 December 1915.
78 Ibid., Birney to Cruikshank, 22 December 1915.
79 Ibid., Birney to Cruikshank, 6 December 1915.
80 Ibid., vol. 4694, 448-14-20, vol. 2, Cruikshank to R.C. Reat, American Consul, 5 May 1915.
81 Ibid., vol. 4696, 448-14-20, vol. 8, Birney to Staff Officer, Internment Operations, 30 December 1915.
82 See Kordan and Melnycky, eds., *In the Shadow of the Rockies*. The photograph appears on page 11.
83 Waiser, *Park Prisoners*, 36-7.
84 NAC, RG 24, Militia and Defence Records, vol. 4695, 448-14-20, vol. 6, Otter to Cruikshank, 27 September 1916.
85 Ibid., Cruikshank to Otter, 28 September 1916.
86 Ibid., vol. 4696, 448-14-20, vol. 7, Cruikshank to Otter, 4 January 1915.
87 Ibid., Otter to Cruikshank, 8 January 1915.
88 Ibid., vol. 4699, 448-14-41, vol. 1, Hingst to Cruikshank, 4 February 1915.
89 Ibid., Riley and McCormick Ltd. to Hingst, 9 February 1915.
90 Ibid., Stewart to Cruikshank, 11 February 1915.
91 Ibid., Otter to Cruikshank, 26 February 1915.
92 Ibid., Otter to Cruikshank, 30 March 1915.
93 Apart from the first breakout, which was not reported in the press, the *Herald* recorded seven separate prisoner escapes verified in the administrative records of the Lethbridge Internment Camp. See the Lethbridge *Daily Herald*, 22 February 1915, 1; 26 August 1915, 1; 13 December 1915, 1; 29 April 1916, 1; 16 June 1916, 1; 21 September 1916, 1; 2 October 1916, 1.
94 NAC, RG 24, Militia and Defence Records, vol. 4695, 448-14-20, Stewart to Cruikshank, 29 November 1914.
95 Lethbridge *Daily Herald*, 22 February 1915, 1.
96 NAC, RG 24, Militia and Defence Records, vol. 448-14-41, vol. 2, Stewart to Cruikshank, 22 February 1915.
97 Lethbridge *Daily Herald*, 22 February 1915, 1.

98 Otter, 'Interment Operations,' 79. As Kordan and Melnycky stated, of the 8,579 interned in Canada, '3,138 could be classified technically as prisoners of war, individuals captured under arms or reservists subject to service in the Austrian or German imperial forces, only 817 were actual servicemen who had been caught (primarily in Caribbean ports) at the onset of hostilities and transferred to Canada for internment.' See Kordan and Melnycky, eds., *In the Shadow of the Rockies*, 12.
99 Lethbridge *Daily Herald*, 29 April 1916, 1.
100 NAC, RG 24, Militia and Defence Records, vol. 4694, 448-14-20, file 3, 'Escape of Prisoners of War 25 & 26-4-16 Board of Enquiry,' 2.
101 Ibid.
102 Ibid., 4.
103 Ibid., 13.
104 Ibid., 4.
105 Ibid., 7-8.
106 Ibid., 3.
107 Ibid.
108 Ibid., 6 and 7.
109 Lethbridge *Daily Herald*, 1 May 1916, 1.
110 Ibid., 11 May 1916, 1.
111 Ibid., 15 June 1916, 1, and NAC, RG 24, Militia and Defence Records, vol. 4694, 448-14-20, file 3, 'Enquiry Into the Escape of Two Prisoners of War, (Jenson and Stovell), June 14th, 1916.'
112 Lethbridge *Daily Herald*, 19 June 1916, 1.
113 Ibid., 21 September 1916, 1, and 2 October 1916, 1.
114 NAC, RG 24, Militia and Defence Records, vol. 4694, 448-14-20, file 3, 'Finding. Court of Enquiry,' 28 April 1916.
115 Ibid., Cruikshank to Date, 23 June 1916.
116 Lethbridge *Daily Herald*, 22 February 1915.
117 Ibid., 25 October 1916, 4.
118 Ibid., 24 October 1916, 1.
119 Ibid., 4 November 1916, 1.

Chapter 5: Conscription Contested

1 Jesuit Archives, Regis College (hereafter JA), Correspondence and Documents, 1918, Bourque to Maj.-Gen. S.C. Mewburn, Department of Militia and Defence, 8 June 1918.
2 Clifford Geertz, *The Interpretation of Cultures* (New York: Basic Books, 1973), 311.
3 A.F. Duguid, *Official History of the Canadian Forces in the Great War, 1914-1919*, vol. 1 (Ottawa: King's Printer, 1938), Appendix 86 reports the initial figure for Canada's First Contingent. One hundred and eighty nurses are included in this total. Recruitment figures fluctuated on a monthly basis from August 1914 to the imposition of conscription three years later. Annual appointments and enlistments were as follows: 1914 (five months): 59,144; 1915: 158,859; 1916: 176,919; and 1917: 63,611. The most dramatic drop occurred between June and October 1916, when monthly additions to the CEF fell from 10,619 to 5,544 respectively. See G.W.L Nicholson, *Canadian Expeditionary Force, 1914-1919: The Official History of the Canadian Army in the First World War* (Ottawa: Queen's Printer, 1962), 546, Appendix C.
4 Nicholson, *Canadian Expeditionary Force*, 221 and Appendix C.
5 Cited in J.L. Granatstein and J.M. Hitsman, *Broken Promises: A History of Conscription in Canada* (Toronto: Oxford University Press, 1977), 64.
6 For Ontario farmers see W.R. Young, 'Conscription, Rural Depopulation, and the Farmers of Ontario, 1917-1919,' *Canadian Historical Review*, 53 (1972): 289-319. For labour see Martin Robin, 'Registration, Conscription, and Independent Labour Politics, 1916-17,' *Canadian Historical Review*, 45 (1966): 101-18. Thomas P. Socknat examines the role of liberal pacifists in 'Canada's Liberal Pacifists and the Great War,' *Journal of Canadian Studies/Revue d'études canadiennes*, vol. 18 (1984): 30-44, and in his full-length study of Canadian pacifism, *Witness against War: Pacifism in Canada, 1900-1945* (Toronto: University of Toronto

Press, 1987), esp. chs. 2 and 3. A general history of conscription in Canada appeared in Granatstein and Hitsman, *Broken Promises*, with chs. 2 and 3 covering the First World War. Studies of specific aspects surrounding the 1917 conscription crisis have appeared in numerous sources. A.M. Willms, in 'Conscription, 1917: A Brief for the Defence,' *Canadian Historical Review*, 37 (1956): 338-51, presented a case sympathetic to the practical aspects of Borden's decision to introduce conscription (which Granatstein and Hitsman later disputed). Various historical accounts of conscription in 1917 appeared in Mason Wade, *The French Canadians 1760-1967*, vol. 2 (1968; rev. ed., Toronto: Macmillan, 1976), ch. 12; Robert Craig Brown and Ramsay Cook, *Canada 1896-1921: A Nation Transformed* (Toronto: McClelland and Stewart, 1974), ch. 13; John English, *The Decline of Politics: The Conservatives and the Party System, 1901-20* (Toronto: University of Toronto Press, 1977), esp. ch. 7; and Desmond Morton, *A Military History of Canada* (Edmonton: Hurtig, 1985), esp. 151-58. Chapter 6 of John Herd Thompson's *The Harvests of War: The Prairie West, 1914-1918* (Toronto: McClelland and Stewart, 1978) and all of Elizabeth H. Armstrong's *The Crisis of Quebec, 1914-1918* (1937; reprint, Toronto: McClelland and Stewart, 1974) provide useful studies of responses to compulsory service in the Prairie provinces and in Quebec respectively.

7 Ramsay Cook, *Canada and the French-Canadian Question* (Toronto: Macmillan, 1966), 35, and Margaret Prang, 'Clerics, Politicians, and the Bilingual Schools Issue in Ontario, 1910-1917,' *Canadian Historical Review* 41 (1960): 281-307.

8 Armstrong, *The Crisis of Quebec*, 152-53.

9 Brian Cameron, 'The Bonne Entente Movement, 1916-1917: From Cooperation to Conscription,' *Journal of Canadian Studies/Revue d'études canadiennes*, 13 (1978), 47. See also Brown and Cook, *Canada 1896-1921*, 265.

10 Office of the Bonne Entente, 'The Bonne Entente: How it Began, What it Has Done and Its Immediate Program' (Toronto: Office of the Bonne Entente, 1916).

11 Cameron, 'The Bonne Entente,' 54.

12 Ibid., 3.

13 *Nouveau Trois-Rivières*, 13 October 1916, 1.

14 Cameron, 'The Bonne Entente,' 45.

15 *Nouveau Trois-Rivières*, 13 October 1916, 1. See also Cameron, 'The Bonne Entente,' 49.

16 Office of the Bonne Entente, *The Bonne Entente*, 5-7.

17 *Bien Public*, 24 May 1917, 1.

18 See Armstrong, *The Crisis of Quebec*, 174-75, and Cameron, 'The Bonne Entente,' 52-53. Both refer to a tense atmosphere surrounding the subsequent meeting of this group in Montreal.

19 Armstrong, *The Crisis of Quebec*, 52-55.

20 Godin was the author of *Mémorial trifluvien*, 2 vols. (Trois-Rivières: n.p., 1933).

21 Archives du Séminaire de Trois-Rivières, FN-0014-P1-131, Fonds Albert Tessier, Louis-Georges Godin à l'abbé Albert Tessier, 16 July 1917.

22 Ibid., FN-0211, Fonds Jacques Bureau, Bureau à Laurier, 17 October 1916.

23 Ibid., Laurier à Bureau, 19 October 1916.

24 Ibid., 'Discours et Votes de Jacques Bureau Contre la Conscription en 1917' (n.p., n.d.).

25 See *Bien Public*, 22 November 1917, 1, for a report on Bureau's uncontested renomination by his riding's Liberal association.

26 See Paul-André Linteau, René Durocher, and Jean-Claude Robert, *Quebec: A History, 1867-1929*, trans. Robert Chodos (Toronto: J. Lorimer, 1983), 200-1. For a more comprehensive examination of the Catholic church's powerful role in shaping Quebec society see Jean Hamelin and Nicole Gagnon, *Histoire du catholicisme québécois*, vol. 1, *1898-1940* (Montreal: Boréal, 1984), esp. chs. 4 and 5.

27 Cited in René Durocher, 'Henri Bourassa, les évêques et la guerre de 1914-1918,' *Canadian Historical Association Papers* (1971), 269.

28 This plan for military conscription for overseas service deals a blow to the integrity of our independent constitution. Conscription does not presently exist in any other British colony. It's possible that the colonies may resort to conscription but such a measure would be taken only for the defence of local borders, never to form troops that would be sent to serve beyond these borders. (Author's translation.) *Bien Public*, 24 May 1917, 1.

29 We know that all the other Dominions have since had their elections, and they didn't consider the state of war as a sufficient motive to abandon all governmental control. (Author's translation.) *Bien Public*, 24 May 1917, 1.
30 Ibid., 31 May 1917, 1.
31 *Bien Public,* 5 July 1917, 1. 'Exactly fifty years after the signing of the Confederation pact, Prime Minister Border, leader of a government whose mandate has expired, is preparing to force a vote that the majority of the people opposes for military conscriptions, as desired by the Imperialists.' (Author's translation.)
32 Ibid., 5 July 1917, 1.
33 Ibid., 7 June 1917, 1.
34 Ibid.
35 Ibid., 2 August 1917, 1.
36 Ibid., 6 September 1917, 1.
37 Wade, *The French Canadians*, vol. 2, 735.
38 Ibid., 226.
39 For a detailed discussion of the Quebec City riot see Jean Provencher, *Québec sous la loi des Mesures de Guerre 1918* (Trois-Rivières: Editions du Boréal Express, 1971).
40 *Bien Public*, 6 September 1917, 1.
41 Armstrong, *The Crisis of Quebec*, 166.
42 *Bien Public*, 7 June 1917, 1. 'If we're to believe the dispatches, such calls fall on well-prepared ground in Toronto. The soldiers who have returned from the front now spend their days breaking up all the anticonscription meetings in that city. Bloody brawls are common and the police have a difficult time protecting the peaceful citizens who express their opinions of the rioters publicly, as is their right. Similar attacks on freedom of speech have been made in Winnipeg and Vancouver; fighting, violence, and ugly scenes have been provoked and perpetrated there by soldiers returned from the front lines.

We truly regret these misplaced and unjustified violent excesses by our military men. The populace is already exasperated with those whom the whole country was supposed to welcome back with sympathy and pride.

These excesses have perhaps come in time to open the eyes of the population. By tolerating such acts of abuse, the authorities have shown how ill-prepared our country is for the military regime to which M. Borden wants to lead us.' (Author's translation.)
43 Ibid., 13 December 1917, 1.
44 James Fentress and Chris Wickham, *Social Memory* (Oxford: Blackwell, 1992), 59.
45 Paul Rutherford has observed that the 'political trauma of 1917 shattered the unity of the Liberal Press.' But since Buchanan owned the *Herald*, its editorial policy simply switched from Liberal to Unionist. Rutherford also noted that, notwithstanding a gradual decline in the party press in this era, 'newspapers were rarely neutral in the political fray. Their publishers were often partisans in their own right, who enjoyed playing politics almost as much as their colonial predecessors.' See Paul Rutherford, *The Making of the Canadian Media* (Toronto: McGraw-Hill Ryerson, 1978), 69-70. An uncritical biography of Buchanan that highlights his career as a politician and newspaper editor was completed by C. Frank Steele in *Prairie Editor: The Life and Times of Buchanan of Lethbridge* (Toronto: Ryerson Press, 1961). For a comprehensive history of the *Herald*, including Buchanan's period, see Georgia G. Fooks, 'A History of the Lethbridge *Herald*, 1905-1975' (Master's thesis, Brigham Young University, 1975).
46 Though Steele does focus on Buchanan's objection to removing the franchise from citizens of enemy origin under the terms of the Military Voter's Act, he pays scant attention to the local contest in the 1917 federal election. Steele erroneously referred to his opponent, L. Lambert Pack, as a 'Laurier Liberal.' See Steele's *Prairie Editor*, 78.
47 On the formation of Union government see, Granatstein and Hitsman, *Broken Promises*, ch. 3, and English *The Decline of Politics*, ch. 7.
48 Brown and Cook, *Canada 1896-1921*, 309.
49 Lethbridge *Telegram*, 14 June 1917, 1.
50 Thomas Socknat, *Witness against War: Pacifism in Canada, 1900-1945* (Toronto: University of Toronto Press, 1987), 65.

51 J. Castell Hopkins, *Canadian Annual Review, 1917* (Toronto: Canadian Annual Review Company, 1918), 348.
52 Granatstein and Hitsman, *Broken Promises*, 70-71.
53 English, *The Decline of Politics*, 178-79.
54 Lethbridge *Daily Herald*, 5 May 1917, 1.
55 Carol Lee Bacchi, *Liberation Deferred? The Ideas of the English-Canadian Suffragists, 1877-1918* (Toronto: University of Toronto Press, 1983), 118.
56 Lethbridge *Daily Herald*, 5 May 1917, 1.
57 Ibid., 11 May 1917, 6.
58 Ibid., 12 May 1917, 9.
59 Ibid., 28 June 1917, 4.
60 Granatstein and Hitsman, *Broken Promises*, 66.
61 Thompson, *The Harvests of War*, 121-22. See also Lethbridge *Daily Herald*, 8 December 1917.
62 The chautauqua movement was founded in 1874 at Chautauqua Lake in New York State. Its aims were directed at adult education through a range of cultural, religious, and recreational activities.
63 Lethbridge *Daily Herald*, 13 August 1917, 1.
64 Ibid.
65 Ibid., 19 November 1917, 1.
66 Ibid., 1 and 4.
67 Ibid., 20 November 1917, 1.
68 Ibid., 19 November 1917, 1 and 4.
69 Ibid., 14 December 1917, 7.
70 Ibid., 21 November 1917, 9.
71 Ibid., 6 December 1917, 4.
72 Ibid., 19 December 1916, 4 (Coaldale); 6 January 1917, 8 (Nobleford); 9 January 1917, 3 (Iron Springs); 13 January 1917, 8 (Barons); 1 February 1917, 6 (Raymond); 13 March 1917, 6 (Magrath); 28 March 1917, 6 (Etzikom); 19 April 1917, 6 (Cardston). The references are to reports for each town concerning either the election of new officers and/or the establishment of a new local.
73 Ibid., 13 March 1917, 6.
74 'Every appeal,' the *Herald* reported, 'was granted on proof of the bona fides of the applicant being submitted.' Ibid., 7 December 1917, 1. See also ibid., 8 December 1917, 11.
75 '"The antipathy of the farmers who have been opposing union government because boys were being drafted off the farms has completely disappeared," declared a well-known farmer to the *Herald* this morning.' See ibid., 7 December 1917, 1.
76 Ibid., 20 September 1917, 1.
77 Ibid., 11 October 1917, 1.
78 Ibid., 11 December 1917, 1.
79 Lethbridge *Telegram*, 14 December 1917, 1.
80 Ibid., 7.
81 Ibid., 1.
82 Lethbridge *Daily Herald*, 18 December 1917, 1.
83 Ibid. The total number of votes reported by the *Daily Herald* the day after the election differs, however, from the final tally. The figures shown here for Pack (2,468 votes) and Buchanan (5,302 votes) are official results taken from the Government of Canada's Parliament of Canada website, <www.parl.gc.ca>.
84 In reference to farmers' responses on a national level, Robert Craig Brown and Ramsay Cook concluded there was 'some support for the Liberals among the rural population, which objected strenuously to the conscription of farmers' sons. Two weeks before voting day, the cabinet passed an Order in Council giving them an exemption, thus neutralizing their opposition.' See Brown and Cook, *Canada 1896-1921*, 273.
85 Lethbridge *Daily Herald*, 18 December 1917, 1.
86 Victor Turner, *Dramas, Fields, and Metaphors: Symbolic Action in Human Society* (Ithaca: Cornell University Press, 1974), 39.

87 For an assessment of censorship and sectarian divisions surrounding the Guelph raid see Brian F. Hogan, 'The Guelph Novitiate Raid: Conscription, Censorship and Bigotry during the Great War,' *Canadian Catholic Historical Study Sessions* 45 (1978), 57-80. A summary of this incident, compiled soon after the event, appeared in J. Castell Hopkins, *Canadian Annual Review, 1918* (Toronto: Canadian Annual Review Company, 1919), 457-59. A brief description of the raid is also found in Leo A. Johnson, *History of Guelph, 1827-1927*, 313-15. Portions of the *Report of the Commission of Enquiry into the Raid on the Jesuit Novitiate at Guelph*, a Royal Commission convened in November 1919 to investigate the affair, are reprinted in Barbara M. Wilson, *Ontario and the First World War, 1914-1918: A Collection of Documents* (Toronto: Champlain Society for the Government of Ontario, University of Toronto Press, 1977), 58-69.

88 Hogan, 'The Guelph Novitiate Raid,' 69-71.

89 A St. Stanislaus novice, George Nunan, recalled that despite the nationwide censorship ban, 'it was known the next morning throughout the town [Guelph].' See JA, Recollections by Marcus Doherty (prepared 19 August 1963) and George Nunan (prepared 21 August 1963), Nunan, 8.

90 Hogan, 'The Guelph Novitiate Raid,' 73.

91 This commission, cited above, was summoned following a five-hour debate sparked by a motion introduced in the House of Commons by Sam Hughes on 7 April 1919. See Hogan, 'The Guelph Novitiate Raid,' 75-76.

92 See Hogan, 'The Guelph Novitiate Raid,' 63.

93 Guelph *Evening Mercury*, 4 October 1917, 1.

94 Cunningham's first term as alderman began in 1924. See Leo A. Johnson, *History of Guelph, 1827-1927* (Guelph: Guelph Historical Society, 1977), Appendices, 369.

95 Guelph *Evening Mercury*, 18 December 1917, 1.

96 Ibid., 17 December 1917, 6. See also 14 December 1917, 1.

97 Ibid., 25 December 1917, 1 and 2.

98 Hogan, 'The Guelph Novitiate Raid,' 63.

99 *Military Service Act, 1917* (Ottawa: King's Printer, 1917).

100 JA, 'Report of the Commissioners of Enquiry into the Raid of the Jesuit Novitiate at Guelph' (n.p.: 1919), 1.

101 JA, Recollections by Marcus Doherty and George Nunan, Nunan, 2.

102 Hogan, 'The Guelph Novitiate Raid,' 59.

103 JA, 'Report of the Commissioners,' 2.

104 Ibid., 2.

105 Ibid., 2-3. On growing local hostility regarding the immunity of the St. Stanislaus students from conscription see Hogan, 'The Guelph Novitiate Raid,' 63-64.

106 Cited in Hogan, 'The Guelph Novitiate Raid,' 62.

107 Ibid., 64.

108 JA, 'Report of the Commissioners,' 3.

109 Ibid., 3-4.

110 Turner, *Dramas, Fields, and Metaphors*, 38.

111 JA, Correspondence and Documents, 1918, Residence list for 7 June 1917.

112 Ibid., Recollections by Marcus Doherty and George Nunan, Doherty, 3-4.

113 Ibid., Nunan, 4.

114 Ibid., Nunan, 5. See also Hogan, 'The Guelph Novitiate Raid,' 65-66 and JA, Correspondence and Documents, 1918, Bourque to Maj.-Gen. S.A. Mewburn, 8 June 1918.

115 JA, Recollections by Marcus Doherty and George Nunan, Doherty, 6-7.

116 Marcus Doherty observed a change in Macaulay's demeanour when he arrived the following day to receive a residence list of the St. Stanislaus community. Doherty described him as 'thoroughly embarrassed and miserable,' a plausible description under the circumstances. See ibid., Doherty, 12.

117 Ibid., Correspondence and Documents, 1918, Mewburn to Bourque, 11 June 1918. On Macaulay's transfer see Hogan, 'The Guelph Raid,' 68.

118 Hogan, 'The Guelph Raid,' 67.

119 JA, The Guelph Raid: Pamphlets, 1918-1920, 'The Raid on the Guelph Novitiate, Astounding Statements,' 1.
120 Guelph *Evening Mercury*, 20 June 1918, 2.
121 Hogan, 'The Guelph Novitiate Raid,' 69.
122 Cited in 'A Statement and Editorial in Connection with the Jesuit Novitiate Case,' 3, in JA, The Guelph Raid: Pamphlets, 1918-1920.
123 Hogan, 'The Guelph Novitiate Raid,' 69.
124 On 20 June 1918, the Guelph *Herald* published a lengthy and reasonably accurate account of the novitiate raid under the caption 'Facts of Novitiate Raid Released by the Censor.' The raid was described as 'fruitless,' and a clear reference was made to an apology received by the novitiate from Department of Militia and Defence officials. See JA, The Guelph Raid: Newspaper Clippings, Guelph *Herald*, 20 June 1918.
125 Hogan, 'The Guelph Novitiate Raid,' 69.
126 JA, The Guelph Raid: Newspaper Clippings, Guelph *Herald*, 24 June 1918.
127 Guelph *Evening Mercury*, 24 June 1918, 1.
128 Ibid.
129 JA, The Guelph Raid: Pamphlets, 1918-1920, 'A Statement and Editorial in Connection with the Jesuit Novitiate Case.'
130 JA, The Guelph Raid: Newspaper Clippings, Guelph *Herald*, 26 June 1918.
131 Ibid., The Guelph Raid: Pamphlets, 1918-1920, *The Facts of the Raid Upon the Jesuit Novitiate* (Toronto: n.p., n.d.), 2.
132 John English, *Shadow of Heaven: The Life of Lester Pearson*, vol. 1, *1897-1948* (Toronto: Lester and Orpen Dennys, 1989), 9.
133 JA, The Guelph Raid: Newspaper Clippings, 1918-1920, Guelph *Herald*, 24 June 1918.
134 Ibid.
135 J.M. Bliss, 'The Methodist Church and World War I,' *The Canadian Historical Review* 49 (1968): 218.
136 Ibid., 230-31.
137 English, *Shadow of Heaven*, 23.
138 JA, The Guelph Raid: Newspaper Clippings, Guelph *Herald*, 25 June 1918.
139 Guelph *Evening Mercury*, 27 June 1918, 1.
140 JA, The Guelph Raid: Newspaper Clippings, Guelph *Herald*, 24 June 1918.

Chapter 6: Gendered Fields

1 Lethbridge *Daily Herald*, 14 August 1915, 1.
2 Ibid., 15 May 1916, 1 and 7; see also *Lethbridge Telegram*, 18 May 1916, 5.
3 For Canada see Jonathan F. Vance, *Death So Noble: Memory, Meaning and the First World War* (Vancouver: UBC Press, 1997).
4 On gender and war see Margaret R. Higonnet et al., eds., *Behind the Lines: Gender and the Two World Wars* (New Haven: Yale University Press, 1987), Miriam Cooke and Angela Woollacott, eds., *Gendering War Talk* (Princeton: Princeton University Press, 1993); and Billie Melman, ed., *Borderlines: Gender and Identities in War and Peace, 1870-1930* (New York and London: Routledge, 1998).
5 Joan W. Scott, 'Rewriting History,' in *Behind the Lines*, ed. Higonnet et al., 25.
6 While civil defence during the First World War was overwhelmingly a male-dominated activity, Barbara Wilson has uncovered 'at least two ladies' rifle clubs in the Toronto area' and 'some women in Hamilton,' under the leadership of Jessie McNab, who 'planned a Ladies' Home Guard.' The unit failed to attract sustained participation and disbanded with McNab's withdrawal. See Barbara M. Wilson, *Ontario and the First World War, 1914-1918: A Collection of Documents* (Toronto: Champlain Society for the Government of Ontario, University of Toronto Press, 1977), lxxxvi-viii.
7 Vera Brittain, *Chronicle of Youth*, ed. Alan Bishop (Glasgow: Fontana/Collins, 1982), 140.
8 Angela Woollacott, *On Her Their Lives Depend: Munitions Workers and the Great War* (Berkeley: University of California Press, 1994). In addition to Higonnet et al., eds., *Behind the Lines*, and Cooke and Woollacott, eds., *Gendering War Talk*, cited above, see Helen M.

Cooper et al., eds., *Arms and the Woman: War, Gender and Literary Representation* (Chapel Hill, NC: University of North Carolina Press, 1989); Gail Braybon, *Women Workers in the First World War: The British Experience* (London: Croom Helm, 1981); and Claire Culleton, 'Gender-Charged Munitions: The Language of World War I Munitions Reports,' *Women's Studies International Forum* 11, 2 (1988): 109-16.

9 Thomas Socknat, *Witness against War: Pacifism in Canada, 1900-1945* (Toronto: University of Toronto Press, 1987), 44-45.

10 Ibid., 59.

11 Veronica Strong-Boag, 'Peace-Making Women: Canada, 1919-1939,' in *Women and Peace: Theoretical, Historical, and Practical Perspectives*, ed. Ruth Roach Pierson (London: Croom Helm, 1987), 170.

12 Barbara Roberts, 'Women's Peace Activism in Canada,' in *Beyond the Vote: Canadian Women and Politics*, ed. Linda Kealey and Joan Sangster (Toronto: University of Toronto Press, 1989), 279-80. See also Barbara Roberts, 'Why Do Women Do Nothing to End the War? Canadian Feminist-Pacifists and the Great War,' CRIAW Paper no. 13 (Ottawa: Canadian Research Institute for the Advancement of Women, 1985).

13 Linda Kealey, *Enlisting for the Cause: Women, Labour, and the Left in Canada, 1890-1920* (Toronto: University of Toronto Press, 1998), 196.

14 Ibid., 197-98.

15 Katie Pickles, *Female Imperialism and National Identity: Imperial Order Daughters of the Empire* (Manchester and New York: Manchester University Press, 2002), 42.

16 See Joanna Bourke, *Dismembering the Male: Men's Bodies, Britain, and the Great War* (Chicago: University of Chicago Press, 1986); and George L. Mosse, *The Image of Man: The Creation of Modern Masculinity* (New York: Oxford University Press, 1996).

17 Contributors to this collection examine evidence from France, Britain, and their colonial possessions, as well as the Middle-East and former Ottoman empire. They also situate, relationally, both masculine and feminine signs and practices in borderline encounters of place and identity. See Melman, ed., *Borderlines*.

18 Scott, 'Rewriting History,' in *Behind the Lines*, ed. Higonnet et al., 26-28.

19 See Cpl. Joe Fitzgerald's comments reprinted in the Guelph *Evening Mercury*, 9 September 1915, 1. The inference that some women might put personal feelings for loved ones ahead of patriotic necessity was frequently raised in the local press. See also 'An Appeal to Young Women' in the Lethbridge *Daily Herald*, 3 February 1916, 5. In addition, local suffrage movements in Lethbridge and Guelph (there was no discernible activity in Trois-Rivières) appeared less active in the early phase of the war, given an absence of articles on women's suffrage, compared to pre-war coverage in the Lethbridge *Daily Herald* and Guelph *Evening Mercury*, from August 1914 to enfranchisement at the provincial and federal levels in 1917.

20 For a still comparatively uncommon review of this for Canada, see Ceta Rankhalawansingh, 'Women during the Great War,' in *Women at Work: Ontario, 1850-1930*, ed. J. Acton et al. (Toronto: Canadian Educational Press, 1974), 261-307. See also Alison Prentice et al., *Canadian Women: A History* (Toronto: Harcourt Brace and Jovanovich, 1988), 141.

21 Mosse, *The Image of Man*, 110.

22 On relationships between androcentric perceptions, practices, and representations of gender see Sandra Lipsitz Bem, *The Lenses of Gender: Transforming the Debate on Sexual Inequality* (New Haven, CT: Yale University Press, 1993).

23 Lethbridge *Daily Herald*, 19 August 1914, 4.

24 J. Castell Hopkins, *The Canadian Annual Review, 1915* (Toronto: Canadian Annual Review Company, 1916), 331.

25 Patriotic organizations in all three cities elected to their executive committees many women who can be readily identified as the spouses of leading business or professional men from each locale. Women not only shared their husbands' social status (their membership was often recorded using their husbands' first names or initials such as Mrs. James Barr or Mrs. George Ross, etc.), but also conferred such respectability to their particular organizations. A commemorative history of Lethbridge's Major Jack Ross Chapter of the IODE, organized in 1917, notes, for instance, that the 'Chapter's first Regent was the late Mrs. G.L. DeVeber, wife of a then prominent Lethbridge Physician and member of the Canadian Senate.' See

GA, Jack Ross Chapter, IODE, *Forty Years History of Major Jack Ross Chapter, Imperial Order Daughters of the Empire, 1917-1957* (n.p., n.d.), P19800046001.
26 Lethbridge *Daily Herald*, 29 April 1915, 1 and 4.
27 Ibid.
28 GA, F.G. Holyoak, *The History of the 39th Battery, Canadian Field Artillery* (1919; reprint, n.p., 1947), 13-14.
29 Lethbridge *Daily Herald*, 29 February 1916, 5.
30 Ibid., and 2 March 1916, 4.
31 Kealey, *Enlisting Women for the Cause*, 198.
32 Lethbridge *Daily Herald*, 22 October 1914, 1.
33 GA, 'Minute Book – Canadian Red Cross Society,' P1698329300.
34 Guelph *Evening Mercury*, 12 September 1914, 1.
35 Ibid., 28 September 1914, 1.
36 Ibid., 9 September 1914, 1.
37 Lethbridge *Daily Herald*, 6 May 1916, 9.
38 NAC, RG 24, Militia and Defence Records, vol. 1858, file 18, 'Canadian Red Cross.'
39 J. Castell Hopkins, *Canadian Annual Review, 1916* (Toronto: Canadian Annual Review Company, 1917), 421.
40 Glenbow Archives, 'Mathesis Club, Lethbridge. Minutes, annual reports, calendars etc., 1912-1980,' BD M-505, Reel #1, 'Constitution, n.d.'
41 Ibid., Report of General Meeting, 30 September 1914, 59.
42 Ibid., Report of General Meeting, 25 November 1914, 66.
43 Ibid., Report of General Meeting, 31 March 1915, 75.
44 On a visit from Dr. Harcourt, identified as a local missionary back from India, see Lethbridge *Daily Herald*, 1 November 1915, 1.
45 Glenbow Archives, 'Mathesis Club, Lethbridge,' Report of General Meeting, 27 October 1915, 99. This entry stated: 'A request from the I.O.D.E. was presented asking as many as possible to avail themselves of hearing Dr. Harcourt's address, "India, her part in the present war,"' with proceeds donated to Lethbridge's CPF.
46 Ibid., 100.
47 The rural area surrounding Trois-Rivières remained even more isolated from active involvement in the war effort. See, for example, Elizabeth H. Armstrong, *The Crisis of Quebec, 1914-1918* (1937; reprint, Toronto: McClelland and Stewart, 1974), 75.
48 While a local Red Cross branch, with a separate ladies committee, did exist in Trois-Rivières, its patriotic work was not prominent. Notice on the Red Cross's work in the city appeared in the *Newcomer*, 10 November 1915, 5.
49 Ibid., 25 November 1914, 4. In addition to selections played by the Union Musicale, some twelve women, francophone and anglophone, provided vocal or instrumental recitals and poetry recitations in both languages. A short comedy was performed in English.
50 University of Guelph Archives, Fireside Circle and College Heights Relief Workers Association, Minutes, 13 October 1915.
51 Ibid., 22 September 1915.
52 Ibid., 20 October 1915.
53 Ibid., 10 November 1915.
54 Margaret S. McCready, 'Adelaide Hoodless, the Women's Institute and women's organization in rural Ontario,' in *Fourth Annual Agricultural History of Ontario Seminar Proceedings, 1979*, ed. Alan A. Brookes. (Guelph: University of Guelph, 1979), 92-96. Wellington County Archives, Women's Institutes, Centre Wellington, Minutes, 1914. See also Wellington County Archives, 'History of the Speedside Women's Institute 1915-1965,' 1-2. In the autumn of 1917, the Dominion Food Controller's office developed a series of 'War Menus,' reprinted in local newspapers, which substituted or rationed increasingly scarce food commodities. See Wilson, *Ontario and the First World War*, xcii.
55 Lethbridge *Daily Herald*, 11 May 1916, 1.
56 Lethbridge *Telegram*, 11 May 1916, 1.
57 Ibid. Paul Fussell's study of the transformation of poetic diction argues that English literature was profoundly affected by the memory of the war. Contrasts in specific vocabularies

and the frequency of certain metaphors found in the 'high diction' of the Victorian era and the modernist prose that emerged are evidence of this transition. See Paul Fussell, *The Great War and Modern Memory* (London: Oxford University Press, 1975).

58 Chris Wickham and James Fentress, *Social Memory* (Oxford: Blackwell, 1992), x.

59 Benedict Anderson, *Imagined Communities: Reflections on the Origin and Spread of Nationalism* (1983; revised and extended edition, London: Verso, 1991), 6. See also John Bodnar, *Remaking America: Public Memory, Commemoration, and Patriotism in the Twentieth Century* (Princeton: Princeton University Press, 1992), 13-14.

60 GA, *Lethbridge Board of Trade, Annual Report 1915*, 2.

61 See Lethbridge *Daily Herald*, 15 May 1916, 1 and 7, and Lethbridge *Telegram*, 18 May 1916, 5.

62 On masculinity and voluntary recruitment, see Paul Maroney, '"The Great Adventure": The Context and Ideology of Recruiting in Ontario, 1914-1917,' *Canadian Historical Review* 77 (1996): 62-98.

63 A.F. Duguid, *Official History of the Canadian Forces in the Great War 1914-1919*, vol. 1 (Ottawa: King's Printer, 1938), 11-12.

64 K.B. Wamsley, 'Cultural Signification and National Ideologies: Rifle-Shooting in Late Nineteenth Century Canada,' *Social History* 20 (1995): 66-67.

65 See Mike O'Brien, 'Manhood and the Militia Myth: Masculinity, Class, and Militarism in Ontario, 1902-1914,' *Labour/Le Travail* 42 (Fall 1998): 115-41.

66 Guelph *Evening Mercury*, 8 September 1914, 5.

67 Ibid., 24 October 1914, 4.

68 Duguid, *Official History*.

69 Ibid., 24 February 1915, 4, and 14 April 1915, 4.

70 *Nouveau Trois-Rivières*, 30 October 1914, 1.

71 *Bien Public*, 24 December 1914, 1.

72 *Newcomer*, 18 November 1914, 5-6.

73 The Hon. Justice Louis-Joseph-Alfred Désy was perhaps best known for his official inquest into alleged corruption within J.-A. Tessier's municipal administration. The Désy Inquest of 1920 led to Tessier's resignation as mayor of Trois-Rivières. See François Roy, 'Le crépuscule d'un rouge: J.-A. Tessier, maire de Trois-Rivières, et l'enquête Désy de 1920,' (Master's thesis, Université du Québec à Trois-Rivières, 1988).

74 A Mr. Robitaille of the Bank of Quebec is listed. See the *Newcomer*, 20 January 1915, 4.

75 Ibid., 3 February 1915, 3.

76 Ibid., 12 January 1915, 3.

77 Ibid., 20 January 1915, 4.

78 Ibid. The list of members, according to the *Newcomer*, showed 'a very large percentage of the working classes.' The paper 'hoped that the class distinctions so rampant in this city will in this case be broken down, and that the young men of the upper classes will also affiliate themselves with the movement, thereby showing that their patriotism is a real, and not an artificial thing.'

79 Ibid., 23 February 1916, 3; 26 April 1916, 3; 3 May 1916, 1.

80 On 'gentry masculinity' see R.W. Connell's discussion of historical themes in his *Masculinities* (Berkeley: University of California Press, 1995), 190-91. See also Michael Roper and John Tosh, 'Introduction,' in *Manful Assertions: Masculinities in Britain since 1800*, ed. Michael Roper and John Tosh (London and New York: Routledge, 1991), 1-24, and J.A. Mangan and James Walvin, 'Introduction,' in *Manliness and Morality: Middle-Class Masculinity in Britain and America 1800-1940* (Manchester: Manchester University Press, 1987), 1-6.

81 Lethbridge *Daily Herald*, 29 June 1915, 1; 6 July 1915, 1; and 20 October 1915, 1, respectively.

82 NAC, RG 24, Militia and Defence Records, vol. 4696, 448-14-21, A.H. McKeown to Lt.-Col. Charles F. Winter, 3 September 1915.

83 Lethbridge *Daily Herald*, 10 July 1915, 1.

84 Ibid., and 14 July 1915, 1.

85 Ibid., 14 July 1915, 1.

86 Ibid., 10 August 1915, 5.
87 Ibid., 19 July 1915, 5.
88 Ibid., 10 August 1915, 5.
89 Ibid., 14 August 1915, 1. Reference to the 'valor' of the ranks and 'beauty' of the cheering line here was indicative of the hegemonic masculinity associated with popular notions of manhood and militarism.
90 Ibid., 22 January 1916, 3.
91 Ibid., 1.
92 Ibid., 23 May 1916, 1.
93 GA, *Lethbridge Board of Trade, Annual Report 1915*, 32.
94 Lethbridge *Daily Herald*, 13 May 1916, 1.
95 Ibid., 12 June 1916, 1.
96 One founding member of the Lethbridge Home Guard claimed that the association was 'composed of over two hundred of our business and professional men.' See NAC, Military and Defence Records, vol. 4696, 448-14-21, A.H. McKeown to Col. E.A. Cruikshank, 3 September 1915. The *Herald* also reported that the 'businessmen of Lethbridge' were 'solidly behind the Home Guard movement' as shown by their attendance at its inaugural meeting. See Lethbridge *Daily Herald*, 10 July 1915, 1.
97 Lethbridge *Daily Herald*, 26 July 1916, 1.
98 Ibid., 10 August 1916, 4.
99 Mosse, *The Image of Man*, 109-10.
100 Joy Parr comments on the possibility of approaching discursive elements that constitute historical experiences as a method of assessing power relations in 'Gender History and Historical Practice,' *Canadian Historical Review* 76 (1995), 365. See also the seminal work of Joan Scott's 'The Evidence of Experience,' *Critical Inquiry* (1991): 773-97.
101 Bourke, *Dismembering the Male*, 251-52.

Chapter 7: Men Like Us

1 Guelph *Evening Mercury*, 2 October 1915, 1 and 5.
2 As one of the most significant aftermaths of the war for all combatant countries, the presence of a cultural 'no-man's land' between the war front and home communities has attracted significant scholarly attention. 'A common feeling among soldiers,' Modris Eksteins wrote, 'was that their experience at the front had created an insurmountable barrier between them and civilians. Communication with home was no longer possible. People simply could not understand what the soldiers had been through, and the soldiers themselves could not articulate their experience appropriately.' See Modris Eksteins, *Rites of Spring: The Great War and the Birth of the Modern Age* (Toronto: Lester and Orpen Dennys, 1989), 228. In his assessment of these distances, Eric J. Leed attributes these 'detachments' to the liminal experiences soldiers activated, from their enlistment to their return: 'Those who returned from the front were often bewildered about where they would fit into the society of their origins, or were convinced that they no longer had a social place to which they might return.' See Eric J. Leed, *No Man's Land: Combat and Identity in World War I* (Cambridge: Cambridge University Press, 1979), 73. The importance of perceptions of the war and its impact on literature and memory in the interwar period has produced significant studies, notably Paul Fussell, *The Great War and Modern Memory* (Oxford: Oxford University Press, 1975); Samuel Hynes, *A War Imagined: The First World War in English Canada* (New York: Atheneum, 1987); George Mosse, *Fallen Soldiers: Reshaping the Memory of the World Wars* (Oxford: Oxford University Press, 1990); Jay Winter, *Sites of Memory, Sites of Mourning: The Great War in European Cultural History* (Cambridge: Cambridge University Press, 1996). For Canada see Alan R. Young, '"We Throw the Torch": Canadian Memorials of the Great War and the Mythology of Heroic Sacrifice,' *Journal of Canadian Studies/Revue d'études canadiennes* 24 (1989/90): 5-28, and Jonathan F. Vance, *Death So Noble: Memory, Meaning, and the First World War* (Vancouver: UBC Press, 1997).
3 Cited in Vance, *Death So Noble*, 100-1.
4 John D. Higinbotham, a pharmacist, left Guelph in 1882, settling briefly in Fort Macleod before establishing his business in Lethbridge. His career and disposition pushed him

toward involvement in numerous associations, national and local. In 1908 he began serving from his frontier apothecary as first vice-president of the Canadian Bible Society. Three years later he was named president of the Alberta Pharmaceutical Association. His wartime voluntarism included helping in the organization of the city's Patriotic Fund and Red Cross, along with assisting in the re-establishment of demobilized soldiers returning to Lethbridge. See Lethbridge *Daily Herald,* 21 October 1908, 1; ibid, 16 March 1911, 10; GA, 'Minute Book – Canadian Red Cross.' *Minutes of Special Meeting of Lethbridge Branch, Canadian Red Cross Society,* 6 May 1919, P196873293000. See also Higinbotham's memoir, *When the West Was Young: Historical Reminiscences of the Early Canadian West* (Toronto: Ryerson Press, 1933).

5 GA, P19735152000, 'Canadians at Lille' by J.D. Higinbotham.

6 Challenges surrounding veteran re-establishment dragged on well into the interwar period. See Desmond Morton and Glenn Wright, *Winning the Second Battle: Canadian Veterans and the Return to Civilian Life, 1915-1930* (Toronto: University of Toronto Press, 1987).

7 Guelph *Evening Mercury,* 26 April 1915, 1.

8 Ibid., 31 May 1915, 1.

9 Ibid., 9 June 1915, 1.

10 This practice began on a large scale during coverage of the Second Battle of Ypres in late April 1915. Both Guelph papers presented initial casualty lists, updated them each day as subsequent lists were received from Ottawa, and featured special coverage of men known to the community.

11 Guelph *Evening Mercury,* 9 June 1915, 1.

12 Ibid., 13 May 1915, 6.

13 Ibid.

14 Ibid., 4 May 1915, 1.

15 For a useful overview on how the sinking of the *Lusitania* was seen by the Allies and by neutrals, see René Albrecht-Carrié's *The Meaning of the First World War* (Englewood Cliffs, NJ: Prentice-Hall, 1965), 79-80.

16 Guelph *Evening Mercury,* 13 May 1915, 3.

17 Ibid., 8 May 1915, 2.

18 Ibid., 17 May 1915, 1.

19 Ibid., 19 May 1915, 1.

20 *Bien Public,* 29 April 1915, 1.

21 *Newcomer,* 26 April 1916, 1.

22 Ibid., 14 June 1916, 2.

23 Guelph *Evening Mercury,* 13 May 1915, 1.

24 Ibid., 29 July 1915, 1.

25 Jeffrey A. Keshen, *Propaganda and Censorship during Canada's Great War* (Edmonton: University of Alberta Press, 1996), see esp. ch. 3.

26 Guelph *Evening Mercury,* 28 July 1915, 2.

27 J. Castell Hopkins, *Canadian Annual Review, 1915* (Toronto 1915), 263.

28 Ibid.

29 Guelph *Evening Mercury,* 2 October 1915, 1.

30 Though the Mercury's report of Nourse's return claimed that 'his bravery was rewarded with the D.S.O. medal,' normally only officers were granted this honour. See Guelph *Evening Mercury,* 2 October 1915, 1.

31 Ibid., 1 and 5.

32 Lethbridge *Daily Herald,* 25 October 1915, 1.

33 Ibid.

34 Lethbridge *Daily Herald,* 8 December 1915, 1.

35 Morton and Wright, *Winning the Second Battle,* 62-3.

36 Lethbridge *Daily Herald,* 8 December 1915, 1.

37 Ibid., 6 November 1915, 1.

38 Ibid., 11 November 1915, 5.

39 Ibid, 4 December 1915, 1.

40 Ibid.

41 Between 1 July 1915 and 31 December 1916, the Military Hospitals Commission recorded 22,742 admissions. See Morton and Wright, *Winning the Second Battle*, Appendices, 234.
42 Lethbridge *Daily Herald*, 23 August 1916, 6.
43 On federal reforms of veterans' pensions see Morton and Wright, *Winning the Second Battle*, 44-61.
44 'Proceedings of the Special Committee Appointed to Consider and Report upon the Rates of Pensions to be Paid to Disabled Soldiers and the Establishment of a Permanent Pensions Board' (Ottawa: King's Printer, 1916), Appendix No. 4, 'Scale of Pensions.'
45 'Proceedings of the Special Committee Appointed to Consider and Report upon the Pension Board, the Pension Regulations, and the sufficiency or otherwise of the relief afforded thereunder.' (Ottawa: King's Printer, 1918), Appendix No. 2, testimony of Norman Knight.
46 Other executives of veteran pensions administration had contributed, 'but the architect,' as Morton and Wright made clear, 'was John Launcelot Todd.' See Morton and Wright, *Winning the Second Battle*, 53.
47 Lethbridge *Daily Herald*, 14 September 1916, 1.
48 Ibid., 24 January 1917, 4.
49 Ibid.
50 Ibid., 14 February 1917, 2, and 17 February 1917, 2.
51 Since October 1915, the provinces were officially saddled with the task of securing employment for returned soldiers. An interprovincial conference held in Ottawa had agreed at that time 'that each province should assume the responsibility of finding employment for discharged soldiers, who, upon their return to Canada, are physically or otherwise fit to assume such employment, and all expenditures necessary in undertaking this duty are borne by the Province.' For Alberta, Howard Stutchbury served as secretary for the provincial central committee of the MHC. See 'Preliminary and Second Report of the Special Committee of the House of Commons of Canada on the Care and Treatment of the Returned Soldiers in Canada' (Ottawa: King's Printer, 1917), 15. Since then, however, no evidence of this committee's efforts in securing employment for Lethbridge veterans can be found; indications from the *Herald*'s editor were that nothing, through any existing bureaucracy, was being done to locate work for the city's ex-soldiers until the Returned Soldiers Bureau was formed in January 1916. It was not until then that Stutchbury's office, along with J.R. Oliver's Returned Soldiers Bureau, actively sought prospective employers' enquiries through advertisements placed in the *Herald*.
52 Lethbridge *Daily Herald*, 14 February 1917, 7.
53 Ibid., 4.
54 *Nouveau Trois-Rivières*, 17 November 1916, 5.
55 Ibid., 1 December 1916, 3.
56 Lethbridge *Daily Herald*, 29 August 1917, 1 and 6.
57 Marnoch also served on the Food Control Board of Canada, was vice-president of the Alberta Food Committee and vice-chairman of the Dominion War Loan Campaign.
58 Lethbridge *Daily Herald*, 4 December 1918, 6.
59 Morton and Wright concluded that calculating 'total disability at the end of the war is surprisingly difficult, since the majority of sick and wounded were considered (and considered themselves) to be fully recovered; only later did they attribute their disability to wartime conditions.' However, the authors reported that by February 1919, 60,203 disability pensions had been awarded. This represented 9.7 percent of the 619,636 total appointments and enlistments in the CEF during the war. On pension disbursements, see Morton and Wright, *Winning the Second Battle*, n. 41, 243-44. The figure for the CEF's total strength appeared in G.W.L. Nicholson, *Canadian Expeditionary Force, 1914-1918: The Official History of the Canadian Army in the First World War* (Ottawa: Queen's Printer, 1962), Appendix C, 546.
60 Lethbridge *Daily Herald*, 30 November 1918, 13.
61 'The Borden government,' Morton and Wright stated, 'stubbornly refused any proposal that might make it the employer of last resort for veterans.' In a similar vein, they revealed later that 'the Military Hospitals Commission had urged, as a transitional measure, such massive public works as the building of a national highway. Such ideas were forgotten

during the wartime prosperity, and they were overshadowed by post-war fiscal anxieties.' See Morton and Wright, *Winning the Second Battle,* 98 and 153.

62 Lethbridge *Telegram,* 23 November 1916, 1.
63 Lethbridge *Daily Herald,* 24 January 1917, 4.
64 Ibid., 8 February 1917, 4. As Morton and Wright stated, 'Worst off were the "functional" or "shell-shock" cases. Whether doctors took them seriously or dismissed them as cowardly malingerers, the consequences were virtually identical.' Granting pensions to these men was discouraged. See Morton and Wright, *Winning the Second Battle,* 75.
65 A major employer's attitude to reintegrating shell-shocked veterans was indicated in a statement issued to supervisors by Canadian Pacific Railway vice-president A.D. MacTier. MacTier warned that ex-soldiers, on the whole, were not 'normal.' 'Do you consider him as an ordinary workman, let him shift for himself and loom on his mistakes only as you would an ordinary employee? If so, you are assuming that he is in all respects just a normal man, and should be able to do the same work as quickly and as well as the average employee. If you do, you are wrong.' MacTier anticipated that getting 'nerve-shattered' veterans back on the job for the CPR would be an uneven success. 'They are [sic] bound to be some exceptions and some men will fail to make good,' he concluded. 'The success or failure of the majority, however, depends on you, and it is your privilege to help your country in this National crisis by endeavoring to make useful citizens out of the nerve-shattered men that are coming back to us from the front.' See 'Proceedings of the Special Committee Appointed by Resolution of the House of Commons, on the 18th of September 1919, and to whom was referred Bill No. 10, An Act to Amend the Department of Soldiers' Civil Re-establishment' (Ottawa: King's Printer, 1919), 935-36.
66 Lethbridge *Daily Herald,* 21 December 1918, 10.
67 Morton and Wright, *Winning the Second Battle,* 113. See also Lethbridge *Daily Herald,* 21 December 1918, 1, and 23 December 1918, 1.
68 Lethbridge *Daily Herald,* 23 December 1918, 10.
69 Ibid., 2.
70 Ibid., 20 December 1918, 12.
71 Ibid., 23 December 1918, 3.
72 *Nouveau Trois-Rivières,* 28 February 1917, 2.
73 Ibid., 13 April 1917, 3.
74 *Newcomer,* 30 May 1917, 4.
75 Ibid., 27 September 1916, 3.
76 A brief description of this event and a reprinted report submitted by Ontario's lieutenant governor on the origin and course of the Toronto riots appears in Barbara M. Wilson, *Ontario and the First World War, 1914-1918: A Collection of Documents* (Toronto: Champlain Society for the Government of Ontario, University of Toronto Press, 1977), lxvii-lxviii and 70-71.
77 *Bien Public,* 8 August 1918, 1.
78 Ibid., 21 November 1918, 1.
79 Ibid., 14 November 1918, 1.
80 Letter from O.F. Ursenbach to *Herald.* See Lethbridge *Daily Herald,* 14 September 1918, 3.
81 Ibid., 3 October 1918, 3.
82 Ibid., 24 September 1918, 3.
83 Jay Cassel, *The Secret Plague: Venereal Disease in Canada, 1838-1939* (Toronto: University of Toronto Press, 1987), chs. 6 and 7. Together, reported cases of syphilis and gonorrhea outpaced the most prevalent disease in the CEF, influenza. See also Morton and Wright, *Winning the Second Battle,* Statistical Appendix, 231.
84 Order-in-Council, PC 1446, Report of the Committee of the Privy Council, submitted by President, Military Hospitals Commission, 29 May 1917, Copy in NAC, RG 38, Department of Veterans Affairs (hereafter Veterans Affairs), vol. 286, Provincial Secretary for Ontario.
85 The term 'military hospitals' in this context refers to 'general treatment hospitals entirely under the control of the Department [Soldiers' Civil Re-Establishment]' as defined by the DSCR: institutions funded by and administered by the state. See House of Commons. Special Committee on Social Civil Re-establishment, *Reports and Proceedings,* 1919, 1040.

86 Veterans Affairs, vol. 286, Dispute with Ontario, 1916-31, 'Memorandum of Agreement between the Military Hospitals Commission of Canada and the Provincial Secretary of Ontario.' The date of this agreement appears in Veterans Affairs, vol. 285, Speedwell Property, N.F. Parkinson to H.C. Nixon, 13 October 1920.
87 Guelph *Evening Mercury*, 3 May 1917, 4.
88 Ibid., 4 May 1917, 1.
89 Ibid.
90 Veterans Affairs, vol. 286, 'Report of Board of Adjustment, re: return of Speedwell Hospital, Guelph to Provincial Government.'
91 Final claims settlements were reached in June 1931. See ibid., Deputy Provincial Secretary to E.H. Scammell, 30 June 1931.
92 Ibid., vol. 286, 'Department of Provincial Secretary, Ontario, and Department of Soldiers Civil Re-Establishment. Summary of Accounts in connection with occupation of the Military Hospitals Commission of the Ontario Reformatory, Guelph (1917 to 1921), and the Ontario Hospital, Whitby (1917 to 1919).'
93 Ibid., vol. 286, Dispute with Ontario, 1916-31, 'Memorandum of Agreement between the Military Hospitals Commission of Canada and the Provincial Secretary of Ontario.' The key clause stated that 'it is expressly provided that such members of the Provincial staff and employees as the Provincial Secretary may deem advisable are to remain there as at present, together with any others who may be placed or sent there by the Province, including the Provincial Farm Director and all shall be free from molestation or interference of any kind by the soldiers or employees or others brought to said premises by the Commission.'
94 This was as of 14 October 1919. See Veterans Affairs, vol. 286, Dispute with Ontario, 1916-31, G.E. Black to F.G. Robinson, 14 October 1919.
95 Ibid., Speedwell Hospital Investigation, J.J. Bayliss to Maj. G.L. Drew, 2 August 1920.
96 Veterans Affairs, vol. 285, Department of Soldiers' Civil Re-establishment, Canada's Work for Disabled Soldiers (Ottawa: King's Printer, 1919), 13.
97 Veterans Affairs, vol. 285, Dispute with Ontario, 1916-31, 'Report of Meeting of Commission of Government and Representatives of Guelph Branch of G.W.V.A.,' 25 November 1919, 5.
98 Ibid., vol. 285, undated copy of GWVA Guelph Branch resolution received by solicitor general.
99 Ibid., vol. 285, A.C. Mackintosh to Hugh Guthrie, 1 October 1919.
100 Robinson sent word to Guthrie of this preliminary departmental investigation 'to let you know meantime that the matter is being actively pursued.' See ibid., F.G. Robinson to Hugh Guthrie, 10 October 1919.
101 Ibid., vol. 285, James A. Lougheed to Hugh Guthrie, 31 October 1919.
102 Ibid., vol. 285, 'Report of Meeting of Commission of Government and Representatives of Guelph Branch of G.W.V.A.,' 25 November 1919, 5.
103 Ibid., 7.
104 Ibid., 5.
105 Ibid., 34.
106 Ibid.
107 Ibid., vol. 286, Dispute with Ontario, 1916-1931, G.E. Black to F.G. Robinson, 27 November 1919.
108 Ibid., vol. 285, 'Report of Meeting of Commission of Government and Representatives of Guelph Branch of G.W.V.A.,' 25 November 1919, 5.
109 Lethbridge *Daily Herald*, 21 December 1918, 15.
110 In his study of Canadian Remembrance Day rituals, Alan R. Young states, 'It is McCrae's poem that has stuck in the popular memory and that is quoted or set to music for Remembrance Day services, its aptness, of course, quite apparent at a time of year when the wearing of poppies is a ritual.' See Young's '"We Throw the Torch,"' 18.
111 McCrae's famous poem 'seems to have had some influence on Canadian war memorials,' Young states. Citing one example, he points out that part of its text was engraved in the Memorial Chamber of Ottawa's Peace Tower. See note in ibid., 27. Paul Fussell refers to its

appeal in Britain, demonstrated by its adoption for commemorative purposes by the British Legion. See Fussell, *The Great War and Modern Memory*, 249.
112 Lethbridge *Daily Herald*, 21 November 1918, 8.
113 Marc Ferro, *The Great War 1914-1918* (1969; reprint, London: Routledge and Keagan Paul, 1973), 151-52.
114 As Robert Graves recalled in his immensely popular war memoir, *Good-Bye to All That* (1929; reprint, Harmondsworth: Penguin, 1983), 78, the 'regimental spirit persistently survived all catastrophes. Our First Battalion, for instance, was practically annihilated within two months of joining the British Expeditionary Force.' After recounting a list of unit carnages he was familiar with from the first battle of Ypres onwards, Graves suggested that during the war 'at least fifteen or twenty thousand men must have passed through each of the two line battalions, whose fighting strength never stood at more than eight hundred.' Consistently, Graves related his own war experience as something that was shaped by his life in the army, not just as a soldier but as a Royal Welsh Fusilier. He went on to recount that in 'the First and Second Battalions, throughout the war, not merely the officers and N.C.O.s knew their regimental history. The men had learned far more about Minden, Albuhera, and Waterloo, and the Battle of the Pyramids, than they had about the fighting on other fronts, or the official causes of the war.' Perhaps this would have been clearer in Lethbridge if the city's GWVA recommended that individual regiments or service units be inscribed, but identifying the battalion in which the 'supreme sacrifice' was made may still have reflected this same sense of identity.
115 Lethbridge *Daily Herald*, 23 November 1918, 14. Among a host of public activities, many war-related, Higinbotham had served as a school board trustee in 1896, 1897, and from 1912 to 1915. See GA, Souvenir Booklet: Lethbridge Public Schools (Lethbridge 1950), P19851045017.
116 Lethbridge *Daily Herald*, 22 November 1918, 10.
117 Ibid., 25 November 1918, 7.
118 This appears to have been a hopeful speculation on Marnoch's part. As of the previous April, the Carnegie Foundation had indicated by letter to city council that an original library fund offer, made to the city fifteen years before, was considered to have lapsed. Furthermore, the Foundation indicated at this time that no grants would be made during wartime as materiel, labour, and financial resources were being directed toward war production. See ibid., 22 April 1918, 9.
119 Ibid., 29 November 1918, 14. A miners' library had been set up in 1893, and the city's YMCA housed the first free library from 1919 to 1921. Lethbridge's first public library building was then completed with the aid of a Carnegie Foundation grant. It was to be named the Carnegie Library, but became the Lethbridge Public Library following a public outcry. Andrew Carnegie was despised by workers in Canada as well as in the United States. See Alex Johnston and Barry R. Peat, *Lethbridge Place Names and Points of Interest* (Lethbridge: Lethbridge Historical Society, 1987), 58.
120 Lethbridge *Daily Herald*, 21 November 1918, 8.
121 Ibid., 22 November 1918, 10.
122 Ibid., 30 November 1918, 14.
123 Ibid., 19 December 1918, 10.
124 Ibid., 27 November 1918, 7.
125 Ibid.
126 Ibid., 21 November 1918, 4.
127 Young, '"We Throw the Torch,"'5. Modris Eksteins suggests that war memorial unveiling ceremonies in every belligerent country did not peak in frequency until 1927. See Eksteins, *Rites of Spring*, 262.
128 Lethbridge *Daily Herald*, 30 December 1918, 5.
129 Ibid., 31 December 1918, 4.
130 Alex Johnston, 'Canada's Wars and the Cenotaph in Galt Gardens, Lethbridge Alberta,' copy of occasional paper published by Lethbridge Historical Society deposited in Sir Alexander Galt Archives.
131 Johnston and Peat, *Lethbridge Place Names*, 37.

Chapter 8: Beyond Hometown Horizons

1 Norbert Elias, *The Society of Individuals*, ed. Michael Schröter, trans. Edmund Jephcott (Oxford: Basil Blackwell, 1991). See also, by the same author, *The Court Society*, trans. Edmund Jephcott (Oxford: Basil Blackwell, 1983); *The Civilizing Process*, trans. Edmund Jephcott, 2 vols. (New York: Pantheon Books, 1982); *The History of Manners*, trans. Edmund Jephcott (Oxford: Basil Blackwell, 1978).

2 Ibid., 19-20.

3 They were met by the wives of Mayor Hardie and the Rev. Charles McKillop. See, for instance, '"Welcome Home" Committee is Needed in City,' Lethbridge *Daily Herald*, 23 January 1919, 3.

4 See Desmond Morton and Glenn Wright, *Winning the Second Battle: Canadian Veterans and the Return to Civilian Life, 1915-1930* (Toronto: University of Toronto Press, 1987).

5 A complete account appears under 'Second Annual Banquet Vets, Successful Affair,' Lethbridge *Daily Herald*, 2 January 1919, 3.

6 In many instances, socially exclusive feasts gave the upper classes in local communities a chance to display themselves in quasi-public forms. Their rituals of toasting, speechmaking, and *haute cuisine* repasts signalled intersecting re-presentations of class, ethnic, and gendered differences, both among participants and later, through public reporting of the event to others, among citizens of generally lower social rank. Boundaries between the ascendant orders and other citizens in a given locale might be delineated through an invitation list or enforced through a restrictive admission or subscription price. From the series of banquets that celebrated Queen Victoria's coronation in 1838, such dinners in towns and cities in British North America, and the grand balls that often accompanied them, became ubiquitous and appealing sites of social mimicry. Gradually, over the long term, more plebeian groups appropriated the outward forms for their own purposes: the nineteenth-century banquet of aristocratic pretensions had become the 'annual dinner' of the early twentieth century. Apart from surviving versions of the debutante's ball, most offshoot ceremonies, hosted variously by businesses, sportsmen's groups, fraternal orders, and ethnic associations, retained forms of masculine signification, where toasts, roasts, and more exuberant expressions of manful assertion might configure head-table performances. For a typology of feasting rituals, see Bonnie Huskins, 'From *Haute Cuisine* to Ox Roasts: Public Feasting and the Negotiation of Class in Mid-19th Century Saint John and Halifax,' *Labour/Le Travail* 37 (Spring 1996): 9-32.

7 Lethbridge *Daily Herald*, 2 January 1919, 3.

8 Ibid.

9 Ibid.

10 Ibid.

11 Elias, *The Court Society*, 144.

12 Elias, *The Society of Individuals*, 18.

13 Lethbridge *Daily Herald*, 19 August 1914, 4.

14 Roger Chartier, *On the Edge of the Cliff: History, Language, and Practices,* trans. Lydia G. Cochrane (Baltimore and London: Johns Hopkins University Press, 1997), 20.

15 Ibid., 22 (emphasis in original).

16 Jay Winter and Jean-Louis Robert, eds., *Capital Cities at War: Paris, London, Berlin, 1914-1919* (Cambridge: Cambridge University Press, 1997), 4.

17 *Newcomer*, 8 September 1915, 6.

18 *Bien Public*, 10 June 1915, 1, and Guelph *Evening Mercury*, 21 October 1914, 4.

Bibliography

Monographs and Collections

Acton, J., et al., eds. *Women at Work: Ontario, 1850-1930*. Toronto: Canadian Educational Press, 1974.

Albrecht-Carrié, René. *The Meaning of the First World War*. Englewood Cliffs, NJ: Prentice-Hall, 1965.

Anderson, Benedict. *Imagined Communities: Reflections on the Origin and Spread of Nationalism*. 1983. Reprint, London: Verso, 1991.

Armstrong, Elizabeth H. *The Crisis of Quebec, 1914-1918*. 1937. Reprint, Toronto: McClelland and Stewart, 1974.

Avery, Donald. *'Dangerous Foreigners': European Immigrant Workers and Labour Radicalism in Canada, 1896-1932*. Toronto: McClelland and Stewart, 1979.

Bacchi, Carol Lee. *Liberation Deferred? The Ideas of the English-Canadian Suffragists, 1877-1918*. Toronto: University of Toronto Press, 1983.

Beaulieu, André, and Jean Hamelin. *Les journaux du Québec de 1764 à 1964*. Quebec: Les Presses de l'Université Laval, 1965.

–. *La presse québécoise: des origines à nos jours*, vol. 4, *1896-1910*, and vol. 5, *1911-1919*. Quebec: Les Presses de l'Université Laval, 1979.

Bell, Catherine. *Ritual Theory, Ritual Practice*. New York: Oxford University Press, 1992.

Bem, Sandra Lipsitz. *The Lenses of Gender: Transforming the Debate on Sexual Inequality*. New Haven, CT: Yale University Press, 1993.

Bercuson, David Jay. *Alberta's Coal Industry, 1919*. Calgary: Historical Society of Alberta, 1978.

Berger, Carl. *The Sense of Power: Studies in the Ideas of Canadian Imperialism, 1867-1914*. Toronto: University of Toronto Press, 1970.

Bloomfield, Elizabeth, and Gilbert Stelter, et al. *Guelph and Wellington County: A Bibliography of Settlement and Development since 1800*. Guelph: Guelph Regional Project, 1988.

–. *Inventory of Primary and Archival Sources: Guelph and Wellington County to 1940*. Guelph: Guelph Regional Project, 1989.

Bocock, Robert. *Rituals in Industrial England: A Sociological Analysis of Ritualism in Modern England*. London: George Allen and Unwin, 1974.

Bodnar, John. *Remaking America: Public Memory, Commemoration, and Patriotism in the Twentieth Century*. Princeton: Princeton University Press, 1992.

Bourdé, Guy, and Hervé Martin, *Les Ecoles historiques*. Paris: Editions du Seuil, 1983.

Bourke, Joanna. *Dismembering the Male: Men's Bodies, Britain, and the Great War*. Chicago: University of Chicago Press, 1996.

Braybon, Gail. *Women Workers in the First World War: The British Experience*. London: Croom Helm, 1981.

Brittain, Vera. *Chronicle of Youth*. Edited by Alan Bishop. Glasgow: Fontana/Collins, 1982.

Brookes, Alan A., ed. *Fourth Annual Agricultural History of Ontario Seminar Proceedings, 1979*. Guelph: University of Guelph, 1979.

Brown, Robert Craig, and Ramsay Cook. *Canada 1896-1921: A Nation Transformed.* Toronto: McClelland and Stewart, 1974.

–. *Robert Laird Borden: A Biography.* 2 vols. Toronto: Macmillan, 1975 and 1980.

Buitenhuis, Peter. *The Great War of Words: British, American, and Canadian Propaganda and Fiction, 1914-1933.* Vancouver: UBC Press, 1987.

Canadian Annual Review. 1914-1918. Toronto: The Canadian Review Company, 1915-1919.

Carter, David J. *Behind Canadian Barbed Wire: Alien Refugee and Prisoner of War Camps in Canada, 1914-1946.* Calgary: Tumbleweed Press, 1980.

Cassel, Jay. *The Secret Plague: Venereal Disease in Canada, 1838-1939.* Toronto: University of Toronto Press, 1987.

Cesarani, David, and Tony Kushner, eds. *The Internment of Aliens in Twentieth Century Britain.* London: Frank Cass, 1993.

Chartier, Roger. *On the Edge of the Cliff: History, Language, and Practices.* Translated by Lydia G. Cochrane. Baltimore and London: Johns Hopkins University Press, 1997.

Cooper, Helen M., Adrienne Munich, and Susan Squier, eds. *Arms and the Woman: War, Gender and Literary Representation.* Chapel Hill, NC: University of North Carolina Press, 1989.

Connell, R.W. *Masculinities.* Berkeley: University of California Press, 1995.

Cook, Ramsay. *Canada and the French-Canadian Question.* Toronto: Macmillan, 1966.

Cooke, Miriam, and Angela Woollacott, eds. *Gendering War Talk.* Princeton: Princeton University Press, 1993.

Craig, Gordon A. *Europe since 1914.* 1961. Rev. ed. New York: Holt, Rinehart and Winston, 1966.

Darnton, Robert. *The Great Cat Massacre and Other Episodes in French Cultural History.* New York: Basic Books, 1984.

Davis, Susan G. *Parades and Power: Street Theatre in Nineteenth-Century Philadelphia.* Philadelphia: Temple University Press, 1986.

den Otter, Andrew A. *Civilizing the West: The Galts and the Development of Western Canada.* Edmonton: University of Alberta Press, 1982.

Derome, L.-J.-A. *Le Canada ecclésiastique: almanach annuaire du clergé canadien, 1917.* Montreal: Librairie Beauchemin, 1917.

Desnoyers, Hélène. *Le 12e Régiment Blindé du Canada: la milice canadienne et le 12e Régiment Blindé du Canada.* Trois-Rivières: Le 12e Régiment Blindé du Canada, 1988.

Duguid, A.F. *Official History of the Canadian Forces in the Great War, 1914-1919.* Vol. 1. Ottawa: King's Printer, 1938.

Eksteins, Modris. *Rites of Spring: The Great War and the Birth of the Modern Age.* Toronto: Lester and Orpen Dennys, 1989.

Elias, Norbert. *The History of Manners.* Translated by Edmund Jephcott. Oxford: Basil Blackwell, 1978.

–. *The Civilizing Process.* Translated by Edmund Jephcott. 2 vols. New York: Pantheon Books, 1982.

–. *The Court Society.* Translated by Edmund Jephcott. Oxford: Basil Blackwell, 1983.

–. *The Society of Individuals.* Edited by Michael Schröter. Translated by Edmund Jephcott. Oxford: Basil Blackwell, 1991.

English, John. *Borden: His Life and Times.* Toronto: McGraw-Hill Ryerson, 1977.

–. *The Decline of Politics: The Conservatives and the Party System, 1901-1920.* Toronto: University of Toronto Press, 1977.

–. *Shadow of Heaven: The Life of Lester Pearson.* Vol. 1, *1897-1948.* Toronto: Lester and Orpen Dennys, 1989.

Fentress, James, and Chris Wickham. *Social Memory.* Oxford: Blackwell, 1992.

Ferro, Marc. *The Great War 1914-1918.* London: Routledge and Keagan Paul, 1973.

Fussell, Paul. *The Great War and Modern Memory.* New York: Oxford University Press, 1975.

Gagnon, Jean-Pierre. *Le 22e Bataillon (canadien-français), 1914-1919: étude socio-militaire.* Quebec: Les Presses de l'Université Laval en collaboration avec le ministère de la Défense nationale et le Centre d'édition du Gouvernement du Canada, 1986.

Gamelin, Alain, et al. *Trois-Rivières illustrée*. Trois-Rivières: La Corporation des fêtes du 350e anniversaire de Trois-Rivières, 1984.
Geertz, Clifford. *The Interpretation of Cultures: Selected Essays*. New York: Basic Books, 1973.
–. *Local Knowledge: Further Essays in Interpretive Anthropology*. New York: Basic Books, 1983.
Godin, Louis-Georges. *Mémorial trifluvien*. 2 vols. Trois-Rivières: Editions du Bien Public, 1932.
Granatstein, J.L., and J.M. Hitsman. *Broken Promises: A History of Conscription in Canada*. Toronto: Oxford University Press, 1977.
Graves, Robert. *Good-Bye to All That*. 1929. Reprint, Harmondsworth: Penguin, 1983.
Hague, D., S. Gould, H.J. Cody, et al., *The Jubilee Volume of Wycliffe College*. Toronto: Toronto Wycliffe College, 1927.
Hamelin, Jean, and Nicole Gagnon. *Histoire du catholicisme québécois*. Vol. 1, *1898-1940*. Montreal: Boréal, 1984.
Hardy, René, and Norman Séguin. *Forêt et société en Mauricie: la formation de la région de Trois-Rivières, 1830-1930*. Montreal: Boréal, 1984.
Hardy, René, Guy Trépanier, and Jacques Belleau. *La Mauricie et les Bois-Francs: inventaire bibliographique, 1760-1975*. Montreal: Boréal, 1977.
Harris, Stephen J. *Canadian Brass: The Making of a Professional Army, 1860-1939*. Toronto: University of Toronto Press, 1988.
Haycock, Ronald. *Sam Hughes: The Public Career of a Controversial Canadian*. Waterloo, ON: Wilfred Laurier Press, 1986.
Higinbotham, John D. *When the West Was Young: Historical Reminiscences of the Early Canadian West*. Toronto: Ryerson, 1933.
Higonnet, Margaret R., et al., eds. *Behind the Lines: Gender and the Two World Wars*. New Haven, CT: Yale University Press, 1987.
Hobsbawm, Eric. *The Age of Empire, 1870-1914*. New York: Pantheon Books, 1987.
–. *Age of Extremes: The Short Twentieth Century, 1914-1918*. London: Abacus, 1994.
Hopkins, J. Castell. *Canada at War: A Record of Heroism and Achievement, 1914-1918*. Toronto: Canadian Annual Review Company, 1919.
Hunt, Lynn, ed. *The New Cultural History*. Berkeley: University of California Press, 1989
Hurtubise, Pierre, et al. *Le laïc dans l'église canadienne-française de 1830 à nos jours*. Montreal: Fides, 1972.
Hynes, Samuel. *A War Imagined: The First World War in English Canada*. New York: Atheneum, 1987.
Jaenan, Cornelius J. *The Belgians in Canada*. Ottawa: Canadian Historical Association, 1991.
Johnson, Leo A. *History of Guelph 1827-1927*. Guelph: Guelph Historical Society, 1977.
Johnston, Alex, and Barry R. Peat. *Lethbridge Place Names and Points of Interest*. Lethbridge: Lethbridge Historical Society, 1987.
Johnston, Alex, and Andy A. den Otter. *Lethbridge: A Centennial History*. Lethbridge: City of Lethbridge and Fort Whoop-Up County Chapter, Historical Society of Lethbridge, 1985.
Jones, David. *Empire of Dust: Settling and Abandoning the Prairie Dry Belt*. Edmonton: University of Alberta Press, 1987.
Kaye, V.J. *Ukrainian Canadians in Canada's Wars*. Toronto: Ukrainian Canadian Research Foundation, 1983.
Kealey, Linda. *Enlisting for the Cause: Women, Labour, and the Left in Canada, 1890-1920*. Toronto: University of Toronto Press, 1998.
Kealey, Linda, and Joan Sangster, eds. *Beyond the Vote: Canadian Women in Politics*. Toronto: University of Toronto Press, 1989.
Keshen, Jeffrey A. *Propaganda and Censorship in Canada's Great War*. Edmonton: University of Alberta Press, 1996.
Kordan, Bohdan S., and Peter Melnycky, eds. *In the Shadow of the Rockies: Diary of the Castle Mountain Internment Camp 1915-1917*. Edmonton: Canadian Institute of Ukrainian Studies, 1991.
Lamy, Jean-Paul, and Guildo Rousseau, eds. *Ringuet en mémoire: 50 ans après* Trente Arpents. Quebec: Pélican/Septentrion, 1989.
Leach, Edmund. *Culture and Communication: The Logic by Which Symbols Are Connected*. Cambridge: Cambridge University Press, 1976.

Leed, Eric J. *No Man's Land: Combat and Identity in World War I.* Cambridge: Cambridge University Press, 1979.
Linteau, Paul-André, René Durocher, and Jean-Claude Robert. *Quebec: A History, 1867-1929.* Translated by Robert Chodos. Toronto: J. Lorimer, 1983.
Luciuk, Lubomyr. *A Time for Atonement: Canada's First National Internment Operations and the Ukrainian Canadians, 1914-1920.* Kingston: Limestone Press, 1988.
McCallum, John. *Unequal Beginnings: Agriculture and Economic Development in Quebec and Ontario until 1870.* Toronto: University of Toronto Press, 1980.
McCormack, A. Ross. *Reformers, Rebels, and Revolutionaries: The Western Canadian Radical Movement, 1899-1919.* Toronto: University of Toronto Press, 1977.
Maltais, Denise, Louise Fréchette, and Louis-René Desurreault. *État général des fonds et collections conservés aux archives du Séminaire de Trois-Rivières.* Trois-Rivières: Séminaire de Trois-Rivières, 1985.
Mangan, J.A., and James Walvin, eds. *Manliness and Morality: Middle-Class Masculinity in Britain and America 1800-1940.* Manchester: Manchester University Press, 1987.
Martynowych, Orest T. *Ukrainians in Canada: The Formative Period, 1891-1924.* Edmonton: Canadian Institute of Ukrainian Studies, 1991.
Melman, Billie, ed. *Borderlines: Genders and Identities in War and Peace, 1870-1930.* New York: Routledge, 1998.
Miller, J.R. *Skyscrapers Hide the Heavens: A History of Indian-White Relations in Canada.* Toronto: University of Toronto Press, 1991.
Morris, Philip H. *The Canadian Patriotic Fund: A Record of Its Activities from 1914 to 1918.* N.p., 1920.
Morton, Desmond. *The Canadian General: Sir William Otter.* Toronto: Hakkert Press, 1974.
–. *A Peculiar Kind of Politics: Canada's Overseas Ministry in the First World War.* Toronto: University of Toronto Press, 1982.
–. *A Military History of Canada.* Edmonton: Hurtig, 1985.
–. *Silent Battle: Canadian Prisoners of War in Germany, 1914-1918.* Toronto: Lester Publishing, 1992.
–. *When Your Number's Up: The Canadian Soldier in the First World War.* Toronto: Random House, 1993.
Morton, Desmond, and J.L. Granatstein, *Marching to Armageddon: Canadians and the Great War, 1914-1919.* Toronto: Lester and Orpen Dennys, 1989.
Morton, Desmond, and Glenn Wright. *Winning the Second Battle: Canadian Veterans and the Return to Civilian Life, 1915-1930.* Toronto: University of Toronto Press, 1987.
Mosse, George L. *Fallen Soldiers: Reshaping the Memory of the World Wars.* Oxford: Oxford University Press, 1990.
–. *The Image of Man: The Creation of Modern Masculinity.* New York and Oxford: Oxford University Press, 1996.
Mukerji, Chandra, and Michael Schudson, eds. *Rethinking Popular Culture: Contemporary Perspectives in Cultural Studies.* Berkeley: University of California Press, 1991.
Nicholson, G.W.L. *Canadian Expeditionary Force, 1914-1919: The Official History of the Canadian Army in the First World War.* Ottawa: Queen's Printer, 1962.
Owram, Doug. *The Government Generation: Canadian Intellectuals and the State, 1900-1945.* Toronto: University of Toronto Press, 1986.
Palmer, Howard. *Patterns of Prejudice: A History of Nativism in Alberta.* Toronto: McClelland and Stewart, 1982.
Palmer, Howard, and Donald Smith, eds. *The New Provinces: Alberta and Saskatchewan, 1905-1980.* Vancouver: Tantalus Research, 1980.
Panayi, Panikos. *The Enemy in Our Midst: Germans in Britain during the First World War.* Oxford and Providence: Berg Publishers, 1991.
–, ed. *Minorities in Wartime: National and Racial Groupings in Europe, North America and Australia during the Two World Wars.* Oxford and Providence: Berg Publishers, 1993.
Pickering, Michael. *History, Experience and Cultural Studies.* New York: St. Martin's Press, 1997.
Pickles, Katie. *Female Imperialism and National Identity: Imperial Order Daughters of the Empire.* Manchester and New York: Manchester University Press, 2002.

Pierson, Ruth Roach, ed. *Women and Peace: Theoretical, Historical, and Practical Perspectives*. London: Croom Helm, 1987.
Prentice, Alison, et al. *Canadian Women: A History*. Toronto: Harcourt Brace Jovanovich, 1988.
Provencher, Jean. *Québec sous la loi des Mesures de Guerre, 1918*. Trois-Rivières: Editions du Boréal Express, 1971.
Ringuet. *Trente arpents*. 1938. Reprint, Montreal: Fides, 1969.
Ritter, Gerhard. *The Sword and the Scepter: The Problem of Militarism in Germany*. Coral Gables, FL: University of Florida Press, 1972.
Roper, Michael, and John Tosh, eds. *Manful Assertions: Masculinities in Britain since 1800*. London and New York: Routledge, 1991.
Rumilly, Robert. *Histoire de la province de Québec: Le Réglement 17*. Montreal: B. Valiquette, 1947.
Rutherford, Paul. *The Making of the Canadian Media*. Toronto: McGraw-Hill Ryerson, 1978.
Ryan, William F. *The Clergy and Economic Growth in Quebec, 1896-1914*. Quebec: Les Presses de l'Université Laval, 1966.
Scott, Frederick George. *The Great War As I Saw It*. Vancouver: Clarke and Stuart, 1934.
Socknat, Thomas P. *Witness against War: Pacifism in Canada, 1900-1945*. Toronto: University of Toronto Press, 1987.
Stacey, C.P. *Canada and the Age of Conflict*. Vol. 1, *1867-1921*. Toronto: Macmillan, 1977.
Steele, C. Frank. *Prairie Editor: The Life and Times of Buchanan of Lethbridge*. Toronto: Ryerson Press, 1961.
Swyripa, F., and J.H. Thompson, eds. *Loyalties in Conflict: Ukrainians in Canada during the Great War*. Edmonton: Canadian Institute of Ukrainian Studies, 1983.
Thompson, John Herd. *The Harvests of War: The Prairie West, 1914-1918*. Toronto: McClelland and Stewart, 1978.
Turner, Edith, ed. *Blazing the Trail: Way Marks in the Exploration of Symbols*. Tucson: University of Arizona Press, 1992.
Turner, Victor. *Dramas, Fields, and Metaphors: Symbolic Action in Human Society*. Ithaca, NY: Cornell University Press, 1974.
–. *The Anthropology of Performance*. New York: PAJ Publications, 1986.
Vance, Jonathan F. *Objects of Concern: Canadian Prisoners of War through the Twentieth Century*. Vancouver: UBC Press, 1994.
–. *Death So Noble: Memory, Meaning and the First World War*. Vancouver: UBC Press, 1997.
Vibert, Elizabeth. *Trader's Tales: Narratives of Cultural Encounters on the Columbian Plateau, 1807-1846*. Norman, OK: University of Oklahoma Press, 1987.
Voisey, Paul. *Vulcan: The Making of a Prairie Community*. Toronto: University of Toronto Press, 1988.
Wade, Mason. *The French Canadians, 1760-1967*. Vol. 2. Rev. ed. Toronto: Macmillan, 1976.
Waiser, Bill. *Park Prisoners: The Untold Story of Western Canada's National Parks, 1915-1946*. Saskatoon: Fifth House, 1995.
Wall, Richard, and Jay Winter, eds. *The Upheaval of War: Family, War and Welfare in Europe, 1914-1918*. Cambridge: Cambridge University Press. 1988.
Wheeler, Margaret, ed. *Lethbridge News 1901-1906 and Lethbridge Daily Herald 1905-1918: A Subject and Bibliographical Index*. Lethbridge: Lethbridge Historical Society, 1987.
Wilson, Barbara M., ed. *Ontario and the First World War, 1914-1918: A Collection of Documents*. Toronto: Champlain Society for the Government of Ontario and University of Toronto Press, 1977.
Winter, Jay. *The Great War and the British People*. Cambridge, MA: Harvard University Press, 1986.
–. *Sites of Memory, Sites of Mourning: The Great War in European Cultural History*. Cambridge: Cambridge University Press, 1995.
Winter, Jay, and Jean-Louis Robert, eds. *Capital Cities at War: Paris, London, Berlin, 1914-1919*. Cambridge: Cambridge University Press, 1997.
Woollacott, Angela. *On Her Their Lives Depend: Munitions Workers and the Great War*. Berkeley: University of California Press, 1994.

Articles and Theses

Artibise, Alan F.J. 'Boosterism and the Development of Prairie Cities.' In *The Prairie West: Historical Readings,* edited by R. Douglas Francis and Howard Palmer. Edmonton: University of Alberta Press, 1992. Appeared originally in Alan F.J. Artibise, ed., *Town and City: Aspects of Western Canadian Urban Development* (Regina: Canadian Plains Research Centre, 1981).

Bassler, Gerhard P. 'The Enemy Alien Experience in Newfoundland 1914-1918.' *Canadian Ethnic Studies/Études ethniques au Canada* 20 (1988): 42-62.

Belleau, Jacques. 'L'industrialisation de Trois-Rivières, 1905-1925.' Master's thesis, l'Université du Québec à Trois-Rivières, 1979.

Bet-El, Ilana R. 'Man and Soldiers: British Conscripts, Concepts of Masculinity, and the Great War.' In *Borderlines: Genders and Identities in War and Peace, 1870-1930,* edited by Billie Melman, 73-94. New York: Routledge, 1998.

Binnema, Theodore. 'Old Swan, Big Man, and Siksika Bands, 1784-1815.' *Canadian Historical Review* 77 (1996): 1-32.

Bliss, J.M. 'The Methodist Church and World War I.' *Canadian Historical Review* 49 (1968): 213-33.

Boudreau, J.A. 'The Enemy Alien Problem in Canada, 1914-1921.' PhD diss., University of California, 1965.

Bourdieu, Pierre. 'Sport and Social Class.' In *Rethinking Popular Culture: Contemporary Perspective in Cultural Studies,* edited by Chandra Mukerji and Michael Schudson, 357-53. Berkeley: University of California Press, 1991.

Brouillette, Normand. 'Le développement industriel d'une région du proche hinterland québécois: La Mauricie, 1900-1975.' PhD diss., McGill University, 1983.

Brown, Robert Craig, and Donald Loveridge. 'Unrequited Faith: Recruiting in the C.E.F., 1914-1918.' *Revue Internationale d'Histoire Militaire* 51 (1982): 53-79.

Cameron, Brian. 'The Bonne Entente Movement, 1916-1917: From Cooperation to Conscription.' *Journal of Canadian Studies/Revue d'études canadiennes* 13 (1978): 42-55.

Chartier, Roger. 'Text, Symbols and Frenchness.' *Journal of Modern History* 57 (1985): 682-95.

Culleton, Claire. 'Gender-Charged Munitions: The Language of World War I Munitions Reports.' *Women's Studies International Forum* 11 (1988): 109-16.

Darnton, Robert. 'The Symbolic Element in History,' *Journal of Modern History* 58 (1986): 218-34.

Dion, Alain. 'L'industrie des pâtes et papiers en Mauricie, 1887-1929.' Master's thesis, l'Université du Québec à Trois-Rivières, 1981.

Durocher, René. 'Henri Bourassa, les évêques et la guerre de 1914-1918.' *Canadian Historical Association Papers* (1971): 248-75.

Desnoyers, Hélène. 'Le logement ouvrier à Trois-Rivières 1845-1945: l'exemple du secteur Hertel.' Master's thesis, l'Université du Québec à Trois-Rivières, 1988.

Fooks, Georgia G. 'A History of the Lethbridge Herald, 1905-1975.' Master's thesis, Brigham Young University, 1975.

Hogan, Brian F. 'The Guelph Novitiate Raid: Conscription, Censorship and Bigotry during the Great War.' *Canadian Catholic Historical Association, Study Sessions* 45 (1978): 57-80.

Huskins, Bonnie. 'From *Haute Cuisine* to Ox Roasts: Public Feasting and the Negotiation of Class in Mid-19th Century Saint John and Halifax.' *Labour/Le Travail* 37 (1996): 9-32.

Kaprielian-Churchill, Isabel. 'Armenian Refugees and Their Entry into Canada, 1919-1930.' *Canadian Historical Review* 71 (1990): 80-108.

Kealey, Gregory S. 'State Repression of Labour and the Left in Canada, 1914-1920: The Impact of the First World War.' *Canadian Historical Review* 73 (1992): 281-314.

Keshen, Jeffrey A. 'All the News That Was Fit to Print: Ernest J. Chambers and Information Control in Canada, 1914-1919.' *Canadian Historical Review* 73 (1992): 315-43.

Kitchen, Martin. 'The German Invasion of Canada in the First World War.' *International History Review* 7 (1985): 245-60.

Kovacs, Martin L. 'Hungarian Communities in Early Alberta and Saskatchewan.' In *The New Provinces: Alberta and Saskatchewan, 1905-1980,* edited by Howard Palmer and Donald Smith, 101-30. Vancouver: Tantalus Research, 1980.

Maroney, Paul. '"The Great Adventure": The Context and Ideology of Recruiting in Ontario, 1914-17.' *Canadian Historical Review* 77 (1996): 62-98.
Morton, Desmond. 'Sir William Otter and Internment Operations in Canada during the First World War.' *Canadian Historical Review* 55 (1974): 32-58.
–. 'The Short, Unhappy Life of the 41st Battalion, CEF.' *Queen's Quarterly* 81 (1974): 70-80.
–. 'The Cadet Movement in the Moment of Canadian Militarism, 1909-1914.' *Journal of Canadian Studies* 13 (1978): 56-68.
Morton, W.L. 'A Century of Plain and Parkland.' In *The Prairie West: Historical Readings,* edited by R. Douglas Francis and Howard Palmer. Edmonton: University of Alberta Press, 1992. Appeared originally in *Alberta Historical Review* 17 (spring 1969): 1-10.
O'Brien, Mike. 'Manhood and the Militia Myth: Masculinity, Class, and Militarism in Ontario, 1902-1914.' *Labour/Le Travail* 42 (1998): 115-41.
Parr, Joy. 'Gender History and Historical Practice.' *Canadian Historical Review* 76 (1995): 354-76.
Prang, Margaret. 'Clerics, Politicians, and the Bilingual Schools Issue in Ontario, 1910-1917.' *Canadian Historical Review* 41 (1960): 281-307.
Rankhalawansingh, Ceta. 'Women during the Great War.' In *Women at Work: Ontario, 1850-1930,* edited by J. Acton et al., 261-307. Toronto: Canadian Educational Press, 1974.
Roberts, Barbara. 'Why Do Women Do Nothing to End the War?': Canadian Feminist-Pacifists and the Great War.' CRIAW Paper no. 13 (Ottawa: Canadian Research Institute for the Advancement of Women, 1985).
–.'Women's Peace Activism in Canada.' In *Beyond the Vote: Canadian Women and Politics,* edited by Linda Kealey and Joan Sangster, 276-308. Toronto: University of Toronto Press, 1989.
Robin, Martin. 'Registration, Conscription and Independent Labour Politics, 1916-1917.' *Canadian Historical Review* 47 (1966): 101-18.
Roy, François. 'Le crépuscule d'un rouge: J.-A. Tessier maire de Trois-Rivières, et l'enquête Désy de 1920.' Master's thesis, l'Université du Québec à Trois-Rivières, 1988.
Rutherford, Paul. 'Introduction.' In Herbert Ames, *The City below the Hill: A Sociological Study of a Portion of the City of Montreal, Canada.* 1897. Reprint, Toronto: University of Toronto Press, 1972, vii-xviii.
Ryan, Mary. 'The American Parade: Representations of the Nineteenth-Century Social Order.' In *The New Cultural History,* edited by Lynn Hunt, 131-53. Berkeley: University of California Press, 1989.
Scott, Joan. 'The Evidence of Experience.' *Critical Inquiry* 17 (1991): 773-97.
–. 'Rewriting History.' In *Behind the Lines: Gender and the Two World Wars,* edited by Margaret R. Higonnet et al., 19-30. New Haven, CT: Yale University Press, 1987.
St. G. Walker, James W. 'Race and Recruitment in World War I: Enlistment of Visible Minorities in the Canadian Expeditionary Force.' *Canadian Historical Review* 70 (1989): 1-26.
Sharpe, C.A. 'Enlistment in the Canadian Expeditionary Force, 1914-1918: A Regional Analysis.' *Journal of Canadian Studies/Revue d'études canadiennes* 18 (1983/84): 15-29.
Socknat, Thomas. 'Canada's Liberal Pacifists and the Great War.' *Journal of Canadian Studies/Revue d'études canadiennes* 18 (1983/84): 30-44.
Stoianovich, Traian. *French Historical Method: The Annales Paradigm.* Ithaca, NY: Cornell University Press, 1976.
Strong-Boag, Veronica. 'Peace-Making Women: Canada, 1919-1939.' In *Women and Peace: Theoretical, Historical, and Practical Perspectives,* edited by Ruth Roach Pierson, 170-91. London: Croom Helm, 1987.
Turner, Victor. 'Variations on a Theme of Liminality.' In *Blazing the Trail: Way Marks in the Exploration of Symbols,* edited by Edith Turner, 48-65. Tucson: University of Arizona Press, 1992.
Wamsley, K.B. 'Cultural Signification and National Ideologies: Rifle-Shooting in Late Nineteenth Century Canada.' *Social History* 20 (1995): 63-72.
Williams, Raymond. 'Base and Superstructure in Marxist Cultural Theory.' In *Rethinking Popular Culture: Contemporary Perspectives in Cultural Studies,* edited by Chandra Mukerji and Michael Schudson, 407-23. Berkeley: University of California Press, 1991.

Willms, A.M. 'Conscription 1917: A Brief for the Defence.' *Canadian Historical Review* 37 (1956): 338-51.

Young, Alan R. '"We Throw the Torch": Canadian Memorials of the Great War and the Mythology of Heroic Sacrifice.' *Journal of Canadian Studies/Revue d'études canadiennes* 24 (1989/90): 5-28.

Young, W.R. 'Conscription, Rural Depopulation and the Farmers of Ontario.' *Canadian Historical Review* 53 (1972): 289-320.

Index

Note: Page numbers in **bold type** indicate illustrations.

Printed and bound in Canada by Friesens

Set in Stone by Artegraphica Design Co. Ltd.

Copy editor: Audrey A. McClellan

Proofreader: Alison Cairns

Indexer: Noeline Bridge

Cartographer: Eric Leinberger